Alone Before God

Pamela Voekel

Alone Before God

The Religious Origins of Modernity in Mexico

DUKE UNIVERSITY PRESS   Durham & London   2002

© 2002 Duke University Press

All rights reserved

Printed in the United States of
America on acid-free paper ∞

Designed by C. H. Westmoreland

Typeset in Quadraat with Post Antiqua
display by Keystone Typesetting, Inc.

Library of Congress Cataloging-
in-Publication Data appear on the
last printed page of this book.

Ten graphs summarizing information
about the wills discussed in this book
appear on the author's Web site at
www.religiousorigins.org.

*Library of Congress Cataloging-in-Publication
Data*

Voekel, Pamela.
Alone Before God : the religious origins
of modernity in Mexico / Pamela Voekel.
p. cm.
Includes bibliographical references and
index.
ISBN 0-8223-2927-1 (cloth : alk. paper)—
ISBN 0-8223-2943-3 (pbk. : alk. paper)
1. Mexico—Church history. 2. Church and
state—Mexico—History. 3. Catholic
Church—Mexico—History. 4. Church and
state—Catholic Church—History.
5. Cemeteries—Social aspects—Mexico—
History. 6. Burial—Social aspects—
Mexico—History. I. Title.
BX1428.3.V64 2002
282′.72—dc21   2002001654

contents

acknowledgments

I didn't want to leave Mexico after completing the research for this book in 1996. The Zapatista rebellion had galvanized Mexico's left, and in the town of Tepotzlán, where I wrote much of this work, my neighbors were giddy with hope for real political change. University of Montana students and some dedicated Missoulians made the transition an easier one. Their passion for Latin America's history and their dogged efforts to globalize the resistance to neoliberalism inspired me during every step of this work. I especially want to thank Melissa Bangs, Kate Keller, Mark Carey, Scott Nicholson, Raquel Castellaños, Joanna Arkema, Camile Becker, Paul Ryan, Jen Sens, Burke Stansbury, Genena Bradley, Egan Bradley, Jordan Dobrovolny, Janet Finn, Andrea Olsen, Lynn Purl, Paul Haber, John Norvell, Kimber Haddix, Leida Martins, and María Bustos-Fernández.

Latin American historians are lucky: many of our most gifted practitioners are as generous as they are talented. Carlos Forment, Sylvia Arrom, William Taylor, Stanley Stein, Nancy Vogely, Linda Arnold, Scarlett O'Phelan Godoy, Anne Rubenstein, William Beezley, and Gil Joseph either greatly improved the manuscript or offered valuable encouragement. Two reviewers at Duke University Press, as well as Valerie Millholland, Miriam Angress, Judith Hoover, and Rebecca Johns-Danes made this a much better book. In Mexico City, I learned a tremendous amount about death in Latin America, as well as some choice Spanish words, from Elsa Malvido and her Seminario de Historia de la Muerte. The Colegio de México's Seminario de Historia de Mentalidades offered key comments that transformed both my research and my thinking. The work owes any sophistication it can claim to the tireless input of Jorge Bracamonte, Fanni Muñoz Cabrera, Cecilia Riquelme, Elliot Young, Isabel Toledo-Young, Liz Norvell, Michael Snodgrass, Anabel Ruíz, and Pablo Piccato: during intense weekend meetings of our splinter faction, their rigorous criticism was rivaled only by their enthusiastic investigations of Mexico City's *bajos fondos*. A special thanks to my *cuates* Jennifer Bowles and Josefina Flores, who tried to warn me, and to Teresa Fernández Leido, Marisa Cerro, Aida Baez Carlos, and Lourdes Rojas, who reminded me that not all of the drama was in the archives. At the University of Montana, the Feminist Research Avengers led by the fearless Anya Jabourl and the spectacular Ken Lockridge proffered sage advice that transformed the work. At the book's most embryonic stage, Ana Alonso and the late Daniel Nugent provided an interdisciplinary frenzy of intellectual excitement in their seminars; I am deeply grateful for the project's exposure to their brilliance. My advisor, Susan Deans-Smith, deserves special praise for her patience and unflagging enthusiasm, as does Sandra Lauderdale-Graham for her insistence that style matters, even in history. Las Reinas, Alex Brown, Rebecca Siegel, María Zalduondo, Danalynn Recer, and especially Jessica Chapin made Texas a hotbed of political and intellectual stimulation. And way back at Mount Holyoke Joan Cocks, Jean Grossholtz, and Teresa Renaker taught me that scholarship and activism are mutually dependent, not mutually exclusive.

The Social Science Research Council, Spain's Ministry of Culture, the Mount Holyoke Class of 1905, the University of Texas, and the University of Montana's wonderful History Department funded the research and writing of this work, and I am deeply grateful for their confidence. Mexico's dedicated and underpaid archivists spent extra time locating documents that proved invaluable. I especially want to thank the entire staff at the Archivo de Notarias in Mexico City.

Finally, my greatest debt is to my family, especially John, John Patrick, Haley, Swen, Penelope, and Hilda Gail. The beautiful and talented Bethany Moreton propelled the book forward and gave it whatever nuance it contains. Only Sor Juana Inez de la Cruz has the eloquence to express my gratitude to her, so I won't even try. Solidarity Forever!

introduction

In 1787, ministers of the Spanish King Charles III outlawed the practice of burying the Empire's dead in or around churches; in its place, the edict ordered the construction of suburban cemeteries throughout the King's domains in Europe and the Americas. A seemingly innocuous measure, the new system of burial grounds struck at the heart of the ancien régime, for it threatened a key medium of displaying and sacralizing social hierarchy and sundered the intimate relationship between the dead and the living that fueled baroque piety. Not surprisingly, the subsequent implementation of the edict provoked impassioned encounters between those with church burial rights and the procemetery faction, who called themselves *sensatos*, or the enlightened ones.

Strictly speaking, the self-styled enlightened could not claim victory in this pitched battle. By the time of Mexico's Independence in 1821, their projected network of verdant, hygienic public burial grounds had suffered overwhelming resistance at the hands of multiple foes. More prosaically, the crusaders were broke. The resulting cemeteries were few and shabby at best.[1]

But the physical reality of suburban cemeteries is only the infrastructure for a far more significant story. The deep background of this civic squabble lay in the urban elites' definitive shift in the early nineteenth century from an external, mediated, and corporate Catholicism to an interior piety, one that elevated the virtues of self-discipline and moderation and focused on a direct, personal relationship to God. Through their numerous procemetery tracts and sermons, New Spain's enlightened promoted a nominally egalitarian theology that attacked the spiritual vacuity of baroque display, the dominant language of Old Regime social hierarchies. At the same time, they advocated an individual spirituality, which helped to splinter the society of orders and estates into one of individuals. Unbeknown to themselves, in fact, those of *piedad ilustrada* (enlightened piety) had lost the battle but won the war.

Any argument concerned with the emergence of the modern, self-regulated individual owes much to Michel Foucault. Lurking below the eighteenth century's liberal and democratic rallying cry to protect the rights and freedoms of the individual from political tyranny, he explains, lay a new set of institutions and practices—asylums, prisons, and hospitals—that employed new techniques of surveillance. These new techniques of power were designed to produce individuals who would internalize morality and to remove from society those who would not. Foucauldian man could regulate and care for himself without supervision; in short, he was capable of this new liberation and political participation, and thus worthy of state protection. Here is an insidious, total form of power: not the power to quash already constituted political subjects, but to create them.

Elsewhere, I have argued that in late eighteenth-century Mexico City the internally regulated individual became an increasingly important index of elite status as corporate forms of identity lost their salience. This self-control was manifested by a heightened command of the body.[2] Patricia Seed, however, is the historian of Latin America who has provided the most thorough cultural examination of the birth of the modern individual, whose reason or interests dominated his passions. In particular, Seed echoed Albert Hirschmann's concern with charting the rise of a "homo economicus," who could be counted on to pursue ruthlessly his economic self-interest.[3] Not Foucault's ubiquitous surveillance, she argues, but the rise of secular reason created this internally tempered self. Whereas late seventeenth-century Mexico City society considered the love felt by young couples to be a sure sign of God's approval of their eventual union in matrimony, by the late eighteenth century this same expression of love signaled the couple's irrational passions unbridled by reason. In the earlier scenario, the Church, the state, and the laity had mobilized against meddlesome parents to protect children's freedom to marry, seeing their passion as a legitimate indicator of their free will, and thus, she argues, of God's will.

By the late eighteenth century, however, a father who disapproved of a suitor's lowly economic or racial background now claimed that this same expression of love clouded his offspring's reason, and both Church and state united with the parents to prevent the union. The passions were no longer a road to God, a sure way of knowing His will, Seed demonstrates.

Rather, they represented a serious social threat that the Christian must overcome through the exercise of secular reason. Contemporaries increasingly defined this reason as economic aggrandizement; children should choose marriage partners whose fortunes matched or surpassed their own. With the economic quickening and increased world market participation of the late eighteenth century, once reviled economic self-interest became a stable and celebrated motivation for human behavior among the Mexico City elite. The reasonable male individual who could be counted on to pursue stable interests underlay New World merchants' desire to swap the restrictions of mercantilism for free trade—an economic system under which people could be relied on to act according to those interests.[4]

Seed, then, provides a deep cultural analysis for the birth of the self-interested economic man whose liberation from corporate shackles and market impediments would subsequently fuel the political utopias of an influential faction of elite Mexican liberals. In his work on José María Luis Mora (1794–1850), the major liberal theorist of the immediate post-Independence period, Charles Hale rightly insists that merely identifying Mora's intellectual influences will not suffice; we must also ask why he embraced certain theorists rather than others. Hale proposes that Mora found particular inspiration in French and especially Spanish writers grappling with the central problem he saw engulfing post-Independence Mexico: first the battle to create representative institutions, then the struggle against the corporate privileges that threatened those institutions.[5] Seed's work bolsters Hale's, suggesting that the economically minded individual at the center of Mora's campaigns against corporate privileges and for free markets had a deep cultural genealogy in Mexico; his liberation was thus "possible because it was conceivable," to employ Roger Chartier's felicitous phrase summarizing the cultural origins of the French Revolution.[6]

But concerned as she is with relations among Church, state, and society, Seed misses that late eighteenth-century reformers within the Church suggested a more spiritual solution to the problem of harnessing these now unruly passions: rigid self-discipline enacted by the light of God's grace. It is the argument of this book that religious origins likewise generated the individual at the heart of the Bourbon assault on corporate privileges as well as these campaigns' intellectual heir, the elite liberal theory of the immediate post-Independence period. Seed is certainly right that her urban elites called on reason to create self-control and moderation, but this reason was not entirely secular, not the "soulless intellect of later rationalism," not inimical to piety. Rather, this moderating force was the divine part of men, God's very presence in their hearts.[7]

Thus, while Mora and other elite liberals sought to free homo economicus from all market impediments to his free pursuit of self-interest, they also pursued the liberation of his spiritual twin: the godly and thus virtuous individual of enlightened Catholicism. The Church's hierarchical mediation with the Divine, impediments to free speech, ascriptive social privileges—all were attacked in the name of freeing the godly conscience from all restraint on its workings and liberating those who displayed godly moderation from all legal fetters to social advancement, while simultaneously placing those who did not firmly under their guidance.

This book, then, explores the role of the new piety in Mexico's shift from a corporate, hierarchical society ruled by a divine monarch during the seventeenth and eighteenth centuries, to the independent republic of 1821, whose elite political discourse stressed the sovereignty of the people, the sanctity of private property, free speech, and representative government, and the exclusion of the demonstrably unvirtuous from enfranchisement or political office.[8] It shares with Foucault, however, a deep distrust of this self-congratulatory liberal rhetoric, whether emanating from the Bourbon state, Veracruz merchants, or Mexico's early elite liberals. I thus heed historian Florencia Mallon's call to chart how such seemingly universalist discourses of individual equality and rights can in reality delegitimate other, more radical visions of citizenship and exclude some from the political process.[9] In both Veracruz and Mexico City, enlightened Catholicism's elite devotees would argue that the moderate—and thus the righteous—should rightly rule those who demonstrated an inability to toe the line drawn by their betters.

A few words of explanation of this shift from legal hierarchy to nominal equality are in order. Until the late eighteenth century, the King's representatives in New Spain proffered no ideology of social equality. This was an ancien régime society whose fixed hierarchies operated with God's approval; the King held sacral status, and society's component parts formed juridically separate entities. The Indians paid tribute to the Crown, and royal laws forbade them to dress like Spaniards, ride horses, or bear arms. As a recognized group, however, they enjoyed access to special tribunals, usufruct rights to village commons, and exemption from the Inquisition and various taxes. Even within this República de los Indios legal hierarchies persisted, for the pre-Conquest nobility were often exempted from the more onerous obligations, such as tribute, and allowed special prerogatives, such as Spanish dress. Spaniards, too, were classified by various political identities. Nobles, soldiers, lawyers, merchants, and priests all had their separate courts and economic prerogatives, and the trade guilds officially monopolized their craft. The racially mixed *castas* faced legal discrimination based on their group identity, being officially barred from most of the guilds and estates. Each person's relationship to the Crown, then, was mediated through his corporate group; New Spain was home to subjects, but no citizens.[10]

Although never static, in the late eighteenth century this hierarchical society began to crumble from pressure from above and below. Bourbon bureaucrats sought to extend state jurisdiction at the expense of the Church, attacked the Mexico City merchant monopoly with a 1789 declaration of free trade, and began to chip away at the artisan guilds' monopolies. At the same time, the carefully delineated República de los Indios and the República de los Españoles began to shade into each other, as the urban casta population grew. The economic quickening of the late eighteenth century led to a new faith in economic interest as a human motivator, and thus economic class began to overshadow ascriptive status as the basis for identity. After independence, the drive to remove the vestiges of this corporate society continued, with the privileges of the Church and army as the principal targets.[11] This book examines reformed piety's role in the battle against corporate privileges and the subsequent struggle to recreate new social distinctions on a different foundation.

At first glance, the cemetery campaign and reformers' efforts to curb the worst excesses of baroque funerals would seem an unlikely investigative pathway into the thorny question of the new piety's larger social and political ramifications. The late eighteenth-century attack on church burials and elaborate funerals, however, represented a strategic strike at the spiritual sanctification of social hierarchy. New Spain's church floors and chapels mapped the society's intricate caste and status categories, as the careful placement of the dead reiterated worldly honors and temporal distinctions. In addition to family privileges, each ethnic and many occupational groups in colonial society had their own economic prerogatives, tax obligations, and even legal rights and court system, and these juridically fixed identities found expression in the careful carving up of church burial space. The clergy's sanctity and corporate status, for example, was demonstrated in their burial under the main altar, close to the Eucharist—a privilege legally denied to the laity. In death as in life, the churches added their blessing to the privileges of the Old Regime's group-based social structure, its floors and chapels fetid simulacra of distinctions among the living.

Funerals also provided the Church with an opportunity to sanctify elites' lofty social position. Elaborate funeral corteges were a common sight on Veracruz and Mexico City streets until the waning years of the colonial period. Although twelve was the usual number, hundreds and even thousands of clergy regularly escorted the dead to the church and prayed at burial ceremonies. With clergy clogging the streets, hundreds of flickering candles, bright cloths, ornate carriages, musical accompaniment, and paid mourners, these funerals stunned the senses of urban crowds, thereby heightening their awe at the power of the seducer and associating him with truly heavenly magnificence.

Resistance to these sensual dramas in particular and the "true piety" that gripped the Empire's self-styled enlightened in general, suggest that Octavio Paz's assertions about the origins of Mexican modernity need to be reassessed. Paz found Spain and her colonies lacking in a "modern moral consciousness," singularly bereft of the self-discipline required for democracy: in Protestant countries and in France, with its influential Jansenist faction, the individualist impulse took hold among the populace before its manifestation in liberalism. By contrast, Catholic Latin America imported modernity; rationalism was an acquired ideology. For Paz, the fundamental difference between Latin American democracy and its Anglo-Saxon version is attributable to the latter's religious origins. The "true piety" of Veracruz and Mexico City sensatos, however, suggests that Mexico's liberalism also had religious roots.[12]

The new piety acted as a solvent on the divinely sanctified social hierarchies of the ancien régime, splintering society into atomized male individuals who felt they owed their social position to their hard work, restraint, and self-control, their interiorization of morality: the very same atomized individuals who wrote and peopled the elite liberals' texts of the ensuing century.[13] Crowded, dazzling funerals indexed a lack of godly moderation. Furthermore, the reformed passed over the Pope and the hierarchy and referred instead to the early Christian councils as their fonts of truth. Reform Catholics justified their extensive participation in the lively public sphere that emerged in Mexico City in the early nineteenth century by underscoring their scriptural erudition and familiarity with Church history as well as their divinely illuminated consciences; thus, this new piety helped justify a new, more participatory politics.

Some of this argument has already found a place in the historiography. Although he focuses on the state's curbing of Church prerogatives and on the intellectual trajectory of a few reform luminaries, David A. Brading notes that the dismantling of the old godly defense of hierarchical society would have failed miserably without the efforts of the "Jansenist" upper clergy, who led the attack on what they regarded as the worst "excesses" of baroque Catholicism.[14] Having asserted this argument, however, Brading does not demonstrate any interest in the fundamental tenets of enlightened Catholicism, in the process of corrosion itself, or in the broader constituency behind the intellectual champions of this new piety. This book attempts to answer some of the questions raised by Brading's provocative assertion that the simple interior piety possessed the capacity to transform larger spiritual and social arrangements.

Scholars of New Spain's Independence period have painted the Church as a conservative force that legitimated the Old Regime, at least until the enlightened and absolutist state provoked its ire. In particular, William B. Taylor, Nancy Farriss, and Francisco Morales have demonstrated that the Bourbon monarchy tightened the noose around its own neck by distancing itself from the divine purpose that had served as its primary justification for rule since the Conquest. In attacking the clergy's privileges and prerogatives, the new secular state cut out its own ideological heart; it alienated and angered the clergy who had served as its primary ideological state apparatus, who had promoted obedience to the King as a fundamental Christian virtue.[15] In a similar vein, Serge Gruzinski argues that for the late eighteenth-century Bourbon state, "The imperatives of civilization progressively replaced those of Christianization" and that this shift fueled the assault on baroque piety.[16] Implicit in their arguments is the notion that the clergy fought a secular state intent on trimming their traditional corporate privileges and dimming the exuberance of baroque Catholicism. This assertion may indeed be true, but it nevertheless considerably obscures the enlightened clergy's own role in crumbling the ancien régime's primary idiom of distinction: baroque display. Likewise, it occludes the sincere Christianity of most reformers. These enlightened men of God sought to lead people down the right road to holiness, not discredit man's bond with the deity as a legitimate justification for political action; they were anything but secular.

Their efforts, then, do not constitute an attack on the Church by a secular state. And indeed, a closer look at the burial campaign reveals that it was not a top-down state imposition on a uniformly recalcitrant populace, as the traditional historiography has depicted the Bourbon reforms; rather, the movement was led by the upper clergy, enlightened bureaucrats, the press, doctors, and, in Veracruz at least, the city's merchants. Indeed, traditional elements within the state bureaucracy actively thwarted cemetery building, proclaiming their allegiance to the old order. At the same time, a portion of Mexico City testators filled their wills with requests for cemetery burials a good twenty years before the cemetery laws were effectively enforced in the 1830s. Most significant, the enlightened subjects who propelled the burial campaign forward during the colonial period did so under the leadership of the Church.

Although the enlightened piety that animated the cemetery campaign had a corrosive effect on the sacral social hierarchy created in part by church burials, it also formed part of a complex causal ecology that threw up new cultural authorities out of the rubble: the *gente sensata*, a culturally self-defined group that objected to both the traditional elite's rule by razzmatazz and the lower classes' immoderate habits. The result was a heightened sense of their social authority. For although in "true religion," pious acts did not necessarily alter one's postmortem fate, upright moral behavior and worldly success were interpreted as a result of one's interior moral transformation; to paraphrase R. H. Tawney's summary of Max Weber's famous thesis, what was rejected as a means to salvation was embraced as a consequence of it.[17] Wealth lost its moral taint, and because the successful bore God's positive stigmata, the poor who fell by the wayside should be under their guidance; clearly, they had not taken God's message to heart, and therefore they might well wear their rags in Hell.

After Independence, certain liberals argued that only the economically successful had the moral fiber for enfranchised citizenship; poverty's etiology clearly lay in the individual's moral failings, not in structural inequalities, and the poor should thus be banished from the political process. These enlightened Catholics also attacked the last vestiges of corporate privilege, which they felt stymied the social leadership of the truly virtuous. One such carefully protected redoubt for the unvirtuous was the Church, which reformers felt squandered its vast income on the sensual opulence and superfluous mediating hierarchy of baroque Catholicism, positively imperiling salvation. It must be reformed, they concluded, so that "true religion" could thrive in Mexico.

Like Gruzinski, Taylor, and Morales, both the distinguished literary critic Jean Franco and the esteemed historian Charles Hale have read these attempted Church reforms as signs of secularization, as evidence for the waning of union with God as an acceptable justification for public conduct and policy. But the reformed of the immediate post-Independence period had reconfigured their relationship with God, not abandoned it; if God illuminated all men from within, then the road to God was not through the Church hierarchy or through "vain and ostentatious" exterior displays of His majesty. The Church should not cloud men's relation with the God in their hearts; it had no need of the excessive bureaucracy and vast sums squandered on liturgical pomp. The imperative was to liberate "true religion" from the Church, which would then exist in a godly and pared-down form. Unlike their French contemporaries, pre- and post-Independence reformers were not engaged in secularization but something more akin to a religious war. In Mexico, the enlightened did not remove themselves from divine sanctification, as Taylor, Farriss, Gruzinski, Hale, and Franco suggest; rather, they employed a different definition of it, and to different ends.

As one would expect from a religious movement, it was the clergy who initially promoted this more austere, individual piety, beginning roughly in the late 1760s. But because of the multilayered causality outlined above, the reformation produced consequences that clerical firebrands neither desired nor anticipated: the weakening of their own authority as the adjudication of political decisions increasingly became the provenance of physical specialists rather than spiritual ones. "True religion's" reformation of the individual produced a cultural sea change that rendered the new empirical medicine credible to enlightened urban elites. This medicine based its claims not on the wisdom of ancient authority but on individual observation.[18] The more critical attitude toward religious authority encouraged a more skeptical attitude toward dogma in science. Furthermore, the new piety had helped to arm this society with a different technique of rule: observing the population rather than performing for it. The theatrical opulence of the baroque funeral indexed a lack of godly moderation; display was redefined as spiritually void. After Independence, doctors' testimony became synonymous with reason; physicians even entered the state mechanism as political leaders, effectively undercutting the clergy's intellectual leadership of Mexico's urban elite. At the same time, science and public health concerns edged out theology as the principal idiom of the burial debate. Years before the liberals completely secularized the cemeteries in 1859, the Church's loss was a foregone conclusion.

Numerous historians have championed Protestantism's paternity of various aspects of modernity, most particularly science, individualism, and capitalism.[19] Catholic Reform piety's procreative powers have received considerably less attention, although their single proponent, Dale Van Kley, makes a spectacular case for the generative powers of Jansenism on the modern political sensibilities that erupted in the French Revolution, particularly the Jansenists' juxtaposition of individual conscience to the will of the absolute monarch and the attendant political decentralization that this helped to create.[20] It is the argument of this book that enlightened piety did have procreative powers and was indeed a factor in the erosion of the hierarchical social relations of the old order. By insinuating that the individual, not the divinely ordained monarch or his clerical hierarchy, was the source of wisdom, "true religion" helped institute a cultural shift that placed the individual at the starting point of knowledge. Reformers' stress on the "inner light" as the surest path to God proved to be an acid bath for a social order that had defined "truth" as the hierarchical authority sanctified by God.

Historians are entirely dependent on their sources, and all sources require critical assessment in their use. Much of this book relies on a statistical analysis of the pious proclivities expressed in 2,100 Mexico City wills. The use of wills as a historical source is replete with problems and pitfalls. These particular documents tell us little about the piety of the majority: the poor. They reveal even less of the religious sensibilities of the desperately impoverished. Furthermore, they illuminate pious gifts and burial preferences expressed by testators but reveal nothing of arrangements made at other times and places during an individual's life. And although the substance of the papers reflects individual initiative, their preambles tell us little beyond which formulaic expressions were favored by which notaries.

Despite these problems, wills read in conjunction with other sources can illuminate much about Mexicans wealthy enough to command respect for their burial choices and to make pious donations. I have supplemented the wills with an array of sermons, tracts, official government correspondence, petitions from the laity to religious and secular authorities, parish burial records, newspapers, legal codes, confraternity records, and evidence from medical institutions, to enumerate just a portion of the documentation.

I have grouped the wills into two databases. The first, and the most often referenced, consists of 350 wills for each of three periods: 1710 to 1720, 1810 to 1820, and 1850 to 1860.[21] Male testators outnumbered females by almost two to one. Merchants, clerics, and state employees were the three largest occupational groups represented in the earlier two periods, with the military and the liberal professions—doctors, lawyers, scribes—replacing clerics and state employees in the top three occupations in the later period. Servants, artisans, and those with agricultural interests—owners of haciendas and smaller properties—rounded out the list of occupations, although roughly half of the wills remained mute on this question. Few testators were identified by their racial classification, although European-born Spaniards constituted 30 percent of the earliest testators sampled and roughly 20 percent of all testators in the middle period, and these testators can be presumed to be white. Indians, blacks, and those of mixed race often were identified as such in the wills in the earlier two periods, but constituted a statistically irrelevant number of the total testators sampled.

The second database of wills comprises fifty wills per decade, drawn from at least five notaries per decade, and beginning in 1620. Its data are thus less fine-grained, and I use it merely to locate the rough timing of large shifts in piety determined from the first database and as a guide to the rough outline of seventeenth-century pious proclivities. In short, the wills offer a window into the shifting pious sensibilities of Mexico City's wealthier residents. Graphs can be found on the Web at *www.religiousorigins.org*.

These qualifications of wealth and urbanity raise some interesting questions: Is urban elites' strong support for the new piety in the late eighteenth century merely the visible tip of a vast iceberg? Did the rural areas find this more interior Christianity compelling? Did the urban underclass, who left few traces in the wills, embrace its tenets? The available evidence suggests the answer is no on all accounts, although this is the first book on this eighteenth-century "Catholic Reformation" in Latin America and no one has addressed this question directly. The extant evidence, however, suggests that Mexico City and Veracruz elites probably floated like large reefs atop an indifferent or hostile ocean; although influential, they were probably not the tips of a massive iceberg.

This is not surprising, given that both cities were demographic anomalies in a predominantly rural New Spain peopled overwhelmingly by Indians and mestizos. The largest city in the New World in 1811, Mexico City claimed whites as half its total of 168,000 residents, in a country where they made up only 18 percent of the overall population; Indians made up only 24 percent of the enormous city, whereas they were 60 percent of the country's inhabitants. Equally anomalous was the economic condition of the capital. The enormous fortunes garnered in the rich silver mines and through merchant speculation found dazzling outlets in the city's advanced school of mining, its Art Academy, Botanical Garden, and university, its twenty-three monasteries, fifteen convents, and twelve hospitals, not to mention its spectacular cathedral and royal palace located in the ample central square. The center of imperial government built on the ruins of the stunning Aztec capital, Mexico City was the architectural gem of the New World.[22]

The port city of Veracruz, on the other hand, was a late eighteenth-century boomtown that grew in response to the 1789 declaration of free trade within the Empire; some scholars even estimate that the city's 1791 population of 4,000 souls swelled to 16,000 by 1803, although more conservative figures show a doubling in the population from 1791 to 1818.[23] Where Mexico City's long-term residents were most likely white or mestizo and relatively well-off, the 1791 Veracruz census demonstrates that most white and mestizo Veracruz males had been born outside the city, with the majority of the whites hailing from Spain. The city's dominant mulatto and black population, by contrast, had much deeper roots: more than half of each group were Veracruz natives.[24] Furthermore, the city's casta residents evidently outnumbered the more peripatetic whites.[25] Thus, Veracruz's stable core population consisted of male and female castas, many of them of African descent.

That Veracruz and Mexico City were demographically unique in New

Spain provides no direct evidence that the new piety appealed uniquely to these cities' elite residents. We have to look for that suggestion elsewhere. Although the cemetery campaign is not a simple referendum on stripped-down Catholicism, it is worth noting that the new burial grounds met with unmitigated hostility in rural areas. More to the point, William B. Taylor's extensive examination of rural piety in the archdioceses of Guadalajara and Mexico City uncovered an Indian population whose religious practice showed no signs of the more individual faith that William B. Christian found challenging the more corporate, communal piety of rural Spain in the same period, the late eighteenth century.[26] Even with Taylor's superb work, however, we are far from the clear geographies of piety indicated by the forced oath to the French Civil Constitution of 1791, with its mandate for a streamlined Church.[27]

If geography offers some suggestive distinctions, so does economic class. Some evidence indicates that the Veracruz poor relished the nominal egalitarianism of the city's new cemetery in the 1790s, or at least reveled in the humiliation of elites consigned to such undistinguished plots. Yet, other evidence points to the opposite conclusion. Juan Viquiera-Alban found that the Bourbon state increased its campaigns against popular forms of religion in Mexico City—processions, fireworks, saints' feasts— in the late eighteenth century, but cautions that a rise in their occurrence or popularity did not necessarily cause this crackdown. Rather, a more "rational" state found them increasingly distasteful and thus policed them more carefully.[28] That some among the popular classes eagerly embraced the sixteenth-century Protestant Reformation should further urge us to caution. Perhaps the distinctive effects of reform piety on the poor of Mexico City and Veracruz simply awaits their historian.[29]

If gauging the reformed piety's popularity outside the narrow confines of Mexico City and Veracruz elites is far from an exact science, then comparisons with other urban areas in the Empire are well-nigh impossible, as there are no extant case studies.[30] Luckily, however, this individual piety was far from an anomaly in the Catholic world of the eighteenth century. Rivers of ink have been spilled in the cause of French Jansenism, but although a few Spanish and Mexican reformers corresponded with their French fellow travelers, the two movements should not be conflated.[31] As Dale Van Kley points out in his magisterial The Religious Origins of the French Revolution, Spanish reformers insinuated themselves into the state in the late eighteenth century, employing it to promote their projects. French Jansenism, on the other hand, attacked the monarchy and the ancien régime's fixed social hierarchies from outside the state apparatus, as English Protestants had done in the mid–seventeenth century.[32] Furthermore, French Jansenists competed with a truly secular cadre of enlightened thinkers, who were both anti-Catholic and anti-Christian. In Mexico, few such secular philosophes existed. Thus, "Jansenism" was perhaps a more influential force in New Spain than in France. This goes a long way toward explaining the thoroughly religious nature of Mexican Church reform after Independence, as well as enlightened Catholicism's significant contribution to Mexico's urban political culture at the turn of the century.

Tackling so large and vexing an intellectual problem as the social effects of the new piety requires clear limits, clearly defined. Because this is the first cultural study of this reformation in the Spanish Empire, the first two chapters carefully explain the theological logic of both baroque and enlightened Catholicism. Chapter 1 treats "baroque" burial practices; the term is meant not as a strict marker of a historical era, but as a descriptor referring to a style of worship and belief that dominated in Mexico City from this study's beginnings in 1620 through the eighteenth century, with some traditionalists persisting throughout the early nineteenth century. Baroque Catholicism was highly communal, stressed the need for priestly and saintly mediation with the Divine, and found in the sensual opulence of the cult a path to knowledge of the Creator. God was an external force who burst into the world through the object domain; Mexico City's numerous relics and images of saints were a concrete, literal channel for His miraculous mercy. Chapter 2 presents the case for the opposition, explaining the intellectual essentials of this Mexican reformation and sketching the general religious context of the late eighteenth century in Mexico City and among the high-ranking state bureaucrats whose reformed sensibilities so influenced the Empire's new burial and funeral laws. The reformed embraced a more direct individual relationship with a God who animated them from within; thus, they advocated a reduced mediatory apparatus, although they never cast the Church as irrelevant to salvation, as had Protestants. These reformers redefined funereal opulence as an index of the lack of moderation that God's presence in the heart provided, and they assiduously avoided it, filling their wills with requests for moderate funerals and humble cemetery burials. For those who saw an omnipresent

God always already present, the suggestion that He would confine His presence to discrete points seemed the grossest superstition, and they eschewed the formerly coveted chapel burials under a saint's protection in favor of common cemeteries. In both these chapters, the sample of 2,100 wills allows us to use death practices as a window into styles of faith.

Chapter 3 brings us to the specific dispute over reformers' pet project: public cemeteries. João Reis's splendid work describes resistance to new suburban cemeteries in Bahia, Brazil, in the early nineteenth century, and stresses reformers' sanitary and financial concerns and protestors' fervent desire for church burials as key to the conflicts. Although health concerns loomed large in Mexico, my research revealed a more fundamentally religious conflict that centered on reformers' desire to lead everyone down the right road to God by creating suburban burial sites far from the superfluous mediating presence of saints' images, clergy, and communicants.[33] Chapters 4 and 5 examine a notorious cemetery struggle in Veracruz as a means of demonstrating the new piety's larger political ramifications. These three chapters together explain why two particularly enthusiastic groups—Bourbon bureaucrats and Veracruz merchants—embraced the new piety. But they also examine the considerable opposition that the reformed faced, both from rural areas and from other urban elites. As Christopher Haigh cautions us in his study of the English Reformation, historical change can seem straightforward only when the opposition is omitted from the story or "treated as silly old fogeys ripe for defeat"; reformations are the work of both "those who grumbled and those who greeted," and we shall see some passionate grumblers in these chapters.[34] Chapter 6 returns to Mexico City, where the simple piety helped birth a lively public sphere of political commentary and critique from roughly 1808 to 1834. Reformers fought to free the godly individual from all restraints on his conscience, including the Church hierarchy, and sought to exclude the immoderate from political participation. They thus launched a thoroughly religious critique of the Church's corporate privileges and prerogatives, seeking to create a truly godly commonwealth.

But if the reform was not a secularizing movement, it did offer aid and comfort to a more secular approach to death. The final two chapters chronicle the transferal of funerals and burials from the provenance of priests to that of licensed doctors as the nineteenth century wore on. Through its reformation of the individual, enlightened Catholicism fertilized the cultural soil for the growth of medical observation as a technique of rule. The new medicine grew alongside the new piety in the tangled garden of the late eighteenth century; therefore, to assign religion a causal role in the former's genesis seems perhaps disingenuous. Surely their mutual distrust of received wisdom conspired to place the individual as the starting place of knowledge, and no doubt it did. But religion, not science, was man's greatest concern; salvation loomed largest, and to impose our own scientific, secular assumptions on theirs is simply anachronistic.

Thus, by this route I argue that the religiously inspired, nominally egalitarian, and individualistic vision of community suggested by enlightened Catholicism provided the cultural matrix for certain elite liberals' post-Independence vision of a nation characterized by claims to the sovereignty and legal equality of all "virtuous" citizens.

chapter 1

The Baroque Backdrop

In the mid–thirteenth century, Spanish King Alfonso the Wise adduced four reasons for preferring church burials over any other final resting place. First, Christians were closer to God than were other sects, and thus their tombs should be closer to churches. Second, church burials provided a salutary reminder to pray for the souls of departed relatives and friends. Third, the dead buried in churches received the aggressive advocacy of the saints in whose honor churches were built. And, finally, bodies placed close to the faithful and protected by their prayers escaped the many devils that plagued suburban burial sites.[1]

Alfonso's concerns would continue to inform Spanish burial laws until the late eighteenth century. A trio of themes clearly underlie the brief list. Most strikingly, physical proximity to designated holy spaces or features is assumed to imply a spiritual advantage, and, conversely, distance from those sanctified points invites danger. Furthermore, spiritual devotion is understood as a collective affair: believers are expected to pray on one another's behalf, and a pantheon of heavenly intercessors processes the requests and transmits them to the Almighty. Finally, believers are assumed to approach God through mediators, who rank above common, fallen man but below the Deity. The concrete, communal, and mediated nature of the sacred was beyond dispute; the question for Alfonso, as for us here, was how to apply these principles to death and burial.

During the seventeenth century and even long after the reform challenge, the Church in New Spain offered its adherents multiple points of access to the sacred. The Catholic world teemed with holy places; the faithful expected—and received—miracles. God erupted into this-worldly life with dogged regularity, and the sacred could flourish within the profane. Humble objects—a shred of cloth, a wafer of unleavened bread, a mason's stone—could be transformed into conduits for heavenly power and could be caressed, ingested, addressed by very mortal men and women. In a world of coarse, immediate pain and few physical comforts, a splinter of the True Cross offered tangible succor for body and soul.

Physical objects contributed to observance in other ways, too. The Church had long recognized the difficulty of communing with God, of concentrating one's full attention on the contemplation of the Divine. Baroque ornamentation was intended to aid in this formidable labor by tantalizing the senses and thereby bending them to the task at hand. If a breathtaking representation of the pieta or a soaring choral Mass wrenched the eyes and ears into a state of adoration, perhaps the heart could follow.

Then, too, the Christian of baroque Catholicism never faced the terrible absolutes of spiritual life unaccompanied. Religious orders and, for the laity, confraternities dedicated to specific saints offered a religious group identity entirely in keeping with the corporate self-conception of seventeenth-century Europe and New Spain; many confraternities organized themselves into these spiritual societies on the basis of their occupations. Moreover, worship itself demanded mass participation. Pilgrimages, holy feasts and festivals, the Mass itself, even ecclesiastically mandated periods of deprivation and mourning—all would have been rendered nonsensical as individual observances. Human company, of course, suffered from severe limitations, but Christians could turn increasingly to the cults of the saints for supernatural advocacy and aid for even such earthbound concerns as scurvy, impotence, and lost money. Weak, fallen, beset by sin and temptation the Christian might well be, but alone? Neither in this world nor the next.

Both trends in Alfonso's formulation, then, reveal the abundance and fragmentation of spiritual power in the Church. The eternal was approached through the external, in ample company and through appropriately ordered channels. Let us turn to the baroque spiritual world of seventeenth- and eighteenth-century Mexico City, using death as our point of entry into New Spain.

Blood, Sweat, and Tears:
Popular Reverence for Relics and Images

The baroque Church in New Spain encountered God's miraculous mercy channeled through a multiplicity of particular places and objects and could point to ample precedence for its beliefs. Europeans had venerated miracle-working bodies or bones of saints and holy people long before the eleventh-century rise in the cult of saints' images, which subsequently grew alongside it.[2] Relics' miraculous healing powers could even point to scriptural authority. The Apostle Paul cures by the laying on of hands, but also by objects he touches: "From his body were brought unto the sick handkerchiefs or aprons, and the diseases departed from them, and the evil spirits went out of them" (Acts 19:12). As Marina Warner argues convincingly, the association of an article with the essence of its former owner can hardly be called exotic; anyone who has ever caressed a beloved's photo or article of clothing, or pestered a celebrity for an autograph, can easily attest to the "simple humanity" of this urge.[3]

But it was the Council of Trent in particular, and the Counterreformation Church in general, that officially endorsed the veneration of sacred relics. Convened between 1545 and 1563, the Council represented a circling of the wagons for the Church; confronted by Protestant attacks and growing defections to the rival camps, the learned Church fathers gathered to elucidate and confirm doctrine. The broader movement to clean up the Church's reputation, the Counterreformation, similarly delved into matters of belief and official observance in defense of the true faith.[4] Consequently, many matters that previously had been left murky and open to individual interpretation became formalized into rigid dogma for the first time.

Relics, then, came in for scrutiny in their turn, and the Church formalized the process for obtaining approval through a bishop. Additional routes for legitimization of relics were provided by the Congregation of Rites and later through the Congregation of Relics and Indulgences. Although the Church now struggled with the laity over whose imprimatur conferred authenticity on holy relics, it did not deny their miraculous powers; rather, it actively encouraged the faithful to seek their powerful aid for their worldly afflictions. Displayed in impressive cases, newly approved relics boasted an official wax seal and red cord.[5] In sixteenth- and seventeenth-century Castile, these relics protected towns from inclement weather, warded off the frequent threats of locusts and drought, and miraculously cured the halt and lame who frequented their ubiquitous shrines.[6]

Despite the stricter authentication process, the traffic in relics stepped up in the late sixteenth century. Alarmed Catholics now rescued these miraculous conduits of divine power from marauding Protestant iconoclasts, spiriting them to safety in Spain and Rome. Cologne's Eleven Thousand Virgins proved a particular boon to the supply, and they and other invaluable treasures received official papal authentication before being sent out to comfort the faithful and bolster the spiritual patronage powers of princes like Spain's Philip IV; Madrid alone boasted the heads of 109 virgins in 1629.[7] The Jesuits joined the Pope and the Spanish Crown as major owners and distributors of these powerful conduits of sacred power, and in 1577 Pope Gregory regaled New Spain with remnants of the apostles and of the doctors of the Church and a thorn taken from Christ's crown. Again in 1584, the Pope showed his generosity to New Spain's Jesuits: in a munificent gesture, he bestowed on them the most prized of all relics, a sliver of the True Cross, as well as a fragment of the Virgin Mary's veil. The latter may not have been exotic; during the High Middle Ages Christians venerated Our Lady's milk, nail parings, and even her hair, in quantities that would have suggested an alarming hirsuteness for the Queen of Heaven could they all have been authenticated![8]

These artifacts of Christendom's holy heritage naturally traversed oceans to reach the far-flung faithful of the Spanish Empire. And even en route to New Spain these holy relics demonstrated their efficacy: the Cross saved the ship from a tempest, and during a subsequent storm the chest guarding the veil refused to budge as desperate sailors jettisoned cargo to save the imperiled vessel; it later whipped up the wind as the ship bobbed helplessly in interminable doldrums. The arrival of these relics occasioned much joy and celebration in the star of Spain's imperial firmament, Mexico City, and their miraculous powers offered hope to those beset with sickness and natural calamity; not long after their arrival, the Jesuits reported, tongues began to tell of the veil's healing powers.[9]

Mexico City, however, was not dependent on imported relics for access to the sacred. With the new guidelines for sainthood, considerable lobbying efforts on behalf of candidates became the rule. In New Spain, from roughly 1740 to 1806, all testators paid a mandatory tax to send advocates to Rome to fight for the canonization of Mexican martyr Felipe de Jesús, who had received beatification in the late sixteenth century.[10] A native son, Felipe worked as a silversmith's apprentice until he entered Puebla's convent of Santa Barbara, which he later fled to travel to Manila as a soldier. After dissipating his small savings, he again took the habit and, now seized with religious fervor, engaged in the fasting and mortification that would bring him closer to God. During his return trip to New Spain in 1600, his boat capsized off the coast of Japan; the Japanese infidels imprisoned the survivors and cut off Felipe's ear. A fellow Christian secreted the grisly souvenir to the Jesuits, who treated it as a holy relic. After a torturous overland march, Felipe and twenty-five others died nailed to crosses, and the faithful collected the martyrs' blood in their hats. Every Friday, they reported, columns of fire and stars of varying colors appeared above the crucifixion site.

In Mexico City, Felipe's body parts graced many churches and convents. The cathedral chapel dedicated to the martyr housed one large and one small bone, the latter resting in an expensive glass case. The chapel of Santa Rosa in the convent of Santo Domingo displayed a cross built from the wood of San Felipe's death cross. The Mexico City Franciscans even boasted a bone shaped in the holy man's image. The Colegio de San Buenaventura, the convent of San Gerónimo, and a Franciscan priory near Toluca all had fingers or small bones from Felipe, and Puebla's convent of Santa Barbara displayed his skin. Mexico City's convent of San Diego had an altar dedicated to all of the twenty-five martyrs who died in Japan, complete with bones.[11]

The beatification of Gregorio López was another seventeenth-century cause supported by mandatory taxes. Asking rhetorically "Who was Gregorio López?" in 1686, chronicler Juan Antonio Rivera explained, "Some say he was Prince Charles, son of Philip II, who had been secretly whisked to Mexico when someone gave the order to hang him."[12] Writing in 1763, Capuchin friar Francisco de Ajofrín noted that López came from Madrid to America, where he "lived as an angel" until he died in his hermit's cave near Mexico City in 1596. The cave continued to attract the faithful, he reported, and López's body rested in a cathedral chapel awaiting his beatification.[13] Franciscan Friar Agustín de Vetancourt raved about the sanctity of López's relics housed in the cathedral's sacristy in 1698, as did observer Juan de Viera in 1777, who noted that it was widely held that the hermit's remains emitted "the smell of saintliness [olor de santidad]."[14] In the late eighteenth century, however, King Charles III ordered the mandas for López's beatification suspended, and Viceroy Matías de Galvez (1783–1784) reissued the order in New Spain.[15]

Official sanctification was one thing; the popular belief in the relics' miraculous powers was quite another. Historian Rosalva Loreto López followed the beatification campaign of one seventeenth-century nun from New Spain's city of Puebla de los Angeles, Mother María de Jesús Tomellin (1582–1637), through three centuries, outlining the miracles the faithful attributed to her. Like Gregorio López, the holy woman emitted an "olor de santidad." Loreto López elaborates on the holy odor: at her death, the nun had been bathed in a thick, sweet-smelling sweat unlike any worldly fragrance, with beads the shape and size of pearls. Pearls had long symbolized sexual purity in Catholic thought, and the sweet fragrance was taken as a sure sign of her saintliness. Bodily putrefaction is the penalty for the Fall, the Church taught; the stench of death often signaled evil in Christian writings. By contrast, the hagiography of saints bursts with fragrant odors and miraculous preservations. Typical of these descriptions, a text from Ecclesiasticus portrays a richly aromatic Virgin Mary: "I gave a sweet smell like cinnamon and aspalathus, and I yielded a pleasant odor like the best myrrh, as galbanum, and onyx, and sweet storax, and as the fume of frankincense in the tabernacle" (Ecclesiasticus 24:15).[16]

Mother María's sweet fragrance, then, signaled her likeness to Our Lady, whose incorrupt body had been borne to heaven in its entirety. The nun's victory over decomposition and death was thus a miracle, a literal infusion of God's saving power into the world. This power leached into physical objects that the holy woman had touched. In particular, earth from her tomb as well as her bodily fluid and other parts had curative powers, a fact not lost on Puebla's faithful. When her body was displayed for the funeral, clerics scrambled to grab the flowers that surrounded her, tore her veil and most of her habit to shreds, and even ripped pieces of skin from her hand. The laity, too, had access to the miraculous cures her relics performed, as nuns from her convent sold relics to the faithful in the form of cloths moistened in the miraculous sweat that the body continued to exude. Here indeed was fervent desire for thaumaturgical channeling of God through objects charged with His sacred essence.

And none could deny the desperate need for such material aid. Racked by frequent plagues, gangrenous sores, and the sudden death of children through illness and accident, Mexico City residents sought God's mercy through direct physical contact with the surfeit of the sacred contained in holy relics—both those officially blessed and those with only the imprimatur of popularity. At his death in roughly 1599, Franciscan Sebastián de Aparicio sweated the familiar aromatic liquid which the faithful, like Veronica wiping Christ's humid brow, mopped up with their handkerchiefs.[17] Like many saints, Aparicio was credited with the cure of particular ailments or problems, his specialty being dead children. One man placed a cloth moistened with the holy man's sweat on the head of his recently deceased child, who immediately revived; bereft parents understandably mobbed his tomb to entreat similar miracles. One child two hours drowned came back to life, and his grateful mother publicized the miracle, as she had promised Aparicio himself.[18]

With ample evidence of these relics' curative powers, Mexico City had become a veritable ossuary by the eighteenth century. The relics of saints and secular dignitaries attracted those who sought succor from sickness or merely a powerful intercessor, and the city's churches and convents competed to have the most holy body parts on display. His namesake confraternity in the Convent of La Enseñanza Antigua tended the index finger and image of San Juan Nepomuceno in the late eighteenth century.[19] In 1722 the cathedral boasted the body of the Carmelite martyr Saint Anastasio, available for public viewing in a silver-trimmed glass coffin.[20] City Councilman Juan Manuel de Aguirre came to rest in the convent of San Francisco in 1729, but the Hospital of la Concepción got his heart.[21] Early in the century the city's churches placed these "inestimable treasures" on display every November 2 for the Feast of All Souls; the *Gacetas de México* noted that so popular had the custom become that even church doors were festooned with body parts.[22]

Images, like relics, offered the faithful direct, tangible conduits to God's mercy, and their caretakers often whisked them through the streets to homes of those stricken with disease so the afflicted could touch them. The Church certainly evinced concern that relics and saints' images acquire official validation, but the theological soundness of their miraculous powers was rarely questioned, and stories of miraculous images abounded in New Spain.[23] One of the most prodigious of these icons in late eighteenth-century Mexico City was a child Jesus bequeathed by an Indian artisan to the convent of San Juan de la Penitencia. During a particularly jarring earthquake, the arch above the image creaked and threatened to collapse, but the diminutive baby Jesus propped it up with two of his small fingers. In 1768, chronicler Juan Manuel de San Vicente, an administrator of the city's comedy coliseum, noted that the feat impressed the faithful, who frequently requested he be brought from his altar to their sick beds.[24]

He was not alone in these missions of mercy. A painting of San Francisco Xavier, famed for having dripped saintly sweat from the canvas, never rested even two days on its altar before being summoned to a sickbed.[25]

Believers contracted for many of these miraculous cures, exchanging gifts, devotion, and promises of publicity for divine attention to their plight. Those who reneged on a vow to a saint risked falling into mortal sin. In 1778, the Mexico City parish of Santa Veracruz had to be amplified to make more room for a life-size image of Our Lady of Soledad regularly showered with gratitude for her miraculous cures. Her devotees adorned her in finery, including a gold crown embedded with the precious stones that symbolized eternity. Indeed, so popular had her cult become that the church expanded to hold the *ex voto* offerings (that is, offerings made in fulfillment of a vow) and paintings that depicted the lame who now walked and the diseased who had recovered from their afflictions through her channeling of God's mercy.[26]

Miraculous images that sweated or wept blood as Christ had in His Passion, curing relics that exuded a saintly odor—here indeed was ample evidence of God's powers at work in the world. God acted through His saints, those who "oozed precious driblets from the great sea of God's mercy" into the world, in historian Peter Brown's felicitous phrase.[27] Protestants had attempted to erase God's eruptions from the physical world. As if in self-defense, images and relics throughout the Catholic world awoke from their Renaissance slumber in the seventeenth century, sweating, weeping, and proffering miraculous cures. Here was baroque religiosity at its height in a pitched battle with austere Protestantism.

From the External to the Eternal: The Sensual Road to Salvation

The Council of Trent had affirmed that, given man's weak nature, visible reminders of God's majesty enhanced our understanding of the Divine.[28] Earlier, I hinted at the ability of these signposts to lead the mind from the terrestrial and mundane upward to an appreciation of God. During the mid–seventeenth century three successive popes confronted the Protestants' sensually ineffable God with the entire splendor at their disposal, funding an architectural extravaganza in Rome that rejected frozen, logical Renaissance designs in favor of soaring columns, swirling movement, and dazzling light.[29] In silver-rich New Spain, the interiors of baroque churches radiated God's majesty.[30] In art, too, God became more physically accessible, more human, more approachable: in Spanish court painter Velazquez's depiction of Vulcan's forge stand figures dressed as Castilian peasants; Caravaggio's religious paintings beckon to the observer; Bernini's Saint Teresa swoons in a quite earthy-looking ecstasy.

Indeed, this theology of external magnificence as a road to the eternal seems to have resonated with particular force in New Spain, where Indian conversion was the principal task at hand. Theatrical renditions of God's majesty provided a bridge of communication across the language and cultural chasm between the neophytes and the proselytizers. Paraliturgies such as dances and theater often proved more effective pedagogical instruments than the catechism, or so many clerics believed. Faced with the daunting task of converting the Pueblo Indians in the early seventeenth century, for example, Franciscan Friar Alonso de Molina paraphrased Trent's theology almost word for word, noting that incense, candles, vestments, and music were essential to "uplift the souls of the Indians and move them toward the things of God because they are by nature lukewarm and forgetful of internal matters and must be helped by means of external displays."[31] In a similar vein, when in 1793 a reformed bishop banned the parade of holy images during Silao's Holy Week, calling their adornment "indecent" and the parade itself an example of the Indians' desire for "uproar, puerile ostentation, and pernicious meetings," Indian confraternity leaders retorted with a theological defense worthy of Trent: without the stimulus of sight, the country folk's faith would wane; their understanding of doctrine came not from simple sermons or the catechism, but from their senses.[32]

Uproar, ostentation, and pernicious meetings, however, seem to have been the order of the day, if the funerals of wealthy Mexicans can be taken as indicative. The populace of Mexico City played frequent audience to innumerable processions and interments that dazzled the senses to the greater glory of God—and the deceased.

Inquisition Judge José Fierro Torres's 1768 funeral provides an example of this unbridled ostentation. Torres's body lay on a polished bed made of West Indian redwood dripping with gold braid and illuminated by candles and torches in ornate silver holders.[33] In a similar case from 1818, another Inquisition judge ordered his heart excised from his body to join other holy relics in the Convent of Santa Teresa la Antigua, where he had served as chaplain for thirty years. The Inquisition placed the remains of his body at the foot of the entrance stairs of their principal gallery, recumbent on silk pillows on an extravagant bier draped with damask and brilliantly illuminated. Nearby tables held a glittering display of silver chalices, gold and silver cloth, and figures of Christ.[34]

Although the cathedral chapter's prestigious clerics favored sober black caskets in the late eighteenth century, they nevertheless demonstrated the sort of unrestrained ostentation in keeping with an epistemology that privileged the external as a road to the eternal. Placed on an elaborate bier draped with bright cloth, the casket was crowned with a black velvet lid enlivened with gold braid; inside, one cleric's final rest was eased with velvet cushions sprouting gold tassels and covered with a gilt-encrusted drape.[35] Bright-colored coffins and flashy funeral attire also characterized the funerals of less distinguished subjects well into the nineteenth century, thanks to the burial insurance offered through confraternity dues. In 1776, a tailors confraternity dedicated to the cult of San Homobono accompanied its dead members to the church after providing a casket, a bright red cloth to cover the body, pillows, silver candle holders, and numerous candles for the trip.[36] Typical of the burial accoutrements offered by most confraternities, the San Sebastián parish brotherhood of Our Lady of Sorrows provided members with an embroidered silk funeral pall, a casket, cushions, and candles with elaborate holders, as well as the group's processional banner for the transportation of the body from the deceased's home to the church.[37]

This splendor reached its apogee, however, in the elaborate funeral beds commissioned by the mighty. Beginning in the early seventeenth century, historian Francisco de la Maza reports, these enormous catafalques shed their former Renaissance austerity and classical style to become sensual extravaganzas. In 1724, for example, King Felipe V's dead son symbolically occupied the central plaza with an enormous trilevel catafalque, its soaring Corinthian columns surmounted by the prince in an open carriage pulled by rearing horses. Paintings, richly adorned images of the saints, thousands of flickering candles, bright cloth, and elaborate baroque sonnets decorated most of these enormous structures, which were prominently displayed in churches.[38]

The sensate splendor of elite funerals also served a social function. Historian José Antonio Maravall makes a strong case that the wildly opulent street theatrics of Crown and high society in the burgeoning cities of seventeenth-century Spain operated on a particular assumption about man's internal nature. The task of those who wished to rule new urban crowds was "not to attempt to suppress the passions nor even stoically to silence them; rather they tried to make use of their force."[39] The idea was to enthrall, to channel the passions to an appreciation of the legitimacy of the powers that flattered them. The baroque was a technique of rule based on a particular notion of the self and its inner workings.

Historian Irving Leonard's own marvelously baroque prose makes him the ideal analyst of the era, and he frequently describes just how dazzling power could be in New Spain. Here he describes Archbishop-Viceroy Fray García Guerra's 1608 entry into Mexico City: "The Liveried magistrates, who had met Fray García on the outskirts of the city, now took positions as a guard of honor. Each held an ornate staff supporting the purple and gold palium with brocade trimmings that sheltered the Archbishop robed in glittering vestments. So massive was this canopy that it required twenty-two of the uniformed *regidores* to hold it aloft in this fashion. This dazzling tableau moved slowly through the streets lined with the awed populace. From the walls, windows, and balconies of the buildings on either side hung rich tapestries and bright-hued bunting."[40] Like the viceroy's entry, elite funerals were intended to awe, to enthrall, to enrapture the senses, to associate the deceased and his family with truly heavenly splendor.

Clearly, baroque funerals had everything to do with the external excitation of the senses as a pathway to God. But another characteristic of these processions competes for our attention: the sheer number of people accompanying the deceased can hardly be ignored. These hordes lead us to Alfonso's second unstated theme, that of the intensely communal nature of baroque Catholicism.

"For Thou Art with Me" Death and the Corporate Spirit

Until the late eighteenth century, few Mexico City residents regarded death as an intimate, introverted family affair, a mere crucible of sentimental crisis: salvation was at stake, and the community's presence was needed to expiate sins. Only the shabbiest of pauper funerals lacked numerous clerics, friends, beggars, family, clients, and perhaps confraternity members. The Church in one of its three manifestations—the saints, the dead, and here the living, or the "Church militant"—united to abbreviate Purgatory's tortures.

These suffrages were particularly crucial at the precise instant of death, the *agonia*, the moment when the senses stopped and the soul passed from the body. Since the twelfth century, Catholics had added individual judgment at the moment of death to the hope of a collective judgment on Christ's return. Now God scrutinized the individual's biography, and heavenly advocates pled his case to the divine tribunal. But first the dying had to face the devil, who appeared at their weakest moment, during the agonia. In this, his last chance to impede salvation, Satan offered an array of tantalizing temptations to the sick, including the hope of eternal life and the company of his loved ones; he also fought for the soul against heavenly angels and the prayers of the living.[41] Pamphlets that circulated in New Spain, such as the French Jesuit Juan Crasset's 1778 treatise on the art of dying, emphasized that all pious acts paled in importance compared to helping the sick die properly, because "the salvation or condemnation of a soul depended on the last battle." Doctors' only real duty lay in convincing the dead to confess, and priests who went to assist the dying "should consider themselves as captains defending a fortress surrounded by a powerful army of enemies."[42]

Particularly in the seventeenth century, many of Mexico City's faithful extended the crucial period for obtaining a reprieve from Purgatory beyond the agonia to include the days immediately following the death. Numerous testators requested Masses to be said or sung immediately after their deaths, even ordering Masses performed simultaneously in numerous churches to speed the process. They also arranged crowded funeral corteges to accompany their body to the church for the funeral and subsequent burial, and ensured that contingents of priests and laymen would pray at their funerals.

In particular, large numbers of religious regularly escorted the dead and prayed at burial ceremonies. In 1640, Bernaude de Medina left instructions in his will for fifty secular clerics and twelve friars from each of the regular orders to accompany his corpse from his house to the church.[43] Wealthy silver merchant Diego del Castillo, who funded the construction of two different churches, paid one hundred clerics to sanctify his death scene.[44] In 1696, Agustín de Medina struck a better deal: he spent the same amount as had Diego del Castillo, but contracted two hundred clerics.[45] To mark the 1677 death of Petronila de las Casas, Mexican martyr San Felipe de Jesús' niece, the populace was treated to a parade of sixty clerics and every Dominican and Dieguino in the city, as well as the palace guard—truly, a feast for the eyes.[46]

Paupers lent God's special favor for the poor to the occasion, and the children of San Juan de Letran were common sights in the funeral processions, imparting to the solemn occasion the holy innocence of children. Founded by the Crown in 1557, by the late eighteenth century the institution served only to supply children for burials, according to one contemporary observer, who noted that a funeral procession was considered sorely lacking in pomp and pizzazz without the unfortunate foundlings.[47] The wealthy also hired professional mourners, who lived off their funeral appearances, and rented mendicants—representatives of poverty's inherent blessedness—from the Royal Poor Hospital in the late eighteenth century, providing them with torches for the procession. Ornate carriages often brought up the rear.[48]

If the deceased belonged to a confraternity, the group's crier advised members of the funeral, and the *cofrades* led the funeral cortege decked out with the brotherhood's insignia.[49] These organizations bespeak the intensely social tendency of the city's religious identity; by the late eighteenth century, 951 registered confraternities operated in the archdiocese of Mexico City. Twelve of the city's fourteen parishes housed brotherhoods, as did seventeen of the twenty-one priories and eighteen of the capital's twenty convents.[50] Most members joined to promote the cult of a particular saint and ensure themselves of a decent burial under that saint's protection, and most confraternities carefully spelled out their burial obligations. In 1759, one typical Franciscan confraternity obliged all members to attend funerals and provided the dead with a coffin, candles for all of the Franciscan brothers to hold during the funeral, and four candles to surround the body during the wake. Cofrades could elect burial in the Franciscan convent, but the brothers accompanied even those buried elsewhere, provided they wore a Franciscan habit.[51] Added inducements to participation were considered prudent: the confraternity of San Homobono promised sixty days of accumulated indulgences for processing at a member's funeral.[52]

Particularly in the seventeenth century, many testators reminded their estate executors to include confraternities in the funeral arrangements. Gerónima Antonia de Alciuar's will declared her membership in the confraternities located in the convents of Nuestra Señora de la Merced and San Juan de Dios, and reminded her family that the membership cards could be found in her possessions if her standing were in any doubt; having paid her dues, she hoped the brotherhoods would comply with their obligations on her death. Widow Juana Rodríguez belonged to three confraternities and insisted on burial in a tomb designated for confraternity members in the Santa Catarina Martir parish chapel of Our Lady of Sorrows. She also urged the other two confraternities to pay her funeral expenses as they had promised in their *patentes*.[53]

Confraternities were not the only groups who accompanied the dead as corporate representatives. The Congregation of San Pedro provided mutual aid to clerics and to those among the laity who could afford the steep 500-peso entry fee charged in 1641. The congregation paid a bell-ringer to convene meetings and to post broadsides announcing members' burials and religious celebrations. Congregants also received individual notification to attend funerals and could even be fined for nonattendance. Clerics received a fee for attending burials and processing in funeral corteges; in 1643 Francisco de Saavedra noted that his twenty-two years of good service had won him the right to attend burials. Clerics valued their colleagues' prayers as the best guarantee of a short stint in Purgatory. Unable to say the Masses assigned to him due to illness, Gaspar de Meua used his will to implore the congregation to honor him with a burial equal to that of the organization's poorer members and to say Masses for his soul.[54]

Loath to leave anything to chance in the accompaniment of the body, at least in the late eighteenth century the deceased's relatives frequently distributed hundreds of cards announcing the obsequies—invitations whose ornate drawings and exaggerated prose were designed to attract as many attendees as possible. The family of the first Marques de Vivinco paid 47 pesos to print 500 cards announcing a 1799 burial; a year later, when a son died, the family again paid for 450 *cartas grandes* and paid one José Cayetano Zara 20 pesos to distribute them.[55] These invitations were often explicit about the sender's motivation for a large turnout; in 1788, Don Miguel Gomez's extended family and friends, for example, desired their guests' presence for the "best showing" of their relative in the Convent of Santa Clara, the number in attendance attesting to his importance and rank.[56]

Mexico City's better-off residents clearly had no shortage of available intercessors, but even in this climate some processions remained truly noteworthy for the sheer number of bodies in attendance. The 1651 funeral cortege of Avaro de Lorenzo dazzled spectators with the presence of the entire Congregation of San Pedro, twelve candle-bearing Dominicans and twelve Franciscans, the provincials of the city's religious orders, and the entire Third Order of San Francisco. According to one observer, "Every cleric in the kingdom attended" the funeral of de Lorenzo, along with numerous secular officials. In 1692, cleric Manuel de Pedraza requested that his body be accompanied by the entire Congregation of San Pedro, the prestigious cathedral confraternity of the Blessed Sacrament, multiple con-fraternities, and the Third Order of Saint Augustine.[57] Wills from this era exhibit the testators' intense preoccupation with this multitude; clearly, to die in colonial Mexico City was to summon the community's collective resources on your behalf. But just as obviously, these dazzling offerings to the glorification of God commanded earthly attention as well, and hardly accidentally. The comforting side of baroque corporate identity was its strength in numbers; the underbelly was its rigid hierarchy.

The First Shall Be First: Mediation and Hierarchy

We have touched on the role of the saints as conduits to the Trinity, and certainly the crowded heaven they populated echoes the communal nature of Catholic practice on earth. The mediated relationship with God that they reinforced, however, became one of the principal victims of Protestant wrath—and, as we shall see in the next chapter, of criticism from within the Church as well. Let us examine the nature of that relationship and the assumptions that supported it.

In her treatment of the cult of the Virgin Mary, Marina Warner quotes at length a Franciscan treatise from the fourteenth century that explains mediation with an arresting image. Imagine that a man has angered the sovereign; what course should he follow in regaining his king's good graces? Surely, a lowly subject would know better than to approach the king in person; rather, "He goes secretly to the Queen and promise a present, then to the earls and barons and does the same, then to the freemen of the household and lastly to the footmen." Similarly, the author helpfully elaborates, we should respect the hierarchy of heaven by bringing such gifts as "prayers, fasting, vigils and alms" to Mary, the Apostles, martyrs, saints, and the poor, all of whom can thus be induced to intercede with Christ the King.[58]

From this formulation of the spiritual realm it was a short logical leap to the priests' similarly intermediate position between believers and Christ. It was against this priestly mediation that Luther scored some of his most dazzling successes, especially given the high tide of anticlericalism among the laity who resented their excesses and venality. The later "priesthood of all believers" of Protestant theology eradicated in a single rhetorical stroke the entire justification for the sacrament of penance and the supposed necessity of clerical absolution.[59]

Furthermore, Protestant reliance on Scripture dealt a dangerous blow to one of the Church's weakest points: the doctrine of Purgatory, which made clerics indispensable and provided a significant source of revenue to an overextended institution. In John Bossy's formulation, Purgatory as a third possible destination for the dead Christian had been "creeping up on Western Christendom since the early Middle Ages" and received invaluable PR through Dante's *Divine Comedy* in 1320. Successive Church councils elaborated the concept from the thirteenth through the sixteenth centuries, evidently guided by rather than forming lay understanding. By the end of the Renaissance, then, the basic outlines were widely accepted: a soul dying in a state of venal sin could expect to spend time in the fiery cave of Purgatory doing penance before achieving Paradise.[60]

Beginning around 1300, the popes evidently entertained a prodigious confidence in their power over this realm as well as that of the living. Close on the heels of this power came that of releasing souls from their torment by way of indulgences. The doctrine of indulgence held that penance owed by one person could be performed and donated by another, assuming a close connection between the two. Indulgence thus added to the existing channels of prayer and sacrifice by which the living could discharge their obligations for the dead. Jesus' self-sacrifice on the cross not only compensated for all believers' sins, it left a surplus of merit unconsumed, which the Church proved willing to transfer to the faithful. And as all the world knows in the wake of Luther's 95 Theses, the Church yielded to the obvious temptation of selling indulgences rather than granting them for penance of prayer and fasting. This practice passed from the unofficial to the official realms of Church practice in 1476, when Pope Sixtus IV decreed that absolute remission of Purgatory would be granted to designated friends and family members in return for contributions to the rebuilding of the church at Saintes in western France. Subsequent sales followed this model, as the jingle apocryphally attributed to Johan Tetzel affirms: "As soon as the coin in the coffer rings/The soul from Purgatory springs."[61]

Mexico City residents' fervent desire for indulgences is nowhere better illustrated than in their enthusiasm for burial habits. Even before being escorted to the church for the funeral services that preceded the burial, and perhaps even before death, the body was dressed in a funeral shroud. The choice of this dress was no light matter. St. Thomas Aquinas had even gone so far as to grant the habit sacramental status, claiming that it could restore the sinful to a state of innocence. During the Middle Ages, many believed that a monastic habit facilitated one's entrance to Heaven. God was a stern judge, and few wished to face Him without a team of celestial advocates to plead on their behalf. A solitary encounter with the Divinity was a most terrifying thought, and the burial shroud of a particular saint was a sure way to grab his or her attention and subsequent intervention in one's plight.[62] In Mexico City, as in many areas of Spain and in Veracruz, the Franciscan habit was the most solicited burial garment. In addition to providing a powerful ally, the Franciscan mortaja (habit) properly blessed by regional officials and worn at the time of death provided the wearer with an unspecified reprieve from Purgatory's torments, as carefully explained in bulls issued by at least four popes.[63] The faithful knew of these indulgences, and several specifically requested the habit of Saint Francis for "the graces and indulgences given to all those buried in said habit."[64]

Although the dying overwhelmingly sought out Saint Francis as their preferred intercessor, some chose other shrouds, perhaps hoping to gain the attention of less occupied advocates. Additionally, religious sometimes opted to be buried in their vestments or the habits of their particular orders. Laymen enjoyed the same privilege relative to their guilds and confraternities; one master tailor, for example, asked to be covered in the tunic of the tailors' Confraternity of the Santísima Trinidad, in a church where he served the Chapel of the Precious Blood of Christ. Several of the faithful left nothing to chance and donned two mortajas for their appearance in front of the heavenly court. A typical matron insisted on the shroud of both San Francisco and Santo Domingo, and a cathedral employee insured the sale of his inheritance to provide him with habits of two different religious orders.[65]

A funeral shroud was not an exotic burial accoutrement that few had seen or pondered before their deaths; Juana Rodríguez, Isabel Rodríguez, Francisco del Castillo, and María Rosa Guerra all instructed their executors to rummage through their clothing to find their mortajas, long since bought and casually included with less ghoulish finery. Guerra even bequeathed a spare shroud to her freed slave, just as she must have handed off her dresses when they went out of style![66] Respect for the custom even persisted in the least likely of circumstances. Several assassins who beat a man to death in 1784 had the patience to dress his body in a funeral shroud modeled on those of condemned prisoners. When the dead man's employer recovered the body, he exchanged that covering for one he must have considered more appropriate, dressing it in a Franciscan habit and paying for a church burial.[67]

In spite of the clear social concern with proper burial dress, however, many found the price prohibitively steep. Certainly, the pooled resources of the confraternities helped some; for the uninsured, peddlers offered a lively traffic in unauthorized garments in the city's markets and plazas. The Archconfraternity of El Cordón de Nuestro Seráfico Padre San Francisco allotted members 12 pesos and 4 reales for a proper convent shroud "to ensure that it carried indulgences." The head of the Franciscans, however, complained that avaricious entrepreneurs had defrauded the order of this important revenue and deprived the faithful of indulgences by fabricating and selling lower-priced habits: "Daily the faithful are buried in Franciscan habits, yet few come to the convent to purchase them," and the prior feared that vendors beguiled their clients into believing that their purchases had been properly blessed and thus carried indulgences.[68]

Some of these habits, however, had perhaps already received an official benediction, as thieves stripped the dead of their garments for resale in the city's informal flea markets. One man complained that San Lázaro's Indian gravediggers had broken into his mother-in-law's coffin and thrown her body into a pit where naked bodies bobbed in the water, as someone had removed and laundered their mortajas to sell them in the market.[69] Those who could not afford even a black market habit flouted the law to beg money for them in the streets. That this practice was seen as legitimate as well as lucrative is revealed in the case of two girls, age twelve and thirteen, who hit the streets in 1784, the elder feigning death while the younger cajoled passers-by into donating for her sister's burial habit.[70]

Mediation, then, formed a crucial support of the baroque Church, in both its clerical and its saintly guises. An awareness of this hierarchical relationship permeates the wills left behind in New Spain during the dominance of baroque Catholicism from this study's beginnings in 1620 until the late eighteenth century. And nowhere is the saints' mediating function clearer than in both notaries' and testators' conception of heaven as a replica of the court of an earthly king. Since the twelfth century, the Church had taught that individuals faced judgment on death in addition to the collective judgment that would occur at Christ's return. Many of the faithful envisioned this judgment as an appearance in front of a heavenly court presided over by a stern and punitive God. To stand alone here was a most frightening thought, especially to a resident of New Spain, who knew firsthand how hair-splitting justice could be. Fortunately, the queen of this court, the Virgin Mary, could be prevailed on to plead one's case, and the lobbying skills of the saints and angels were also readily available to the faithful. In the advocation section of the will, the notaries asked Mexico City testators to name intercessors for their appointment in the celestial court, and Heaven's Queen, guardian angels, the Archangel Michael, and the saint whose name the testator bore were all frequently mentioned, as well as other saints to whom they had a special devotion.

In accordance with contemporary Church teachings, wealthy testators bedecked Mary and the saints in the sartorial splendor befitting their lofty court position. Seventeen percent of the testators canvassed for the period 1710 to 1720 left such gifts for holy images; as we shall see, this percentage declined precipitously among their later counterparts. Buried in the Augustinian convent in the presence of the entire Mexico City nobility in 1722, one Maria Antonia de Mendrice bequeathed an astonishing 63,570 pearls to adorn the image of the Virgen de los Angeles.[71] In a more typical bequest, another well-born lady willed a silk tunic woven with "the finest adornment" to the Jesus of Nazareth venerated in the convent of Santa Catarina; Our Lady of the Rosary received an antique diamond necklace, a bracelet, and three threads of fat pearls; and a painted image of Saint Francis of Paula came into enough fine silver for a new frame.[72] The eighteen angels bedecked in pearls and diamonds bespoke another communicant's generosity as they danced attendance on the saints' images processed through the streets on Good Friday in the 1760s.[73] In Veracruz, several confraternities sent invitations to city dignitaries to join them in similarly adorning the angels who regularly graced that city's religious processions in the late eighteenth century.[74] In this way, wealthy and pious testators could serve as conduits, bringing God's splendor to earth where the faithful could see it; in the process, the wealthy could also display their own association with the exalted hierarchy of heaven.

As in any status-based society, the circle of saints demanded exclusivity to maintain its lofty position. The Council of Trent proved instrumental in regulating admission to this most exclusive of confraternities, condemning apocryphal saints, and in 1587 the embattled Church moved against saints' cults that lacked official approval. From this time forward a rigorous legal investigation, featuring advocates for the cult as well as a "devil's advocate" who represented the opposition, judged the candidates on their performance of miracles, doctrinal purity, and heroic virtue.[75] Only when a candidate had passed this initial beatification process was he or she elevated for canonization by the Pope. But although Trent and later reformers tightened their control over the sorting-out process and attempted to curb the worst cases of idolatry, the influential Council issued no explicit condemnation of ordinary Catholics' practices concerning saints. Pilgrimages, the cult of favor-dispensing images, appending ex voto offerings to images, the cult of relics—all of these practices continued unchecked. By regulating sainthood, indeed, the Church endorsed it with renewed confidence.[76]

The hierarchical nature of the baroque Church and the supernatural world it purported to represent can hardly be in doubt. Let us now look specifically at the case of burials in New Spain for the practical effects of this theology. The contemporary logic of death offers us an entryway by combining the concrete, the communal, and the hierarchical in a single locale.

Church Burials: Locating the External and the Corporate

The practice of burying the dead in parish churches, monasteries, and convents arrived in America with the Spanish, who had accommodated their dead in temples since at least the eighth century. Indeed, in stark contrast to Bourbon King Charles III's aggressive cemetery advocacy, the Crown initially threw its weight behind church burials in the Indies. Royal edicts encouraged bishops not to impede anyone from obtaining a church crypt in 1583, and even chastised the Franciscans in 1660 for charging exorbitant fees that indirectly discouraged church interment.[77]

In contemporary cosmology, the logic was self-evident. Churches, as consecrated spaces and as the collection point for sacred objects and images, were naturally more holy than other locales. Similar conceptions motivated pilgrimages both to miraculous European sites and to the Holy Land.[78] The act of consecration rendered the very bricks and mortar of the building qualitatively different from common stones, just as the Host was transformed from mere bread to the Body of Christ.

If certain places were holier than others, then it followed that some locations were so far removed from the sacred as to be downright dangerous. One religious order so feared the devils who beset their brothers' remains in a neglected and lonely tomb that in 1787 they moved the bones to the glittering chapel of Our Lady of Sorrows. The bodies left the "nefarious company of demons that regularly visited even those buried in sacred ground," to be placed where the prayers of the devout and good works for the "souls trapped in the prison of Purgatory" would abbreviate their tortures. In the new chapel, the brothers would be under the protection of the Virgin Mary, to whom the chapel was dedicated, and could count on the aid of the saints whose "sacred relics" decorated the chapel's altar. Preacher José Francisco Valdés concluded that the move benefited the dead friars enormously.[79] The chapel's rich adornment testified to the saint's popularity, and the numerous candles and lamps cast the heavenly light that deterred the devil. Bodies buried in the more popular locale would benefit from the prayers of those devoted to the Virgin.

But while demons still frolicked around isolated bodies, nowhere were Mexico City testators more in agreement with Alfonso the Wise than in their fervent quest for heavenly protectors, and their wills brim with requests to be buried near particular images housed in churches and chapels. The wish for a heavenly advocate, for the succor of prayers by the congregation, and for protection from demons manifested itself in requests for burial in a crypt directly under an advocate's protection.

Recall that testators typically named celestial advocates in their will. Why, then, did they insist on the additional trouble and expense of burial near images of what were so often the same advocates? The desire for physical proximity to these holy images and the relics was fueled by the belief that God revealed His majesty to the world through the object domain, and saints and their relics were high in the hierarchy of sacrally charged locations. Cleric Josef de la Peña, a Spaniard from Galicia, requested burial in the chapel of Our Lady of Antigua and implored the Cathedral Chapter not to impede his wishes because of his "special devotion to this image." The widow Juana de Abila Tirado sponsored the altar

CHURCH/CHAPEL BURIAL

of San Ecce Homo in the church of the Immaculate Conception and had personally adorned the saint with candlesticks and draperies; it was her dying wish that both she and her family rest there.[80] The shifting popularity of particular advocates awaits its historian, but many late eighteenth-century testators requested the protection of the Virgin of Guadalupe, the patroness of New Spain; typical of her devotees was Creole Manuel Antonio Mateos, who in 1802 selected burial by her altar in the convent of La Merced.[81] Adhering to the older style in burial preference, in 1824 the archbishop's secretary and an ex-administrator of the Convent of Regina Celi expressed his fervent desire to be laid to rest "near one of the altars where the faithful adore Our Holy Mother of Sorrows or Our Lady of Light."[82]

Many testators in fact militated for extremely specific burial spots as close to a saintly image as possible. Josefa Rita Rondon did not want to be buried somewhere in the vicinity of Our Lady of Sorrows: she wanted to rest directly under her feet, and felt confident that the cathedral would honor her wishes because she had spent generously on Masses and celebrations. In 1720, Anna Maria Guerrero Hinojasa Cordova specified burial in a crypt whose entrance fell *inside* the railing of the altar of Our Lady of Sorrows; if her wishes were not respected, however, she requested at the very least to rest inside the railing of the altar to another saint in the same church. The Santa Veracruz parish confraternity of San Francisco Javier had a three-tiered burial plan in their chapel: clerical members of the confraternity rested in tombs in the presbytery, confraternity officials near the altar steps, and all other members in a crypt under the chapel's entrance.[83] Similarly, the Confraternity of the Precious Blood of Christ, located in Santa Catarina parish, buried rectors and majordomos in their chapel's presbytery, while lesser officials rested at the foot of the presbytery stairs, and the bulk of the membership occupied the chapel's nave.[84]

In funerals and church burials, then, those lucky enough to command respect for their final wishes united the dominant themes of baroque spirituality. On the one hand, they paid homage to external nodes of sacred power by demanding access to saints' images and earthly relics; on the other, they summoned the collective efforts of the visible and invisible Church to speed them on their way and intercede on their behalf. In so doing, of course, the dead themselves became yet another external inducement to pious observance: how much easier for a communicant to remember his religious duties when kneeling directly over another's mortal remains!

But this complex web of spiritual functions could hardly exist in a vacuum. The combined elements of external display and communal mediation were simultaneously carrying out a social mission, albeit less explicitly. The hidden agenda is thus our next concern.

Baroque Spirituality and the Social Order

In and of themselves, the burial habits of New Spain's elite are of interest only to devotees of the colonial Empire, or to those of a ghoulish turn of fancy. But it is my argument that these practices and the changes they underwent at the hands of reformers reveal a fundamental shift in how men related to God and notions of community that often is attributed only to Protestant history. Looking outside the Church to the surrounding social order allows us to begin that exploration.

If the devout chose their tombs to ensure numerous suffrages and effective, energetic advocates for their immortal souls, they also did so with an eye toward a display of their social position. New Spain's church floors and chapels mapped the society's intricate caste and status categories, as the careful placement of the dead reiterated worldly honors and temporal distinctions. As Francisco Antonio Lorenzana candidly noted in his capacity as archbishop of Toledo, Spain, "The Church uses burials and the ritual honoring of cadavers to distinguish not only kings and sovereigns, but individuals and social groups."[85] In addition to noble family privileges, each ethnic and many occupational groups in colonial society had their own economic prerogatives, tax obligations, and even legal rights and separate court systems, and these juridically fixed identities found expression in the careful carving up of church burial spaces according to their distance from sacrally charged locations. In death as in life, the Church sanctified the privileges of the ancien régime's group-based social structure, its floors and chapels guides to distinctions among the living.

In particular, Church burials charted the ancien régime's carefully delineated caste distinctions. Members of the República de los Indios bore its special privileges and obligations, such as tribute payment and exemption from the Inquisition's jurisdiction. These Indians likewise rested in specially designated tombs in the regular orders' churches, usually in the

[handwritten margin note: SOCIAL POSITION CONFIRMED IN DEATH (TRAPPINGS)]

exterior cemetery or in an outdoor chapel that reflected their lowly status.[86] The official 1669 schedule of burial fees is insistently specific: those of Spanish descent paid 4 pesos to be buried in the space stretching from the altar to the middle of the church; poorer whites and mestizos needed 20 reales to rest in tombs under the center area to the door; mulattos paid 12 reales for a similar privilege; Indians paid 1 peso. The common cemetery adjacent to the church housed the impecunious dead at no cost. By 1787, these fees remained virtually unchanged.[87] These were steep but not exorbitant prices for the time, when the annual subsistence-level income for one person in Mexico City hovered around a mere 34 pesos, and artisans, who rarely had full-time employment, earned from one-half to 1 peso daily.[88]

Elite families represented their social position by requesting burial in family crypts. No official price list existed for these prestigious locations; a 1555 law prohibited the laity from selling church burial sites to each other, and one in 1565 banned prelates from granting anyone perpetual family rights to interment in chapels without a written permission from a bishop.[89] Nevertheless, the law appears to have been flouted with impunity. Indeed, the Church required a "customary donation" to obtain a burial spot, implying that the custom was so widespread as to command a generally recognized price.[90] Numerous testators expressed their desire to rest in family tombs or family chapels, the latter an expensive proposition that involved maintaining the chapel's decorations and founding or perpetuating a salaried chaplaincy. One wealthy owner of a sugar mill modestly declared that as an "unworthy patron" of the convent of Our Lady of Mercy he wished his son to inherit his tomb in the convent's church. In 1661, Gabriel Guerero de Luna instructed his estate executors to place his body in the Santo Domingo chapel of Our Lady of Atocha in his ancestral crypt; almost fifty years later, a village mayor who may have been his descendant requested burial in the same chapel.[91]

Church burial spaces not only charted ethnic and family privilege but provided a key site for the display of corporate identities. The regular orders, particularly the Franciscans, housed numerous tombs designated to hold members of particular corporate entities. The Mexico City Merchants Guild, which held an officially sanctioned monopoly on trade in New Spain until 1789, buried its leaders in a Franciscan tomb otherwise reserved for the order's brothers. In a 1686 request, Merchant Guild prior Juan Jiménez de Siles declared his desire to "benefit from the proximity to the holy men resting in said burial spot." The rank-and-file Guild members rested in the Chapel of Our Lady of the Immaculate Conception in the same convent; 140 years after Jiménez de Siles's request, merchant Francisco Chavarri desired burial under this chapel, citing his membership in the Guild as his motivation. The Royal Mint also boasted its own tomb for both employees and their wives; in 1661 Doña Francisca Velasco identified strongly enough with her husband's employer to request burial in the crypt despite her mate's evident desertion. Both the Mexico City and Veracruz City Councils possessed their own chapels, and Mexico City's San Francisco Convent had a tomb for the Colegio de Abogados, prestigiously situated behind the Altar of the Sacred Trinity. Trade guild members also sought the comfort of group burial; in 1743 a Castilian silversmith requested burial in a tomb reserved for members of that high-status trade, which was officially closed to anyone not of Spanish descent. Juana Alvarez de Valdés, the unmarried rector of a school for girls, insisted she be interred in the tomb designated for the institution's dignitaries.[92] To repose among one's fellows was evidently a great comfort to those for whom death was a familiar companion.

The clergy's sanctity and corporate status found expression in their burial under the main altar, a privilege legally denied to the laity. The cathedral chapter buried its distinguished members in the first crypt in front of the main altar on the side of the chapel of San Felipe in the late eighteenth century. Although a layperson, as a high-ranking official of both the Tailors Guild and the Archconfraternity of the Holy Trinity, in 1790 Rafael Puentes, alias "Pamplona," thought he deserved burial near the church's main altar. His advocates continued to insist on this privilege despite the consolation of Puentes's elaborate funeral, which included a church draped in black bunting, numerous torches and candles, and the offer of burial below an altar to Our Lady of Mercy. The Trinitarians flatly denied Pamplona burial by the main altar, citing precedence, evidence from a recent excavation of the site revealing that only priests' rotting bodies rested there.[93] Church burials thus offered a map of society's fundamental social arrangements, of its strict legal division into hierarchical corporate and caste groups. Through burials carefully arranged by their distance from sacrally charged locations such as the main altar or a saint's chapel, the Church sanctified these distinctions and asserted God's approval for them.

As we have seen, baroque Catholicism's priestly and saintly mediation, its unbridled opulence, its highly communal notion of salvation, and its miraculous infusions of the Divine into the mundane world all bore the tacit or explicit approval of both Church and state. Mexico City's colonial residents expected miracles, and the highest powers found this confidence eminently reasonable. The baroque was far from a socially neutral path to the sacred; in particular, its wild opulence was premised, as Maravall suggests, on the belief that stimulating the senses led to awe at the power of the seducer. But in the late eighteenth century a new form of devotion challenged the fundamental tenets of baroque Catholicism. The resulting conflict consumed influential portions of urban society and prompted a reevaluation of the Church's essential components—and of the justification for and techniques of social rule.

chapter 2

The Reformation in Mexico City

Indisputably, the Protestant Reformation is Europe's best-known response to prevailing Catholic currents during the middle centuries of the second millennium. Following Weber's famous thesis, the Reformation subsequently has accrued credit for the Enlightenment form of governance and the development of capitalism. Implicitly, then, Catholic Europe and its colonies have languished in the wake of Protestantism, forever a day late and a dollar short in the twentieth-century sweepstakes of national cohesion and democratic stability. By this line of reasoning, a nation forever in thrall to prerationalist modes of thought and extravagant public display can hardly be expected to tread the straight and narrow path of individual liberty, with all its presumed benefits.

In this context, the Counter-Reformation that developed within the Catholic Church itself is often regarded as an attempt by the losing concern to offer an improved product to the public and win back its market share, if you will. As we saw in the preceding chapter, the Council of Trent and the attendant Counter-Reformation sought to clarify and regularize doctrine, as well as to remedy flagrant misbehavior by the clergy. This project of the sixteenth and early seventeenth centuries, however, did not go far enough for some eighteenth-century Catholic reformers in the Spanish Empire, those who represented, in their words, "la piedad illustrada": enlightened piety.

As the name suggests, this new form of pious observance implied many of the same rationalist currents that culminated in Protestantism itself. It is my contention that these currents profoundly influenced the development of modern sensibilities in Mexico, long after the theological debate itself had cooled. In this chapter, we take a look at the emergence of the "new" piety, itself actually a reformulation of quite ancient religious thought, in the years 1767 to 1827. Most significant for our purposes, this enlightened Catholicism militated vigorously against several central features of baroque religiosity: its external sensuality, its communality, and its mediating hierarchy. In their place, it proffered an internal, individual, and direct spirituality that exalted moderation, reason, and discipline above all other Christian virtues. In so doing, the new piety challenged baroque techniques of rule and the divine sanctification of ossified social hierarchies and enshrined individual moral moderation as the true justification for social rule.

Augustine versus Pelagius: The Heart of the Struggle

In his indispensable guides to the theological issues of the Protestant Reformation, Alister E. McGrath lays out an argument in Christianity whose roots extend at least to the fourth century after Christ. At the crux of this dispute lay the notion of grace and its subsidiary, the doctrine of justification. "Grace" in this context referred to God's inexplicable clemency toward flawed and sinful mankind; "justification" boiled down to the requirements for salvation. In other words, and understandably, Christians were consumed with the question of how such a lowly creature as man could hope to enter into a relationship with God and thereby obtain the gift of His grace, salvation.[1]

Two competing schools of thought dominated this debate. Augustine of Hippo's writings encouraged the concept of salvation through grace alone; that is, human beings could not in any sense "earn" salvation, trapped as we are by our puny, sinful natures. Therefore, salvation must be a gift of God's grace, an undeserved bounty that the Almighty could bestow or withhold as He saw fit, but not in response to human efforts to win His favor. The doctrine of salvation through grace bore its ultimate fruit in the Protestant Reformation, but has flourished in less radical form in the Church of its birth across the centuries since Augustine.

The rival doctrine of "salvation by merit" is represented by Pelagius, to the point that Augustine's original works on grace and justification are referred to collectively as the "anti-Pelagian writings." Pelagius held a much brighter view of human capacity, and argued that God had revealed the requirements necessary for man to achieve Heaven. In this more two-sided relationship, man had but to strive for a moral life as laid out in Scriptural guidelines and, essentially, God would keep His end of the bargain.[2] In short, whereas Pelagius celebrated human autonomy and the benefits of good works for salvation, St. Augustine professed the belief that eternal life was a gift, not a reward.[3]

The medieval Church came down officially on the side of Augustinian grace, and Pelagianism was branded heretical. But the Church's official pro-Augustine stance reflected all the confusion inherent in medieval theology. Students of Augustinian thought in that era were confronted with a bewildering diversity of works claiming the imprimatur of Augustine's authorship. Moreover, even the works that subsequently proved authentic were fragmentary, physically isolated from one another, and often written in response to other theologians whose terms Augustine had been forced to adopt, to the confusion of commentators writing centuries later. Consequently, the Church professed fealty to Augustine in some areas without a clear understanding of the African saint's actual position. Such was the case for the doctrine of salvation through grace alone. Only the intense source-critical analysis that arose in the late Middle Ages allowed for some elucidation, and by that time, practices had grown up within the Church that enabled Protestants to attack Catholicism as insufficiently Augustinian, its official line notwithstanding.[4] After all, what could be more inimical to the idea of unearned grace than the sale of indulgences considered in the preceding chapter?

But Protestants were not the only ones troubled by this disjuncture between theory and practice. Rather, they were merely those who saw the problem as irresolvable within the existing structure of the Church, and so left it to begin anew. In so doing, as Benjamin Warfield points out, they elevated Augustine's precept of salvation through grace alone over another of his doctrines: that of the necessity of the Church for salvation.[5] Another group of reform-minded Christians, however, chose an alternative path and fought to honor salvation by grace within the Church. That fight took them to places inimical to the baroque piety explored in the first chapter. It was these early sixteenth-century Catholic reformers, particularly Erasmus of Rotterdam, whom our eighteenth-century enlightened Catholics found intellectually inspirational.

"Enlightened Piety" and the Pelagian Controversy

St. Augustine's insistence on the necessity of efficacious grace provided the core of Catholic Reform piety in the late eighteenth-century Spanish Empire. For Protestant John Calvin, God bestowed saving grace on men long before their actual physical existence in the world, and thus all of men's good works—their implorings, prayers, and charitable donations—were for naught in their quest for salvation. God's freely given grace was irresistible; man was helpless; and Calvin advised that "we must leave to God alone the knowledge of his church, whose foundation is his secret election."[6] God issued immutable decrees of divine grace for the elect and eternal damnation for the reprobate.

Grace was not so immutable for the Spanish Empire's eighteenth-century Catholic reformers. Although God singled out some for salvation, providing them with their "inner light," He also granted or retracted that gift during an individual's lifetime, and thus works had salvific efficacy—though only if inspired by love for God. But herein lay the rub: love of God came from God's previous gift, the "inner light." In 1777, Archbishop Alsonso Nuñez de Haro y Peralta neatly summarized his take on Augustinian grace thus: "Given that God is justice, then by essence, there is not nor can there be good intentions without love, and our intentions are more, or less, good according to the greater or lesser extension of this holy love."[7] The laws God inscribed in Christian hearts, in their souls, were nothing more than the very presence of the Holy Spirit, and this presence spread *caridad* (true charity or love) in the heart. Without this presence in the soul, no love of God or His laws; without such love, no grace.

Although reformers regularly lauded St. Augustine as their inspiration, they also cited works by Erasmus and the sixteenth-century Spanish writers he influenced, especially Fray Luis de Grenada and Fray Luis de León, as precedents for their controversial stance on grace and free will.[8] And in this reliance, they revealed that one's interior state was not only part of the preparation for grace, but was the true sign of grace received. In his 1579 *The Names of Christ*, Fray Luis de León explained that Christ acted on the soul not through fear of external punishment but through an interior and prior unmerited grace: "Christ writes upon our will what the old law givers wrote upon paper and ink, or upon stone with a chisel." For those few "justified by faith," this grace does not inspire fear of God's wrath, but rather "spreads such honey in our souls that it turns our minds towards goodness and justice and makes us wish for the victory of the good and the fair."[9] Thus, God's freely given grace worked an internal moral transformation in men, who then performed good acts inspired by God's prior love rather than fear of external punishment or desire for earthly glory.

Because God illuminated men from within, reformers urged the faithful down a radically different path to God than that trod by baroque Catholics:

knowledge of God began with knowledge of the self, not exterior and theatrical signs of God's majesty. Only God's grace could bridge the cognitive gulf between Him and fallen man. This He made available in the merits of Christ and in the saving death on the Cross, thereby providing men with an "inner light" to understand the Word. Now knowledge of God began not with the exterior object domain, but within. His prior love was the foundation of true religion and was "inscribed by the finger of God, that is by the Holy Spirit, in Christians' hearts."[10]

For some reformers, to know oneself was to follow one's conscience. Council of Castile President Pedro Rodríguez de Campomanes (perhaps the most influential of the Spanish Empire's Catholic reformers) opened his most consulted work by informing Christians on precisely how to live a godly existence: "The good Christian will consult his conscience in order to live in accordance with divine precepts and the morals advocated by Jesus Christ. This divine law is so perfect, that it not only moderates the unruly passions . . . but also dictates true charity towards one's fellow man."[11]

The Rejection of the External

Archbishop Núñez de Haro y Peralta outlined a clear path to salvation for the souls in his care. When God formed a new alliance with man through Christ's sacrifice, He shunned the loud theatrics that had heralded the arrival of the old laws. The Israelites had been "a people stubborn and rebellious, carnal, base, and completely lacking in the true understanding of spiritual things." In addressing such a "primitive people," God could not expect true understanding, and so He dazzled their senses and struck terror into their hearts: "The mountains trembled, the thunder crackled, and the lightning illuminated the sky."[12] Formerly, God announced His presence with external signs that overwhelmed man's senses, erupting into the physical world at particular times and places. The mysterious ladder that appeared to Jacob, the burning bush that spoke to Moses, the thick cloud that filled Solomon's temple—all this confused, agitated, and terrified the people and forced priests to flee the temple, but did little to foment their true understanding of God.[13] Christ's saving sacrifice opened the door for genuine comprehension of His dictates, and thus men could and should move beyond the inferior knowledge provided by sensual rapture to His dazzling exterior manifestations.

The written word was now to be the prime vehicle for the disclosure of the divine. Theology is a science that reveals God to man, explained divinity student and later rebel parish priest Guanajuato Miguel Hidalgo y Costilla in a 1784 thesis; thus, there was no way to acquire theological wisdom other than "consulting the Holy Scripture and tradition, because God is sensually ineffable and superior to any human intelligence, and thus we only know His majesty through what He has deigned to reveal to us."[14] Critical to the importance of the revealed written word was the 1783 Inquisition decision to allow the Bible to be read in the vernacular and its 1789 permission for the publication of a Castilian Bible—decisions that, as we shall see, ultimately helped crack the clerical monopoly on religious interpretation, opening the way to individual evaluation of dogma.[15]

The imperative, then, was to discourage the faithful from the external prods to piety that kept them from a more internal moral struggle and from serious reflection on the simple scriptural precepts preached by the new piety's promoters. The voice of the reformed, and a venue for the musings of some of the Empire's most influential burial reformers, Madrid's journal El Censor (1781–1787), fabricated a facetious letter and attributed it to a certain benighted confraternity majordomo baffled by his parish's recent arrival: a dedicated reformed priest. It seems that El Censor's hero, the priest, had banned or sold off most of the church's ornamentation, including blond wigs for an image of the baby Jesus, a silver staircase, wooden angels, and a parade float with life-size representations of the stages of Christ's Passion. If the eyes should not be overwhelmed, then neither should the ears, and so the priest also sold the parish's loud musical instruments. Elsewhere, El Censor explained the priest's logic: far from elevating the soul to the contemplation of the Divine, loud "theatrical music" merely flattered the senses and excited "the delinquent passions." Tidiness, cleanliness, order, and above all silence, the priest insisted, should replace ornamentation and instruments; these alone constituted worship pleasing to God.[16]

In reformulating sensual stimulation as an impediment rather than a segue to God, reformers such as Archbishop Nuñez de Haro y Peralta, Hidalgo, and the editors of El Censor placed themselves squarely within a late eighteenth-century shift in the accepted way of obtaining union with the Divine. For the case of New Spain, this shift found its historian in Patricia Seed, who found that elite Mexico City residents redefined the passions unbridled by secular reason as unruly threats to social order rather than indicators of God's will.[17] But enlightened Catholics insisted on a more demanding taskmaster than secular reason: rigid self-discipline enabled by God's light to the soul.

For these reformers, the true Christian was the man who demonstrated the now supreme Christian virtue of stoic moderation that signaled His interior mortification of the senses—not the man whose exterior pious works contributed to the clamor and ostentation of worship. Perhaps ironically, these truly Christian virtues could themselves be displayed for the edification of the unreformed, not least through opposition to previous forms of display. To set a spiritual example of moderation and true devotion, the ecclesiastical hierarchy rejected the theatrical extravagance that they felt had formerly characterized pastoral visits. In 1771 Mexico's Fourth Provincial Council, presided over by Mexican Archbishop and later Spanish Cardinal Francisco Antonio Lorenzana, noted that "moderation edifies the faithful" and that carriages and other hoopla constituted a scandal.[18] During the same era, Puebla's Bishop Francisco Fabián y Fuero shunned the invitations, fireworks, crowds, and bell-ringing that traditionally greeted an archbishop's pastoral visit, noting that all the uproar merely "distracted from the visit's true purpose, which was to reform customs and provide spiritual solace to the faithful."[19] Archbishop Nuñez de Haro y Peralta feared that festivities occluded Christ's simple moral dictates, and he banned the customary triumphal arches, fireworks, and dances from his pastoral visits; as had Fabián y Fuero, he insisted on humble accommodations uncluttered by special pillows or wall hangings. To demonstrate the moderation in all things that all should aspire to, the bishops likewise demanded a modest table rather than the customary lavish banquets.[20]

Nowhere is reformers' distaste for exterior goads to spirituality more evident than in their belief that only genuine contrition, not fear of punishment, could purify the soul. Penance and repentance inspired by God-given love designated true contrition, whereas seeking absolution or modifying one's behavior out of terror of God's exterior wrath demonstrated mere attrition and thus did nothing for the believer's soul. Reformers read about the contrition debate in published sermons and tracts, including the *Catechism of Madrid*, authored by the tutor to the children of King Charles III. *El Catecismo* argued that only tortured remorse for offending God constituted true contrition.[21] Following this logic, reformers counseled sacramental stinginess, citing sixteenth-century theologian Fr. Luis de León's advice that withholding absolution forced the penitent to dwell on his mistakes and thus to "truly understand his error and to work more feverishly for his health and for the ultimate and complete renovation of his soul."[22] Acts of adoration and repentance, Núñez de Haro y Peralta advised, "were only pleasing to God if motivated by sincerity."[23] Following this logic, some prelates advocated curbing the public's access to the Eucharist—a sacramental reprieve for sin—to encourage their flock toward a more systematic program of spiritual exercises.[24]

Speaking figuratively in a 1767 tract, New Spain's Archbishop Lorenzana noted that no serious examination of conscience would occur as long as some confessors continued to offer the sacraments indiscriminately and thus "provided the sinful with pillows so that they recline, and . . . failed to reprimand vices."[25] Reformers wished to shift the emphasis in sacramental penance from routine completion of the prescribed penance following confession to interior discipline preceding it. In so aspiring, they sought to inculcate what they felt was a more systematic interior morality. By deliberately withholding the sacraments, Catholic reformers arrived by a perhaps more circuitous path to a theological destination inhabited by Protestants: for the true Christian, spiritual and thus moral health should be rigorously and internally imposed.

Reformers understood that on this issue they were skating dangerously close to the Protestant heresy of the sacraments' utter worthlessness for salvation and the attendant hostility toward the Church's necessary mediation between the soul and God. The Council of Trent declared anathema Martin Luther's belief that expressing contrition out of fear of punishment rather than love merely made the penitent a hypocrite, an even greater sinner. Núñez de Haro y Peralta carefully linked his stance on contrition to Trent's teachings, meticulously noting that the Council did indeed insist on the necessity of God's prior love for true contrition. Trent had declared that fear of punishment could be a gift of God, an impulse of the Holy Ghost, "who does not indeed as yet dwell in the penitent, but only moves him, whereby the penitent being assisted prepares a way for himself unto justice."[26] The penitent is thus previously disposed to obtain the grace of God in the sacrament of penance. Núñez de Haro y Peralta concurred with Trent, citing Augustine that "only the love of God, although tenuous and remiss [remiso], together with the hatred and detestation of sin, make our conversion certain and our penitence true."[27] In short, Protestants felt that God had to dwell in the heart for true contrition, and that, because His presence or absence was decided well before one's earthly existence, the sacraments were entirely superfluous. In contrast, the archbishop stressed that the penitent moved by the Holy Spirit could pave the way for God to dwell in his heart by taking the sacrament. For Catholic reformers seeking a way to stay true to their conscience and yet rest in the bosom of the Church, the distinction was a vital one.

The Unmediated Relationship

Although carefully distancing themselves from Protestant heresies, in embracing their version of Augustine's notion of grace so fervently, the Catholic reformers produced radical consequences indeed. Because God bestowed salvation through grace in the prepared heart and through that alone, and because the road to God was thus within, much of the Church's formerly necessary mediation between the individual soul and the Divine summarily evaporated. External mediation came to be tagged as so much blasphemy and superstition, especially where the mediation of the saints was concerned. From the fundamental reform tenet of individual responsibility and from the criminalization of the unbridled senses, there naturally followed considerable antipathy toward the saints' critical mediation with God in general and toward the practice of adorning them in opulence in particular. The saints' popular function as conduits of palpable divine power reformers flatly redefined as an affront to God's omnipotence, as a superstitious sacrilege that confined Him more to some places than others. The faithful should indeed look to the saints, but not as purveyors of miracles; rather, a radically reduced number of saints should serve as moral exemplars, paragons of the now supreme virtues of moderation and restraint.[28]

The voice of the reform clergy and their fellow traveler, Madrid's *Mercurio Histórico y Político*, routinely bewailed the proliferation of religious cults. In 1787, the Madrid weekly published a denunciation of the Jesuit-promoted Cult of the Sacred Heart by Italian reform bishop Scipione de'Ricci (1741–1810), who had presided over the controversial 1786 synod of Pistoia that chided the Pope for encouraging these new devotions not discussed in the Holy Scriptures or the works of the early Church Fathers.[29] Not prone to excess verbiage, de'Ricci noted that "devotions have mushroomed with the passage of the centuries . . . leading us to agree with St. Augustine's assessment of his own epoch that there exist people who transform religion into pure whim."[30] Echoing this sentiment, Archbishop Nuñez de Haro y Peralta advised his flock to shun *doctrinas nuevas*, demonic doctrines that aroused the ears of those who loved "novelty, opulence, and sensuality," and instead devote themselves to Christ's teachings as interpreted by the early Church Fathers. "The Apostolic Canon should be our recourse, the word of God our spiritual sustenance, the sacraments our remedy, and Jesus Christ the only door through which we enter the celestial kingdom," the archbishop declared.[31] The early Church had instructed the faithful to pray only to God; under no circumstances should anyone "permit even the most minimal [doctrinal] novelty" to distract them from this focus on Christ's redemptive sacrifice. Thus, His Excellency helped reduce his bishoprics' 951 confraternities to 450, attempting to focus worship away from a proliferating number of saints.[32]

As part of their mission to return the Church to its early pristine purity, to remove the centuries' accumulated clutter that stood between God and the individual, reformers sought to eliminate all of the celebrations that they felt clogged the liturgical calendar and scattered the honor rightly belonging only to God to multiple recipients less deserving. Furthermore, the often raucous nature of saints' festivals did nothing for the self-discipline that God's inner light could provide, and indeed could lead to sensual corruption. Bishop Fabián y Fuero declared that, given the vanity and dissipation of his flock, only the minimum number of fiestas should transpire in the city's neighborhoods, and these few should be held "with the utmost religiosity and discretion."[33] In 1793, Viceroy Revillagigedo issued an edict banning all religious festivals except Christmas, Corpus Christi, and the festivals of the virgins of Carmen, Los Angeles, and Pilar.[34] It is highly doubtful that Revillagigedo's edict succeeded; numerous testators sponsored saints' celebrations after the edict, and when faced with a Crown order to reduce the number of fiestas, the cathedral chapter wasted no time in appealing to the King to preserve the festivals of San Pedro and San Felipe de Jesús.[35]

Reformers had much to say about the benefits of unmediated worship centered on Christ, but they proved especially garrulous on the practice of adorning images. Without doubt, some of their critique centered on concerns common to reformers since Trent, especially the fear that the laity worshiped the images themselves rather than what they represented, but much reflected their particular campaign to remove all barriers to "true" interior worship.

In the same contrived letter to *El Censor* that we earlier heard decrying elaborate decoration, the befuddled parishioner laments that in his crusade for moderation, the new priest had prohibited his flock from dressing a Virgin in a lavish silk and gold dress bequeathed by a grateful noblewoman. The Virgin should provide an example of real Christian virtue, the editor lectured this stubborn traditionalist, and thus her clothing should be simple; the senses should not be excited by opulent display, particularly not in church.[36] Indeed, the paper insinuated that the Virgin's resplendent attire could transform her into nothing less than a "vile whore" who tantalized the faithful into lust![37] Here indeed the Empire's enlightened Catholics broke with those of more baroque sensibilities.

Mexico City reformers demonstrated little patience with the extravagance that diluted the true worship of God. In the late eighteenth century, the Mexico City cathedral chapter stepped up its efforts to canonize San Felipe de Jesús, reminding Archbishop Nuñez de Haro y Peralta that two centuries had passed since his beatification and encouraging him to influence the King to petition the Pope. The archbishop and the viceroy reluctantly granted the cathedral chapter's request for a license to collect alms, and in 1797 the clerics named Joaquín José Ladron de Guevara as collection supervisor. By 1802, however, Guevara's zealous and festive approach antagonized those of piedad ilustrada, and a royal edict ordered a halt to the "excesses." It seems that Guevara had sent his team of collectors to certain homes every eight days and harassed the artisan guilds into building an image depicting various stages of Felipe's life, a project that occasioned squabbles between the lawyers and silversmiths guilds. The city glowed with special illumination for nine nights, and the confraternities, guilds, and Indian neighborhoods marched in the parade—all due to Guevara's enthusiasm. The King and the Council of the Indies demanded that he be removed from his post and that the procession display tasteful and moderate solemnity, with only the Franciscans and Dominicans—and not the guilds, confraternities and Indians—participating.[38] The visual depictions of Felipe's life, the brilliant illumination, and the phalanx of clerics, Indians, and guilds—all of this detracted from the modesty and moderation stressed by reformers. The presence on the streets of Guevara's boisterous minions now amounted to a provocation.

The reformed critique of the popular cult of the saints, however, went beyond curbing celebratory opulence. From the belief in the Word as the primary domain of disclosure of God's grace logically followed the demotion of miracles and favors performed by saints' images, holy relics, and indeed any physical object except the Eucharist. Once welcome manifestations of the divine presence on earth, for reformers they now counted as mere "superstitions." Because God's prior love undergirded man's very perception of the world, circumscribing His power to particular locations, objects, or saintly mediators grossly mocked divine omnipotence. Prolific pamphleteer and Mexico's first novelist José Joaquin Fernández de Lizardi (1777–1827) proved both blunt and satirical on this point: "The real Christian knows the economy of the Supreme Being, His presence, and that He has no need to revoke the laws of nature that He initially established." Miracle-mongers, the "crass ignorant," El Pensador (Lizardi) explained, envisioned a God who repented of His initial natural laws, or who, conversely, could not control them. In short, these rubes conjured "an impotent and ignorant being," not the true God.[39] In his short stint as Pope, the wrong-headed Leon XII had already canonized a Jesuit, Fernández de Lizardi explained in an 1827 article, a Jesuit whose most impressive miracle failed to impress El Pensador Méxicano. It seems this holy man had upbraided a group of Italian diners he discovered eating chicken on a Friday. When the group ignored him and then laughed at his warnings, he gave his official blessing to the birds, which rose from their plates. "The miracle is clear, there can be no doubt," roared the facetious El Pensador, "and anyone who makes roast or cooked chickens fly, should be placed on the altars."[40] An all-powerful God, "a God who was everywhere," to quote Mexico's Archbishop Francisco Javier Lizana y Beaumont (1803–1811), a God who illuminated men from within, had no need for dramatic explosions into the mundane world, displays that contravened reformers' and Augustine's most fundamental notion of how man knew God: "Do not go outward; return within yourself. In the inward man dwells truth."[41]

As in any broadly based movement, some participants proved more consistently orthodox than others. In particular, reformers were not always of one mind on the question of God's physical manifestations in the world, and the purists gained the upper hand only with time. While all within the reform camp stressed devotion to the Eucharist, some also found evidence that other physical objects could also channel God's mercy; they followed Trent's and the Counter-Reformation's precedent in distinguishing between the Church's legitimate use of the sacred and the laity's misguided appropriations. Presided over by reform firebrand Archbishop Lorenzana, Mexico's 1771 Fourth Provincial Council roundly condemned the "ignorant" laity who sought protection against accidental death by attaching scraps of written Scripture or orations to their chests or by painting sacred images on their body. However, the synod's quarrel with these practices had more to do with just *who* conjured God's presence than with the conjuring itself; on the same page, these learned theologians reiterated their belief in the powers of the Agnus Dei, a waxen image of the Lamb of God consecrated by the Pope.[42] The Church had promoted these miraculous objects throughout its domains and the Mexican council thus merely reiterated dominant Church teachings.[43] The hallmark of the Catholic reformers, after all, was their desire to retain the structure and function of the Church while promoting a radically pared-down style of worship; not surprisingly, this attempt occasionally led them into some interesting logical cul-de-sacs.

As the reform movement gained momentum in the early nineteenth century, however, God's miraculous interventions into the world increasingly disappeared—at least from reformers' point of view. The exterior object domain of the world held no special sacred charge for those who felt that the Holy Spirit illuminated them from within, and they carefully spelled out the difference between the enlightened community and the spiritually benighted, the latter often cast as under the sway of the regular orders. Where the Council of Trent—in a compromise reformers had to eschew, while in general trying to cling to Trent as a fig leaf of legitimacy—had allowed the faithful to seek cures from the saints for particular maladies and had lauded relics' miraculous powers, Fernández de Lizardi's satiric 1827 last testament echoed Erasmus in ridiculing the "superstitious powers that Christians attributed to the saints," assigning to each the cure of a particular malady, even appealing to advocates famed for "warding off scorpions and rats."[44] God did not erupt into the world at multiple points, for He was always already there in the reformed believer's heart.

In short, whereas some early Protestants had engaged in raucous acts of destructive iconoclasm and Fernández de Lizardi heaped sarcasm on the saints' ability to channel God's mercy to earth, more theologically sober reformers like Archbishop Haro y Peralta, Viceroy Revillagigedo, and even *El Censor* adopted a subtler tack. Straddling the rail between full-scale Protestant radicalism and the necessary retrenchment of Trent, these enlightened Catholics promoted a classic model of institutional reform based on change from within the existing structure. Rather than embarking on the quixotic task of banning the saints from Catholic worship, they curbed their numbers and tried to mold their meaning for their own ends, stressing their interior moral virtues over their miraculous powers and brokerage functions with the Almighty.[45]

The Enlightened Individual:
Community and Hierarchy in Reform Catholicism

The mediation of the faithful between the soul and God went the way of the saints in reform thought. By stressing the interior disposition as the critical component of salvation, the reform piety implied a distrust of the community's—and even the Church's—ability to intervene in the individual's postmortem plight. Huge funeral contingents might console the living, but they did nothing to alter the dead's fate, insisted Crown advisor and influential burial reformer Baltasar Melchor Gaspar María de Jovellanos, who frequently cited Augustine as his inspiration.[46] A most biting satirist, Fernández de Lizardi went even further, ridiculing typical funeral corteges as graced not by the exemplary Church militant united to rescue a soul, but by "a smattering of old men stuffed into colored frocks, known as Trinitarians, followed by a clutch of clerics and numerous *monigotes* [professional mourners] behind which trailed the cadaver and a few carriages."[47] In a similar vein, Viceroy Revillagigedo sought to diminish the regular orders' presence in death rites, banning the friars from their traditional nocturnal forays to deliver the sacraments to the dying or to accompany elites' cadavers to monastic institutions.[48] In these examples, the individual's responsibility for his own salvation was laid bare: it was not to be had through exterior penance or unthinking consumption of the sacraments, still less could it be obtained exclusively through the Church's indulgences or prayers. Suffrages—Masses, orations, alms—were simply too little, too late for the man who had not relentlessly enacted the dominance of the spirit over the lusts of the flesh, who had not seized responsibility for his interior state. Here, too, reformers showed a striking similarity to Protestants, who were isolated from each other and from the dead in their individual, unmediated relation to God. After all, what could be the point of a community's praying for a soul whose fate had been predetermined?

From this emphasis on the individual's relationship to God and the importance of Scripture naturally flowed hostility to worldly spiritual hierarchy. The doctrine of papal infallibility in particular came under fire. If the just looked inward to find inspiration and could reflect directly on His word written in the vernacular, then why should the Pope—or anyone else, for that matter—be placed above the individual believer's own conscience? Although few reformers did more than hint at the inviolability of the lay religious conscience before the nineteenth century, many openly questioned papal infallibility and elaborated a conception of ecclesiastical authority based on the serious study of the Church Fathers and the early councils. In the later eighteenth century, reformers lobbied successfully for the study of ecclesiastical history and early Church councils and discipline, all of which were added to university theology curriculums throughout the Empire.[49]

Behind reformers' adoration for the early councils lurked a thinly disguised attack on papal pretensions. With their numerous clerical, and even lay, participants, these Church councils arrived at truth through heated debate and discussion and thus implicitly challenged the Pope, as well as scholastic respect for authority generally. Jovellanos felt that scholasticism threatened theological studies by discouraging individual evaluation of the Bible, patristic writings, and Church councils in favor of its own sophistic musings.[50] Indeed, this illustrious secular reformer explicitly advocated the evaluation of Church doctrine through knowledge of the councils, especially those held in Spain, and advised aspiring theologians that only the Bible ranked above the councils in importance—with the Pope presumably running a distant third.[51] Thus, reformers' oft-repeated injunction to "return to the pristine purity" of the early Church, with its conciliar authority structure, struck a blow against the very pinnacle of the Church hierarchy: the Holy Father.[52] But it did so entirely within the conceptual framework of Church governance; the reformers, after all, were hardly advocating the Protestant "priesthood of all believers" or putting matters of theology up for popular referendum.

As the self-styled enlightened attempted to return Mexico City's late

eighteenth-century Church to its pristine purity by attacking religious en-
crustations, they found themselves confronted with a populace with a
penchant for the sensual stimulus of liturgical and paraliturgical extravagance and thoroughly mired in *amor propio* (self love). But attack they did.
An idyllic conception of the early Church provided reformers with a foil for
the cluttered corruption of the present, a common language that identified
reformers to each other, and a justification that their projects were
grounded in scriptural imperatives. Reformers rallied to the cause of restoring the primitive discipline that characterized the early Church and
thereby rescuing it from the corrupt proliferation of saints, pilgrimages,
relics, and superfluous rank. To return to this Apostolic Age of Christocentric purity, it was necessary to scrape off the religious accretions of the
centuries like barnacles off a boat. Like Erasmus in the sixteenth century,
reformers believed that "it is at the very sources that one extracts pure
doctrine."[53]

Protestant, Jesuit, Jansenist: The Contemporary Religious Context

If the patristic past provided reformers with their utopian vision, the Jesuits
played the opposite role, that of stalking alter ego—even after their 1767
expulsion from the Empire. Where reformers championed their version of
Augustine's notion of Grace, the Jesuits fell under Pelagius's spell, advocating man's role in his own salvation, his free will. They belittled
reformers' stress on the importance of the soul's interior disposition for
salvation, and argued that from this fundamental error all others sprang.
The Jesuits counseled frequent communion and fear of God's wrath as
sufficient motivation for confession and rejected the immutable truths of
early Church councils in favor of probalism, the belief in mutable truths.[54]
Linking Jesuit probalism to the contrition debate, Archbishop Lorenzana
claimed that probalism encouraged the frequent, even daily confession
that in his view discouraged interior moral struggle. His contemporaries
had more access to the sacraments, priests, and confessors, and worshiped in richly adorned temples, but despite all this, few Christians fervently complied with their duties or enacted a true "reformation of customs."[55] In 1768, eight years before expelling the Jesuits from the Empire,
the King issued a royal edict warning universities to be on guard against
probalism.[56] Finally, while the enlightened sought to peel away the cen-

turies' residue of umpteen cults, the Jesuits actively promoted their cult of the Sacred Heart of Jesus and other *devociones nuevas*, found neither in the sacred books nor in the apostolic canon.[57] Although one could certainly quibble about the veracity of reformers' accusations, what is clear is that the Jesuits provided enlightened Catholics with an inverse mirror for their own beliefs.

If the spats between the Jesuits and the self-styled enlightened sound familiar, they should: the conflicts replayed in Catholic form some of the fundamental theological disputes fanned by the Protestant Reformation. Like our Catholic reformers, Protestants regarded the early Church as a paragon of virtue, praising its parsimony, its lack of miraculous relics, images, and superfluous hierarchies. The Catholic Church had relaxed into idolatry and needed to return to the strict discipline and austerity of earlier centuries, as our reformers also insisted. Thus, Protestants promoted an unmediated and individual bond with God, which inspired their riotous sixteenth-century iconoclasm: the images torn from churches, the religious paintings defecated on in the streets, the priests roughed up by swirling crowds.[58] And given their stance on grace, influential Protestants, like our reformers, stressed the utter worthlessness of exterior pious works not motivated by God's prior love to the soul. "It is a great offense against God," averred Spanish enlightened Catholic intellectual Josefa Amar y Borbón, "to believe that he is content with merely exterior practices and formulaic devotions, in which the heart plays no role, because the moderation of desires and subjection of the will does not occur."[59] This position echoed Calvin's assertion two centuries earlier that "there is nothing which God more abominates than when men endeavor to cloak themselves by substituting signs and appearances for integrity of the heart," as well as Protestant precursor Martin Luther's belief that faith was "nothing else but truth of the heart."[60]

But if Catholic Reformism bore an eerie similarity to early Protestantism, in the Spanish Empire the movement was tempered not only by a pragmatic fear of the Inquisition (although reformers infiltrated even this institution) but also by a deliberate and sincere Catholicism. Reformers, after all, were led by bishops, archbishops, and parish priests, in addition to well-placed secular officials. New Spain's and the Empire's reformers eschewed the most radical Calvinist doctrine of justification by faith alone and continued to preach the importance of good works for salvation, although they stressed their utter worthlessness if performed "out of fear of God's wrath rather than out of conscience."[61] Although iconoclasts the enlightened may have been, there was no image burning in New Spain or anywhere in the Empire. True, ultra-enthusiasts railed against "superstitious" practices and advocated a return to the core truth of the Scriptures and the simplicity of the early Church. But it was the seemingly infinite exterior spurs to piety and worldly manifestations of the Divinity that they wished to be shorn of, not the Church's entire structure or all its images. If the Protestant relationship to the Church was like peeling an onion, leaving nothing but the holder alone before God, then enlightened reformers were stripping an artichoke to its significant doctrinal and institutional heart. Thus, proponents of "true religion" could encourage a more individual and interior piety while at the same time promoting, say, the cult of the Eucharist—and do so without any qualm of intellectual casuistry. His presence infused the physical object of the Host, and this core truth could not be eliminated, nor could the institution that conducted the ritual.

Although this Catholic reform movement demonstrated considerable doctrinal overlap with Protestantism, it bore an even more striking resemblance to French Jansenism, and indeed "Jansenist" was the epithet most often hurled at reformers by their Jesuit and Inquisitorial enemies. Seventeenth-century Flemish theologian Cornelius Jansen's weighty 1640 tome *Augustinius* provided the clarion declaration of reform principles, reading Augustine as the champion of predestination over free will.[62] In Jansenist thought, the theological centrality of the interior disposition led one to stress mortification of the passions as the means to clear the road to an understanding of His word. Jansenists thus sought to curb or postpone access to the sacraments to allow for systematic and individual moral struggle.

Reformers in Spain and her Empire did indeed read French Jansenists such as the oft-cited Abbé Fleury, who advocated the return of the Church to its pristine purity. Indeed, the Bourbon state's most illustrious reformers, including the aptly named exemplar of Christocentric worship Baltasar Melchor Gaspar María de Jovellanos, regularly discussed doctrine at the salon of the Countess of Montijo, who corresponded with French Jansenist Abbé Clément de Bizon. But it would be a serious mistake to see the Spanish Empire's reformers as a merely derivative or imitative movement, a weak offshoot of the French. As we have seen, partisans of "true religion" were part of an international Hispanic Catholic current; they claimed sixteenth-century theologians such as Erasmus and the Spanish Fr. Luis de León in their camp, while also drawing sustenance from their contemporaries in Italy.[63]

There is another, and perhaps more important reason for not conflating French Jansenism with the "true religion" of the Spanish Empire's self-defined enlightened Catholics. As Dale Van Kley points out in *The Religious Origins of the French Revolution*, Spanish reformers, unlike French Jansenists, insinuated themselves into the state in the late eighteenth century, employing it to promote their projects. Appointment to a see or transfer to another diocese was a royal prerogative, which had been extended in Spain to include the right of presentation to all canons, prebends, and benefices, and the Council of Castile itself served as the main administrative body. The result of this selection process was the creation of a loyal secular Church bureaucracy, exemplified by archbishops like the sycophantic Francis Bocanegra of Santiago, who adroitly side-stepped orthodoxy to declare that "if we imitate our king we shall all be perfect."[64] Spanish secular religious likewise had much to gain from their cozy relation to the Crown: royal protection provided a degree of autonomy from Rome by, among other measures, mandating royal approval prior to the publication of papal edicts.[65] Thus, the carefully selected secular clergy numbered among enlightened Catholicism's staunchest proponents, prompting and colluding with government officials to promote health and sanitation, as well as to dismantle the elaborate ceremonial edifice of baroque piety.[66] Even more striking, religious reformers stood front and center in most of the Spanish monarchy's enlightened projects. Charles III surrounded himself with reformers, among the most famous being Jovellanos, who later served as Minister of Grace and Justice (1797–1798), a post that placed him in control of the Empire's religious affairs. French Jansenism, on the other hand, had attacked the monarchy and the ancien régime's fixed social hierarchies from outside the state apparatus.[67]

Reformers' distrust of the external as a path to the eternal did not lead them to a pessimistic retreat from worldly temptations, to a cloistered existence walled off from the world, and this partially explains their aggressive public advocacy. Rather, they stressed individual subjection of the senses to rigid godly discipline. Thus, for reformers like Haro y Peralta, monastic separation from the world's temptations was no longer the loftiest path to the Divine; the temptations of the world need not be entirely rejected to be subjected. Self-mastery could and should be wrought from within. God was not out there but inside, shaping man's will, and His presence led to a moderated existence. Here indeed was a version of Max Weber's "this-worldly asceticism."[68] To be in reason's thrall was to be in God's.

Sight was the "most lively, most rapid, and most difficult to contain of all the senses," Núñez de Haro y Peralta argued, but contained it could be, and he carefully delineated two ways of looking: that required by necessity and inspired by "urbanity" and "good breeding," in which the eyes conserved "modesty and the opportune gravity"; and its opposite, the wandering eye that lingered on "objects that incited the passions."[69] Indeed, rather than retreat to an isolated existence, as had some despairing seventeenth-century French Jansenists, enlightened Catholics enthusiastically promoted the epoch's ubiquitous social engineering projects designed to lead the benighted to a life of godly moderation.

Just such an effort was the growing campaign to curb funeral and burial "abuses." The baroque Catholicism we saw in the first chapter was far from a socially neutral path to the sacred. In declaring the spiritual vacuity of exuberant baroque forms of worship, reformers attacked what had formerly been a primary medium for displaying and justifying the fixed social inequalities of the ancien régime. Thus, the enlightened piety discredited baroque display of God's majesty as a technique of rule at the same time that it whittled away at His approval of juridically fixed social inequalities. In the next section, we examine the practical efforts that effected these changes, both implicit and explicit.

Squelching Exuberance:
The Official War on Funereal Extravagance

It began in 1768, when the Mexico City Council warned Viceroy Antonio María de Bucareli y Ursúa that exaggerated funerals still plagued the city despite their prohibition in 1695. His Excellency promptly took official heed of this irregularity, reissuing earlier decrees and establishing stricter rules to trim what reformers considered burial abuses. This prompt action merely exemplifies a growing trend toward official action, which promoted enlightened sensibilities and vigorously discouraged their baroque competition.

The official campaign was no attempt to exercise a government monopoly on funeral pomp or prevent subjects from appropriating honors rightly belonging only to the monarch or his representatives. Rather, even the death of a good Christian king or his family member should rightly be an occasion for a didactic display of the now supreme Christian virtue of moderation. Royal deaths were no longer to provide occasions for "immoderate" expenditures that "squandered the savings" of all classes of people. Taking aim against bright colors and rich fabrics, Viceroy Bucareli's edict ordered grieving women to limit themselves to simple black dresses and thin shawls. Men should appear in long black capes and skirts cascading to the feet, and under no circumstances should masters spend money on special mourning attire for servants.[70] Indeed, simple black attire to commemorate the death of all vassals, even the most prestigious nobles, was mandated. Long capes, wool or flannel pants, and hats without silk linings could be donned by grieving fathers, mothers, siblings, grandparents, spouses, and in-laws, but not by the family's servants or by entire corporate entities.[71]

Even more alarming than immoderate mourning expenses, the 1778 Mexico City Council felt, were the many ornate caskets paraded through the city's streets in funeral corteges. The most elaborate were lined with lacy sheets and draped with opulent velvet threaded with gold and silver designs, for which the council feared that elites spent up to 1,000 pesos.[72] Viceroy Bucareli's edict reiterated earlier laws that lambasted these "vain" demonstrations, favoring instead unadorned black cloth and plain sheets, it being improper to employ spectacular colors "in the instrument that is the origin of the greatest sadness."[73] A subsequent edict restated a 500-peso fine for displaying embroidered sheets.[74] All of the immoderate "excess" bespoke the amor propio of a lost soul whose last act was merely an attempt to distract others from taming the passions.

Determined to inculcate his flock with the supreme virtue of Christian moderation, Puebla's Archbishop Fabián y Fuero sought to limit any opportunity for the display of vanity or the profanation of the house of God, banning elaborate funeral beds from his diocese in 1769. Luxuriously draped with bright red damask, these *imperiales*, as they were called, would disappear to be replaced with a demonstration of the deceased's modesty and restraint rather than his vanity; all caskets were henceforth to rest unassumingly on the floor or on an ordinary table draped with black cloth.[75]

Viceroy Bucareli's 1778 edict opened with the dire warning that all of this flash imperiled the souls of the deceased; in 1792, Havana's Bishop Felipe Joseph de Tres-Palacios y Verdeja banned silver and gold from coffins, noting that "pomp leads the vain to shameful vices and the loss of their souls." Striking a more temperate note, Archbishop Fabián y Fuero advised that the opulence "profaned the house of God."[76] Thus, the stakes were high, and Reform Catholics could not wait for the reprobate to control themselves: in 1793, Viceroy Revillagigedo declared a state license necessary for all funerals involving the "distinction of a funeral bed" and obliged the city's religious to confess to any infractions. The edict's principal target was the regular orders, which reformers regarded as the major directors of the baroque theatrics that imperiled salvation. The Franciscans admitted to conducting numerous ceremonies with the honor but assured the viceroy that all had been duly approved; the Augustinians adamantly insisted that they routinely solicited both ecclesiastical and viceregal permission before such burials.[77] Thus, those of *piedad ilustrada* (enlightened piety), as they described themselves, put both Church and state authority to work restoring the Church to its original purity.

The press also provided a powerful tool to promote the reform agenda. An anonymous turn-of-the-century contributor to Mexico City's *Diario de México* expressed unease with music that led the ears astray, lamenting that so many trumpets and other "belligerent" instruments now blasted during funeral corteges that they had come to resemble "fandangos" and "battles staged for the theater" rather than serious and sentimental events. The paper's editor agreed, noting that "well-directed" music could properly move the listener but that trumpet blasts and other raucous music should be reserved for the countryside. Even the bells that had reminded the faithful to pray for the soul of the departed incited reformers, who issued numerous edicts against "excess" bell ringing.[78]

Baroque prose irked *Diario's* enlightened readers as much as did elaborate music. The welter of detail and the dyspeptic sentimentality of funeral invitations rendered God's simple dictums indecipherable, opined the enlightened. One anonymous contributor, for example, blasted baroque funeral invitations for their annoying verbiage. "Why should funeral invitations employ so many useless words? Why do they inevitably include long lists of the invited, rather than merely the principal mourner's name?" he wondered, concluding that the time had come "to simplify everything, time to overcome superfluity in all endeavors."[79]

The stress on the true understanding of God's simple moral precepts as preached by the reformed inspired their stinging critique of baroque oratory. Exhortations to scriptural morality conveyed in plain speech: that alone constituted preachers' true purpose, and reformers decried the "pompous descriptions" and "rarefied allegories" that they felt dominated sermons.[80] Convoluted displays of erudition were the oral analogue of baroque prose; they occluded the transparent truths contained in the Scriptures. If all men illuminated by God's light could reflect on His injunctions, then oratory and intellectual brilliance lay not in word games but in clear Scripture-based homilies.

Thus, the worst transgressions against the imperative of funeral moderation incited reprimands from the state in the years bracketing the turn of the century. The Audiencia (High Court) and the Council of the Indies chastised José Joaquín Ladrón de Guevara, a Cathedral prebendary and the son of prominent Creole Audiencia Regent Baltasar Ladrón de Guevara, for transforming an 1805 family funeral into a vulgar street festival. Guevara's penchant for pomp was well-known to the Council of the Indies, who had already upbraided him for his efforts on behalf of St. Felipe de Jesus' canonization, an event that included images, floats, the presence of religious and political communities, three bands, and a picket of soldiers, as historian David A. Brading vividly describes.[81] In the case of the funeral, Guevara had printed and distributed numerous invitations, contacted the city's confraternities, religious communities, and political bodies, and then liberally distributed candles to the assembled, whom he paraded on an extended funeral march through the city—all without the Audiencia's consent. Thoroughly annoyed, the Council warned Guevara against future spectacles and ordered all subsequent funeral corteges contained to the streets leading directly from the house to the church.[82]

The antics of the Marquesa de Xaral de Berrio's family similarly provoked reformers' ire. Bordered with metal braid, lined with chambray sheets, and covered with elaborately embroidered cloth, the Marquesa's coffin particularly irritated the Council, who reminded Viceroy Iturrigaray that flashy caskets and sheets carried a 500-peso fine. Indeed, the last rites of wealthy subjects like the Marquesa provided a constant source of annoyance for the self-defined enlightened, who believed that for a typical funeral the deceased paid 8 pesos for parish rights and 50 pesos for accompanying clerics; sent 350 invitations; paid numerous poorhouse residents 3 pesos apiece; placed twelve torches on the tomb and four candlesticks on the altar; distributed thirty one-pound candles to Audiencia and cathedral chapter members, four half-pound flames to the doormen, and numerous candles to those assembled in the Church; lavished 100 pesos on the religious orders present; and paid the gravediggers a modest sum—most of which violated the numerous state edicts enjoining pomp in funeral splendor.[83] Indeed, the impetus for the city council's letter encouraging Viceroy Bucareli to publish his 1778 edict on burial extravagances had been a heated discussion of the "excesses" the council witnessed in the funerals and burials of the Count of Miravalle, the Marques de Prado Alegre, and the Marquesa de San Francisco de Guardiola.[84] It is probable that these three titled subjects were brought for burial in a funeral cortege followed by elaborate carriages, and the 1778 edict specifically chastised the wealthy that paraded and postured in mourning coaches.[85]

The official apparatuses of state, Church, and press, then, actively promoted the restrained piety of the "enlightened" reforms, both on general principles and in response to specific cases. But it is a historical commonplace that laws and official exhortations often indicate the unpopularity of the required behavior, not its prevalence. Were the public pronouncements of a minority falling on deaf ears? As it turns out, in this case, they clearly were not, for we can turn to other sources of evidence for verification of the principles' broader influence.

The New Fashion in Funerals

Building momentum in the late eighteenth century and peaking during the decades surrounding Mexico's 1821 Independence from Spain, numerous testators insisted that their funeral arrangements eschew all worldly vanity and instead announce their Christian humility and moderation. While many of their predecessors and a small minority of their contemporaries dazzled spectators with gilded coffins and trumpets, clerical throngs and confraternities, these Reform Catholics proved equally flamboyant in their modesty. In particular, many testators embraced the critique of elaborate funerals as mere displays of amor propio.

In a request typical of the many who now desired moderation, surgeon Rafael Sagas in 1816 asked to be sepulchered in the cemetery of San Lázaro "without any pomp and with the greatest possible humility." Similarly, an unmarried woman from San Juan Teotihuacan, Agustína de Olvera y Alzibar, was willing to leave the disposition of her remains to the discretion of her estate executors, but only with the understanding that they "omit all superfluous expenses that smacked of pomp or temporal vanity." And José Galindez, from Spain's Basque region, wanted his death ceremonies "without any pomp or circumstance whatsoever" and with the "most moderation possible."[86]

Whereas Sagas, Olvera y Alzibar, and Galindez made adamant but somewhat vague requests for funereal modesty, others left more specific instructions about what should properly be included in or omitted from the more restrained ceremonies. Candles, bells, elaborate caskets, and raucous music came in for particular criticism. Spaniard Manuel de Marroquín insisted on burial in an "ordinary wooden coffin," without any prior bell ringing or distribution of invitations to the ceremony, which was to be executed with the "utmost secrecy and moderation." In his 1796 will, José Vicente Rodríguez rejected even an ordinary coffin for his funeral; whereas some reformed testators wished to be laid out on woven mats (*petates*), he opted instead to be placed on the uncovered floor.[87]

In the years bracketing the turn of the century, increasing numbers of testators echoed these sentiments. In contrast to the 1710–1720 period, when about 5 percent of testators requested simpler ceremonies, from 1810 to 1820 roughly 36 percent did so, the culmination of a rise that had begun with a trickle in the 1780s, a mere fifteen years after Archbishop Lorenzana began his tenure in the city.

The growing popularity of the sparser ceremonies was apparent to contemporaries. Even before accepting his job as city attorney in 1817, José Bernardo Baz had frequently heard clerics disparaged for levying exorbitant fees for the now common simple funerals. It seems that the new ceremonies had been omitted from the official burial price list (*arancel*) issued in 1757. To stop the grousing about their appropriate price, he suggested that the Mexico City Council request that the Audiencia add them to the official fee schedule. Concurring with Baz, the city council noted that because private funerals had entered into "general practice," clerical fees had become "material for scandal for some and the cause of constant griping for the majority of the population."[88] The source of such widespread disquiet: the clergy charged the same prices for luxurious rituals (*de pompa*) as for the secret ones (*funerales secretos*) that lacked the key elements of the elaborate funeral cortege.[89]

The ensuing scuffle between the priests of the cathedral parish of El Sagrario and the Mexico City Council over the proper fees for the simple ceremonies reveals that two equally passionate and sincere notions of salvation's true path were at loggerheads in Mexico City. The city council insisted that the minimalist ceremonies were dictated by "a truly Christian humility." Roiling throughout the parish clerics' terse, carefully worded retort, their contempt for the simpler last rites bubbled over in their assertion that "no matter how common, they are irrational and repugnant to decorum and should be destroyed by the roots." Learned theologians, they argued, concurred that priests should override wills that rejected "clerical accompaniment at the funeral, the traditional candles, or the singing of psalms," in short, the "ceremony established by the Church." By this reckoning from those with a vested interest in maintaining pomp, the "pretext of humility" to gain the remission of sin led the reformed to reject the ceremonies that truly remitted sins; thus, "in an attempt to please God [the deceased] cease to do what really pleases Him."[90]

The novelty of this situation, however, lay not in the occurrence of the secret funerals per se, but in their huge popularity. A sprinkling of turn-of-the-seventeenth-century testators had indeed deliberately embraced the more modest ceremonies, even employing the adamant rhetoric that would become so prevalent in Mexico City's wills one century later; but most testators before the late eighteenth century elected the sparser rites out of economic necessity. In 1693, for example, Spanish Captain Don Av de Venabides wanted no "pomp or fuss [*fausto*]" during his burial, no invitations sent, and only the presence of the parish guide cross and twelve people for his funeral cortege. Similarly, Ana de Los Angeles, a married native of Seville and mother of three, entreated her son to arrange for church charity for her funeral and Masses in 1642. Los Angeles lamented that her husband's extreme poverty prohibited her from burial with "even the most moderate pomp," and reminded her son that "God would reward him" for honoring his filial duty to bury her.[91]

Whereas earlier testators like Los Angeles stressed poverty as the impetus for a humble burial, turn-of-the-nineteenth-century testators pointed to an equally irresistible imperative: the dictates of their conscience. Mexico City native María Nicolasa Larrión requested burial in any one of the city's church cemeteries without any ceremony whatsoever, in a manner similar to that of the poorest of the poor, "for reasons of conscience."

Indicating his preference for the "most humble shroud of San Francisco," as well as for bypassing the church for immediate burial in the cemetery, like the poor who were routinely buried there, Juan Antonio Martínez Valdés went on to "appeal to the consciences" of his wife, children, and estate executors that they resist the vanity that would impel them to ignore his express wishes; rather than succumb to any funeral frippery, his family should order Masses for his soul and help the poor. In what later became perhaps the period's most publicized case of funeral modesty, the Count of Nuestra Señora de Regla left instructions worth repeating for the sheer drama of the Count's humility and the importance he placed on conscience. Rather than carry his body to a church for funeral services, his survivors were requested to see that "four unaccompanied servants whisk his body in a covered box to the cemetery of Santa María, where a parish vicar will be waiting to pray while the body is covered with earth. For this purpose, the hole will be dug prior to his arrival and the cleric paid what is owed to him." The Count further specified only "moderate" mourning expenditures and ordered his household not to advise anyone of the death until several days had passed. He further warned his executors not to modify even the slightest detail of his requests. Not only did their conscience dictate their strict compliance to his desire for moderation, but anything ordered by a testator became thereafter an unquestionable law.[92]

In following the dictates of their own conscience and in urging others to follow theirs, Larrión, Martínez, and the Count of Nuestra Señora de Regla displayed their adherence to a fundamental tenet of Reform Catholicism: the belief in God's internal illumination of the faithful. This was not a secular, post-Freudian conscience that these sincere Catholics followed, but God's laws written in their hearts; recall, for example, Campomanes's advice to the good Christian that he need only consult "his conscience in order to live in accordance with divine precepts and the morals advocated by Jesus Christ."[93]

In a further testament to enlightened precepts, the humble testators also turned death into a far more solitary event. The Trinitarians, the confraternities, the mourning carriages, the children of San Juan de Letran, the numerous invited friends and family—all of these groups evaporated from the reformed funerals in response to adamant exhortations from the testators. In 1818, notary Francisco Jiménez served notice to his wife and son that they not "print invitations, rent or borrow carriages, invite mourners, . . . or notify the Colegio de Escribanos [the notary school] of the ceremonies." Numerous testators requested "no accompaniment whatsoever" and even demanded that the church door remain closed during their funeral to ensure that no one would enter. In one typical 1818 case, Bárbara Rodríguez de Velasco wanted to be whisked to her parish church in a simple box carried by four pallbearers unaccompanied by anyone else, and buried there in the "humble shroud" of San Francisco with the door closed and no pomp whatsoever.[94] Consistent with reform teachings, however, testators dispensed only with what they regarded as superfluous intercession, not the core rites, and several requested that their funeral be "without any pomp or ceremonies other than those explicitly established by the Church."[95]

But, as concerned as they were with lack of funereal pomp, they were positively consumed with what came after their humble and ill-attended funerals; their wills demonstrate an adamant humility about burial location. Their more direct relationship with the Almighty, as well as a desire to imitate the Christ at the center of their worship, led Reform Catholics to eschew burial under a saint's protection in favor of the common cemetery or an unspecified location in a parish church. A quick look at the numbers outlines the story. In the years 1710 to 1720, 45 percent of the 350 testators sampled indicated a preference for a particular burial location; of those, 73 percent had clearly specified an altar or other area under an image's protection in a chapel. These numbers begin to shift dramatically in the 1780s. By the 1810s, of the 55 percent who did specify a burial location, only 23 percent designated a particular saint's chapel or, less frequently, another location within the church of their choice.

More interesting, of course, is where these early nineteenth-century testators did want to be buried and why: "in whichever of the city's church cemeteries"; "in the parish church closest to where I die"; "in the cemetery like the true poor"; "in the cemetery of San Lázaro"—these were typical declarations. The San Lázaro cemetery was no Elysian field; mud-spattered pigs and mangy dogs rooted in the offal and fed off the bones that jutted up from the mud, contemporaries reported, and half-clad bodies bobbed in pools of rancid water. Here indeed was a resting spot worthy of the humble.[96] Prior to this period, church cemeteries located in front of or alongside churches had welcomed only the poorest of the poor, mostly the city's swarthy underclass, forced by scant finances to rest in a place that many of the city's elite testators considered to be outside the protection of the church and its saints. Only a statistically insignificant handful of the most destitute testators requested cemeteries as their final resting place from 1710 to 1720, a figure that rose to 13 percent among the reform-minded 1810–1820 testators. And this, years before the cemetery laws were enforced, which seems to have begun in the 1830s. In choosing a cemetery or an unspecified location in the parish over burial near a particular image, reformed testators rejected one way of knowing God to embrace another: they eschewed the saints' lawyering skills for an unmediated relationship with God, and they undermined the traditional hierarchy of sacred spaces to declare their belief that God's love did not burst into the world through the conduit of saints' images and holy relics, but illuminated their hearts.

There can be no doubt, then, that in terms of death rites, reformers had made considerable headway toward their goal of restoring Mexico City's Church to its early discipline by the second decade of the nineteenth century. Now a sizable portion of testators rejected baroque display as "vain" exterior works and organized their funerals to reflect their Christian humility. They had turned inward to live in accordance with the dictates of their conscience, and they wanted their funeral to illustrate the moderation they had so earnestly acquired through the discipline that others would do well to imitate. But, as we have seen, burial rites were only one site of struggle; the faithful had multiple venues in which to demonstrate their adoration for the city's numerous holy images and their fervent desire for their mediation with God—including their own home—and to express their need for the community's intervention with the Divine. Did testators merely redirect their loyalty to the exterior cult of the saints to venues other than funerals and burial sites?

The evidence suggests not. Many early nineteenth-century testators embraced the imperative to moderation as it applied to other concerns. Not only did fewer testators leave gifts to adorn the saints, they also shunned the confraternities dedicated to their cult. Where 18 percent of the wills sampled between 1710 and 1720 bequeathed gifts that enhanced the exterior cult of images, the same number of early nineteenth-century wills revealed that only 4 percent of testators included this pious directive.

Confraternities, too, lost adherents in the early nineteenth century. Most religious brotherhoods sponsored the cult of a particular patron saint or advocation of Christ or Mary, and spent fulsomely for the lights and ornamentation of their chapels and for festivals in their honor, which were invariably accompanied by the noisy salute of firecrackers that Fabían y Fuero and Núñez de Haro y Peralta both had banned from their pastoral visits. Where roughly 24 percent of the earlier testators indicated their confraternity membership, only 2 percent did so during the later period. Furthermore, gifts to churches of privately owned religious images declined as well, albeit only slightly.

By the early nineteenth century, then, the glittering opulence of Mexico City's cult of the saints had dimmed. Reform Catholics were finding intercession with the Divine less urgent. There was even a noticeable drop in the percentage of testators ordering Masses for their souls. Particularly dramatic, however, was the decline in the desire for Masses said at a particular altar or dedicated to a particular saint, suggesting that more of the faithful agreed with Núñez de Haro y Peralta that "Jesus Christ should be the only door through which we enter the celestial kingdom."[97] Of the 52 percent of 1710–1720 testators who ordered Masses, roughly 20 percent named a specific altar. This proportion fell to 7 percent of the 39 percent who ordered Masses a century later, as Reform Catholics increasingly spurned the need for saintly mediation with the Divine. Many, however, continued to request some form of Mass for their soul, reflecting their respect for this Christ-centered sacrament.

That turn-of-the-century testators eschewed the more sensual aspects of baroque Catholicism and found the need for a heavenly advocate less compelling evinces their more individual and unmediated relationship with the Holy Spirit that inhabited their hearts. By rejecting sensuality, they displayed His binding effect on man's sinful will. The faithful could and should establish a direct relationship with God with the aid of only the most basic of mediatory rites, those they associated with the Church's early centuries.

Thus, on the eve of Independence, the Church was not a peaceful fraternity of the faithful, but a house divided. On one side stood those of tempered pious sensibilities—tempered, in their own assessment, by the internally imposed discipline that mortified the senses. On the other side, equally sincere in their quest to know God, stood those for whom God reigned from his throne in heaven but whose power and majesty was immanent in the world through the mediation of the saints, the miraculous relics housed in churches, and the sense-dazzling majesty of the holy cults.

In this theatrical magnificence, of course, lay a technique of rule based on the notion of seducing the senses to produce awe at the power of the seducer and to associate him with the Divinity. For the reformed, however, this pious project categorically led the faithful away from following the dictates of their divinely illuminated conscience. Both sides hurled invective at the other, and Mexico City's streets and churches became a ceremonial battleground. The challengers seemed the most vituperative, frequently suggesting that the righteousness of reform projects should be self-evident to all intelligent people.

In the middle stood the majority, who now evinced more mixed pious sensibilities than had the earlier baroque testators or who displayed diffidence toward burials and pious giving, leaving these decisions to their estate executors. The number of enlightened Catholics had certainly increased over the hundred years that lay between the first decades of the eighteenth and nineteenth centuries, perhaps fivefold if we take the humble funeral as our measuring stick, or roughly threefold if we use diffidence toward burial near an image as our gauge; allegiance to the enhancement of the majesty of worship, estimated by gifts to images, also declined fourfold. Many seem to have embraced reform tenets, but this is not to suggest that the pared-down piety replaced its more established rival overnight, or even that it ever completely unseated the older style altogether. Rather, the spiritual struggle continued, with minorities committed in roughly equal numbers to the two extremes and the majority inhabiting a middle region of more mixed sensibilities.

The 1795 will of casta and widow María Guadalupe Ambriz provides a case in point. Demonstrating the burial arrangements common to reform Catholics, Ambriz elected to rest in an unspecified location in her parish and indicated her desire for a modest funeral without "any pomp whatsoever." Her pious bequests, however, signal her adoration for Our Lady of Guadalupe and the Christ of Chalma, an important pilgrimage site, and she had Masses said to these two intercessors and left interest-bearing capital for candles, firecrackers, and flowers for the annual fiesta for Guadalupe that she had long hosted in her own home. Her possessions included small plots of land in the neighborhood of San Miguel, a house, and images of both Guadalupe and Saint Gertrude.[98] Ambriz bolstered the statistical ranks of those who elected an unostentatious funeral and did not choose a particular chapel for burial, but demonstrated considerable enthusiasm for the more sensually stimulating worship—including the dreaded firecrackers—discouraged by reformers. If Ambriz embraced some aspects of the reformers' agenda, she flatly rejected most of it.

Contemporaries felt that lurking underneath the religious sensibilities dividing the more polarized faithful lay differences in economic and social status. At the turn of the century, reformers promoted the construction of suburban cemeteries to end "vain" funereal displays, to restore the Church to its pristine purity, and to promote public health.[99] In 1779, Nuñez de Haro y Peralta regarded social elites as the cemeteries' principal opponents, stating that no general cemetery had been built because "the important subjects and the wealthy have their own burial crypts in churches, and in Dominican, Franciscan, and Augustinian Third Order chapels . . . and they harbor a repugnance for the measure."[100] Years later, Augustin de Rivero attributed the cemetery campaign's lethargy in Mexico City to the many people who were "preoccupied only for themselves, for their noble circumstances and wealth, and who had a poor understanding of true religion."[101]

Exasperated with the sputtering results and the endless thwarting of efforts by scant finances, testy elites, or just plain foot dragging, some reformers felt that rather than continue to antagonize the privileged, concessions should be made to help win them over to cemetery burial. In a report to the 1821 Mexico City Council, a lawyer and honorary city councilman who had spent three years in prison for his Independence sentiments proposed the construction of special tombs in a new general cemetery to entice the wealthy, "who are the group that most energetically defies the burial laws, some of them because they have Third Order or Confraternity tombs and because of other motivations inspired by their amor propio, which leads them to believe that it is a slight for their parents or relatives to be interred without distinction in the general cemetery."[102] The archbishop's and the two city councilmen's identification of the wealthy as the burial reformers' chief nemesis jibes with the 1777 city council's concern over the opulent funerals of several prominent ascriptive elites, the Count of Miravalle, the Marques de Prado Alegre, and the Marquesa de San Francisco de Guardiola, and with Guevara's street theatrics for San Felipe de Jesús.[103] These cases render credible reformers' sense that social elites continued unabated in their desire to bring God's flamboyant majesty to earth, setting a poor example of the supreme Christian virtues of humility and moderation.

But who was the Count of Regla, one of the wealthiest men in New Spain and the humble exemplar who wanted a funeral shorn of all pomp? Or High Court Judge Xavier Alvarez de Méndez, who wanted to rest next to the Count? Who, indeed, was King Charles III? The King not only built a suburban cemetery outside his palace and elected burial there, but in New Spain his death set an example of the moderation that reformers attempted to impose on all Mexico City residents. Charles III's neoclassical funeral catalfaque "was disillusioning for its simplicity."[104] The Count, the Judge, and the King: this was no scrappy coterie of self-made men who found in the new piety's individualism an ideological affirmation for their social ascension without the benefit of ascriptive privileges. Surely this was no rising bourgeoisie trying to aggrandize their own power by discrediting elite spirituality. If Haro y Peralta felt the wealthy foiled their plans to return the Church to its original purity, the lofty social position of those who elected the sparser ceremonies alarmed the clerics of El Sagrario, as we have seen; moreover, their 1817 city council opponents never once contradicted their analysis, as indeed several prominent city council members had themselves elected secret funerals the year before.[105] What emerges, then, is a widening chasm among the elite Mexico City testators, as some were as flamboyant in their modesty as were others in their splendor.

What was at issue was not precisely who would rule, but with what justification and with what techniques of power. In embracing the simple funerals, testators spurned an important technique for the divine sanctification of social position. In their set-to with the Mexico City Council over fees for the modest ceremonies, the crux of the parish priests' defense had been that Church authorities unanimously concurred that funeral pomp should mirror social position, measured, in their terms, by "the faculties and dignity of the dead" as well as their monetary fortune. Simple funerals contravened this most basic and timeworn principle and thus were illegal. That funeral pomp had marked social status in the past and should continue to reflect the deceased's worldly position in the present seemed an unassailable truth to the Sagrario's parish priests.[106]

In their dramatic rejection of corporate tombs under a saint's protection in favor of cemeteries, the reformed testators themselves were expressing more than their individual relationship with God; perhaps ironically, they were also establishing a new group identity. Although it is merely suggestive, based as it is on such small numbers, consider the following. Inspired by the Count of Regla's pious example, a cluster of testators expressed their desire for burial next to this exemplar of true piety. Guillermo Gregoni, for example, sought to be planted "in the cemetery grave immediately next to that of the Count of Regla." Wealthy, powerful, and prominent, Audiencia Judge Francisco Xavier Alvarez de Méndez, too, could easily have afforded burial in an exclusive chapel; instead, in 1810 he chose a humble funeral and cemetery grave adjacent to the Count's.[107] What social group here expressed its esprit de corps? A group defined by the common spiritual and moral enlightenment of its individual members. In a sense, their burial choice did indicate their lofty social position, but inhabiting those heights, as we shall see, increasingly rested on a different justification: not birthright or corporate privilege, but the godly moderation and humility that these testators displayed—virtues that discredited baroque display as a technique of rule.

But that we cannot simply peel back the pious pronouncements to reveal some underlying socioeconomic or status structure differentiating the two groups should not lead us to jettison this analytical quest. Some groups did display more of an affinity for the new piety than did others; in particular, state bureaucrats seemed overly represented among the reformed, and high-ranking reformers such as the Count of Campomanes and Viceroy Revillagigedo flexed state power to encourage everyone to embrace "true religion." In the next chapter we begin our exploration of their enthusiasm and their opponents' zeal to diffuse it.

chapter 3

Freeing the Virtuous Individual

The cemetery battles that shook the Spanish Empire in the late eighteenth and early nineteenth centuries reveal the extent to which the enlightened defined themselves as a cohesive group with a social mission. Their adherence to the new interior piety fueled their increasing rejection of church burials in favor of common cemeteries. Grounding their status in their moral fitness to oversee the era's ubiquitous projects for promoting industry and population growth, the enlightened redefined church burials from pious acts that abetted salvation and sanctified one's social authority to mere displays of vanity and ostentation. The cemetery campaign represented a frontal assault on the representational practices of the ancien régime's spiritually sanctified corporate gradations and the dawn of a new justification for rule.

But in New Spain's rural areas, and in Spain, indeed throughout the Empire, resistance proved fierce. Although the greatest jewel in the Crown, New Spain was just one piece of a vast Empire. To employ Peter Guardino's felicitous phrase, to understand political outcomes, we must consider the too-often invisible dissenters "camped out on legislators' minds." These were not only in New Spain, but throughout the King's dominions.

The New Geography of Death

Although multiple outposts of the Spanish Empire were grappling with the cemetery issue throughout the era, it was the well-publicized 1781 epidemic that ravaged the Basque town of Paisages that initially provoked the official state concern that we see resonating throughout the Empire.[1] The disaster particularly galvanized King Charles III's enlightened coterie of Church and state officials. They placed the blame for the epidemic squarely on the shoulders of the carelessly packed cadavers and energetically exploited the tragedy to spark an official government inquiry into church burials.[2]

The task of compiling testimony on burial practices fell to the over-worked Council of Castile, already burdened with responsibility for guilds, prisons, asylums, and even ecclesiastical matters such as Spanish relations with the papacy. Its members included technocratic lawyers and a sprink-ling of aristocrats and clerics.[3] Secretary of State (1776–1792) José Moñino y Redondo, the Count of Floridablanca, urged the Council to first canvass the opinions of Spain's bishops and archbishops before composing a plan to prevent future disasters.

The Council of Castile's well-researched final report on church burials included the testimony of the religious authorities suggested by Florida-blanca, as well as the recommendations of other experts; those cited in-cluded the Economic Societies of the Friends of the Country, the Madrid Medical Academy, and the Royal Academy of History, as well as various European courts that had already created suburban cemeteries in their own countries.[4] Intertwined with fashionable concern for public health were equally serious appeals to the imperatives of "true piety." To both the religious and the secular experts, the two themes appear not so much compatible as inseparable. Throughout the reports, the injunctions of enlightened piety marched side by side with the latest medical theories. For our purposes, they are more easily examined separately; this chapter con-centrates on the piety that animated the cemetery campaign, and a subse-quent chapter analyzes the medical evidence. However, this separation of the two realms is not meant to suggest that secular knowledge had de-clared war on pious wisdom. To the contrary, combatants drew their battle lines not between "secular" and "religious" but between the two different definitions of piety we have just considered.

Although all of the experts consulted by the Council of Castile wished to banish the dead for reasons of physical health, even those most concerned with the sickness wrought by corroding cadavers continued to justify the new cemeteries with reference to their spiritual propriety. All agreed that the utopia to be recreated was the discipline of the early Church, and bishops and secular authorities alike energetically mined ecclesiastical history for nuggets to demonstrate that early Church discipline proscribed in-temple burials. Even Saint Paul was buried in the Via Ostiense, after all, and 74,000 martyrs reposed in the Appian road—not in churches. More-over, the reformers argued, the periodic Church councils, such as that of Braga in 561, had unanimously rejected church burials down through the ages and had reiterated this point by providing funeral benedictions for cemeteries but not for churches.[5] Crown attorney Jovellanos's 1783 disquisition on general cemeteries dealt briefly with the testimony of "the best modern physicists" before launching into a lengthy historical exegesis of Catholic doctrine, in which he declared the physical proximity of the dead to the living irrelevant to the salvation of souls from Purgatory. Interment in urban areas dated from only the thirteenth century and represented a type of secular vanity, reported Jovellanos.[6] The Council of Castile's three attorneys optimistically noted that the public's repugnance for suburban cemeteries would easily dissipate if clerics would just prevail on their flocks to live according to the Church's early discipline.[7]

Many of the authorities consulted by the Council of Castile feared that the more prominent faithful would reject suburban cemeteries as dishonorable, although most felt that this vanity (amor propio) should not be indulged. The Archbishop of Malaga, for example, thundered at his flock that the "honor and esteem that you so covet in burials, [are] in reality nothing less than vanity and pretension carried on even after death."[8] Echoing these sentiments, Crown advisor the Count of Cobarrús argued that "it is essential that burials be uniform to overcome the sacrilegious distinctions desired by our ridiculous vanity."[9] In a similar vein, the Bishop of Huesca praised cemeteries as a means to "contain the ambition of those desirous of perpetual sepulchral rights in church or anywhere else that places them in a position superior to others."[10] The principal objective of burial reform, as parish priest Francisco Xavier de Espinosa y Aguilera carefully explained, was not to ignore the dead, but to eliminate the luxury and vanity that exacerbated the distinctions between rich and poor, nobles and plebes.[11] Casting one's body into the cemetery with the poor would be a testimony to the new interior virtues and a denouncement of "ostentatious" and unearned social distinctions.

Reformers quickly learned, however, that their brand of piety and their seemingly egalitarian vision could not be easily foisted on a hierarchical society, and elaborate compromises were proffered to appease the leery. Realpolitik frequently undermined reformers' utopias in the cemetery campaign. One anonymous author suggested to the Council of Castile that the dead first decompose in grounds outside the city and that one day a year be set aside for confraternities, religious communities, and parishes to harvest the desiccated remains and place them in churches; unclaimed bodies would remain in the cemetery.[12] Similarly worried that parishioners would shun the new cemeteries or, worse yet, clandestinely bury their dead in private gardens or bribe their way into church tombs, as had occurred during an epidemic in Seville, many of the prelates polled by the Council of Castile reluctantly arrived at the same conclusion: the distinctions represented in church should be reproduced in the new cemeteries, at least temporarily, and only later, when the faithful had become accustomed to the new burial grounds, should all honors be abolished.[13] Despite Jovellanos's quip that "vanity rather than true devotion" lay behind the "tasteless" display of social distinctions in cemeteries, Charles III's 1787 edict permitted tombs for confraternities, parishes, the regular orders, and elite families.[14]

Despite reformers' careful compromises, however, the opposition remained hostile. To support their case, opponents seized on the bishops' economic trepidation and even contested their interpretations of early ecclesiastical councils. In opting for the latter defense, of course, cemetery opponents accepted the terms of the debate set by reformers, their stress on the early Church as the utopia to be reestablished. Church history was far from consensual on the burial issue: if Saint Efren, who labeled himself "an insignificant corrupted worm," thought temple burial an affront to his Christian humility, a mere eighteen years later a determined Saint Ambrose insisted on resting under the Milan cathedral's central altar. Not content with these observations, critics turned the radicals' discomfort with visual spurs to appreciation of the Divinity against them, noting that all of the concern about pestiferous cadavers contravened the wisdom that "veneration for the house of God was inspired not by the temple's exterior, cleanliness, or ornamentation but by the faithful's sentiments and humility."[15] For the most part, however, cemetery opponents on the Council of Castile lavished praise on the dead's didactic presence, believing that in-church burials promoted "mystical reflection," and fretted that the banishment of the defunct from public spaces would lead to a diminution of the Masses and pious gifts that constituted the bulk of funds in most parishes. Finally, unwavering that temple burial was synonymous with a belief in Purgatory and resentful of threats to limit funerals to odd hours when only small audiences could be mustered, conservatives on the Council of Castile vetoed the cemetery measure after seven years of debate.[16]

But the King's enlightened ministers and attorneys proved more influential, persuading him to officially prohibit temple burials and order the construction of suburban cemeteries where all would repose "regardless of status or privileges," as they so hopefully noted. Emphasizing the dead's threat to public health and the Church's "primitive discipline" as imperatives, radical ideologues imposed their vision of society by legislative fiat. Construction was to begin immediately in areas that had experienced epidemics, preferably in hermitages with already extant chapels so that the faithful would not fret that the new burial grounds banished them from the protection of the saints. The cost was to be borne by the Church, and the blueprints devised by priests in consultation with *corregidores*, regional Crown officials.[17]

It is important to note, however, that the 1787 Royal Cemetery Order contained carefully crafted compromises with traditionalists' preoccupations, the most important being that those who had purchased perpetual rights to a burial vault before the edict's promulgation would retain them. The edict also noted that suburban cemeteries would not leave their occupants languishing in Purgatory: as consecrated ground, they guaranteed the efficacy of prayers. And, although the regular orders lost their burial privileges, the Academy of History assured cemetery critics that each parish and order would continue to celebrate funeral Masses with the body present and have a designated space in the cemetery for its defunct parishioners or patrons; Church benefactors' remains could continue to rest in chapels.[18]

The Empire's Enlightened Cemetery Proponents

In the years following the 1787 decree, numerous enlightened coteries began cemetery construction in the Spanish Empire, citing the new piety and public health as their motivation. Mexico City offered but one battlefield in a larger war; Cuba, too, could boast men of enlightened sensibilities. Organized into a Royal Economic Society beginning in 1792, Dr. Tomás Romay, the poet Sequeira y Arango, and their associates lobbied for a suburban cemetery, but the measure floundered until 1802, when the group named Bishop Joseph Díaz de Espada y Landa its leader. The bishop began his presidential tenure with a lecture on the Church's primitive discipline, canon burial laws, and "reason"—all of which roundly condemned church burials. He also solved the financial problems that had stymied construction, providing money for a cemetery blueprint to be drawn up, and successfully lobbied the Havana Cathedral Chapter for additional construction funds. Ecclesiastical and secular cemetery collaborators received an additional boost from the 1804 Royal Cemetery Edict, and in 1806 the dead trundled through the new cemetery's gates, passing under a large chiseled sign that read "For religion and public health."[19]

The centerpiece of the cemetery's inauguration was the ceremonial transportation of the remains of Governor Diego Manrique and Archbishop Joseph González Candamo from a poorhouse (Casa de Benifencia) chapel to the suburban burial ground. A speech on that occasion encouraged attendance at the ceremony for the edification provided by these men's "modesty and Christian humility."[20] But while the bishop lauded reform values, he also mounted an attack on more "traditional" religious practices, banning the confraternities dressed in festive tunics that regularly accompanied bodies to the church for burial, except in groups of four or fewer; he also prohibited the cofrades from exacting a fee for their services.[21] The cemetery embodied the new piety's egalitarianism and emphasis on an unmediated and individual relationship with the Divinity; no images graced its interior, and the bishop stressed that all of the faithful should pay the same price for burials, a measure consistent with canon law, and one he felt would end arbitrary charges. Most important, everyone should be buried in the cemetery: no one, not even nuns, should be exempted.[22] To ensure that no baroque rituals defamed this hard-won testament to enlightened Catholicism, the official cemetery rules encouraged redoubled efforts to ensure that "neither vanity nor affection lead to the luxury and pomp that profane religious burials."[23]

Shorn of the saints and far from the churches where the Church militant congregated, for many of Havana's faithful the cemetery was spiritually denuded, not piously parsimonious. Their resistance began immediately. The new cemetery was a provocation, a positive threat to salvation, and the more socially privileged, it seems, resented the cemetery's implicit egalitarianism, whereas the regular orders fretted about the lost burial fees. The Franciscans led the opposition, earning the King's opprobrium in an 1807 order that praised the cemetery.[24] The privileged and other clerics were not far behind. Cathedral cleric Antonio Odoándo de Balmeseda informed the Council of the Indies that in their zeal to bury everyone in the cemetery, reformers overstepped the law's bounds.[25]

Also animated by the new piety, Lima's reform coterie proved every bit as influential as that of Havana, inaugurating their city's general cemetery in 1808. Roaming the outback of Catholic orthodoxy in his address on that occasion, the Lima archbishop reminded listeners that Augustine had deemed burial location irrelevant to salvation and that Pope Gregory had taken Augustine one step farther, declaring that "exterior ceremonies" merely signaled the reprobates' presumption and vanity, and actually lessened their chances for salvation.[26] Cemeteries, the archbishop concluded, were sanctified by both reason and the "true piety" espoused by Augustine and Pope Gregory.

In Montevideo, a parish church and the Franciscans competed for bodies, between them burying around 215 corpses annually; after a glut of cadavers in 1789 and 1790, the city council and the town's doctors decided to bury all residents, even the Franciscan Tertiaries' distinguished members, in a provisional cemetery. A month later, however, the Franciscans honored Melchor González's will and buried him in their church, prompting the parish priest to remind them that the gente sensata (the enlightened, the intelligent) unanimously backed the new cemetery. A general cemetery was not built in Montevideo until after the 1809 English invasion and fire.[27]

If indeed a new category arose in the Spanish domains of the late eighteenth century, how can we account for this development? What in enlightened faith so appealed to the men we see arguing passionately for humble funerals and egalitarian burial grounds?

In arguing the case of the English Protestants, Christopher Hill has suggested that doctrines stressing the motivations of the heart flourish in periods of rapid social change and appeal to new social groups seeking to justify their repudiation of traditional authorities.[28] The imperatives of an interior and godly conscience give sacral weight to dissenters; God illuminates them, how can men stand in their way? How does this model apply to the case at hand? The "true piety" that animated the cemetery campaign certainly provided a powerful weapon against elite pretensions. From the standpoint of reform spirituality, those who paraded clerical throngs through the street or rested in ornate caskets were morally suspect. Had they taken God's word to heart? Had they labored to tame their passions? Probably not, or they would not have been engaged in such splendorous display in the first place. Furthermore, the righteous who did find God in their hearts could and should speak the truth that they found there; "true piety" could potentially desacralize everything that stood between the individual conscience and God. It would appear, then, that the "true piety" of the enlightened reform fits Hill's definition of a doctrine of the heart.

But the Spanish Empire's proponents of the new piety seem to defy the second half of Hill's equation, at least at first glance. Bishops and high-level government proponents of the new cemeteries, indeed the King himself, stood at the very pinnacle of the secular and ecclesiastical hierarchy. Surely this was no "rising class," for how much higher could they have risen?

However, in Spain, the clerical hierarchy was not an aristocratic preserve but a solid career choice of the well-educated, studious sons of the often impoverished lower and middle nobility. Similarly, the most enlightened of the King's bureaucrats often hailed from the lesser nobility and had attended the universities rather than the prestigious *colegios* that educated the privileged scions of the aristocracy. In short, many enlightened reformers had earned their positions through disciplined individual effort and accomplishment rather than birthright. Campomanes himself exemplifies their typical trajectory. Taking advantage of a 1771 law that intentionally broke the colegio graduates' hold on power by opening all civil and ecclesiastical offices to university alumni, he catapulted himself from a poor *hidalgo* family in Asturias to the presidency of the Council of Castile in 1783.[29] As historian Jorge Cejudo López succinctly describes them, many late eighteenth-century bureaucrats symbolized an ascendant social and professional sector with a natural aversion to old elites whose interests "coincided with those of the *colegios mayores* and the Jesuits who had often controlled these institutions."[30] Reformers, in other words, fulfill Hill's definition of a new social group.

The career of Salamanca's Bishop Felipe Bertrán, known for his personal austerity and modest table, illustrates Cejudo López's argument for a fundamental antagonism between those of enlightened piety and the theatrical "elites" so demonized by cemetery proponents.[31] Appointed by Charles III to the post of Inquisitor General, Bertrán used his position to approve the publication of a vernacular Bible. His sermons rehearsed the fundamental tenets of reform piety, railing against vanity and citing Fr. Luis de Grenada and Saint Augustine as inspirations for his view that only "God knew the real number of those predestined for salvation, but it was manifest truth that the reprobate far outnumbered the chosen."[32] Collaborating with university graduate and Secretary of Grace and Justice Manuel de Roda to reform the colegios mayores in 1771, Bertrán offered the following justification for his involvement in the campaign: "Be he noble or plebeian, although the graduate may have spent all his days and nights and exhausted his energy in study . . . if he was unable to gain entry to a Colegio Mayor the most that he could hope for in a civil career would be an *alcalde*'s office or a miserable post of corregidor, or a temporary appointment in the administration."[33] Clearly, in His Excellency's eyes, disciplined labor merited a higher order of reward, and the nobility's "playing fields of Eton" criteria were standing in the way of justice.

There is certainly evidence that the new piety appealed to these hard-working but stifled men personified by Campomanes and Roda and championed by Bertrán, the self-made men who had risen through the ranks of the Bourbons' new aristocracy of merit. This frustrated class of men thus mounted the most powerful of attacks on their social superiors: a religious one. Those compelled by vanity to elect elaborate burials demonstrated not their sanctity, but their reprobate status; they announced not their social worth but their unworthiness to oversee the new projects of moral and economic reform. The *gente sensata* had reconceived man's connection with God, and baroque piety became fake, misleading, even idolatrous, and those who engaged in it equally so.

It is important to note, however, that in the case of the late eighteenth-century Spanish Empire, the new piety did not merely appeal to a preexisting group that shared a position in the socioeconomic, status, or even institutional structure. Rather, the new piety actively abetted the creation of new social actors. The *gente de luces* (the enlightened) were united less by social or institutional position or even economic interests than by their common view of themselves as the culturally enlightened. This point is most evident in addressing the anomalous actors in the drama; several of the most prominent cemetery stalwarts, including Jovellanos and Cabarrús, hailed from the privileged nobility, yet advocated a diminution of its prerogatives. Conversely, some of the conservative defenders of noble prerogative had attained their rank through commercial success.

That the new piety actually galvanized and defined group members can be further seen in the widely publicized cases of ascriptive elites who embraced its tenets. The Duke of Osuna and an anonymous lieutenant-

general, for example, both earned the Bishop of Seville's praise for refusing elaborate funerals and church burials, a statement of their rank, he felt,
and opting instead for cemetery interment, an expression of their "humility" and enlightened piety.[34] Dr. Fernández also lauded the Duke and
Duchess of Osuna's cemetery burial but reminded readers that the most
"shining example" was set by Charles III, who had opted to rest in the
cemetery he had ordered built outside of the Escorial Palace.[35] We have
already seen the Count of Regla's inspirational pious example in New
Spain and heard clerics comment on an increasingly common elite penchant for the modest funerals and cemetery burials there. This was not
casual nonchalance about postmortem fate, a secular indifference to salvation, but flamboyant modesty: that the Duke, the Duchess, and the King
himself would choose cemetery burials declared their adherence to the new
piety. But while welcoming the titled to their ranks and exploiting them for
publicity, the enlightened defined themselves as a porous group independent of their inherited position in the ancien régime's fixed social hierarchies that they so diligently worked to dismantle.

Nor did institutional affiliation define the enlightened. Burial tracts invariably referred rather unceremoniously to the enlightened as a self-
defined cultural group. The Archbishop of Orihuela recounted to the
Count of Floridablanca that "all those of good judgment and true piety"
clamored for an immediate solution to the burial problem, and Salamanca's archbishop noted that the stench of rotting bodies in church was a
common complaint of every *hombre sensato*.[36] Dividing society into the
learned and the ignorant, the pious and those mired in amor propio, of
course, constituted a radical break with the vision of an ossified community divided into estates and corporations. It implied mobility and offered
the literate a certain freedom of choice to embrace or reject the cultural
attributes of the enlightened: a noble, even the highest aristocrat, could be
a convert. And as we shall see later, even the deserving poor could aspire to
join the elect.

The Challenge of Cultural Cohesion

A self-defined group with no organic cohesion faces obvious problems of
maintaining internal connections, and the gente sensata met these chal-
lenges with all the new tools of the Enlightenment. A fluid communication

network that knit together readers with a shared sensibility about cemeteries and other enlightened projects facilitated their self-identification.
Advocates demonstrated a familiarity with the latest European studies,
corresponded with each other, and allied with the most radical elements
within the state administration.

In their energetic efforts to influence opinion, authors churned out both
translations and original works. In a single volume exemplary of the type,
one polyglot translator published an Italian academic burial tract, a pastoral letter from the Archbishop of Toulouse, and Church historian Ramón
Cabrera's examination of canon law on burials.[37] Spaniards pondered
French doctor Janin's notion that vinegar provided a powerful antidote to
fetid air, reading his work in a state-sponsored translation. The doctor had
driven a sewage cart liberally doused with vinegar through the streets of
Paris at 2 in the afternoon without anyone's divining its contents; after
repeated experiments, he enthusiastically advocated the liquid as a panacea
for all sources of noxious air, including the dead.[38] In a tour de force of pan-
European erudition, the Royal Academy of History's well-documented 1781
published treatise demonstrated familiarity with the works of Benito Bails,
Boerhaave, Van Swieten, Sauvages, Hoffmann, Verheyen, Ramazini Sánchez Riveyro, Pringle, Joseph Haberman, Tissot, Mead, Vicq d'Azyr, and
the medical institutes of Vienna and Paris.[39] The expanded press and personal correspondence also linked the Empire's learned. Jovellanos noted
that both the Gazeta de Madrid and the Mercurio de España printed and discussed the Parliament of Paris's 1765 edict banning temple burials, and
papers in both Spain and New Spain kept readers abreast of the cemetery
campaign, often providing elaborate and alarmist rationales for their construction.[40]

The sixty-six Economic Societies of the Friends of the Country (Amigos
del Pais) founded between 1775 and 1800, however, were the Spanish
Empire's new channels of enlightenment par excellence. The societies
provided their members with an institutional structure from which to
promote the age's ubiquitous moral reform projects. The nobility was
energetically recruited and the societies comprised these "enlightened"
nobles, reformist ecclesiastics, and assorted "middle-class" elements, according to historian Robert Jones Schafer. The societies dedicated themselves to fomenting practical economic development and imbuing the
populace with a work ethic. These industrious reformers set up "patriotic

schools" to teach spinning and the catechism, penned useful agricultural reports, and devised elaborate plans to put vagrants to work. Reflecting the enlightened's emphasis on moral reform, in 1781 the chapter rewarded Juan Sempere y Guarinos first place in an essay contest on the subject of mendicancy. Guarinos found poverty's origin in the moral failures of the poor, their unwillingness rather than their inability to work. Prior efforts to curb vagabondage, Guarinos continued eloquently, had failed because of false piety, namely, the injunction to "Give properly without looking to whom," which merely encouraged continued sloth; spiritual transformation, not indiscriminate charity, was the real solution. Guarinos doubtless found little to criticize in Madrid, where the society chapter trained the poorhouse residents in textile manufacture.[41]

The cemetery campaign found enthusiastic adherents in the economic societies, as we have seen in the case of Havana. Unsolicited, in 1781 the Sociedad Economica del Principe de Asturias informed the Council of Castile that the King's interest in general cemeteries merited the applause of all "enlightened people [gentes de luces]." In Madrid at least, those tended to be the most thoroughly imbued with the new piety: cemetery advocate the Count of Campomanes founded the Madrid society in 1775, Francisco de Cabarrús presented his 1778 defense of free trade with America to the group, and Jovellanos later served as its president; suspected Jansenist and salon hostess the Countess of Montijo did a stint as secretary of the group's women's auxiliary.[42] Clustered in the economic societies, those of enlightened piety sought to impose their vision of society on the recalcitrant while actively promoting a new aristocracy of "all reasonable men."

Resistance from Above and Below

Meanwhile, outside the debating rooms of the official policymakers, the coteries of enlightened urban elites, and some Mexico City testators, the grumblers expressed their discontent with the new burial grounds. In a case of unsuccessful elite resistance in 1807 Cordoba, a marquise's grieving son secretly buried his aristocratic mother in a convent; accompanied by an armed guard, the local corregidor immediately disinterred her body and paraded it to the cemetery, where, he declared, "all persons were to be buried no matter how distinguished or illustrious."[43] The well-heeled of

Seville also hated the new cemeteries, refusing during the 1800 epidemic to accept their exclusion from "holy ground" or their placement in common graves, "where their relatives were confused with the plebe."[44] Explicitly charged with promoting his town's new cemetery, Crown official the Marquis de Candia mulcted several miscreants caught conducting clandestine church burials, but allegedly shelled out for his own wife and child to rest in the prestigious Franciscan convent. Other residents proved more cagey, engaging in more clever subterfuge than did the embattled Marquis: the family of Don Teodoro Roy processed an empty coffin to the town's "shabby" cemetery to divert the authorities' attention during his elaborate funeral and convent burial.[45] Burial reformers could find ample evidence that burial location and funeral pomp were jealously guarded by traditional elites who refused to accept the egalitarianism implicit in the new cemeteries.

That regular orders shared elites' hatred for the cemetery project should come as no surprise: the regulars' housed many of the Empire's most illustrious dead, and burial fees represented an important source of the orders' funds. Furthermore, and perhaps more important, reformers felt that the regular orders enthusiastically supported baroque piety, with its emphasis on sensual apprehension of God's majesty and the need for mediation, and thus encouraged both elaborate funerals and the desire for burial under a saint's protection. The reformed thus cast the regular orders as their principal nemesis in their battle; they demonstrated little patience with the friars' dillydallying, even issuing a May 1804 order granting secular powers the authority to forcibly extract cadavers sepulchered in convents. Even worse for the friars, enlightened bureaucrats blamed the regular orders for the foot-dragging that constituted the primary response to the 1804 Cemetery Edict, and banned them from constructing their own suburban cemeteries.[46]

This zeal, however, was soon tempered by pragmatism, specifically, a desire not to tread too hard on Church jurisdiction. In Madrid, armed and enthusiastic secular officials had stormed a convent and exhumed the clandestinely buried body of a high-ranking religious; to avoid such obvious scandals, in 1807 the King required that his underlings obtain an ecclesiastical license before disinterring cadavers. In a decision made the same year, the Crown granted the Archbishop of Toledo's request to allow archbishops to be buried in churches, but denied a petition for the regular orders to continue to be buried in cloister.[47] Indeed, it was not until 1818 that King Ferdinand, desperate for allies in his battle against post-Cadiz Cortes liberals, revoked the 1807 decisions and permitted religious to be buried in their cloisters.[48] Reformers, of course, had anticipated that the regular orders would be shaken by the measure. Jovellanos, the attorneys of the Council of Castile, and the Bishop of Segovia all argued, however, that banishing the dead from convents and monasteries would put an end to the unseemly public burial disputes between the regular and secular clergy—and, we might add, considerably dilute their ability to bestow God's approval on what reformers regarded as vain social pretensions.[49]

Whereas most of the Empire's bishops and the regular orders arrayed themselves into opposing camps on the cemetery issue, the lower secular clergy proved divided on the issue. Burial fees provided a significant part of the income of priests, who usually got the short end of the stick in their competition with bishops, cathedral chapters, and diocesan administrations for a share of the tithe. In Segovia, to cite just one example, parish priests constituted the overwhelming majority of clerics but enjoyed only 28 percent of tithes. Furthermore, throughout the Empire, where ecclesiastical riches were overwhelmingly concentrated in urban areas, even economically desperate unbeneficed priests refused appointments to the numerous rural parishes that simply could not support them.[50]

Predictably, then, many parish priests proved less than enthralled by the cemetery project and led their flocks into battle to protect the dead from banishment. The bishops of Osma and Burgos reported that many of their dioceses' lower clergy lived off burial fees. In Pancorbo ecclesiastics organized a boycott of the new cemetery, even overruling wills that requested the new burial ground. Emboldened by his participation in this giddy collective effort, priest Felipe Oquendo advanced the struggle by herding his cattle into the cemetery to graze, thereby converting the town into "the laughing stock of the county" and preventing residents from "grasping the measure's utility."[51]

In New Spain, too, suburban cemeteries worried impecunious parish priests and seemed to have held little appeal for their rural parishioners. In 1809, Archbishop (1803–1811) and briefly Viceroy (1809–1810) Francisco Javier de Lizana y Beaumont took advantage of what he saw as a lull in the Independence-era hostilities to encourage his suffragen to step up cemetery construction. Early Christians, those pure exemplars who "never adopted superstitious or barbarous practices," had buried their dead with decency and respect outside of towns, and his flock should do the same, especially given the numerous dilapidated parishes with wood floors, or none at all, parishes where one could not dig up even a handful of earth free of skeletal fragments. Furthermore, the bishop instructed the faithful, "God was everywhere," not just in the parish church—a rendition of re-form tenets that, if taken to its logical conclusion, undermined the hier-archical sacrality of space that fueled church burials as well as the tradi-tional Catholic ordering of towns and cities.[52] In the past, the haze of superstition and idolatry had obscured the dictates of natural reason. Eager to implement the measure, the bishop hoped that the priests' reports would illuminate the "mentality of both the educated and the ignorant" so that he could devise a practical strategy to overcome "the masses' un-founded preoccupations" concerning cemeteries."[53]

Huascazaloya parish priest Josef de Alcarate's response to Archbishop Lizana y Beaumont reveals his fear of his flock's "unfounded preoccupa-tions" as well as his trepidation about his own income. The arancel, the official fee list, priced burials according to the tomb's distance from the main altar, and Alcarate hoped these divisions would continue in the proposed cemetery. More important, the bishop's orders should be tacked to the church door so that the parishioners did not blame the area's much-maligned priests for the sure-to-be-unpopular measure. Also pleading poverty, parish priest José María Vigra reported that during repairs to his Iguala church he had used its adjacent cemetery as a stop-gap measure, but faced raucous opposition during every burial. He feared that if his flock learned of the bishop's suburban cemetery plans—that they would not even be sepulchered near their loved ones in the temple—they would cease giving to the Church entirely.[54]

Like his colleagues in Huascazoloya and Iguala, parish priest Idelfonso de Esquivel y Vargas of Tepexic del Rio worried that the type of flamboyant modesty "demonstrated by the wealthy Count of Regla" would have disas-trous consequences for his parish, where priests lived off the occasional elaborate funeral; he himself barely had enough to eat after paying for church maintenance. Between the money exported to Spain to fight the French invasion, a disastrous harvest, and the Indian governor's unwilling-ness to fund the cemetery, the parish had no resources, and Vargas pro-posed using the church's existing adjacent cemetery rather than building a new suburban burial ground. Indeed, religious in Liapunto, Salvatierra, and Irapuato had successfully pled poverty to avoid cemetery construction—a legitimate claim, at least in Irapuato, where thirty-two secular clergy competed for the alms of the few followers.[55] In Celaya, priest José Ignacio Silva shunned the new cemetery and continued to preside over church burials.[56] The clergy hated the cemeteries because, José Ignacio Roca speculated, they diminished income from temple burials and priests' fees.[57] Indeed, the official fee schedule (arancel) in the area divided churches into four sections, charging from 20 pesos for burial near the altar to 1 peso for spaces near the entrance, all of which represented a considerable contribution to ecclesiastical coffers, as did funerals themselves, which in Iripuato could cost up to 40 pesos for elaborate ceremonies with musicians and numerous Masses. In the Bajío, where impoverished clerics could not muster even enough money for their own burial, general cemeteries represented a further blow to already scarce revenues.[58]

Scarce funds were the central issue in Durango as well, where the population lived dispersed on small ranches, with perhaps twenty or thirty families clustered together in each area's central town. Most of these farmers lacked the funds to pay for burials, much less to make large pious bequests, and churches were little more than adobe huts, a cross haphazardly protruding from the roof, a few frayed adornments. Priests eked out a miserable existence, some on the brink of starvation, and few parishioners confessed before death or received the sacraments. Although the bishop rather half-heartedly suggested a baptismal campaign to raise cemetery funds, he noted that even if a few head towns built cemeteries, it would be impossible to enforce the measure on haciendas and in the smaller villages.[59]

Despite their shared financial woes, however, other parish priests energetically advocated the new cemeteries and the reform piety that prompted their construction. As we have seen, the erudite Francisco Xavier de Espinosa y Aguilera, parish priest of Cortes de la Frontera, raked across the latest scientific studies and early Church history to make his procemetery case to the Council of Castile, and corresponded with others of like mind.[60] Similarly, El Carpio's parish priest argued that the town's small church "emitted odors that caused dizziness and stomach pain," and exhorted his flock to overcome their "superstitions" and exile corpses from the temple.[61] And, as we shall see, Veracruz's indefatigable parish priest José María Laso de la Vega led a cemetery movement that rent the city's social fabric asunder, as those of more baroque sensibilities mustered all of their forces to oppose the reformers' new burial ground.

The upper echelons of the Church hierarchy were not entirely oblivious to the economic fears that stalked the lower clergy. Certainly, most prelates hoped that cemeteries would end the false indulgences peddled by unscrupulous churches and monasteries, curb worldly vanity, encourage a more interior piety, and end the competition between the regular and secular clergy for burial fees. But at the same time, these religious dreaded a radical diminution of funds from in-church interments, elaborate funerals, Masses, orations, and alms. Already alarmed by a trend toward fewer requests for Masses in the decades prior to the cemetery campaign, Avila's cathedral chapter argued that the dead visually reminded the living of their obligation to lessen Purgatory's tortures; their removal would constitute a serious blow to already declining revenues. So, too, the bishops of Zamora and Calahorra feared that cemetery construction meant an end to the custom of adorning caskets with *ofrendas* (offers of unconsecrated wine and bread) as gifts for officiating priests. But the most adamant statement came from the Bishop of Pamplona, who tagged cemeteries as "ruinous for parish priests" because they lived from baptism, marriage, and burial fees; he feared that without the right to private in-church tombs, the faithful would cease to give to the Church.[62] The Bishop of Vich noted that the faithful sought church burial for the indulgences that it often carried, and recommended that the King petition the Pope for indulgences for cemetery chapel altars to ensure a steady flow of donations.[63] Even the most pro-cemetery bishops harbored the lingering fear that if the dead were out of sight they would be out of mind, causing severely reduced revenues.[64]

For most of Spain's clerical hierarchy polled by the Council of Castile, and for many of its parish priests, however, fear of diminished funds was superseded by the rejection of visual incentives to faith. In their formulation, God was at war with Mammon in this dispute, and they knew whose side they were on. Linking this sentiment to the cemetery campaign, the Bishop of Teruel acknowledged that the dead in church provoked pious giving, but added that cemeteries would accustom the faithful to a more pure, interior religion.[65] He evidently considered that pious goal worth the price.

Fierce resistance from the rural areas, the regular orders, and traditional elites, as well as a devastating 1804 plague, inspired the Council to investigate why the 1787 and 1789 Cemetery Edicts had elicited such minimal compliance and to chart a new course of action. No surprise here: the Council concluded that those twin bugbears of the enlightened—the superstitious masses and vain, theatrical elite—had deliberately stymied their pet project; as well, some of the blame fell to scant finances. A Crown attorney's elaborate report cited the "ignorance and trivial concerns of the common people [*gente vulgar*]," but noted that their resistance had fizzled out over time. Lack of funds, on the other hand, had thwarted even the best-intentioned efforts. Reflecting the enlightened fashion for simplicity, Arjona proposed that towns build cemeteries without "luxury or magnificence" to save money, which should be raised from well-endowed cathedral chapters and new taxes on wills, estates, or the dead themselves. The "egoism of elites," their amor propio, however, constituted the heart of the problem and justified redoubled state efforts. It was now time, so the attorney urged, to take enforcement out of the hands of the overworked and distracted Council of Castile and give it to appointed ministers empowered to deal directly with local authorities. The Council agreed and designated four officials to foment cemetery construction throughout Spain.[66]

The new cemetery officials came armed with fresh ammunition in the form of an 1804 Royal Cemetery Edict that augmented the powers of the secular authorities in general and of doctors in particular. The Council of Castile ordered that doctors certify all new burial sites and that civil architects create all cemetery plans.[67] That the new edict considerably increased outside interference in local burial decisions can be seen in the case of the town of Zujar. In response to the 1787 edict, the town council and parish officials had sent resolutions to the archbishop and to the area's corregidor, but then quarreled on the proposed site and tabled the measure because of scant funds. In 1804, the *cabildo* (city council) and the parish priest finally agreed on the hermitage of San Angel, which received the seal of approval from the town's licensed doctor. Zujar's city and church officials then wrote to the archbishop to urge him to order the impoverished parish to donate the land for the project; the archbishop agreed, and sent the entire bundle of correspondence to Antonio Villanueva, who had been recently appointed by the Council of Castile to oversee cemetery construction in the area. The parish reluctantly turned over the land, but as late as 1815 the *ayuntamiento* (city council) was still petitioning the area's intendant for construction funds.[68] Indeed, despite the *Gazeta de Madrid*'s March 1805 optimism that Spain was witnessing a flurry of cemetery constructions, "freeing itself by this measure from the serious dangers that had afflicted it," progress proved somewhat halting. Valencia's general cemetery opened in 1807, but parish burials continued; Madrid had to wait until the 1808 invasion of Napoleon for cemetery construction to begin; and Leon's populace boycotted the municipal cemetery inaugurated in 1809.[69]

Beginning in 1808, however, the fortunes of enlightened burial reformers rose when Napoleon's troops seized Madrid, forcing King Ferdinand's abdication and prompting a fractious public debate on the location of political sovereignty in the monarch's absence. Having previously distanced itself from divine legitimization through baroque ritual by promoting an individualist theology that undermined hierarchical authority by sanctifying the individual conscience, enlightened Crown and Church officials now witnessed the logical culmination of their efforts in the regional juntas (1808–1809) and the Spanish Cortes (1810–1814). Although junta participants ordered themselves by the Old Regime estates of the clergy, military, nobility, the high court, and commerce, all eventually concurred on one point: with the monarch gone, sovereignty resided with the people. Under the constant critique of a militant press and a "public" loosely organized in tertulias (literary salons) and reading societies, the regional juntas quickly permutated into the Spanish Cortes, dominated by the enlightened clergy and representing not privileged estates but "the comun." Its well-publicized debates, laced with references to "citizens" and "individuals," and its edicts dismantling corporate privileges and establishing the legal equality of all nationals heralded the end of the protracted struggle both deliberately and unwittingly begun by enlightened Church and state ideologues against the Old Regime's fixed social hierarchies.[70]

As an institution informed by a modern vision of society based on sovereign, unfettered individuals, the liberal Cadiz Cortes that ruled the Empire during the King's abdication championed general cemeteries where all would repose regardless of "status or privileges." In November 1813 the Cortes granted Spanish and American civil authorities one month to create provisional cemeteries, threatening to punish the recalcitrant under the authority granted to them by the Constitution.[71] Viceroy Félix

María Calleja del Rey immediately forwarded the order to the bishops and intendants of Yucatan, Guadalajara, Leon, and Durango, and to Mexico City's archbishop-elect. While all swore to enforce the measure, and the archbishop assured the viceroy that the suburban cemeteries of San Lázaro, San Salvador, and San Andres already welcomed many of the capital's dead, it was Guanajuato intendant Fernando Perez Marañon who most energetically embraced the project in New Spain, setting off a tumultuous confrontation with his area's already beleaguered clerics.[72]

A paradigm of the enlightened ideologues who held the new intendancy positions, Marañon placed "reason, humanity, and decency" atop his list of reasons dictating an assault on "the barbarous abuse of burying the dead in churches." In a highly provocative move, Marañon designated an abandoned rural temple and suburban chapel as provisional cemeteries; a suburban site previously reserved for the city's insolvent poor was designated as the future general cemetery. To help overcome what he underestimated as a "general dislike" of his plan and to provide an example of the new Christian virtues, Marañon's sister received the rather dubious distinction of first buried in the new general cemetery. His brother, an Inquisition official, soon joined his sister, despite his dying wish for church burial. Well-pleased with his efforts, the intendant reported to Viceroy Calleja that these examples would convince all of the cemetery's merit.[73]

His next report was less sanguine. The prior of the convent of San Diego had solicited the viceroy's permission to bury within its cloister and Marañon feared a capitulation would incite "thousands and thousands of reclamations from *mayordomos, sindicios*, ministers of the Third Orders, confraternity members, ecclesiastical benefactors, and those who had purchased church tombs"—precisely those groups that defended temple burial most vociferously throughout the Empire. While the viceroy ignored the provincial's plea, the regular orders and the laity revolted against the new cemeteries, engaging in clandestine burials and other subterfuge. The ever-vigilant Marañon surprised San Diego's Friar José Dionio Yepes in a midnight burial of a religious, and with the aid of Ecclesiastical Judge Dr. Antonio Lavarrieta—who, like Marañon, frequented Guanajuato's enlightened circles and energetically advocated cemetery reform—attempted to bring Yepes to justice. The dispute was eventually referred to the viceroy. In a similar case, the civil authorities shocked San Sebastián's prior, who had surreptitiously buried Lino Urusua's wife's body, by ordering her exhumed from the convent's floor and summarily and publicly transported to the general cemetery. The friar protested that disinterment carried the penalty of excommunication, that he had an ecclesiastical license for the burial, and that, most important, church burials continued in all of the towns under Marañon's jurisdiction.[74]

Ferdinand's triumphant 1814 return to the throne, however, and his subsequent dissolution of the radical Cortes, gave cemetery opponents a reprieve in their battle with enlightened civil and Church authorities. Lamenting that their dead were being "extracted from the cloister to be placed in general cemeteries by men of questionable discretion," the Empire's regular orders appealed to the sympathetic King, who exempted them from the general rule in an 1818 edict that was promptly reissued in America.[75]

The tumult provoked by the new cemeteries in New Spain's rural areas and the hinterlands of Spain stands in stark contrast to eighteenth-century French citydwellers' diffidence, and is more consistent with rural Guatemalans' fierce resistance charted by Douglass Sullivan-Gonzalez.[76] Michel Vovelle argues that Robespierre's "de-Christianization" campaign of year II was not an abrupt imposition on a benighted Provence population; religious fervor had grown tepid a good fifty years before the Revolution and citizens reacted with indifference to suburban burial sites. Parisians proved equally nonplussed by the new general cemeteries constructed in the late eighteenth century. Pierre Chaunu charted a waning interest in church and convent burial in the eighteenth-century, from 41 percent to only 20 percent of testators opting for temple interment over the course of the century. Despite the clergy's dire warnings of popular upheaval, the destruction of Paris's massive St. Innocents cemetery provoked no resistance.[77]

As we have seen, traditional elites and that favorite target of reformers' wrath, the regular orders, proved the most actively resistant to the new cemeteries. But in their sermons, reports, and exhortations, reformers believed that they fought a Janus-faced battle against the plebe's so-called irrational superstitions and "egotistical elites' " penchant for pomp; they spelled out their own identity in opposition to their nemeses above and below them in the social hierarchy. And, although prominent in the Bourbon bureaucracy, reformers were also well represented in the press, the Church hierarchy, and to a lesser extent among parish priests, and in the new enlightened economic societies. The cemetery skirmishes that shook the Spanish Empire were hardly a secularizing move on the part of the Bourbon state, designed to deflate the privileges of the Church by de-sacralizing death.

The Ghost in the Bourbon Machine:
Piety and the Broader Project of Reform

The reformers' struggle to assert the demands of the new piety did not stop at the doors of the cathedral, or even at the cemetery. Far from being an arid theological debate, the campaign for funereal modesty attacked the very institution of fixed social hierarchy. The Catholic reformers wielded this weapon against entrenched, hereditary elite status, but only superficially in the name of radical egalitarianism. Rather, they envisioned a society of self-made men of reason, whose interior pious virtues and spiritual en-lightenment would produce economic success and hence well-earned so-cial power. All obstacles to this individual's rise had to be summarily removed, and ascriptive social status stood most glaringly in the way. Reformers employed the language of reform piety to critique all obstacles to the enthronement of the virtuous, self-disciplined individual as society's fundamental constituent.

The scourge of "superstition" and exuberant religion, and the voice of the reform clergy, El *Censor* satirized the idle nobility (*nobilidad ociosa*) and heaped praise on the self-made man. In a typical article, a noble insults a virtuous and prosperous commoner as a "new man." The man retorts with pride that he might be new, "which is to say that I came into the world before my fortune . . . that I am an original, not a copy . . . I am new, it's true."[78] El *Censor*'s editor found the burial theatrics that expressed social hierarchies as morally ociosa (lazy) as the nobility. The idle nobility was as undeserving of its worldly status as were those who engaged in flamboyant piety: neither had struggled to tame their "disorderly appetites," neither had disciplined themselves, and, perhaps most important, they were often one and the same. Reformers' juxtaposition of interior virtue to vain exte-rior acts expanded beyond religion to include critiques of all those whose status was not acquired but given at birth. In the pages of El *Censor*, Jovellanos ridiculed a noble as "a pretty, perfumed, sugar-pastry fop / whose noble dress is to cover vile thoughts."[79]

Although the nobility should lose its special privileges, as befits a religious movement, they were invited to join the reform camp and redefine
their social authority on the basis of virtue. Listen to Jovellanos in a 1787 *El
Censor* article: "Let common men burst boldly forth and seize honors and
titles, splendor, noble rank. Let all in infamous confusion sink, and do
away with classes and estates. Virtue alone can be their guard and shield;
without her, let all end and come to naught."

Reformers' efforts to free the virtuous from their social shackles extended far beyond the construction of cemeteries that would reflect and
promote their vision of right order in society and its proper mode of
expression. True, their efforts often met with opposition from within both
the Church and the state, and their campaigns often proved resounding
failures. Nonetheless, it remains undeniably significant that in the late
eighteenth century Bourbon bureaucrats unleashed a legislative barrage
against corporate privileges, especially those of the nobility and the
Church. The campaign was designed to create a more just meritocracy, a
society based not on ossified rank but on individual merit, on interior
virtue, not exterior display of status. Responsible for his spiritual salvation,
the individual should also seize hold of his social and economic salvation,
and thus all obstacles to the social ascent of the internally regulated individual should be summarily abolished. New Spain's energetic Viceroy
Revillagigedo, an active proponent of the new cemeteries and a champion
of restoring the Church to its early glory, neatly summarized this goal when
he decried "the damage caused to vassals by the unequal conditions that
distinctions and exemptions [*fueros*] introduce between them."[80]

In particular, well-placed bureaucrats in both the Church and the state
sought to reduce the numbers and power of the conservative clergy and the
nobility, who they believed stymied the nation's economic advancement.
Having long shed its military justification, the nobility lost its fiscal exemptions, and even its closed status, as the Bourbon state opened rank to those
who engaged in commerce. The new upward mobility clearly mocked the
society of estates.[81] According to enlightened Church and state bureaucrats, the retrograde elements of the Church, particularly the regular orders, sanctified the elite's social position through church burials, siphoned
money away from government coffers through the tithe, prevented the free
circulation of land and capital, and interposed both educational and judicial barriers between sovereign and subject. Most alarming, however, these

conservatives undermined the Empire's social fiber: they proffered indiscriminate and conspicuous charity that discouraged the necessary moral transformation that inspired honest work.[82]

In New Spain, the Bourbon social "homogenization" project, as historian Antonio Elorza so aptly tagged it for the Spanish case, focused on the indigenous and casta population, previously isolated by both protective and restrictive legislation as well as by language.[83] The state lifted bans on "people of reason" residing in Indian communities, legislated against debt peonage to ensure freedom of movement, and sent funds to Spain's Bank of San Carlos to prevent their expenditure on raucous religious rituals unbecoming to the rational lifestyle they now believed Indians capable of leading.[84] At the same time, new cultural and class categories jockeyed to replace the besieged caste system: Mexico Intendant Bernardo Bonavia proposed exempting from tribute Indians who dressed like *gente de razon*, the Count of Aranda insisted that educated castas merited consideration for government posts, and the state sold official certificates proclaiming the purchaser's whiteness to anyone who could afford them (*gracias al sacar*).[85]

Language also proved a central issue in the social leveling campaign. Whereas early evangelists had mastered indigenous languages, reformers perceived the myriad Indian tongues, as well as regional languages such as Basque and Catalan, as threatening the generalized public culture they sought to superimpose over ethnic and regional particularities. The campaign began with a 1770 royal edict empowering colonial officials to eradicate all languages other than Castilian.[86] New grammar schools (*escuelas pias*), designed to liberate children from "the laziness which inclines them to vice and which causes them to become, when adults, not only useless but dangerous to the republic," taught the language and insisted to parents that children needed Spanish for their "civil conduct with all people."[87] Informed by a vision of society where the individual, not the order, caste, or corporation, constituted the fundamental constituent, reformers sought to eliminate all barriers to individual advancement.

Although the burial reformers thus clearly rejected the Church's traditional means of sanctioning social hierarchy, it might seem a stretch to imagine their attacking the privileges of the very clerical hierarchy in whose ranks so many of them served.[88] Nancy Farriss has more than done justice to this extensive diminution of clerical privileges in the late eighteenth century, and thus the specifics of that entire campaign will not detain us here. One aspect of the campaign will have to suffice to illustrate the overall tenor. With blatant disregard for the Council of Trent's affirmation of criminal asylum's divine origin, in 1773 the Crown prohibited flight to convents and churches located near prisons and reduced the number of edifices that could harbor outlaws to just one or two per town. The monarch also recommended that the secular, not the ultramontane regular clergy, administer asylum.[89] Emboldened by the state's tacit approval, secular officials began to more aggressively pursue miscreants hidden on ecclesiastical property. In a 1782 Mexico City case, Acordada constables sneaked up on a refugee from secular justice as he lounged against a parish's cemetery fence. Despite his repeated shouts of "I call the Church," the officers chased Juan Duran through neighboring streets and whisked him off to prison. Duran eventually won his appeal and returned to asylum, but parish priest Francisco Javier Bedoya contended that no precedent existed for Juan's incarceration: the police had often observed refugees in the cemetery on their daily rounds but had respected their right to protection.[90] The campaign to extend state jurisdiction to every nook and cranny of the Empire intensified with the 1787 royal order authorizing secular authorities to extract all refugees from churches, albeit with prior notice to ecclesiastical officials.[91]

As with the nobility and the saints, however, the idea was not to eliminate priests' social powers, but to reconfigure them. They should be less mediators between man and God—for this was less necessary, as we have seen— and more promoters of Christian virtues, moral exemplars and teachers.[92] At first blush, that most of the Church hierarchs polled by the Council of Castile would so enthusiastically shed their lucrative and prestigious director's role in the visual theatrics of Church burials and funerals seems surprising, to say the least. Their social leadership, however, was not terminated at this time, but rather transformed, as they began to supervise the numerous projects to *reformar costumbres*. The customs in question related to economic life and the work ethic, and their excellencies took a very hands-on approach to promoting their visions for both. The Bishop of Barcelona and the Archbishop of Grenada both instigated cemetery construction years before it became a topic of debate in the Council of Castile; the Bishop of Orihuel founded a cigarette factory to promote industrious habits; and Cardinal Francisco Antonio Lorenzana, after presiding over Mexico's Fourth Provincial Council and establishing a poorhouse in Mex-

ico City, transformed the Alcázar into a workhouse and revived the area's
flagging silk industry. The lower clergy also eagerly fomented industry; the
Sunday homily, after all, continued to influence far more people than did
the enlightened press. Council of Castile President Campomanes therefore
shrewdly recommended that priests learn the latest advances in cottage
industry to convey the information to parishioners (while cemetery reformers likewise relied on sympathetic homilists to sway their listeners).[93]
The parish priest subsequently enshrined as Mexico's greatest Independence hero, Miguel Hidalgo y Costilla, who we last heard warning his
parishioners away from baroque ornamentation, clearly embraced Campomanes's reconfiguration of priests' functions, redirecting his flock's energy toward the recommended practical economic projects, including or-
chards, a wine press, silk worms, and a pottery.[94] Who better to oversee
moral transformation projects than those who had subjected themselves to
strict morality and rigorous discipline, to a life lived in accordance with the
dictates of conscience?

But despite their campaigns to eliminate ascriptive privileges, it would
be a mistake to read the reformers as radical egalitarians intent on economic leveling; the last were by no means to be first, at least not here on
earth. Rather, many reformers predicted that their assault on privilege
would result in the rise of the virtuous, the moderate, the most frugal and
energetic and the fall of the exuberantly extravagant or the permanently
feckless. In a just meritocracy, El *Censor* opined, the wealthy would and
should dominate government posts because "the rich are the most qualified to hold them as they have proven themselves the most talented and
dedicated [*aplicados*] and thus the most virtuous."[95] Here was a work ethic
worthy of Max Weber!

That wealth and virtue were so readily conflated, that poverty so clearly
signaled moral turpitude—in short, that morality could be so closely associated with industry—sprang from eighteenth-century novelties. The interior moral transformation encouraged by the new piety focused so relentlessly on energetic labor in part because new economic theories colluded
with the reform movement to inspire efforts to up the populace's productivity. During the eighteenth century, factory productivity, crop yields, and
the number of the King's vassals replaced the accumulation of gold and
silver as the measure of wealth.[96] As the president of the Council of Castile
succinctly put it, "A numerous and directed populace is the greatest good

of a state, and the foundation of its true power."[97] This rationale of state stood in stark relief to the sixteenth-century conversion mission touted as the "greatest good" in the *requeremento* read to newly conquered subjects.[98] Indeed, when Spain signed peace treaties with Turkey, Tripoli, and Argel (1782, 1784, and 1786, respectively), a foreign policy based on proselytizing and defending the faith officially came to a close.[99] The result was a new devotion to removing economic barriers and creating eager and capable workers. As early as 1719, Father Juan Cabrera's widely read *Crisis política* outlined the state's responsibility for nurturing its subjects' prosperity.[100] And in his influential 1762 *Proyecto económico*, Crown economist Bernardo Ward, who we will later hear decrying the saints' sartorial splendor, urged the government to challenge its citizens' mores "because if we do not inculcate in them work habits, we will never be able to introduce the spirit of industry; and without this spirit all our efforts to improve agriculture, skilled occupations, factories, and commerce will be of little use."[101] Acordada official Hipolito Villarroel, whose sensationalist tract limned the vices of Mexico City's poor, also plaited together economic, moral, and state advancement, recommending programs to combat laziness because "government's greatest good lies in encouraging people to work in their respective offices and trades, in order that they contribute to the good of the state."[102]

From a twenty-first-century perspective, the determined campaign to end the Church's implicit approval of worldly social rank through church burials and the new stress on creating a more productive populace seem to demonstrate that some bureaucrats were determined to shuck a divine mandate for rule in favor of a more secular justification: the state's ability to abet the productivity of populace and nation, to promote "useful" projects.[103] The evidence from the cemetery campaign suggests a different interpretation. The burial reformers who weighed in to the Council of Castile, after all, were motivated largely by a new piety that stressed the value of interior moral transformation. Cemeteries, they hoped, would end the vain display of worldly distinctions in church burials and encourage a more internal moral struggle. Thus, at the same time that the new piety inspired an attack on the Church's traditional sanctification of social hierarchies, it provided its adherents with a powerful moral—and strictly religious—imperative for their own leadership of social engineering projects. This was no secularization of the right to rule: the reformers' knowledge and subsequent worldly success sprang from their definitively un-worldly religious quest for salvation. They had taken God's message to heart, they had reflected and understood His moral injunctions, they had read the Bible and the Church councils, they had diligently examined the rectitude of their motivations, and they had prospered; thus they should rightfully guide others to the light.

Conclusions

Historians have described the Bourbon homogenization project as an at-tack by the state against corporate privileges, notably those of the Church. Such an interpretation would likewise identify the cemetery reform move-ment as an attempt to force nonchurch burials on an entrenched Church hierarchy. But we have seen how the reformers' own self-definition paints quite a different picture. The self-proclaimed "men of reason" could be found not only within the ranks of the press, but also in positions of influence throughout both the Church and the state apparatuses. The proponents of the new piety defined themselves as a class, therefore, not by profession, institutional affiliation, or rank at birth. Rather, they pointed to their common moral enlightenment, which they posited against the elites' vanity on the one hand, and the craven, uncomprehending superstition of the poor on the other. Predictably, then, champions and opponents of the suburban burials waged their battles at all levels of administration, both imperial and clerical; in the eyes of its authors, the new plan was a project not of some monolithic state, but of reasonable, enlightened men wher-ever they could be found.

The new religious sensibility that fueled the cemetery campaign was an active agent in the creation of a would-be ruling class that justified its social leadership not by birthright but by the newly important Christian virtues of self-discipline, moderation, and enlightened erudition. Through personal correspondence, the press, and the new economic societies, this group forged its sense of identity, an identity based on pious sensibility and capital rather than on an inherited position in a juridically fixed and spir-itually sanctified social hierarchy. Critical to the cultural sensibility of the enlightened was an adherence to a new piety that rejected theatricality in favor of the interiorization of religion. Rising through the ranks of the Bourbons' more rational bureaucracy because of their erudition rather than their aristocratic birth, enlightened Crown officials, particularly the upper clergy, rejected the theatrical display of social position in church burials and elaborate funerals; their status, after all, was based on their moral authority and on the attendant imperative to observe, analyze, and improve the population. In the cemetery campaign, the predominant language of reformers' social leveling efforts was piety, a piety that galvanized the enlightened and sacralized—not secularized—their new social authority. Equally important, although the gente de luces may have dominated the state, they faced considerable conservative opposition from within even the highest level of government all the way down to city councils. Such broadly distributed resistance demonstrates that cemetery reform was the project of a rising class, a class intent on redefining the justification for rule, not a top-down imposition of a monolithic and despotic state. During their own cemetery battle, Veracruz's merchants and reform clerics would find powerful allies in the Bourbon state, but so too would their conservative opponents. It is to that city that we now turn for a careful examination of this process.

chapter 4

The Battle for Church Burials

The one-size-fits-all burial grounds threatened the elaborate visual display of social hierarchy in church tombs and imperiled the traditionally well-attended funerals: How many fellow-subjects could be expected to turn out and pray for your soul if your funeral afforded no greater diversion than a dusty walk to the suburbs and an interment short on pomp and circumstance? How could a humble casta remember his place if your ultimate end were no more inspiring than his own? And how could the living keep their attention on the afterlife without the dead's constant presence to remind them of their own mortality? Not surprisingly, the 1790 construction of a suburban cemetery in Veracruz provoked impassioned encounters between those with church burial rights and the city's procemetery faction. The resultant cemeteries proved sparse and unkempt, merely relocating the threat to public health rather than eradicating it.

The intensity of Veracruz's burial battles stemmed from two antagonistic notions of piety, two conflicting interpretations of Salvation's true path. In an era of intense preoccupation with the soul, such a conflict was far from an esoteric sideshow; rather, it illuminates the fault lines of pre-Independence Mexico in much the way that contemporary struggles over abortion or welfare reform reveal fundamental currents in fin de siècle United States. This chapter examines the principal protagonists of the Veracruz cemetery skirmishes: the hospitals, confraternities, regular orders, and elites with prior burial privileges. The subsequent chapter explains the causes and consequences of Veracruz's enlightened merchants' firm adherence to the new piety.

The Cemetery Skirmishes

As we have seen in Mexico City, funerals provided the Church with an opportunity to sanctify elites' lofty social position. Although twelve was the usual number, hundreds and even thousands of clergy regularly escorted the dead from their home to the church and prayed at burial ceremonies. Imagine, for example, the riveting effect of the Countess Luisa de Albornoz y Legazpi's 1653 funeral. Her entourage included the viceroy, the entire nobility, and every cleric in the city; an ornate carriage attended by twelve torch-bearing pages brought the body to the Franciscan monastery for burial in the sacristy.[1] In Veracruz, fewer religious were available for the elaborate corteges so prevalent in Mexico City's streets and churches until the late eighteenth century, but veracruzanos still managed to round up impressive funeral contingents. The wealthy also contracted monigotes, poor denizens who lived off their funeral appearances, and pious brotherhoods swelled funeral contingents; numerous testators noted confraternity memberships in their will, and most of these organizations promised their members a well-attended funeral as a final act of brotherly love.

As in Mexico City, the regular orders in Veracruz directed the local theater of power. Traditional elites—those of noble birth, ostentatious wealth, and fair skin—coveted burial under the protection of the friars' chapels and altars; not surprisingly, this demand for hallowed ground allowed its caretakers to charge stiff fees for its use. For Veracruz's most expensive burial real estate—the area from the presbytery to the matrix of the church—the friars charged at least one hundred times the daily wage of a Mexico City artisan.[2] Franciscan coffers in particular received additional revenues from the sale of their habits as funeral shrouds, overwhelmingly the most popular of the available options in burial dress.

But the Franciscans were hardly exceptional: Veracruz's other religious also did a brisk business with the well heeled. Don Antonio de la Ganda came to rest in Santo Domingo's Virgin of the Rosary Chapel; within twenty-four hours, three different religious orders were praying Masses for his soul. In a creative deathbed bargain, Don Pedro de Caldes bequeathed ample funds to fuel the lamp that continuously illuminated the Blessed Sacrament in the church of Our Lady of Mercy, where he coincidentally sought burial.[3] In short, the new cemetery threatened not only the friars' own time-honored right to interment in cloister, but their substantial burial earnings and their important role in sanctifying the social precedence of Veracruz's elites.

Scandal and subterfuge rocked Veracruz after the cemetery's April 1790 inauguration and the subsequent ban on temple burials. Led by the regular orders, resistance began with foot-dragging and escalated into outright disobedience. The Bethlehemites, for example, self-confidently declared that the Royal Cemetery Edict affected only the laity and not the religious themselves.[4] Alarmed by the friars' recalcitrance, Viceroy Revillagigedo immediately convened the clerical hierarchy resident in Mexico City to convince them to alert their wayward Veracruz brethren to the "utility and will of the King" represented by the cemetery edict.[5]

Given the sensato-dominated state's unwillingness to brook opposition from the ultramontane regular orders, it should come as no surprise that the leaders summoned by Revillagigedo enthusiastically pledged allegiance to the cause; these were the same authorities who had expelled the Jesuits from the Empire in 1767, after all.[6] Indeed, in language as brass as that deployed by the most ardent cemetery proponents, Mexico City's Augustinian provincial Tomas Mercado lectured his Veracruz inferior on the deadly gases exuded by decaying corpses, reminding him that "true piety" and reason accorded with the cemetery, and that "nothing was more important to the religious mission than encouraging subordination to both the secular and religious authorities." Rather than foment dissent, the Veracruz Augustinians should disabuse the faithful of their belief that Masses and orations worked better with the dead present, and employ their authority in "sacred exhortations" in favor of the cemetery.[7] Supremely satisfied with the hierarchy's response, and with the instructions they immediately dispatched to Veracruz's increasingly distraught friars, Viceroy Revillagigedo remained confident of the project's success.

Veracruz's embattled religious, however, refused to go to the graveyard without a fight. News of the Augustinian hierarchy's adamant support for the new burial ground ricocheted through the city, prompting the priors of La Merced and San Francisco to hide their own superiors' procemetery instructions so as not to further fan the "flames of sedition" flickering among their subjects. A rattled José María Laso de la Vega, the city's reform-minded mulatto parish priest, doubted he could enforce the measure without resort to violence, which Viceroy Revillagigedo had expressly forbidden in favor of "reason" and "prudence." Further adding to the parish priest's anxiety was the rumor that *sugetos visibles* (the prominent, the well-known) had colluded with the friars to bury young children in the city's monastic houses. These elite miscreants explained that they themselves supported the cemetery and had merely sought temple burials to console their heartbroken wives, but Laso de la Vega wasn't buying it; he feared that this civil disobedience would resuscitate the horror for the cemetery that he had only recently begun to stifle.[8]

The *cura*'s (parish priest) trepidations proved well founded. In December 1790, six months after the cemetery's opening, zealous Governor Intendent Miguel de Corral discovered that the Dominicans had surreptitiously buried Friar Maríano Cabeza de Vaca in their church's sacristy, an act attended by an impressive number of Veracruz's religious.[9] To make matters worse, the burial had been preceded by a secret session of the city's friars, who had conspired to shun the new cemetery. The fallout from the event deteriorated into finger pointing and backstabbing, as the communities scrambled to justify their flagrant disobedience in the face of Corral's unrelenting investigation. Amid this rather bewildering array of excuses, accusations, and evasions, however, one point was clear: even if the majority of the religious would not publicly back the Dominicans, they had indeed attended both the funeral and the secret meeting, thus lending at least symbolic support to Cabeza de Vaca's scandalous burial.

Emboldened by the regular orders' defiance, and aided by their connivance, Veracruz's traditional elites joined the brothers to fight for the church burials so critical to salvation—and their social status. The April 1790 death of Barbara Bauza, wealthy benefactress and wife of a prominent and pious trader, provoked the opening salvo in the elites' defense of their church crypts.[10] Arguing that the law explicitly exempted Church benefactors, Bauza's relatives demanded that her recently buried body remain in its Franciscan tomb. Similar cases followed in rapid succession.[11]

Other members of Veracruz's privileged preferred to flee rather than risk the cemetery or disinterment. Laso de la Vega's assistant reported that after confessing and accepting the Eucharist, a dying woman had abandoned her deathbed and escaped by carriage to nearby Boca del Rió, where she hoped to obtain a church burial. The Veracruz City Council reported that these protests confirmed most residents' belief that the site served merely as an ignominious dumping ground for paupers or an overflow space for epidemic victims and was thus unfit for the town's more respectable residents.[12]

An alarmed Viceroy Revillagigedo found backing among Laso de la Vega and others of "enlightened piety." To combat these fears, he convened Veracruz's religious to convince them that "utility, the will of the King, and the good of humanity" dictated support for the new cemetery. The beleaguered regulars eventually capitulated, but only on the condition that the burial ground marked the same privileges and distinctions formerly represented in churches and monasteries, a compromise hammered out previously in Spain but conveniently overlooked by the Veracruz enlightened.[13] Viceroy Revillagigedo reluctantly sent instructions for the construction of burial vaults for confraternities, privileged families, the regular orders, and the secular clergy, and placed each group in charge of adorning its own tombs—seemingly a significant setback for the radicals' vision of a cemetery where elaborate displays of status would be eradicated.[14]

But was it? Probably not, and for one principal reason: although with Revillagigedo's concessions the cemetery displayed the corporate power of ecclesiastical institutions and confraternities and the inherited privileges of certain families, it was outside of town, where few could see it. The arrangement by corporate hierarchy served not merely to satisfy some internal sense of order on the part of the elite, but to instruct the populace about this order and its divine sanction. The best proof of this self-conscious pedagogy lies in the elite's reaction to their intact but invisible burial privileges: their hatred for the cemetery intensified despite Viceroy Revillagigedo's concessions. To express their displeasure with the lack of "decency and pomp" in the new funerals and burials, Veracruz elites sought revenge against their principal nemesis: parish priest Laso de la Vega. This cura perceived their goal as nothing less than "the ruin of the parish and its dependents." To combat his fervor, the elite resorted to a financial boycott, a truly inspired strategy, as all parish priests depended heavily on funeral revenues for parish maintenance. In an elaborate 1790 maneuver they conspired to request Masses only from the regular orders and to *fingirse pobres de solemnidad* (pretend to be poor) to oblige the parish to inter their dead for free or at a reduced rate—a potentially ruinous measure, as elites had always paid the highest burial and funeral fees.[15]

In their insistence on pauper funerals, the protesters took advantage of a Church law that dictated that all Catholics rest in consecrated ground, denying space only to infidels and excommunicates and charging the parish with ensuring decent burials for the poor.[16] In an ironic move, some Veracruz elites shunned what remained of the rituals of precedence that accompanied in-church burial; this poor-mouthing allowed them to flex their financial muscle for Laso de la Vega's edification. Just before the cemetery's construction, Don Francisco Zaragoza had buried his mother-in-law with all the fanfare corresponding to her prominent social position—and consequently filled the cura's pockets in the process. His sister-in-law's death, however, provided him with the occasion to protest the new burial grounds: Zaragoza ordered the parish's sacristan to escort his sister-in-law in secret from his house to the cemetery at 5 in the morning and forbade him to process with the body to the church door, as this would involve paying accompanying priests. Laso de la Vega noted that even the poorest of his parishioners received better treatment than Zaragoza's sister-in-law and he hoped that with time "God would touch the protesters' interior and make them see the injustice of their antics." In the meantime, suspecting that the city's notaries had abetted the testators' clever defiance, Laso de la Vega and the intendent governor convened the group and threatened them with punishment.[17]

With the viceroy, the bishop, local state officials, and the parish priest aligned against them, however, Veracruz's outraged elites knew that boycotting the parish was insufficient. They found a sympathetic ally in the conservative Council of the Indies, which had only recently been converted into an appeals court for American grievances. Major players in the internment wars—Barbara Bauza's family, the confraternities, the hospitals, and the Veracruz City Council, among others—petitioned for exemption from the cemetery and meticulously recounted the squabbles scandalizing the city.[18]

The city council had opened its anticemetery campaign by retracting its former support for the new burial ground, sheepishly noting that its own members would prefer burial in the parish's San Sebastián chapel.[19] But it was the December 2 burial of an alderman that fired the city councilors' long-smoldering resistance to the boiling point and prompted their immediate appeal to the King for their burial privileges. After learning that Councilman Esteve would not be buried in the city council's parish crypt, the deceased's father insisted on burying him in the new cemetery with the absolute minimum of accompaniment and funeral pomp, a tactic designed not to display his adherence to the new piety but to withhold funeral fees from the unpopular Laso de la Vega. At least some of Esteve's fellow aldermen, however, wanted to provide him with "the honors corresponding to a member of the illustrious body [the city council]" and placed guards outside his house to prevent a less-than-spectacular funeral.[20] Both Esteve's father's and the council's actions reveal the importance of the visible, theatrical sanctification of social authority: Esteve's cortege and funeral, and an elaborate in-church burial, both displayed the religious'—and thus God's—approval of the councilman's authority.

That Veracruz's political authorities relied on perceptible spiritual sanctification to justify their leadership can be further seen in the city council's involvement in the cult of San Sebastián. A healer known for his effective advocacy for the sick, San Sebastián was particularly adored in plague-afflicted Veracruz, where yellow fever, black vomit, and other diseases periodically ravaged the eighteenth-century population.[21] The besieged city needed Sebastián's help, and the cabildo took its sponsorship of the cult seriously, sending alms collectors shouting through the streets on a weekly basis.[22] This money funded the saint's annual procession, which occurred on his feast day, January 21, an elaborate affair indeed. Clerics, confraternities, and the regular orders accompanied the Sebastián image from his suburban hermitage to the centrally located parish, while the faithful, particularly the city's black and mulatto residents, clogged the streets and adorned their houses with curtains and altars. The city council commissioned ornate carriages for its own members and for religious dignitaries, and regaled all communicants with expensive refreshments.[23] In short, sponsorship of the San Sebastián cult provided municipal authorities with numerous venues to display their largesse, their divinely approved precedence, and their crucial brokerage function with the Almighty.

Thus, in their petition to the King to preserve their burial rights in the parish's glittering chapel of San Sebastián, the councilmen spared no detail, complaining that inhabitants had been repulsed by the macabre sight of the hospitals' uncovered dead trundled through the streets to the cemetery, where forced laborers discarded them nonchalantly at the gate or buried them in shallow graves so that the buzzards picked at their rancid remains. Ignorant of the exact content of the council's report, Viceroy Revillagigedo confidently dismissed the protesters. The cabildo members predictably dug in their heels, hiring a lobbyist in Madrid and conducting further investigations in Veracruz to cement their case for church burial.[24]

While the city's anticemetery petitioners awaited the Crown's response, the battle intensified in the months that followed. Jocular, candle-bearing groups occupied the city's avenues to engage in funeral processions that mocked the corteges shambling from the parish to the cemetery. In retaliation for the laity's appeals to his superiors, and to combat the opposition now spilling into the streets, Laso de la Vega took to haranguing his flock from the pulpit. To further underscore his point, the priest buried his own father in the cemetery rather than next to the bones of his long-dead mother resting under the Dominicans' church floor.[25] The opposition, however, remained unconvinced; after the cura's third sermon appealing to utility and "true piety," an anonymous group of parishioners affixed a pasquinade to the church door declaring the cemetery to be little more than a glorified "corral."[26]

These minor skirmishes set the stage for the arrival of the October 1791 royal order informing Revillagigedo that "in order to curb the excesses we are seeing," those with extant burial privileges in religious edifices should not be impeded from enjoying them. As they had during the high-level cemetery debate in Spain, Bourbon bureaucrats divided on the cemetery issue. Rather than being a project of the state, "Bourbon" cemetery reform in New Spain likewise constituted a battle between two factions found both within the official bureaucracies and among private citizens: ancien régime traditionalists on the one hand, a rising enlightened camp on the other. Viewed as the products of a monolith, the state's positions look erratic and contradictory, but as battles in a tug-of-war between conflicting groups, they make perfect sense.

First and foremost, the edict rebuked Revillagigedo and his allies for acting precipitously in building the cemetery without respect for the 1789 Royal Order, which had merely solicited reports on cemeteries' feasibility, not ordered their construction. Furthermore, the enlightened had acted unilaterally, failing to consult with the religious orders or with individuals and confraternities with extant burial privileges.[27] Stung by this criticism but undaunted, the viceroy sent elaborate reports to the Council of the Indies and sought to influence enlightened royal ministers.[28]

In the confusion that followed Charles IV's decision to allow cemetery exemptions, it became apparent that the machinations of the privileged lurked behind the cabildo's appeal to retain its seven San Sebastián chapel crypts. The three proprietary councilmen alone encouraged popular grievances and had filed the complaints without the other members' consent, rendering the appeal legally invalid.[29] The now openly procemetery city councilors claimed that a heated discussion had indeed occurred during a council meeting, but "those [aldermen] who coveted a distinguished burial" had been appeased by the compromise of burial rights in the suburban San Sebastián hermitage, and the entire municipal council had consented to forward this request to the authorities. Only later did they learn that Perpetual Councilman Juan José de Echeverría had betrayed them and instead appealed to the King for parish—not hermitage—burial. In the process he had adduced a series of horrors that afflicted the cemetery, including protruding bones and uncovered, rotting bodies.[30] These complaints were common to cemetery critics, and Laso de la Vega noted that it would not surprise him if the "lazy" and the "preoccupied" had themselves purposely strewn the bones about to discredit the new cemetery.[31]

The three rogue councilors proceeded to transform the dull investigative hearing of Echeverria's misdeeds into a raucous procemetery forum, citing the cemetery's public health benefits and arguing that souls would continue to receive effective suffrages even if their bodies were not under parishioners' feet. The procemetery faction's account revealed their firm adherence to "true piety," with its stress on self-imposed moral transformation: "If a man who places himself at the feet of an altar to beseech his creator's favor cannot remember an obligation, he should expect very little from a mere oration."[32] In search of evidence to invalidate the royal order, Revillagigedo demanded a copy of City Councilman Echeverría's clandestine appeal to King Charles IV.[33]

Viceroy Revillagigedo opted for his own interpretation of the October 1791 Burial Edict: the cemetery would continue to welcome all of Veracruz's dead except those who had founded religious edifices or had been officially declared "saintly" by the Church; in short, everyone would be buried there. Revillagigedo's disobedience of an explicit royal order was motivated in part by his knowledge that Veracruz's popular classes—who usually had received burial in the parish's exterior cemetery, and who had been extras, never stars, in the city's baroque death dramas—relished the cemetery's explicit egalitarianism and would cease to support the site should traditional elites be exempted. Puebla's Bishop Biempico y Sotomayor echoed Revillagigedo's sentiments, exhorting his fellow religious to embrace the cemetery and convince their flocks that "vain distinctions should not be carried on after death." Only martyrs and the saintly deserved to be sepulchered in churches. Finally, in a bold invocation of reformers' favorite imperative, the bishop thundered that "all ecclesiastical rules [on burials] were nullified by the order to restore the primitive governance [*disciplina*] of the Church."[34]

As soon became clear, the permanent aldermen were not Veracruz's only politically intrepid conservative group; other petitions belatedly surfaced as the Council of the Indies' cemetery exemptions trickled into Veracruz.

Inspired by Laso de la Vega's defiance, the enlightened ignored the King's explicit exemption orders, however, and the disputes dragged on. The confraternities now took up the banner of resistance.

Their resistance proved formidable indeed, as the city claimed numerous brotherhoods. Although a seventeenth-century pirate raid had destroyed important documents and earlier ecclesiastical licenses, an official 1791 investigation uncovered three brotherhoods in the convent of San Francisco, two in the convent of Santo Domingo, and one each in the Convent of La Merced and the chapel of El Señor del Buen Viaje, as well as six parish organizations, for a total of thirteen confraternities serving a city of roughly four thousand residents.[35]

Both the impressive rates of enrollment in the organizations and the vast sums they spent on liturgical celebration require some explanation. The confraternities operated in an atmosphere of constant absorption in the fate of one's immortal soul and represented a lay effort to back up standard clerical functions. Membership in a confraternity linked a believer to a network of fellows pledged to devotions on behalf of the souls in Purgatory, whose ranks you would almost surely eventually join yourself. As they did in Mexico City, confraternities in Veracruz controlled urban and rural real estate and received numerous bequests from the faithful.[36] Confraternities also relied on membership fees for the revenues spent on the cult of their patron saint and on members' funerals. In exchange for a lifetime of small fees, for example, the Confraternity of Our Father Jesus of Nazareth of the Three Falls promised María Regina Salao 22 pesos for her burial, funeral shroud, bells, tomb candles, and a Mass sung for her soul in the chapel of Our Father Jesus.

Similarly concerned with postmortem fate was the Confraternity of San Benito de Palermo, whose bell-ringer wound his way through Veracruz's streets to advise members of their obligation to pray and chant for departed souls on the Octave of the Commemoration of the Dead.[37] As stipulated in Alexander VII's 1674 papal bull, the Church remitted San Benito de Palermo members' sins when they joined the group. Any of a host of acts earned a member sixty days' pardon from penitence: funeral participation, meetings to implement pious works, religious processions, escorting the consecrated Host when it went out on Viaticum, reciting five times the Our Father or Hail Mary for the souls of dead cofrades, housing poor travelers. Furthermore, those who gathered in the confraternity's chapel on May 4 to pray for heresy's extirpation, the Pope's health, or the Church's general exaltation earned a seven-year reprieve from Purgatory's torments. The confraternity provided all new members with a patente detailing their rewards and obligations. The coveted in-church burial and funeral services so critical to abbreviating a stint in limbo were carefully detailed in San Benito de Palermo's patente, which, in exchange for various fees, promised 22 pesos for interment and funeral fees.[38]

With their promise of ample suffrages, a decent burial under the chapel of the group's patron saint, and the attentive advocacy of this saint during each member's appearance in the heavenly court, confraternities attracted members from across the social spectrum, although not from the desperately poor, who found the fees prohibitive. Energetic city council member Pedro Antonio de Garay y Llano, who signed the 1781 petition for a Veracruz merchant guild, founded the Franciscan convent confraternity of La Escuela de Cristo in 1792.[39] Other merchants also played prominent roles in the city's confraternities. Juan de Vieyra y Sousa and Antonio Frediani, for example, both served as majordomos of the confraternity of Nuestro Padre Jesus Nazareno, located in the convent of Padres Predicadores. The Franciscans housed the prestigious members of the Franciscan Tertiaries as well as the city's tailors, who ran the confraternity of San Diego de Alcalá. Numerous Veracruz residents held multiple memberships, an indication that many brotherhoods' composition cut across class and status lines. Doña Beatriz de Real, for example, belonged to two confraternities in the convent of Predicadores, four parish organizations, two confraternities housed in the convent of La Merced, and the Franciscan Tertiaries. Don Francisco José de Ortega paid weekly dues to no fewer than seven brotherhoods, who together provided an enormous sum for his funeral expenses.[40]

Between their adoration of patron saints and their belief in the efficacy of prayers and saintly intercession for the departed, the confraternities proved a stringent irritant to the enlightened's pious sensibilities; recall, for example, Archbishop Nuñez de Haro y Peralta's peremptory reduction of his diocese's confraternities by half. Confraternities did nothing to promote serious moral struggle through individual adherence to God's light; indeed, high-level reformers such as cemetery champion Campomanes felt that their "exorbitant and vain" expenditures on liturgical celebration positively detracted from that most important project. There was nothing wrong with seeking mediation with the Divine, of course, but efforts should focus on Christ as represented in the Eucharist rather than the plethora of saints promoted by the confraternities, and the Count of Floridablanca noted that these "superstitious and false devotions fomented and maintained laziness and vice."[41] The Count of Campomanes emphatically shared this sentiment and saw a particular danger in the members' enthusiasm for the Seven Acts of Mercy, one of which, of course, was almsgiving. In a sentiment worthy of our own contemporary scene, Campomanes opined that charity encouraged begging, whereas restraint might spark the poor to a rational moral transformation and consequent economic self-sufficiency.[42] The deserving poor should be given the education and skills to prosper—a hand up, not a handout, as the current parlance would have it.

All of the confraternities celebrated their patron saint's holiday, but Corpus Christi provided an occasion for especially frenetic participation in public religious ritual. First instituted by Pope Urban in 1264, Corpus Christi became the critical celebration of the Catholic calendar after the Council of Trent stressed the Doctrine of Substantiation in the face of the formidable Protestant challenge.[43] In Veracruz, parish confraternities staged a procession commemorating Christ's holy burial, adorning the parish's wooden angels and lining up to parade behind banners. The city's most distinguished residents headed the procession, carrying the Franciscans' Holy Cross from its chapel and leading the confraternities.[44] Thus, as during Holy Week, the city's brotherhoods transformed Veracruz's streets into a stage for the pomp and splendor of baroque procession and its attendant sanctification of social hierarchy and explicit melding of political and religious authority.

In Veracruz, the enlightened's unease with the confraternities' excesses had been felt long before the cemetery campaign. The promotion of the cult of the Eucharist found expression in the city in the form a parish confraternity founded in 1789 and dedicated to the Blessed Sacrament, to which one benefactor designated 50 pesos annually for the adornment of the case (sagrario) displaying the Host.[45] These Slaves of the Blessed Sacrament included thirty-one of Veracruz's most distinguished residents, each of whom served as carriage driver one day a month, escorting the Host to the homes of the sick and dying.[46] Even earlier, in 1776, however, Campomanes's and Floridablanca's sentiments reverberated in New Spain in the form of a requirement that all confraternities obtain a Crown license; a

1791 law mandated a royal official's presence at every gathering.[47] The crackdown continued in 1796 with the order that all brotherhoods submit their constitution for review by the Council of the Indies, which often refused their licensing requests.[48]

The two sides squared off: the enlightened expressed misgivings about the confraternities' preferred path to salvation; across the chasm, many Veracruz cofrades recoiled from the cemetery campaign and, by association, from the new fashion in piety. How could they accept as legitimate a theological innovation that threatened their only means to shortening their family's sojourns in Purgatory (to say nothing of their own)? Hence their pasquinades, their clandestine church burials, their impassioned pleas to higher-ups for exemptions; salvation was at stake, and the militant faithful had banded together in dedication to a patron saint to obtain it. The urgency of this quest, the passion that ignited the disputes, stemmed from a fundamental—and perhaps ultimately irreconcilable—disagreement with the enlightened over the bricks and mortar that smoothed the road to Heaven. Imagine the angst, if not the sheer terror, of a poor tailor, a typical member of the San Diego de Alcalá confraternity, on learning that his carefully scrimped weekly fees would no longer guarantee a resting spot under a saint's protection, would no longer assure him of the promised chapel burial where the faithful would daily be reminded to pray for his soul.

Given the stakes, then, the confraternities' rebellion against the cemetery should come as no surprise. In reaction to the late eighteenth-century Crown campaign to monitor the confraternities more closely, the Veracruz brotherhood of San Benito de Palermo petitioned the Council of the Indies to renew its constitution; predictably, their burial policy became a serious source of contention. Allocating substantial monies for the members' elaborate monastery burials, the clause was rejected by the Council; henceforth, it ruled, dead cofrades belonged in the general cemetery, which "benefited public health." The parish brotherhood of San José joined the San Benito de Palermo confraternity in the anticemetery crusade, successfully petitioning King Charles IV to open a new crypt next to their chapel's main altar, a request that provoked the wrath of Viceroy Revillagigedo, who challenged the King's favorable decision. Employing a language that revealed his own penchant for the new piety, Revillagigedo informed the Council of the Indies that the confraternity's request violated "the historic discipline of the Church." Although in 1799 Viceroy Aranza confirmed Revillagigedo's decision, the case was not definitively decided in the enlightened viceroy's favor until 1803, well after his term had ended in 1794.[49]

Elite Franciscan Tertiaries provided the hospitals and the confraternities of San Benito de Palermo and San Joséf with additional anticemetery allies.[50] Although laymen and laywomen made up the bulk of their memberships, and although they offered funeral benefits, the Third Orders were not confraternities, as Pope Benedict XIV made clear in his 1725 bull, "Patena sedis." Unlike the brotherhoods, the Third Orders required profession and a one-year novitiate and offered funeral shrouds like those of the military orders. Third Order members, according to Pope Climente VII's special decree later ratified by Pope Innocencio, enjoyed all of the privileges, favors, immunities, and prerogatives of the San Franciscan friars and the nuns of Santa Clara, but resided in their own home rather than in cloister.[51] Like the confraternities, however, the orders—which in New Spain included Santo Domingo, San Francisco, San Augustine, Nuestra Señora de la Merced, and the Carmelites—knew definitively that suffrages opened the door to heaven. All members were required to attend funerals with candles in hand and to pray fifty psalms or recite the Paternoster fifty times for the newly deceased, although strict compliance was almost impossible given the group's vast membership.[52] The Franciscans also mandated that the enlisted don the San Francisco burial shroud; failure to comply led the order to boycott the funeral. Most important, in Veracruz all Franciscan Tertiaries could elect burial in the group's richly adorned chapel, and both male and female officeholders and instructors could opt for a presbytery crypt. All participants counted on three Masses after their death as well as the daily Mass said for both the living and the defunct, and officers received "honorable suffrages" attended by their families and the entire brotherhood, as well as an additional three Masses.[53]

The new cemetery particularly irked Veracruz's Franciscan Tertiaries, whose defunct members rested in the group's impressive chapel.[54] Located immediately behind the monastery's central altar, the chapel boasted both a sacristy and a large meeting room, and its adornment, as one traveler marveled, easily rivaled the glittering opulence of the Mexico City silversmiths' cathedral chapel.[55] Third Order members' wills further testify to their wealth and privilege, designating lavish bequests to family, Church, and charity. José García de la Larra requested as many Masses as could possibly be recited the day of his May 1778 funeral and ordered an additional six hundred recited immediately thereafter. Inquisition commissioner Don Miguel Francisco de Herrera preferred burial in the Franciscan Tertiaries' chapel, but noted that he would settle for a tomb in the parish presbytery, which gleamed with exquisite marble imported from Europe. Herrera's funeral procession wound its way from the Franciscans' chapel to the parish and included Veracruz's entire clerical community as well as the Inquisition, who sat in the presbytery, as Herrera had specifically instructed. The clerics returned to the parish the following day to say an additional one hundred Masses and to distribute alms to one hundred beggars. Not all Franciscan Tertiaries demonstrated such largesse on their deaths, but, as Herrera's and others' wills indicate, the rich and powerful were well-represented in the Third Order of San Francisco.[56]

Powerful and prominent, Veracruz's Franciscan Tertiaries seemed stunned by the enlightened's aggressive cemetery offensive but quickly recouped, deploying their considerable cultural capital to send a series of written protests to secular authorities. To justify retaining their tombs, the Tertiaries emphasized their consistent upkeep of the chapel and a fifty-seven-year-old burial record (1733–1790). Unmoved, Veracruz's intendant governor warned Viceroy Revillagigedo that continuing the brothers' chapel burial privileges would incite an avalanche of petitions to join the order, mitigating the new cemetery's salubrious effects. The bishop concurred with the governor's assessment and added that neither the religious themselves nor the Tertiaries merited exemption and that the Cemetery Edict overrode all temple burial rights. Not surprisingly, Viceroy Revillagigedo invoked the dictates of public health to shoot down the prestigious Third Order members' petition for burial rights.[57]

Hospital burial had a long history in the Indies, and the Veracruz hospitals joined elite families, the regular orders, and the Third Orders and confraternities to oppose the new cemetery. In 1622 Bishop Don Alonso de la Mota y Escobar cited a 1612 papal bull as precedence for granting Veracruz's Hospital de San Juan de Montesclaros the right to inter their own dead.[58] But the Pope's bull and the bishop's decision both failed to impress the enlightened, who countered these authorities with the imperatives of the new piety and public health to bolster their case. Antonio María Fernández easily imagined the "infinity of putrid miasmas" exuded by the four hundred bodies accommodated annually under the Hospital of San Juan de Montes Claros and by the forty dead women the Hospital of Nuestra Señora de Loreto buried yearly—not to mention the troops fermenting under the Royal Hospital of San Carlos and the bodies decaying under the Bethlehemites' small convalescent facility.[59]

The hospitals' principal grievance centered on finances, as the new cemetery threatened burial fees and pious donations. The Royal Navy paid the Hospital of San Carlos, which tended to the numerous troops billeted in the insalubrious city, 10 pesos for its sailors' funeral and suffrages, a custom dating from at least 1700. After much bickering, in 1790 the parish and the hospital hammered out a compromise whereby the bulk of the 10 pesos donated by the Royal Navy went equally to the parish priest, the hospital, and the cemetery chaplain, with the remaining pittance divided among singers, sacristans, gravediggers, and bell ringers. Still, despite the compromise, the reigning peace was an uneasy one, punctuated with flareups: conflicts among regular and hospital orders, each proclaiming their right to carry the cross in funeral corteges; squabbles between hospital and parish over the solvents' funeral fees; and mutual accusations of haphazard, unsanitary cemetery burials.[60]

Yet, for all this, the hospital dead were not among those exempted from the cemetery by Charles IV's 1794 order. But, as the regular orders, the confraternities, and Veracruz's elite families had already demonstrated, burial customs proved intractable to mere legislative fiat, and skirmishes between the hospitals and the parish dragged on. In one typical exchange, a hospital prior pleaded with the authorities to allow him to sepulcher the dead in the hospital on the entirely plausible grounds that the acting parish priest, Bartolome Borrero, was likewise defying the law and burying his wealthy parishioners in the church! Both miscreants were promptly upbraided and expressed contrition, but simultaneously engaged in footdragging measures to stall their opponents; although the conflict's resolution remains unclear, such resistance, like that of the regular orders and Veracruz's elite families, demonstrates the considerable forces arrayed against the enlightened.[61]

The intensity of the sepulchral skirmishes that shook Veracruz in the early 1790s indexes a more profound social conflict. At stake in the burial battle was not only the traditional religious sanctification of political rule and social hierarchy, but the dead's function as the critical mnemonic device for the Church's elaborate rescue efforts on behalf of Purgatory's suffering souls. Traditional elites' resistance to the cemetery is easy to understand: the suburban burial grounds directly and explicitly threatened their principal idiom of distinction and technique of rule. Veracruzanos' fervent desire for suffrages, and their fear that exiling the dead would remove them from the community's prayers and the saints' protections, as well as the hospitals' and friars' fears of reduced burial revenues, are equally comprehensible. The enlightened's rejection of lavish funerals and their firm cemetery support is more difficult to account for, and it is to this dilemma that we now turn.

chapter 5

Piety, Power, and Politics

Amid the din of protestation in the previous chapter, the voice of the reformers is barely discernible: Viceroy Revillagigedo's reformist rallying call to restore the Church to its pristine purity, Bishop Salvador Biempico y Sotomayor's rantings against vanity. But in fact, Veracruz's zealous reformers were every bit as loud and cacophonous as their opponents.

In Veracruz, the new piety constituted part of the complex causal ecology propelling the city's enlightened to shun baroque display as spiritually vacuous. Rather than make a spectacle of themselves—or make themselves through spectacle—Veracruz's self-styled enlightened (sensatos) adopted a different, but equally religious, justification and technique for rule: by taking God's message to heart, by disciplining and moderating their senses and worldly pleasures, they had prospered through individual effort and good conduct. They now peered down on those who apparently would not or could not receive the Word, those who therefore needed the enlightened to inculcate them with the values of hard work and sobriety. Adherence to enlightened piety became both a marker of cultural identity and the critical justification for their rule, a mechanism through which this emerging group distinguished itself from both the traditional elites it fought to discredit and the popular classes it wished to rule.

Critical to understanding these self-defined sensatos' rejection of theatrical display is the new enlightened piety that gripped veracruzanos in the late eighteenth century. In-church burials and elaborate funerals demonstrated not sanctity and strict adherence to Church teachings, but possible moral depravity. Concurring with his counterparts in Spain and Mexico City, Puebla's Bishop Biempico y Sotomayor satirized Veracruz's cemetery oppo-

Portions of this chapter appeared in William H. Beezley and Linda A. Curcio-Nagy, ed., *Latin American Popular Culture: An Introduction* (Wilmington, DE: SR Books, 2000), 1–25.

nents' pretensions as motivated by both "the spirit of vanity and the desire to distinguish themselves" and by their stubborn suspicion that the new burial grounds could not accommodate the "odious distinctions" they so coveted. Veracruz's religious, rather than encourage such wrong-headedness, should remind the benighted that "death makes everyone equal and the vain distinctions of this world cannot be continued into the next."[1]

All of the funereal hubbub insinuated the deceased's probable moral vacuity: "strict adherence to the discipline advocated by the early Church," "modesty in exterior display," "prudence," "interior composure"—these were the virtues Bishop Biempico y Sotomayor urged upon the faithful. Well-acquainted with the Royal Academy of History's strong cemetery advocacy, as well as with the works of authors repeatedly cited in reform circles, Biempico y Sotomayor felt the theatrical compliance to religion's exterior forms distracted the faithful from the real work of moral transformation; he urged the enlightened to prevail over "the capricious and blind preoccupations of those who, lacking education, prefer the indulgence of their vain, ambitious and particular desires over the public and common good of the state and religion."[2]

Yet, for all his eloquence and energetic advocacy, in Veracruz the real virtuoso of the new piety was not the bishop, but mulatto parish priest Laso de la Vega, who seized every opportunity to sing the new piety's praises. In a characteristically controversial move, Laso de la Vega opened a special 1793 paean to the Virgin of Guadalupe by warning his unsuspecting parishioners of the evils of lavish burials: "What vain instructions the great and powerful of this world leave in order to win the esteem of their fellow men, building churches with elaborate tombs for the rest and repose of their cadavers. But does not all this, when examined with a strong light, reveal itself to be nothing more than a diaphanous cloud of smoke. . . . [A]s grand as their patrimony on earth may have been, they cannot make their remains last even one moment more than dictated by the rules of corruption and their bodies' own defective nature, nor can their earthly glory be locked inside their tomb along with them."[3] Elaborate tombs. Festering bodies. Vain pretensions of grandeur. Although certainly more eloquently than most, Laso de la Vega expressed the heart of the reformers' stinging religious critique of their more flamboyant opponents.

Although many reformers hinted at Augustine's influence on their thought, Laso de la Vega, like Núñez de Haro y Peralta, expressed his unbridled enthusiasm for the illustrious Church Father and a return to an earlier, simpler Church. Here is the priest's assessment of the saint, given in a 1780 sermon in his honor: "Augustine, reformer of the primitive faith, and the surest channel through which flows the crystalline water of its virtues . . . the lucid shadow of the divinity himself . . . the very soul of Catholicism. He founded two monasteries in Hipona, the fruit of which was the total reform of customs, and the restitution of Christianity to its primitive colors."[4] The implications of Augustine's doctrine of individual illumination, with its implicit critique of much of the Church's necessary intercession for salvation, had potentially radical implications, as we have seen. As in Spain and its provincial capitals, enlightened intellectuals' vocal opposition to worldly vanity and the visual display of God's majesty did not fall on deaf ears in Veracruz. The radical rise in the number of wills requesting a moderate funeral illustrates this startling sea change. Whereas only around 2 percent of all testators from 1740 to 1779 requested a modest burial, by the peak of the cemetery controversy from 1790 to 1799 20.3 percent of all testators demanded sparse funerals.[5]

Piety rather than economy or diffidence toward burials motivated the modesty movement. Testators who chose the sparser funeral ceremonies rejected the numerous priests and confraternities that accompanied the dead to the church for burial, an elaborate funeral ceremony, or both. Imbued with the new piety, these propertied veracruzanos spurned the need for excessive priestly mediation at the same time that they rejected theatrical religion as a legitimate pathway to God, or a legitimate display of the social position. In Veracruz, as in Mexico City, examples abounded: one wealthy widow proved positively exaggerated in her modesty, insisting that her body be illuminated by only four one pound candles before interment in the suburban cemetery without a cacophony of church bells or any other "demonstrations of luxury." Similarly, Juan Bautista de Alvizuri insisted on burial near the cemetery's door without bells or "any other luxury"; only the parish priest and a few acolytes were to accompany his body out of the city gates to the cemetery.[6]

This widespread support for this "true piety" was not lost on Archbishop Biempico y Sotomayor, who rallied his allies to testify in writing against Councilman Echeverria's controversial report to the King. The comments demonstrate their authors' hostility toward those with prior burial rights and toward visually dazzling pious displays in the streets. If the wealthy felt they helped to bring God's majesty down from heaven for the edification of all, they were sadly misguided, for their antics merely displayed their amor propio. Of the eighteen men summoned by the bishop, five were doctors, three worked for the new Junta de Policía, three held cabildo posts, one had a Church career, and two participated in international trade. Despite their diverse occupations, the witnesses all rehearsed the fundamental tenets of the new piety and of reform thought on cemeteries, and all agreed that City Councilman Echeverría's report had distorted, exaggerated, and just plain fabricated the cemetery's evils.

Recall that Echeverría had adduced a Pandora's box of horrors unleashed upon Veracruz by the new suburban burial ground: bodies dumped unceremoniously at the cemetery gate, circling buzzards, grasping clergy, hospital dead bouncing through the cobblestone streets on uncovered carts, and an outraged opposition sundering the city's social fabric all appeared in the permanent alderman's report. The bishop's team of witnesses set out to debunk Echeverría's allegations, which they regarded as a farrago of lies and misrepresentations. City council *síndico personero* Eligio Uztáriz retorted that a covered cart escorted by two sentinels ferried the hospitals' bodies out of town, where a permanently stationed gatekeeper immediately notified a clerical assistant to perform the funeral service—bodies were most certainly not dumped at the gate, as Echeverría insisted. Furthermore, far from representing consensus opinion, cemetery aversion afflicted only those who had parish or convent burial rights.[7] Intendancy Treasurer José María Laso Vacarino also acknowledged that clerics indeed charged a peso for the trip to the cemetery, but placed the blame squarely on those who, "desirous of distinguishing themselves with more fuss [fausto] and pomp than the norm, and not content with a vast number of clerics to carry the body from their house to the parish, stubbornly insist that a swarm of religious accompany their loved one to the cemetery."[8]

If the witnesses called by the bishop to respond to Echeverría's report all shared a horror of decaying bodies, an assumption of medicine's cultural authority, and an uneasiness with superfluous mediation with the Almighty, nowhere were they more united than in their consensus that burial battles pitted the enlightened and the popular classes against the city's more baroque elites. As did reformers throughout the empire, Veracruz's enlightened coterie believed that the righteousness of their piety was self-evident and that the privileged refused to heed the call of reason; cleric

Manuel María Laso Nacariño, for example, noted that "all reasonable men [hombres sensatos] should be indifferent to cemetery burial."[9] Councilman Eligio de Uztáriz reported that wealthy subjects (*subjetos con caudales*) created the disturbances and that Juana Miranda's and Barbara Bauza's illustrious relatives' protests had galvanized the opposition and destroyed the uneasy peace that he claimed had reigned for two years after the cemetery's construction. Eligio Fernández and Laso Vacariño echoed Uztáriz's insistence that the privileged hated the cemetery, but Francisco Antonio de la Torre noted that the initial general aversion to the site had waned, leaving the wealthy as the only opponents—a phenomenon that a Junta de Policía member attributed to the lower classes' initial belief that the cemetery would be reserved for the poor. Once it became evident that everyone, "without regard to status," would be marched to the cemetery, the popular classes enthusiastically supported the site.[10]

The new piety's fundamental tenets—rational individual judgment and self-control guided by God's light, moderation, hostility to elaborate display of social position or visible inducements to faith—were critical to the enlightened's sense of an "us" arrayed against a "them" who did not share their pious sensibilities. Summing up the 1790s cemetery skirmishes that had polarized Veracruz, the 1806 city council claimed that the vain desire of some to maintain their burial privileges, the confraternities' poor understanding of "true worship," and the indiscrete zeal of certain ecclesiastics had provoked scuffles during every burial. "Those of enlightened piety," the council confessed, had been the new burial ground's only consistent backers, an analysis that echoed the bishop's 1791 assertion that the cemetery merited and had received the support of all "prudent enlightened people free of vulgar preoccupations."[11]

According to contemporary testimony, then, the popularity of the "true piety" that gripped veracruzanos in the late eighteenth century explains the city's procemetery stalwarts. But to accept this answer unexamined is to ignore the more complex interplay of historical cause and effect: Why this brand of piety, why now, why among these people? As in Spain and the Empire, doctors, enlightened secular clergymen, and government bureaucrats represented ascendant social groups whose status was now firmly rooted in the social engineering projects so characteristic of the epoch in general, and of post-1790 Veracruz in particular. In the port city, exploding numbers of new merchants joined these groups to constitute a critical mass of individuals who demonstrated an affinity for the new piety.[12] The new piety gave the enlightened a language to dignify their attacks on the wealthy, whose stubborn insistence on Church burial demonstrated nothing more than their amor propio, their alienation from God, their failure to take His message to heart. In Veracruz, the now familiar cabal of enlightened state officials and reform-minded clerics led the cemetery movement. But, as we have seen, "prudent enlightened people" could be culled from the ranks of the prominent; even the flashiest traditionalists could get themselves under control through spiritual exercises, eschew their thespian tendencies, and experience a true conversion of the heart. And in Veracruz, those with caudales, many of the city's rising merchants, did just that. The question, of course, is why.

The Veracruz Merchant Community

To understand the merchants' affinity for the new piety, we first have to come to grips with their rising economic fortunes in Veracruz as well as their tenuous cultural authority in the city. Veracruz's burgeoning merchant community began to coalesce as an entity chary of the Mexico City merchant guild, who had an official monopoly on foreign and domestic trade, well before the official 1789 promulgation of free trade between New Spain and the Spanish Empire. Indeed, free trade merely formalized a practice that had been accelerating over the course of the eighteenth century. The critical event in the loosening of the Mexico City monopoly and the attendant increase in Veracruz merchant autonomy was the 1728 transfer of the trade fair from Mexico City to Veracruz's neighbor, the bosky retreat of Jalapa, which allowed Veracruz residents to establish their own relations with merchants from the Iberian peninsula and to shed their role as mere agents for Mexico City interests.[13] The gradual unraveling of the trade system of convoyed fleets further added to the woes of the Mexico City monopoly. Eighteenth-century English naval superiority made the use of individual ships rather than large fleets a more pragmatic defensive strategy; as a consequence, only thirteen of these large convoys docked in New Spain between 1720 and 1778.[14] In 1772, Charles III officially terminated the fleet system, establishing in its place officially licensed ships, thereby cutting off Mexico City merchants' ability to purchase the entire enormous cargoes and opening the trade to a wider variety of merchants, particularly those located in Veracruz and Jalapa.[15] Equally distressing for the monopolists, New Spain's thriving and increasingly diverse economy made a centralized distribution system based in Mexico City untenable; as early as the 1760s, for example, Veracruz merchants acted as direct intermediaries between peninsular traders and Oaxaca's prosperous cochineal producers.[16]

The Crown formalized this indirect assault on the Mexico City trade monopoly in a spate of late eighteenth-century legislation. The opening initiative: official Crown representative José de Gálvez's 1767 measure allowing Veracruz interests to funnel European merchandise directly to the Yucatan and Campeche.[17] A cascade of deregulation legislation soon followed: in 1774 the Crown permitted the exchange of products among New Spain, Peru, and New Grenada, provided they did not compete with Spanish imports; in 1789 free trade within the Empire, which had been in effect in most of Spain's other colonies since 1778, was extended to New Spain; and in 1791 Spain's allies obtained entrance to the New World's markets, a privilege that was quickly extended to the allies' colonies in 1795.[18]

Whereas the loosening of trade regulations ended the monopoly held by Mexico City and Cadiz's entrenched merchant communities, in Veracruz commerce boomed. From 1790 to 1799 ninety-nine ships arrived in the port annually, and this number nearly doubled between 1800 and 1810, when 173 vessels plied their wares to traders each year.[19] Veracruz's commerce not only expanded, it diversified; indeed, so international had the city's trade become that by 1808 only 29 of the 193 ships that landed in the city had originally disembarked from Spain.[20] Veracruz, long formally a mere entrepôt for the Cadiz–Mexico City trade, now became an official commercial center in its own right. In 1777, even before the trade boom, the commander of the last fleet to reach Veracruz described it as a bustling port: "Given that the city is the only port for large embarkations and the place where the fleets from Europe have always unloaded, Veracruz participates heavily in the commerce of these goods. . . . Inhabitants make their purchases directly, and then later, during the off-season sell to populations in the interior. . . . In the same way they buy cheap grain and anil and sell it to Europeans for their return trip."[21]

By the early nineteenth century, at least 232 domestic and international merchants participated in activities like those described by Ulloa, and eighty to ninety small retailers tested their skills in the city's lively economy, which engaged a staggering two-thirds of the adult male population in trade-related occupations. Most important, the principal beneficiaries of this trade bonanza were those previously excluded by the monopoly system.[22]

Eight years before the official 1789 free trade proclamation, Veracruz's merchant community came together to defend its interests, petitioning the Crown for their own guild similar to that of Mexico City.[23] More important for our purposes, the merchants left evidence of their stance on the new cemetery and thus, indirectly, their opinions on the reform piety that animated its construction. Nine of the twenty-six merchants who signed the 1781 document played parts in the cemetery dramas of the early 1790s: six of them staunchly defended church burial rights, and three of them bolstered the ranks of the enlightened opposition. Clearly, to be a merchant was not necessarily to be enlightened; the real story lies in the shifts in attitudes over time.

On the one hand, the merchants who defended church and convent burials in the final decades of the eighteenth century did so with vehemence. Antonio Saenz de Santa María, it should be recalled, surreptitiously buried his child in one of the city's convents. Another member of the merchant-dominated city council, Juan José de Echeverría, secretly wrote to the King to protect the cabildo's parish tombs.[24] To a man, in fact, the anticemetery petitioners were vocal, high-profile architects of the resistance. Acting to protect the burial rights that they or their loved ones already held and possessing the know-how and influence to gain the King's ear, these Veracruz traders spearheaded the efforts against the cemetery.

On the other hand, three of the 1781 merchant petitioners numbered among the cemetery's enlightened advocates. City Council Official Eligio Uztáriz testified enthusiastically against Permanent Alderman Echeverría's woeful assessment of the cemetery and strident defense of city council parish burial rights, and joined Bishop Biempico y Sotomayor's carefully selected team of witnesses in blasting the spiritual and health dangers of temple interment. The miasmic exhalations produced by the dead corroding under the city's hospitals particularly irritated alderman and merchant Antonio María Fernández, whose 1789 report to the city council reads like a gente sensata manifesto, with the elaborate cult of the saints, unlicensed healers and midwives, stinking sewage, and that favorite bugbear of the enlightened, the vagrant poor, playing their accustomed roles as the city's moral saboteurs.[25] Finally, in the very eye of the cemetery storm stood petitioner and merchant Miguel Ignacio de Miranda, parish majordomo and Laso de la Vega's right-hand man from the cemetery campaign's 1789 initiation.[26]

But by the time of the 1795 establishment of the Veracruz merchant consulate, the ratio of enlightened to cemetery opponents had begun to reverse itself. Of twenty-six official guild members, half left documented evidence of their cemetery stance: seven strongly advocated the project, a mere five clearly opposed it, and one waffled, his actions demonstrating pure ambivalence. Predictably, the five demonstrated impassioned vigor in defending the burial arrangements that they perceived as their surest path out of Purgatory.[27]

Most of the 1795 merchant guild members who participated in the cemetery skirmishes, however, did so on the side of the enlightened. Junta de Policía and guild members José Ignacio Pabón, Remigio Fernández, and Juan Manuel Muñoz all appeared as witnesses in Bishop Biempico y Mayor's campaign to discredit Echeverría's clandestine correspondence with peninsular authorities. Fernández often suffocated during Mass in the parish due to the malodorous cadavers; Muñoz declared that the poor's cemetery opposition abated when it became clear that everyone, without exception, would be buried there.[28] Three merchant guild members, all witnesses called by Bishop Biempico y Sotomayor to discredit Echeverría's report, backed the cemetery on a unanimous three-point platform: the safeguarding of public health, the necessity of overcoming the "vanity" of a selfish minority, and the dictates of primitive Church discipline. It was José Ignacio de Urlarte, however, who most succinctly expressed the group's esprit de corp in his statement that "the sensatos are in favor of the cemetery, those with burial rights are opposed."[29] These guild members, of course, were not the only Veracruz merchants inflating sensato ranks: City Councilman Francisco Antonio de la Torre, for example, declared the wealthy to be the only glitch in the otherwise smooth cemetery construction project.[30] Behind these merchants' statements, the rough cultural outline of the sensatos' identity can be clearly discerned: their self-identification as a group opposed to the vanity of "the wealthy and privileged," their adherence to "enlightened piety," and their firm allegiance to the dictates of public health all stand out as critical markers of group identification.

But can we conclude from the strong opinions of these eight enlightened businessmen that most of the city's rising merchants embraced the new piety's implicit individualism and potential to justify their own social authority? Not yet. And not without further corroborative evidence.

This evidence is found in the stunning events of the opening decade of the nineteenth century. In 1803, the Veracruz Merchant Guild not only officially advocated cemetery burial, but also declared its intention to build a new cemetery with improved sanitary conditions. Acting for "the good of humanity" and "the conservation of public health," as well as to "restore the Church's primitive discipline," the 1804 merchant-dominated city council renounced its burial privileges in San Sebastián Chapel and strongly urged others to do the same. The parish priest and the distinguished members of the Confraternity of the Blessed Sacrament, established in 1789 as part of the enlightened's promotion of Eucharistic devotion, added their voices to those of the cabildo.[31] Emboldened by the May 1804 royal order for cemetery construction, the twelve aldermen pledged that "no one, not even a viceroy, would be buried within city walls."[32] To sway the benighted and to "remedy the clergy's neglect," municipal authorities followed the merchant guild's lead, voting to build a new cemetery and to fund the beautification of the old by designating an alderman to oversee permanently both maintenance and burials. More than ten men were immediately contracted to perform the work.[33] Not to be outdone, an independent group of wealthy merchants publicly declared that neither they nor their families would accept church burial, hoping by their example to persuade the "common folk" to overcome their "superstitions."[34] Thus, by 1804, the institutional voices of the merchant community—the city council and the guild—had definitively declared for the cemetery to a chorus of public support from Veracruz's other traders.

But why? What had transpired in the twenty-three short years between the 1781 guild petition, with its small handful of enlightened signers, and the merchants' consensus rejection of church burials in 1804?

As Christopher Hill has argued for the case of English Protestants, doctrines that stress the importance of interior motivations known only to God flourish in periods of rapid social change and appeal to new social groups seeking to justify their repudiation of traditional authorities.[35] Appeals to godly conscience to resist authority, appeals to an illuminated conscience: these prove to be potent rallying cries. Veracruz merchants, like Bourbon bureaucrats, certainly fit Hill's description of a new social group emerging during a time of social flux. In the port city, exploding numbers of new merchants plied their trade in the world market at the turn of the nineteenth century. And these merchants were most assuredly engaged in challenging the traditional trade monopoly held by Mexico City merchants. As we have seen, the new piety provided the era's most devastating breed of social critique: a religious one. Elites who indulged themselves in excessive display shouted not God's approval of their social position, but their vacuous interiors, their potentially reprobate status. Thus, on the one hand, Veracruz's booming economy produced a critical mass of individuals whose new wealth placed them, at least potentially, outside the ancien régime's social structure. On the other hand, the new piety offered a rousing indictment of that social order's primary means of justification: the visual display of God's majesty. Despite spirited opposition from within the ranks, the merchants as a group seem to have seized this new tool, which bolstered their authority and discredited their opponents. But as we have also seen, many of the cemetery opponents and proponents were drawn from the same economic group: the city's more prominent merchants. Thus, this was no battle between a rising bourgeoisie and "old wealth," but a shift in how elites would justify their social authority and how they would wield power: not by the discredited baroque display but through observing and disciplining their social inferior. But the new piety alone cannot explain this shift, which can be attributed only to a complex causal ecology of which the new piety was merely a dominant but not solitary part.

Retreat from the Streets:
The Plebe Teaches the Sensatos to Rule

The shift from display to discipline as a technique of rule stemmed in part from elites' uneasy relationship with Veracruz's long-resident urban poor; their discomfort only increased with the large numbers of migrants fleeing crisis conditions in the surrounding countryside to seek employment in the city's new boom economy.[36] Thus, the new merchants' cultural authority was tenuous at best in Veracruz, seriously compromised by their inferior numbers and recent appearance on the city's scene; after all, the mere presence of a class that considers itself fit to dominate by no means ensures its domination. As the immigrants and resident poor strained power previously exercised through intimate patronage and face-to-face contact, these predominantly Spanish merchants found combating the poor's cultural mores a formidable task. They were further hindered by the friars, traditionally perceived as allies of the poor. In that role, the clerics had undertaken to heal the rifts between wealthier, whiter residents and members of the city's swarthy underclass through indiscriminate charity. The enlightened felt that this approach merely encouraged the poor's torpor. Rather than comforting the large number of new "vagrants" in their lowly station, the friars should cede their positions to the morally enlightened. These energetic Christians would then urge their charges toward a more profound and lasting internal transformation, which would give the poor the moral fiber necessary to escape degradation.

First and foremost, Veracruz's would-be rulers had to contend with an underclass with deeper roots in the city than their own. Where Mexico City's long-term residents were most likely white or mestizo and relatively well-off, the 1791 Veracruz census demonstrates that most white and mestizo Veracruz males had been born outside the city, with the majority of the whites hailing from Spain. The city's mulatto and black population, by contrast, had much deeper roots: more than half of each group were Veracruz natives.[37] Furthermore, the city's casta residents evidently outnumbered the more peripatetic whites.[38] Thus, Veracruz's stable core population consisted of male and female castas.

Late eighteenth-century censuses, of course, are not reliable and generally raise more questions than they answer: Whose categories are being employed, the census taker's or those of his subjects?[39] But, despite the census's pitfalls, residents' and travelers' impressions of Veracruz confirm rather than contradict it, and therefore lend credibility to at least the gist of its findings. Veracruz's core population of blacks and mulattos impressed 1697 Italian traveler Giovanni Francesco Gemelli Carreri, who declared that the evanescent white population disappeared into the interior as the fleet disappeared over the horizon, not to be seen again until its return, leaving blacks to dominate the city.[40] As the only port for arriving slave cruisers, Veracruz housed the recent arrivals until they made their wrenching journey inland or to coastal plantations; some of these Africans undoubtedly remained in the port to work as stevedores and servants. In 1654 Jesuit Andres de Rivas boasted of his glorious mission to baptize these 3,000 to 4,000 slaves who yearly arrived from Angola, the Congo, Guinea, and other parts of Africa. In 1815 rebel prisoner Antonio López Matoso echoed the wisdom of the previous centuries in his statement that "buzzards and men here are black, some in their soul, others in their body."[41]

The city's insalubrious conditions and inclement weather partially account for the dearth of permanent resident Spaniards and Creoles, who felt themselves to be poorly suited to tropical conditions. Travelers unanimously gasped in horror at the city's festering environs. As early as 1623 Thomas Gage noticed the "standing bogs" on the southwest side of the city, which exacerbated the already sticky air and the unhealthy climate that he blamed for the scant population.[42] For Europeans, the port proved a veritable tomb during the frequent bouts of black vomit. In 1763 a visiting Father Francisco de Ajofrín noted, "European arrivals maintain their robustness and color for a mere six or eight months until the constant sweating slowly saps their vitality."[43] The only relief from the heat came in the form of freezing northern winds that hurled down without warning upon the city, scattering sand and sending enormous waves crashing over the embankments.[44] Not surprisingly, throughout much of the eighteenth century, those with the economic wherewithal to escape the city did so, leaving mulattos and other castas as Veracruz's core population.

The large number of long-term casta residents, however, does not fully account for their high level of cultural and economic clout in the city. To understand this we have to grapple with the poor's relationship to the city's wealthier and whiter denizens. On the one hand, many black slaves and some Indians, free blacks, and mulattos lived with their elite employers, forming the sorts of vertical links of dependence between rich and poor that so characterized early eighteenth-century Mexico City.[45] Merchant and City Councilman Sebastián Fernández de Bobadilla, the tireless defender of his family's church tomb, for example, claimed two slaves and five Indian servants in his extended household; fellow cemetery critic and merchant guild participant Domingo Lagoa de Miranda counted on four slaves; and accountant Juan Matías de Lacunra had three male servants and four maids, among them a slave, a free black, and a free parda. On the other hand, blacks, Indians, mulattos, and castas constituted a considerable presence among the city's small-scale independent artisans. Pardos José Ortiz and José Villanueva competed for customers on the same street as five other shoemakers, among them one casta, one white, one Indian, and two other pardos. There were, however, limits to social mobility. Although a handful of pardos and mulattos numbered among the city's carpenters and tailors, Spaniards dominated the more prestigious and profitable silversmith and watchmaker businesses clustered along Santo Domingo street, all of whose twenty-seven residents were listed as white in the 1797 census.[46]

Many of Veracruz's resident poor, however, were neither independent craftsmen nor intimately embroiled with the city's minority white population. Instead, they toiled on the docks in large work teams (roughly one hundred men) loading and unloading the ships, the lifeblood of the city. And they acted in concert to protect their interests. The merchant guild scrambled to diffuse the subversive potential of stevedore captain José Cayetano Cordova's 1796 petition for guild status under maritime law, which would have allowed him to control the docks, to doom lucrative cargoes to rot at the workers' whim, and to set the prices of each cart of merchandise moved to waiting warehouses. Charged by the merchants' guild with investigating Cordova's petition, merchants Tomás de Aguirre and José Ignacio de Uriarte declared that the stevedores were land workers and thus ineligible for consideration under maritime law. Furthermore, the experience of numerous port cities demonstrated that graft and corruption by dock guilds often paralyzed trade, thwarting merchants' interests.[47]

Receiving no surcease from the city council or the merchants' guild (*consulado*), workers and their often dubious representatives nevertheless continued to defend their interests.[48] In 1804, work crew captain Francisco de Paula Garay noted a "state of abandon" on the docks. His charges, who unloaded the King's ships for a fraction of the fees paid by private vessels, often left their tasks to work for the highest bidder—or not at all. To remedy this situation, he proposed that his crew receive an exclusive monopoly on all loading and unloading in the port and that the merchants' guild establish an official fee list for all merchandise.[49]

If the stevedores' petition provides a foggy glimpse of the underclass acting in concert to defend its economic interests, the poor's cultural impact on the city comes more sharply into focus. In particular, several early eighteenth-century Inquisition proceedings against black and casta *curanderos* (healers) indicate that elites tapped their powers, and that many veracruzanos regarded the Inquisition, indeed the entire Church, as a sort of malpractice review board to be called in only if a curer's magic failed. When artillery specialist Francisco Zalas had a run of bad luck at the gambling tables, he knew to seek help from casta Madre Chepa; she presented him with a magic amulet consisting of a stone wrapped in a cloth together with a mysterious white powder. His confidence restored, Zalas returned to cards with the necklace in place, but continued to lose. He therefore concluded that indulging in such superstition constituted a sin and promptly sought a priest's absolution, with uncomfortable results for the Madre. Doña María Rendon, the widow of a navy admiral, had a similar epiphany when she called in Madre Chepa to help one of her unmarried slaves give birth. To aid the slave's quest for a husband, the curandera provided her with magical powders and vowed to bring her a special live animal whose urine had divinatory powers. When the promised animal failed to materialize, Doña María denounced Madre Chepa to the Inquisition.[50]

That the city's casta curanderos provided services to clients across the social spectrum can also be seen in the case of Juan Luis, a slave curandero. After exhausting the cures for bone pain proffered by the local apothecary, white tailor Fernando Alcoba took his neighbor's advice and called in Juan Luis, who had a stellar reputation as a bone healer. As merely one part of an elaborate process, Juan Luis sucked live worms from his patient's head and feet. Although Alcoba's motivations for ultimately denouncing the curandero are unknown, his initial reliance on the slave's wisdom, and Madre Chepa's clients' faith in her services, together evince the cultural clout brandished by black, casta, and poor veracruzanos.[51]

Veracruz's large, stable, and culturally influential casta population and numerous white immigrants were not the city's only distinguishing features that militated against urban underclass quiescence. Recall that late eighteenth-century Veracruz, like New Spain's other urban areas, experienced a large infusion of rural refugees. In late eighteenth-century Mexico City, these new urbanites strained the elaborate networks of patronage and protection that vertically linked the poor to their elite patrons and employers.[52] Operating smack in the historic center of state power, however, Mexico City authorities immediately forged a relationship with the new urban indigent who fell outside of traditional patronage networks. Beginning in the 1760s, the state established charitable and rehabilitative institutions such as the poorhouse (Hospicio de Pobres), pawnshop (Monte de Piedad), and foundling home (Casa de Expósitos) and offered employment in the enormous Royal Tobacco monopoly and in trades formerly restricted to guild members. An expanded police force that aggressively pursued malefactors and mediated disputes among the poor further focused their hopes on the state as a resource to mitigate their misery.[53]

Not so in Veracruz, where only two public works had been completed by 1789 and where the regular and hospital orders, not secular officials, dispensed charity to the small number of destitute.[54] Thus, in the late eighteenth century, Veracruz's new merchants confronted a stable, culturally and economically influential resident population of castas, as well as a steady stream of what they considered unruly rural refugees—the undeserving, vagrant poor—without the infrastructure of charities and police forces that greeted Mexico City's migrant poor. This relationship is critical to understanding the merchants' subsequent rejection of church burials and elaborate funerals and the visual, theatrical display of social status that they represented. For as the enlightened grappled to refashion the underclass into disciplined workers by transforming Veracruz in accordance with Enlightenment strictures, the special pressures of their environment compressed these efforts into an observable time frame; we can actually follow them as they scurry to establish schools and charities, to expand the police force, to install street lamps for easier surveillance, to wrest control of the hospitals from the regular orders. In so doing, they forged themselves as a self-conscious class that observed, edified, and physically cared for those they deemed their cultural inferiors. They learned to wield their moral authority through observation of their social inferiors, rather than through the discredited baroque display. And all within a generation.

Embracing the new individualist theology, which both justified and inspired many veracruzanos' economic ascension, the enlightened stressed poverty's moral etiology and the individual's responsibility for his economic plight. Thus, the result of the new piety was, in Antonio Gramsci's terms, the creation of a new moral-political ethos. As Gramsci points out, a dominant class must not only impose its rule via the state, but also demonstrate its capacity for intellectual and moral leadership. The enlightened claimed their particular ethos as universal because the status of "enlightened" was putatively available to all who embraced the group's cultural attributes.[55] Their self-confident moral authority derived from their assiduous and individual "moderation of desires and subjection of the will"— that is, from their adherence to the new religious sensibility. Thus qualified, they could undertake to reform both the burial customs of elites and the poor's undesirable mores.

It was this Enlightenment meliorism that inspired elites' thirst to refashion the city and its poor, not through indiscriminate charity but
through moral transformation. In 1789, City Councilman Antonio María
Fernández lamented that vagrants abounded in the city. But rather than
laud poverty's inherent blessedness and gently apply the balm of charity to
heal the rifts between rich and poor, he tagged these immigrants "the lazy
of both sexes" and advocated the construction of a poorhouse where the
truly needy would be separated from pretenders. Furthermore, more
schools under secular tutelage should be built to discourage the laggards'
children from emulating their parents. Finally, he recommended that surveillance of the poor be stepped up through the establishment of neighborhood police (Alcaldes de Barrio) and the installation of numerous street
lamps.[56]

The late eighteenth century witnessed a boom in secular institutions
designed to inculcate the poor with the enlightened's values, institutions
overwhelmingly directed by the sensatos themselves. In 1787, backed by
the donations of numerous merchants, Laso de la Vega and a small group
of leading citizens organized themselves into the Sociedad de Amigos del
País (Society of Friends of the Country) and founded a "patriotic school"
patterned after those being formed by enlightened groups in Spain, Havana, Oaxaca, and Puebla.[57] Campomanes's *Discurso sobre el fomento de la
industria popular* had promoted these schools, and in Veracruz, in addition
to grammar, writing, and math, the school taught reform piety in the form
of Church history and moral education.[58] In a similar vein, the sensatos
staffed the Junta de Policía, which initially oversaw the placement of cob-
blestones on the city's scraggly streets and, despite budget woes, later
undertook other city improvement projects; Bishop Biempico y Sotomayor
relied on the expert testimony of several Junta members to discredit City
Councilman Echeverría's anticemetery allegations.[59] The prominent Cossío House traders sponsored an indigents' home, which encouraged work
and prohibited gambling and prostitution, and in 1801 influential residents
spurred the city council's creation of a poorhouse (Casa de Misercordia),
staffed by the laity rather than the clergy and featuring large looms for
spinning cotton.[60]

But nowhere was the sensatos' civic participation more apparent than in
their systematic wresting of control of the city's hospitals from the regular
and hospital orders, who they felt employed these institutions to shelter
undeserving beggars rather than cure the sick.[61] In 1791 a loosely organized

group of enlightened ousted the Hipolite friars from the Hospital of Our Lady of Loreto, and the ayuntamiento backed their takeover by refusing the friars entry, even after the Audiencia (High Court) approved their return.[62] In 1798, the city council and the merchants guild pooled their resources to open the Hospital of San Sebastián, under lay rather than religious auspices, and in 1805 prominent residents and the municipal council petitioned Viceroy Iturrigaray to close the Church's Hospital of San Juan de Montes Claros, whose central location they now deemed a public health risk.[63] Thus, although the secular authorities' support for religious festivals like that of San Sebastián barely wavered and elite leadership in the confraternities continued, the new civic improvement projects offered an alternative source of social status. Here was a venue not to display God's sanctification of social authority, but to exercise it. Enlightened merchants could exercise—or, perhaps better put, create—their new moral authority by observing, educating, and curing others, by leading the dissolute to a more moderate existence, rather than by strutting their status through the streets in religious procession.

The city itself became a place for the sensatos to hone new techniques of power by observation rather than display, a didactic space for inculcating everyone with enlightened values. Whereas in Mexico City, Viceroy Revillagigedo had employed state power to install street lanterns, in Veracruz enlightened residents pooled their resources to pay for illumination, and by 1802 the city boasted 226 lamps, a team of caretakers, and a city councilman who oversaw both maintenance and repairs. The enlightened further combated untidiness and disorder—and the deeper fecklessness they signaled—with stepped-up sanitary measures, such as garbage carts that ferried refuse out of the city to be dumped in the sea and a 1797 order enjoining all residents to sweep in front of their houses on Wednesdays and Saturdays.[64] With these measures, the eyes of power zoomed in on the picayune details of daily life and expanded the sensatos' purview into the black of night, when revelers spilled out of the taverns to stagger home.

To enforce these more intrusive measures, to ensure that someone was observing the sundry unemployed residents who now eluded surveillance in elite households or shops, the Veracruz City Council established the Alcaldes de Barrio, the neighborhood police who had patrolled Mexico City streets since 1782. Designed to "prevent scandals, repress vices, extinguish laziness, and foment industry," the police force was manned by "honorable citizens" with the moral authority to provide an example to their charges. And, to further facilitate rational surveillance, the 1797 aldermen discussed dividing the city into four major police precincts, each divided into two minor wards.[65] In each case, Veracruz's sensatos themselves enthusiastically organized the new instruments of order; the Enlightenment in Veracruz was not an unwanted state imposition but the pet project of the rising merchant-dominated enlightened class, a class that forged the city as it created itself.

A flood of immigrants. A stable population of culturally influential castas. Organized dockworkers. Veracruz's underclass cannot be described as docile, and the city's new merchants scrambled to construct the charities, lights, and police forces that would ensure an urban environment and population conducive to their increased participation in the world market. Fired by an individualist piety that stressed self-imposed discipline, the enlightened deduced a moral justification for rule. From there it was a short step to usurping the religious' role as charitable providers and placing themselves in an unmediated, educative relationship with the city's underclass. Authority coursed through these newly carved channels and simultaneously ebbed from the old ones.

But this outcome was hardly preordained. Veracruz's newly wealthy could have fought to purchase prestigious church burial sites, and they most certainly could have sunk their fresh capital into elaborate, well-attended funerals. But instead, they loudly and publicly declared their support for the new cemetery and filled their wills with requests for humble funerals. In their relation with the city's restive underclass, the sensatos had explicitly rejected the community-based salvation and visual mnemonics represented by church burials. In its place they erected a more individualist piety whose emphasis on the internalization of religious moral maxims gave them the justification to supervise others who had not taken the message to heart, or who, being women, could not do so.

This individualist theology and its attendant moral earnestness led to a more optimistic outlook on men's ability to transform themselves and others. It thus culminated not only in hostility toward the immutable essences that undergirded Old Regime identities, most notably the belief that "the poor will always be with us," but also in a disparagement of fixed social relations as poverty's etiology. If the illuminated self determined one's earthly and otherworldly destiny, then the category of "downtrodden" must be as empty as that of "nobility." In responding to the stevedores' petition examined earlier, the merchants revealed the ugly underside of this individualism that animated the sensatos' attack on corporate privileges and monopolies, such as the one previously held by the Mexico City merchants. The irony apparently lost on him, merchant guild spokesman Francisco García Puertas replied to the workers' request for a monopoly by declaring that "these types of privileges are odious." Thus, at the same time that the enlightened dismantled a rigidly hierarchical group-based society in the interest of freeing individual initiative, they simultaneously cut off avenues for the economically disadvantaged to act collectively, and even began to blame the poor for their condition: for if one could rise by individual effort, then one remained mired in poverty due to individual indolence. But let Puertas speak for himself: "Despite the enormous quantity of money paid to stevedores, they are poor and dress shabbily, and when they fall sick they go door to door begging alms, or to the hospital if they are too weak—all of which can be blamed on their bad conduct as well as their unwillingness to establish a fund for the sick and debilitated."[66] City Councilman Martín Sánchez Serrano shared Puertas's adherence to the tenets of enlightened individualism, attacking workers' desire for a monopoly on the grounds that "nobody can impede a man from dedicating himself to the job that offers the best remuneration . . . especially not in Veracruz where . . . those with prudence and good conduct have moved up and into better positions." Serrano implied, of course, that only the undisciplined tarried long in poverty or poorly paid positions. The municipal authorities and the merchants guild demonstrated their faith in this new litmus test of moral, and thus spiritual, fiber by voting to choke off any possibility of collective advancement.[67] That the stevedores' labor lined other pockets proved impossible to ponder; the stress on individual moral character led almost inexorably to the dismissal of structural economic equalities as a source of poverty. Here we see the sort of moral anesthesia required for laissez-faire capitalism.

El *Censor*, the voice of piedad ilustrada, had anticipated this belief in the virtuous rich, this new justification for social authority, by a good thirty years. In an October 1786 editorial typical of those that filled its pages, the paper noted that in a society with no legal fetters on personal advancement, the rich would logically occupy the most important government posts. Far from a travesty, this plutocracy was just, because "where wealth resulted from industriousness, the rich proved the most worthy of rule, because by their accumulation they had demonstrated themselves to be the most talented, the most energetic, and consequently the most virtuous."[68]

In Veracruz's self-congratulatory enlightened we have the fundamental constituent of modernity: the man who believes he has cut all of the threads binding him to the social fabric, who conceives of himself as a fully sovereign individual.

At first blush, that Catholicism could act as midwife to an individualist morality seems improbable, to say the least. In the most famous account of Protestantism's central role in the rise of capitalism, Max Weber details the life of the isolated Protestant, who, cut off from salvation through the Church or through the prayers of the faithful, must tread a lonely path to meet his predestined and irresistible postmortem destiny. Without the sacraments to compensate for spiritual lapses and unable to alter his fate through good works, the Protestant is seized by the most profound anxiety: How am I to know what God has willed for me? The answer, according to Weber, is that the very works so worthless to salvation become a sign of the state of grace. Those who prosper must be the elect.[69]

Catholic Reform piety, of course, could not offer even this fragile assurance of salvation, for God could withdraw the gift of grace and works did indeed have salvific powers if performed with the correct interior disposition. Worldly success could not be read as an assurance of God's favor because His decree could change; continued charitable works were required to obtain or maintain salvation. Herein lay the crux of some reformer's theological pessimism surrounding man's capacity to aid his own salvation: only those chosen by God, those inspired by His love, could perform the required deeds with the proper motivation—hence Catholic reformers' implacable hostility toward the Jesuits. The Society of Jesus advocated a more humanistic Christianity, one larded with what reformers regarded as neo-Pelagian errors. Chief among these was the principle that all men could will to do good or evil; God did not bestow on a few lucky souls the gift of grace but merely foresaw and then rewarded or punished men's actions. The result of this pessimism in seventeenth-century France, so Dale Van Kley convincingly argues, was the Jansenists' retreat into despair and an isolated monastic existence—a far cry from Weber's striving, worldly Protestants.[70]

The self-assurance of Veracruz's pious merchants did indeed stem from a sanctification of worldly activity, but not exactly in the way described by Weber. Its etiology lay instead in the new piety's emphasis on necessary moral transformation, on righteous intentions, which became powerful, albeit tautological, justifications for social leadership. Although one's capacity for moral transformation—one's inner light—was a gift from God, and its presence or absence thus ultimately uncertain, what was certain was that the path to God lay within. Thus, those who showed signs (torpor, histrionics) of straying from that clear path could be readily identified. Who better to help these wanderers get a hold of themselves than those who had taken God's message to heart and who demonstrated this interior quest through their self-control and moderation? As we have seen, a number of groups—*manteista* bureaucrats, reform-minded clerics, Veracruz merchants—found in interior moral transformation a powerful weapon to forge their own social authority and to discredit that of others.

The city's ubiquitous undeserving poor, however, were not the only group that provided an inverse mirror for the enlightened's sense of moral superiority; the self-defined sensatos also remained suspicious of women's ability to get themselves under control without firm guidance. As did Spain's burial reformers, New Spain's enlightened authors and orators unflaggingly associated the old exterior piety with women, whom they portrayed as incapable of interior self-control and reflection and as more wedded to tradition and superstition than were men. Bishop Biempico y Sotomayor, for example, noted that the city's distinguished cemetery opponents had been led astray by "the flimsy piety of women who regarded the suburban cemetery as outside the protection of God and his saints." Similarly, Mexico City reformer Augustín de Rivero noted that it was mostly women who stubbornly insisted that suffrages worked better if the dead remained under the church floor.[71]

Ironically, it was the enlightened Josefa Amar y Borbón, Madrid Economic Society member and friend to salon hostess the Countess of Montijo, who most thoroughly tarred her own sex with the brush of excess. In her advice to young mothers on their children's moral education, Borbón noted that it would be best to insist that "real devotion and virtue consist not in the exterior formula of visiting numerous churches and reciting many orations, a vice more common to women than to men . . . what is important is to cement in them that true and solid virtue consists in practicing good and abhorring bad, in controlling one's passions, in mortifying one's appetites, in practicing charity, and above all in complying with one's obligations."[72]

Thus, cemetery advocates such as Laso de la Vega and Agustín de Rivero, who labeled anticemetery women "superstitious," appealed to a masculinity that stressed interior virtues, rational, technical control of oneself and nature—not unbridled aggression or ritualized chivalry—to convince them of the new piety's merits. So, although the identity category of sensato was seemingly open to all, authors and orators rhetorically linked the new piety with masculinity and thereby heightened its seductiveness for men by suggesting its rejection by most women. The causal ecology underpinning the sensatos' cemetery advocacy, however, is far more lush, far more tangled than the hopelessly intertwined elements of the new piety and a rising merchant class energetically seeking to dominate Veracruz's underclass. Passionately involved in guiding others to moral improvement, the enlightened found the dead's presence in the center of the city an affront, a statement of their power's limited parameters, their inability to transcend mortality. In stark contrast to the ancien régime pattern of fixed social identities, enlightened identity depended on the desire to improve one's own life—and the ability to do so. Thus, the dead's presence served the enlightened less as a prod to pray for others' eternal life than as a reminder of their ultimate mortality, their inability to prolong their own and others' worldly existence.

In the ideal city, the living rather than the dead would occupy the enlightened's line of vision, as a testament to their transformative power. After the opening of the Veracruz cemetery, the hospitals disgorged the dead into the city. Uncovered bodies borne on porters' shoulders jogged through the streets and out the main gates—a horrifying spectacle for the new architects of enlightened urbanization, as well as a powerful image seized on by cemetery critics to discredit the new burial ground.[73] The solution: covered caskets or carts, which saved the sensatos from a now horrifying glimpse of their own mortality.

Thus, the enlightened's social meliorism had a physical as well as a spiritual dimension. The authority of medical specialists grew apace with the new piety and ultimately outstripped the latter. The subtleties of this complicated relationship should become clearer in the final chapters, in which we explore rising medical "expertise" and popular resistance to it. If Veracruz's merchants highjacked the radical egalitarianism implicit in this new individualistic piety, so too did a number of elite theorists in Mexico City. It is to this development that we now turn.

chapter 6

The Ideology Articulated

So far, we have established that the reformed Christianity claimed champions in late colonial New Spain, fueling their social agendas and ecclesiastical politics as well as their spiritual lives. Proponents of this stripped-down Catholicism worked cheek by jowl with theological conservatives in the parallel power structures of Church and state, and their quarrels with their misguided colleagues filled reams of paper and months of debate. But in the early nineteenth century, the colony's formal political realm split wide open. In the almost unrecognizable landscape of independent Mexico, enlightened Catholic principles emerged in the halls of power and public opinion—altered by the experience, to be sure, pressed into unaccustomed service, but still easily recognizable as the new piety. In this chapter, we follow the Augustinian impulse into its political incarnation through two of the new republic's most influential liberals, and connect their work to evidence from a wider public.

In 1808, French troops spilled over the border into Spain and forced both Ferdinand VII and Carlos IV to renounce their rights to the Spanish throne, which Napoleon promptly bestowed on his brother Joseph. Although no one yet called for independence or even an end to royal rule in New Spain, the episode ignited a full-blown crisis of sovereignty. Delegates from Spain's provincial juntas descended on the colonial capital seeking recognition as the new legitimate authorities. Rather than recognize these officials, the Mexico City Council urged the viceroy to establish a separate junta to rule in the King's name; a group of peninsular merchants responded by violently deposing Viceroy Iturrigaray and replacing him with their own candidate until an official replacement, Francisco Javier Venegas, arrived in 1810.

At this juncture, parish priest Miguel de Hidalgo emerged at the head of a peasant army determined to wrest sovereignty from these peninsular usurpers. Marching with Hidalgo under the banner of the deposed Ferdinand VII were numerous parish priests aggrieved by the Bourbon assault on their prerogatives and income. Hidalgo's program grew increasingly radical in the crucible of battle, however, and by 1810 some rebels were calling for independence and the expulsion of all Spaniards. The rebels failed to rouse the peasantry of the Central Valley, however, and Hidalgo's planned attack on the capital dissolved into retreat, desertion, and ultimately a grisly execution of the principals. On the heels of this disaster, however, another parish priest emerged as the standard-bearer of the revolt. Father José María Morelos y Pavón convened a congress in Chilpancingo in 1813 after several years of hard-won victories on the part of his insurgent army. There the rebels declared Mexico's independence and called for a representative government and an end to the legal caste system. They were defeated, but even after Ferdinand VII's restoration in 1814, the fighting continued; now the question of legitimate sovereignty was fanned by a group of Spanish liberals, who in 1820 forced Ferdinand to recognize the Constitution of 1812. Only after eleven years of chaotic strife could a truce be reached: under the Plan de Iguala, Mexico would be an independent constitutional monarchy. By 1824, the monarchists had thoroughly discredited themselves: Mexico was transformed into a genuine republic. The Constitution closely resembled that of Spain, with several notable exceptions: all Mexican men could vote and the Church regained its corporate privileges and prerogatives.

In response to these two decades of political upheaval, a vibrant public sphere of written political criticism emerged in Mexico City. Debate raged over the obvious linchpin of postmonarchical governance: Who should rule and with what justification? In this context, the state's prime ideological apparatus, the Church, logically came under scrutiny. Barely a century earlier, Mexicans had remained passive spectators during the War of Spanish Succession; no such lively public sphere had responded to that crisis of governance.[1] But now new printing presses churned out unprecedented recommendations for every facet of Church governance and religious practice, an assault that would have been inconceivable just a generation before.[2] This deluge of opinion that accompanied Independence, the emboldened literate urban laity that publicly critiqued the Church, the resolution of the problem of sovereignty in favor of the people and not a monarch, and the paradoxical efforts of certain elite liberals to exclude most of their countrymen from the benefits of citizenship—all of this must be seen as logical extensions of the new piety that had emerged in the previous five decades.

Meet the Press: Dominant Voices in the New Public Sphere

Historian Francois-Xavier Guerra locates the origins of this profusion of public debate in the new voluntary associations, which opened their membership to all individuals who could make a reasonable argument regardless of their Old Regime status, and thus provided the training ground for modern politics. Gestating clandestinely during the reign of enlightened despotism, such groups had strutted into the open in Spain after the 1808 monarchical crisis. But the clubs constituted only the form of participatory government, not its ideological content; by Guerra's line of reasoning, the latter had to arrive from abroad. Pamphlets and periodicals from Spain began to alight in the New World, promoting a revolutionary concept of society based on sovereign individuals. Thus, by this explanation, Spain and Europe generally radiated the Enlightenment outward; indeed, Guerra maintains that except for the ruminations of a few isolated Spanish Americans alert to French or North American ideas, new modern visions of community washed ashore in Spanish America only in 1808.[3] Guerra even signals New Spain's numerous religious titles as compared to France's as indicators of modernity's retardation in Mexico. In fact, as we shall see, they signaled just the opposite.

Many readers knew one of the most prolific participants in this unprecedented ferment, José Joaquín Fernández de Lizardi (1777–1827), by his pen name, El Pensador Mexicano (the Mexican Thinker). Scholars of Lizardi's work, and of the lively world of letters of which he formed a central part, have attributed this boom of political polemic to a new faith in transparent secular reason. All were capable of reason; anyone could publicly train its bright light on decisions of formerly sacred authorities. In a similar vein, literary critics almost unanimously concur that behind Lizardi's critique of both monarchy and papacy lurked the influence of European Enlightenment luminaries like Voltaire.[4]

Lizardi may have piped this antiauthoritarian tune the loudest, but other influential moderns accompanied him with gusto. The major elite liberal theorist of the period, Doctor of Theology José María Luis Mora, found multiple outlets for his concerns in the altered climate of Independence.

Mora dominated the new republic's first constitutional congress with his eloquent paeans to individual sovereignty and larded his widely circulated journals and pamphlets with the same reasoned rhetoric. Mora's liberalism moved into the heart of the new political establishment when he assumed the post of chief councilor to Valentín Gómez Farías during the radical government of 1832–1834.

Mexican liberalism's most distinguished historian, Charles Hale, reads Mora as a champion of secularization; according to Hale, Mora bent his multiple channels of influence to the task of "fashioning a society where the religious values and the Church as an institution would be of little consequence in the action of individuals."[5] Certainly both these men seem to wring the same themes from the age as their liberal contemporaries in Europe and North America. Beyond a doubt, Mora, Lizardi, and other Mexican liberals sought to reduce the powers of the Church while bolstering those of the state, often with a passion bordering on the fanatical.

But it was not a "secular" state they wished to create. Far from exemplifying imported Enlightenment precepts, these men and many like them represented a new religious sensibility in the act of raising up its heir: the sovereign individual who was to dominate elite liberal thought until the Revolution. Not rationalist concerns but insistently Christian ones formed both their text and their credentials for speaking with authority in the new public arena. Mora's writings reveal an enlightened Catholic who sought to establish a religious commonwealth ruled by godly secular magistrates. His was not a battle between secular and religious but between the "true religion" of the gente sensata and that of the baroque, hierarchical Church. In this, Mora resembled the Protestant reformer Zwingli more than the atheistic Bentham whom Hale suggests as an intellectual influence, although he convincingly establishes Mora's debt to that influential secular reformer. In his battle against the remnants of corporate privilege, Mora undeniably sought to free homo economicus from all impediments to the pursuit of individual self-interest. But by his own lights, that struggle could not be separated from its corollary: the liberation of the godly self-disciplined from the Church's barriers to freedom of conscience.

Nor can we conclude that Mora strove to impose a "new secular morality," removed from the tyranny of the Church, as Hale suggests. Although Mora noted that public morality would improve when all Mexicans distinguished between Christianity and civil law and respected the latter, this observation was a small nugget encrusted in a larger discussion of the masses' inability to recognize the difference between the Church and real religion. By Mora's lights, the folk remained mired in baroque Catholicism, with its miraculous saints and opulent rituals, whereas the "wise" understood that eschewing pomp did not make one a heretic, but a better Christian. This exterior religion smothered conscience and led to destructive social vices, to immorality. Here and elsewhere he hints that the true task was not a purely civil morality, but the imposition of the real religion that induced self-control.[6] All "true lovers of the real religion of Jesus Christ and of their country's prosperity" should be interested in sustaining both, he declared in 1834. Why? "Because without religion, without the religious cult, there could be no society or public morality in civilized countries." The unreformed Church, not Christianity itself, was the obstacle to morality. This Christianity, however, had been smothered by superstition and clerical ambition and avarice. Thus, to free the faith from "the tyranny of the Church" was to disarm the impious, who carped incessantly about its financial and clerical abuses. Only a purified religion could withstand the assaults of the ungodly and simultaneously "solidly establish the civil rights of nations and governments and public prosperity."[7]

If anything, Lizardi justified his public voice with even more nakedly religious qualifications than did Mora. In his bold attacks on established authority, the Mexican Thinker scarcely made a move without citing Scripture and the early Church councils, unless it was to refer to his own divinely inspired will. That he did so in service to strikingly modern political concepts signals no inconsistency or self-contradiction but rather a process of modernization that differs from sectarian Protestant or deist preconceptions about the mutual incompatibility of Catholicism and modern rationalism. Alternatively, some observers have misinterpreted the Mexican intellectuals' "new concepts of civilization" and "norms of public conduct" as fashions from France, where the bourgeoisie spurned the aristocracy's conspicuous consumption and theatrics in favor of austere dress and composed mien. Lizardi and some of his elite contemporaries did indeed frown on the "public display of the sentiments," but not because they were now considered "vulgar" and "embarrassing" to elites chagrined by sneers from foreign visitors. Rather, displays of pomp and excessive sentimentality outraged reform sensibilities. Indulgence in sensual depravity demonstrated a state of nonresistance to the world's sensual pleasures and thus an alienation from God.[8] Historian Jean Franco correctly asserts that Lizardi's oeuvre reveals his firm conviction that social leadership should be entrusted to "individuals who know how to postpone pleasure for the good of society." Likewise, she establishes that El Pensador Mexicano considered himself a lay priest "with a responsibility to preach the new values of work and discipline."[9] But, as the bishops' flamboyant display of moderation that we saw earlier made clear, self-restraint was the fruit of true Christianity and could be displayed for the faithful through unflinching opposition to immoderation in all its forms.

Despite the overwhelming evidence, then, scholars have slighted the underlying religious impetus for these weighty theorists' public polemic in general, and the content of their political writings in particular. Franco sums up the dominant interpretation in her unequivocal assertion that Lizardi belonged "to a new generation whose intellectual formation presupposed access to a body of secular knowledge (of European origin) which offered, in a rational language, a new criteria for public conduct and private life." This distinguished literary critic supports her claim in part by referring to Lizardi's 1812 imprisonment for criticizing a viceregal edict, which allowed the military courts to judge rebel clerics. Such an act, she maintains, demonstrates his membership in this new secular intelligentsia that had broken with the clergy, whose point of reference remained theology. In contrast to these men of God, Lizardi "based his authority on knowledge acquired in the works of lay authors."[10] But no philosophes appear in Lizardi's appeal to the viceroy to revoke the odious edict. Rather, Lizardi noted that the viceroy had no jurisdiction over these rebellious ecclesiastics because "the holy fathers, the councils and canons, and all of the authority of the Church" prohibited it. Lizardi likewise quoted generously from Scripture, striking a characteristically dramatic note in his advice to the viceroy not to spill the blood of these clerics as "Cain spilled that of Abel."[11] His knowledge of the Church councils and the Scriptures— not European Enlightenment luminaries—underlay this liberal critique of the viceroy.[12]

Indeed, Lizardi repeatedly disavowed any association with the Enlightenment's more irreligious critics, and situated himself within the reform current of the Church. Defending his novels El periquillo sarniento (The itching parrot) and La Quioxtita from Fernando Demetrio González's accusation of blasphemy, Lizardi responded that he too knew "how to cite texts and not the texts of Voltaire or Diderot or other Lutherans and Calvinists . . . but those of the Holy Scripture, whose irrefutable truths you cannot obfuscate even under a cloak of heavy, hooded clothing."[13] Elsewhere, El Pensador went further, vigorously tarring the Enlightenment with the brush of godlessness. These impious deists and materialists, these putative "sages of the nineteenth century," could not countenance the "brake that our religion puts on the abuses of the passions." Utterly unregulated by God's will, they savaged with haughty impudence the Holy Scriptures, ecclesiastical canons and statutes, and other aspects of the faith. If instead all Christians exercised holy restraint, Lizardi continued, if they all had the "spirit, science, and virtue of the Jerónimos, Ambrosios, Agustinos, Basilios and Bernardos, it would cease to matter that hell vomited forth Voltaires, Rousseaus, D'Alberts, Montesquieus, Federicos and Diderots." How much more clearly could the author distance himself from the heretics who "freely criticize the Church in London, Paris, and Philadelphia"?[14] For Lizardi, as for Mora and many others in these pages, the new liberal political possibilities followed naturally from the tenets of their piety, and therein lay their justification. Not deracinated sons of the European Enlightenment, these luminaries were instead the unexpected New World spawn of enlightened Catholicism.

The Intellectuals on the Offensive:
Attacks on Church, Monarch, and Nobility

Above all, the Scriptures provided Lizardi and Mora with a sturdy soap box from which to attack revered authorities. Now available in the vernacular, freed from the authoritative glosses of the schoolmen, and transparent to the internally illuminated individual, the Bible served Lizardi as a source of unassailable imperatives to moralizing. An 1824 pastoral from the Bishop of Sonora prompted a telling response in this regard. The letter labeled those who defied the King as God's enemies, and an impassioned Lizardi attacked it by directing his readers to the real authority on matters theological. Surely, El Pensador sardonically noted, the benighted bishop understood that "God detests the government of kings," because the Scriptures showed that when the Israelites requested a monarch, God punished them. When they subsequently implored Samuel to prevail on Him for an end to their suffering, they admitted that "we have added to all of our many sins one more: that of asking for a king."[15] Monarchy was not divinely ordained but sinful, and the Bishop of Sonora ignored this clear scriptural message to his peril. Lizardi's scriptural and historical erudition thus punctured the Church hierarchy's exclusive interpretive claims as well as the King's pretensions to divine sanctification.

For Mora, too, the Scriptures offered transparent access to God's imperatives, and, befitting a true man of God, he railed against the ignorant clergy who thwarted the Bible's circulation among the laity. To forward this end, he pledged in 1829 to abet the efforts of the British and Foreign Bible Society, which distributed Catholic Bibles to Mexicans despite Church opposition. The "real lovers of Christianity," he assured the society, would battle so that religious education would in the future center on the reading of Divine Scripture rather than catechisms, those mere "words of men."[16] Thus, the allegedly secular Mora arrived at a conclusion similar to that of the sixteenth-century Protestant reformer Zwingli, who decried Church tradition as not God's word but that of flawed mortals. Zwingli, of course, took the critique to its logical conclusion: brandishing his Bible, he advocated the establishment of a theocratic state where ministers and magistrates would enact the self-evident scriptural precepts long since abandoned by the Church.[17]

Likewise girded in the armor of the Word, the Mexican intellectuals turned reform tenets against even the most sacred authorities. The popes, Lizardi asserted, had exploited the "ignorance and unbridled passions" that prevailed during the Middle Ages to insinuate themselves into the pinnacle of the Church hierarchy, thence to trumpet their infallibility. In a scandalous reversal of the proper flow of authority, during this dark time the bishops had begun to think of themselves as the pope's vassals and slaves, even referring to him as "His Majesty"![18] The Holy Fathers, then, had manufactured their own claims to unassailable authority; the early Church councils, Lizardi declared, clearly restricted the role of these servants of the servants of God.

As we have seen, this return to primitive conciliar authority and early Church discipline is a perennial theme in enlightened Catholicism, but Lizardi gave it voice in new literary forms. In an 1825 pamphlet, he has a wise sexton tell a doubtful countryman that he can rightfully ignore Leo XII's encyclical urging Mexicans to return to Ferdinand VII's monarchical fold. The Pope usurped his authority, the sexton asserts, but his interlocutor need not take his word for it; rather, "Read ecclesiastical history—which I did not write—and you will see not only this, but his even more scandalous excesses."[19]

Although Lizardi himself did not write ecclesiastical history either, he most certainly read it carefully. Devoted almost in its entirety to an account of the papacy through the centuries, his 1826–1827 periodical the *Correo Semanario de México* opened with a salvo that summed up the tenor of the entire twenty-pamphlet series: numerous doctrinal works, he thundered, revealed the popes' illegitimate authority! Jesus Christ had granted no express concessions to the popes, and the Holy Scriptures, the New Testament, Saint Peter, and the consistent practice of the early centuries did not affirm their lofty position. Lizardi concluded that "there are not nor can there be other founts of the truth" than these, and so appeals to other sources were meaningless.[20]

Prune the Church's right to taxes and property, Mora argued with equal stridency. Preaching the Divine Word, administering the sacraments, and attending to matters directly related to God's cult: these had been the Church's only prerogatives during its glorious early centuries. It was only during the infamous reign of Emperor Constantine that clerics obtained riches and the right to punish malefactors, as well as other civil privileges. But if rights came from the temporal powers, then they could be revoked by the temporal powers. One needed only the most superficial knowledge of the Bible and the divine religion of Christ, Mora asserted, to grasp that the Church was entitled only to the faithful's voluntary donations for its ministers' immediate consumption.[21]

Significantly, the Church's corporate privileges fell under attack most strongly during the 1833 administration of President Valentin Gómez Farías and his chief advisor, Mora. Monastic vows were declared a matter of individual conscience, and thus the state would not aid the Church in enforcing them. Obligatory tithing was abolished, along with other mandatory Church donations. The government bandied about proposals to seize Church wealth and plans to create state dioceses where bishops would live off "modest incomes." The president's men even entertained thoughts of whittling down the bloated calendar of saints' celebrations. Taking their cue from the executive's National Palace, emboldened state legislatures in Mexico, Puebla, and Veracruz prohibited pilgrimages to shrines, required state approval for confraternities, prohibited the collection of Church taxes, and closed convents and church schools.[22]

The devotees of "true religion" found weighty spokesmen in Lizardi and Mora, but their contribution to immediate post-Independence political culture is most vividly apparent during the patronage debate, as Michael Costeloe has demonstrated. The Spanish King had long held the right of presentation to ecclesiastical benefices, the *patronato*. In this arrangement, the Crown presented candidates for a major benefice, such as a bishopric, to the Pope for official approval. Candidates for lower-level positions were presented to the local bishop rather than to the Holy Father. Mexico, however, began its independence under a pope who refused to acknowledge its separation from Spain. King Ferdinand VII therefore continued to claim the right of presentation to all benefices, and his cooperation was not forthcoming; by 1829 Mexico found itself bereft of bishops.[23] Thus, the state and the Mexican Church had to resolve the problem of ecclesiastical appointments. It was precisely this debate on patronage that the reformed transformed into a raucous referendum on the very nature of Church authority.[24] Post-Independence Mexican urban elites like Lizardi and Mora were not engaged in secularization—a disenfranchisement of man's right relationship with God as a motive of action—but something more akin to a religious war.

The congressional committee's 1824 report reflected the ideas of its most flamboyant and well-known member, the loquacious Fray Servando Teresa de Mier. A renegade Dominican and an avowed Jansenist, Mier brought an unabashedly reformed sensibility to the debate. Declaring that Trent had rightly acted in the face of "the diabolical Protestant reforms," he further opined that the august council should have gone farther and scraped off the accumulated dross of man-made error. Now Mexico should reclaim the old and true rules of the Church, as had the 316 fathers of the Council of Pistoia and the bishops and constitutional clergy of France.[25] But in the France of the *philosophes*, the left "frequently allowed itself to burst out with laughter" at the "antiquated foolishness" of the Jansenists involved in crafting the civil constitution, jeering openly at their biblical references and their preoccupation with old battles against the Jesuits, at least according to one unsympathetic participant.[26]

In Mexico, however, nobody was laughing at Mier. The committee's report of 1823 predictably located patronage with the civil authorities, but went further. It was essential to restore primitive ecclesiastical discipline, particularly a system of ecclesiastical elections. At the lowest level this process would involve even parishioners, in addition to local, municipal, and state authorities. The eventual report that appeared the following year jettisoned this scheme as imprudent, but insisted that patronage was a temporal prerogative, not a papal one. A tacit compromise prevailed; the state would exercise the patronato, but without any formal, legal declaration.

Predictably enough, Lizardi and Mora's public critique of "sensual excess" found its most comfortable target in the hierarchy of unearned social distinction. As enlightened Catholics, they cast jaundiced eyes on status and wealth based on birth or corporate privilege rather than on the righteous fruits of Christian moderation. The nobility's theatrical opulence, their penchant for pomp and immoderate expenditure, bespoke their hollow interiors. Lizardi's 1816 novel El periquillo sarniento took advantage of the new literary form to make this point.

The story's antihero is Periquillo, a wastrel who stubbornly resists gainful employment in a trade despite repeated wise counsel. Providentially, he washes up on an island, home of a just meritocracy. A wise Chinese king rules this utopia, where thrifty artisans compose the population. Periquillo pretends to be a count; when the wise ruler asks about New Spain's nobles, "born and not self-made," the protagonist replies that "they do nothing but amuse themselves: they promenade, and at most, work at whatever will not exhaust their fortune. If you could see the houses of some of the counts and nobles in my land, if you could sit at their tables, if you could observe their luxury . . . the magnificence of their persons, the equipment of their coaches, the richness of their liveries . . . you would be surprised."[27]

If the misguided Periquillo admired all of this unbridled opulence, of course, then the virtuous reader should not. The condemnation of the nobility's empty interiors intensifies after our protagonist escorts the island's wise ruler back to New Spain. Here Lizardi contrasts theatrical display and luxury to true devotion. Periquillo explains to the foreigner that many "great families" retain a home chaplain for "adornment," to which the incredulous visitor replies with a characteristically didactic restatement of the antihero's blithe revelation: "In your land the rich keep ministers of religion in their homes more out of luxury and vanity than devotion; that these men serve to flatter rather than correct their masters', their patrons', or whatever-you-call-them's vices?"[28]

For Lizardi as for enlightened Catholics generally, all of this opulence signaled a lack of moral moderation; thus, the nobility should cede their social leadership to those, like Lizardi, who demonstrated the proper control over themselves. Indeed, these empty titles constituted an affront to republican virtue. In an 1825 dialogue Lizardi's countryman suggests that as a republic Mexico should abolish titles like marquis and count because they smack of vassalage. The sexton agrees wholeheartedly, tagging these distinctions as vanities and silliness that "Solomon, the most powerful of kings, knew after enjoying the fruits of the world, according to the Scriptures. I would be ashamed if they called me count or marquis, because wise men would recognize me as a *majadero*, as someone who wanted to distinguish myself with an empty and insignificant little name."[29]

Others with corporate privileges also came in for criticism. After Mexico's 1821 Independence, the liberal newspaper El Fenix de la Libertad chastised the army's penchant for excessive display, contrasting the pomp of the monarchy and the nobility's vanity with the simple virtues that should reign in a republic. Mimicking viceregal mores, the army indulged in richly adorned uniforms, which not only set a bad example but also indicated their "effeminate" nature. The author warned that while the Romans rejected excess they remained invincible, but with its introduction began their fall, and the same would happen to Mexico, "where we have men more comfortable in a dressing room than in battle." It was time to end luxury and vanity so that Mexico could count on "men who were not effeminate, who thought more about their obligations than about obtaining outfits to attend tertulias."[30]

Few members of any society, of course, leave such clear paper trails to their mentalités as do published intellectuals. The elaborate, detailed wills of the upper classes form one of the few clues to the popularity of enlightened Catholic notions among a wider audience. An analysis of the wills from this period and beyond to 1860 suggests that Lizardi, Mora, Mier, and their peers were not speaking into a vacuum. Their changed attitude to exterior display found its way into the files of Mexico City's nineteenth-century notaries; samples from the early decades of the 1800s echo Lizardi's suspicion of the theatrics of both the rich and the poor. Doubtless aware of the documents' significance, Lizardi in 1827 published a satirical will bequeathing "a multitude of churches, hermitages, and convents of religious of both sexes," but "very little religion." Processions, bells, firecrackers, and festivals abounded, he continued, but little progress had been made toward the modification of bad habits or the inculcation of a true fear of God.[31]

Most nineteenth-century testators firmly rejected the sensuality of the exterior cult as well as excess mediation with the Almighty, as we have already seen. Where 73 percent of the earlier 1710–1720 testators who had indicated a burial preference had pledged fealty to the saints or to another particularly charged burial location within a church, only 23 percent of the middle period wills did so. This figure plummeted to 12 percent of the testators during the 1850s. Less reliance on the saints as mediators with God is echoed in the decline in interest in Masses said in a particular saint's chapel or other spot in the church. Although the number of the faithful who designated particular churches for Masses fell off only slightly, from 29 to 22 percent, the number locating those Masses in specified chapels within these churches mirrored the precipitous decline in specific burial locations: from 20 to 7 to just 5 percent of all testators. The 36 percent of testators who insisted on a moderate funeral during the 1810–1820 period fell slightly, to 28 percent, from 1850 to 1860. Nor did gifts to adorn sacred images rebound to its high of 18 percent during the 1710–1720 period, dropping to a mere 3 percent of the 1850–1860 group. This sea change in pious giving becomes even more dramatic, however, when the total number of testators who made pious bequests is calculated: the numbers dropped over the century and a half under study from 39 percent to 21 percent to 17 percent.[32]

Like the archbishops' flamboyant displays of godly moderation we saw earlier, the wealthy testators' shift away from showy legacies provided outward signs of a pure interior state. This trend offered good Christians a mechanism for mutual recognition, a new norm of public conduct. And if only the truly Christian could see whom to count among their number, they also arrogated to themselves the exclusive right to read the signs of godlessness. Now gifts that enhanced the exterior religious cult demonstrated the reprobate's amor propio. The Count of Campomanes had praised alms to the deserving poor and warned that other pious offerings lost their merit because they were frequently accompanied by a spirit of amor propio; but the wise benefactor could avoid this pitfall by offering succor that fomented familial industry.[33]

And what constituted this dangerous love of self? Citing Saint Augustine, Archbishop Nuñez de Haro y Peralta explained that amor propio endangered men's souls through their enthrallment to worldly social distinctions. To act in accordance with God's will it was necessary to "conserve in the heart a rectitude, a purity, a fervor that dominates imperiously over our amor propio and all of our passions, and that orders our actions and movements."[34] Two cities have been formed by two loves, declared Saint Augustine: "The humble city is the society of holy men and good angels; the proud city is the society of wicked men and evil angels. The one city began with the love of God; the other had its beginnings in the love of self."[35] Lizardi did not have to look across the ocean to France for new norms of public conduct: they were being preached from the pulpits of Mexico City.

As we saw in Lizardi's intrepid written critiques of ancien régime authorities and praise for republican government, enlightened Catholicism stood front and center in what most scholars have deemed Lizardi's imported secular concerns. In his discussion of patriotism, Lizardi revealed his debt to the reformed Church yet again: the amor propio of the ungodly undermined love of country and suffocated Mexico's budding nationalism. As literary critic Nancy Vogely points out, Lizardi found selfishness at the root of many North Americans' tepid patriotism. But this self-love was not some Freudian malaise; rather, as El Pensador explained, egoismo was "the art of making oneself the center of everything surrounding one; or, more clearly: it is the fifth essence of amor propio . . . the perfect egoist contains within himself his country, law, religion, and family."[36] Mexicans professed to be great lovers of their country, he explained elsewhere, but proved to be less enamored of their countrymen: wealthy Americans did not "succor the poor, or civilize them, or instruct them."[37] Thus, those who exhibited the self-control that reformers juxtaposed to amor propio were the community; all others were moral saboteurs and should be under their guidance.

Lizardi's consuming concern with stinginess and vanity was shared not only by a healthy proportion of testators but also by other participants in Mexico City's public sphere. The evils of lavish display and the virtue of moderation were frequently rehearsed themes in the *Diario de México*, which had the largest circulation of the capital's new periodicals.[38] In an 1808 article advocating simple uniform dress for "the economy of families and the moderation of luxury," the author cited Fray Luis de León's observation that women were the guiltiest of "fomenting luxury with their bobbles and adornments." Indeed, he went on, some were so out of control that they employed "more dangerous" means, so that "hombres de bien" were scandalized even to lay eyes on them. In another article typical of the genre, an author laments the "luxury" that he felt had crept into Holy Week: while Our Lady draped in black shed tender tears for her son, Christians insulted God's temple by "putting all of their passions into motion," preening in the most expensive clothing and effecting a superior, haughty demeanor. Pious souls who felt themselves tempted by this luxury should stay at home, pray to God, and be prepared to suffer the destruction of the exterior cult with the confidence that "nobody can rob them of the cult of the heart."[39]

Vanity and luxury were also the themes of an 1811 fable printed in the *Diario*. Born in the populous city of "Vanidopolis" in the province of "Showiness," Luxury's parents were Laziness and Insanity, his running mates and instructors El amor propio and Novelty. Seduced by a foreign girl named La moda and known for her significant investments in expensive fashion, Luxury marries and the pair gives birth to little Deuda (debt) and Trampa (deception). The good queen, Healthy Conscience, finally ends the tale by expelling the family from her dominions.[40] Like Lizardi and Mora, the *Diario* deplored these customs in a religious vocabulary, not a French one.

The Spanish Empire's enlightened Catholics provided the precedent for Mexico City intellectuals' critique of the nobility's inner vacuity. These reformers trained the ammunition of their faith against entrenched, corporate elite status, but only superficially in the name of radical egalitarianism. Rather, they envisioned a society of self-made men of godly moderation, whose interior pious virtues and spiritual enlightenment would produce economic success and hence well-earned social power. All obstacles to this individual's rise had to be summarily removed, and chief among them stood ascriptive social status.

Caridad: The Bridge to Individual Sovereignty

Below the surface of this public rancor at superfluous Church hierarchies, monarchy, and papacy lurked enlightened Catholicism's most fundamental constituent: the individual, internally illuminated and thus virtuous. Both Lizardi's and Mora's writings strove inexorably to desanctify anything standing between the individual conscience and God. In their stern interpretation, divinity did not cascade downward from Heaven to coagulate around kings and popes for distribution among those they ruled. Like other reformed Catholics, they effectively reconfigured God's presence in the world. Recall that reform luminaries had rerouted the path to God from outward through the Church hierarchy to inward through the illuminated conscience. Recall that Pedro Rodríguez Campomanes, president of the Council of Castile, found this path clear and uncluttered: "The good Christian will consult his conscience in order to live in accordance with divine precepts and the morals advocated by Jesus Christ."[41]

Mora took this precept to its logical conclusion: the Church hierarchy distracted the godly from truly Christian morals! Clerics felt "an invincible repugnance" toward freedom of worship and the liberty of thought and the press, because these "principles and the institutions that guaranteed them destroyed or weakened their control over conscience." The liberation of conscience, then, became a distinctly religious imperative for the diminution of clerical privileges. The clergy, Mora explained in the same passage, hated legal equality because it dissolved the hierarchies and fueros that supported their power as a class. Religion was a matter of conscience, and thus monks should be free to reject monastic vows, taxes paid to the Church should be entirely voluntary, and clerics should be equal citizens with other Mexicans.[42]

This reconfiguration of the path to God leaps out from El Pensador's public musings on the proper government for the young republic. In one bold foray, Lizardi declared that the Bishop of Sonora worshiped Ferdinand VII as an idol. Already everywhere in His creation, God was no more present in the King than anywhere else; the King was "an imperceptible atom" in relation to Him. The misguided bishop, however, had forgotten these simple truths and "wanted Americans to kneel down on the earth in front of his idol, Ferdinand, and to seat him on the same throne as the Eternal. What blasphemy!"[43]

But if sovereignty did not reside in the King, where did it lie? Sovereignty certainly derived from God, but, as we have seen, for enlightened Catholics God did not reign from "out there" but made a home within the illuminated individual. As Lizardi explained, "Sovereignty is nothing but the exercise of the will, and as every man has a will, every man has his own sovereignty." In a republic, men did not surrender this God-given sovereignty but only temporarily entrusted it to others for the greater good of all. Furthermore, those who questioned the godliness of republican government ignored the Scriptures and early Church precedent, for during this happy time Saint Peter refused to dictate political decisions as a monarch, and instead "convened the apostles and the clergy (just as the president of the Republic can convene deputies and senators for extraordinary sessions) and to discuss matters, and decide the best plan by a majority vote, which then became law."[44]

The evidence of their own words leaves little room for doubt. Clearly, Lizardi and Mora joined other enlightened Catholics in attacking the sclerotic legal hierarchies of the ancien régime in the name of the new piety's fundamental unit: the virtuous individual. El Pensador states as much in his 1820 reply to a clerical opponent who had labeled him a mere "plebe," implicitly unqualified to voice public criticism. This accusation failed to faze Lizardi, who responded that "true nobility, even before God, consists in virtue. And who is first and most saintly before God? He who has the most *caridad*."[45]

How did Lizardi and other reform Catholics define this caridad that crowned the individual as his own monarch? The Scriptures provided them a clear answer, for the Almighty did not mince words. Love of our neighbors and even enemies constitutes the bedrock of faith: "This is what Jesus Christ preached, this is the true merit of religion."[46] The Christian could manifest this love only through generosity to others, especially the poor. Lizardi latched onto this precept with vigor, making repeated invidious comparisons between the wasteful and vain ostentation of the exterior cult and gifts to the needy. Again echoing the flamboyant moderation of Mexico City's reformed archbishops, in 1813 Lizardi questioned whether the Church needed so much luxury, "vanity," and profusion in the homes of the magistrates of a religion founded by a Teacher of poverty and humility. He concluded it did not. All of this hoopla and expense constituted a scandal prejudicial to the nation; the wealth should instead be invested in the real treasures of the Church, the "treasures that Saint Lazarus presented to the greedy tyrant (the poor)."[47]

Both Lizardi and Mora frequently rehearsed this critical distinction between the spiritually vacuous exterior cult and true charity. Indeed, one of the things that often drove Lizardi to distraction was that many of the indolent rich confessed and feigned virtue on the outside, despite their haughtiness toward the poor. "Did not their confessors warn them," he thundered, "that where there was no generosity there was no charity, and where there was no charity there was no virtue?"[48] In El *periquillo sarniento*

Lizardi noted that "the poor's tears honored the dead, and demonstrated the deceased's caridad and beneficence." Moreover, they assured eternal salvation more truly than did "all of the pomp, vanity, and showiness of a lavish funeral and burial."[49] The majesty of the exterior cult froze wealth that was better spent on Christianity's simple kerigmatic truth: the love of one's neighbor.[50]

Mora concurred. The saints' festivals sponsored by the confraternities and religious orders squandered money on unproductive ornamentation and mere diversions such as fireworks and lighting, sums better spent on hospices, hospitals, and other beneficial works. As the "living temples of God," the poor should be preferred to the pomp and luxury of the cult. No less an authority than Augustine had taught as much by dramatic example, "breaking sacred vessels of precious metal to distribute them to the needy."[51] In a critique that would have stung the moderate and urbane Archbishops Haro y Peralta and Lorenzana, Mora contrasted dutiful parish priests who dispensed the essential sacraments to the clerical hierarchy's "excesses." Before the reign of the current archbishop, Mexico had not witnessed a truly apostolic pastoral visit; rather, the bishops traveled to receive gifts from the faithful rather than to tend to their spiritual needs, and, most alarmingly, they did so with an ostentation and pomp unworthy of "episcopal moderation."

For Lizardi, Mora, and others of "enlightened piety," however, the truly Christian imperative was not to give indiscriminately: only the "true poor" were the "living image of God." If the nobility needed spiritually enlightened pedagogues like Lizardi to temper their opulent theatrics, so too did their inferiors. If God illuminated some men from within, then the corporate category of "poor" was as spiritually empty as that of "monarch" or "nobility," and indeed their rags could be read as a sign of profligacy and immoderation. Some among the poor, both men maintained, also showed clear signs of being sunken in sensual depravity, albeit of a different sort.

In one of the numerous didactic episodes in El periquillo sarniento, the dissipated Periquillo falls in with a scraggly group of men and women who make their living begging on Mexico City's streets. The crutches, eye patches, and rags donned by these vagrants, however, emphatically do not signal their closeness to God because of their distance from worldly riches. In the privacy of the beggars' lair, our protagonist discovers crutches stacked against the walls and ointments to feign hideous skin sores; he learns that a beggar woman pinches her infant to produce his plaintive cries. Periquillo's host in this den of thieves explains that by pretending to be blind, lame, or leprous, they maximize their take and net enough to slake their powerful thirsts. All of these theatrics, and the further feckless-ness they financed, merely "robbed the honest poor" of their sustenance, Lizardi concluded.[52]

Lizardi and Mora could claim many fellow travelers in this preoccupation with true charity, as the early nineteenth century witnessed a sea change in pious giving away from the exterior cult and toward the poor. A study of the pious gifts designated in 350 wills from each of the decades 1710–1720, 1810–1820, and 1850–1860 details the story. During the initial period of 1710–1720, for example, only 33 of the 138 testators who designated pious bequests gave at least one gift to the poor. But one hundred years later, of the 65 testators who made pious bequests, 49 left gifts to the poor. Overall, of the 350 testators sampled for each period, only 11 percent of all of the early testators and 12 percent of the later testators designated gifts for the poor. Yet the percentage of gifts to social inferiors out of all pious bequests rose dramatically, from 26 to 76 percent. This trend continued into the nineteenth century: during the period 1850–1860, a full 67 percent of Mexico City residents leaving bequests designated the poor as recipients, with over half of these giving exclusively to the downtrodden. Thus, al-though pious giving steadily declined, we should be cautious about at-tributing this trend to secularization, for the total number of gifts to the poor rose in the middle period and fell only slightly in the later period as compared to the 1710–1720 testators.[53] The culprit, I suggest, was not growing nonchalance about salvation, but a changing interpretation of how to effect it—or, perhaps, manifest it.

El Pensador's intellectual debt to early exemplars of the reform current is clear. Crown economist Bernardo Ward's unflinching critique of adorn-ments in Spain appeared in a celebrated 1762 tract that proffered advice to the monarch and his representatives on how to revive Spain's flagging industry. This influential work merits quoting at length for its rehearsal of the imperative to restore the Church to its austere early glory before the proliferation of saints and for its advice on what constituted a truly pious bequest: "In France the cult of the Divine is not less majestic, but is less costly than here. There temples have the sturdy adornment that comes from architecture, sculpture and other noble arts . . . the faithful do not dress them [images of saints] or place diamonds on them, because the wise and devout of that country know that it is more in accordance with the principles of our religion, and the practice and governance of the primitive Church [*disciplina antigua*], to apply these riches to the living image of God, to those in whose person one actually dresses and feeds Jesus Christ, that is, to the true poor."[54]

A closer look at a few representative wills demonstrates this profound shift in pious sensibilities advocated by Ward and later echoed by Lizardi. Cristobal Peña, a native of Toluca, noted in his will that he had filed for divorce from his wife, whom he accused of trying to poison him with venom. After indicating his preference for a modest funeral and leaving his burial location to his estate executor's whim, in 1831 he left small amounts to his two brothers, 100 pesos to a woman who had tended him during his illness, and 50 pesos to the poor, to be distributed not by the clergy, but by his estate executors.[55] Café owner José Mariano Fernández de Cordova also found gifts to the poor a more efficacious salvatory gesture than contributions to the cult of worship, and in 1830, after requesting a cemetery burial, bequeathed 100 pesos to destitute individuals chosen by his estate executors. Some testators funneled their gifts through the new public institutions concerned with regulating the indigent. In 1859, Guadalupe Ceballos endowed permanent funds for the Hospicio de Pobres in León, the hospitals of San Juan de Dios in León and San Lázaro in Mexico City, and the child care activities of the Sisters of Charity in Mexico City; any residue from her estate was to go to an unspecified group of the poor.[56]

Comparing the wills of two wealthy testators demonstrates the sea change in pious sensibilities that accelerated at the end of the eighteenth century and reached its crescendo in the early nineteenth. In her 1717 will, Mexico City native María Josefa de Avendaño y Orduña requested burial under an altar to the Holy Christ, whose cult she sponsored in the convent of Nuestra Señora de la Pura y Limpia Concepción. She left 3,000 pesos for her funeral, which she ordered conducted with "all possible decency." She left a small bequest to the poor to be distributed the day of her death, and a small donation for "poor girls" and prisoners, but reserved the bulk of her tremendous fortune to enliven the liturgical calendar, dress the saints, and illuminate and decorate the city's churches in the form of the following bequests: the interest from 2,000 pesos for lamp oil to illuminate various altars, including the one under which she rested; endowments for over fifteen saints' feasts, including one for Saint Joseph, "her protector and lawyer"; money for several chaplaincies to be established to pray for her own and others' souls; and more than 100 paintings of holy people, many of them with gilded frames. Further gifts added to the overall luster, including a bronze bell, metal chairs imported from Moscow, a gilded stand for the missal, four gilded torch holders, and even a fount of holy water to be placed near a chapel of Our Lady of the Immaculate Conception.[57] In his 1815 will, by way of contrast, Spaniard Manuel de Marroquín requested "no pomp whatsoever" and a simple wooden coffin. Prisoners received 3,400 pesos; priests were instructed to distribute another 3,200 to the poor, and the regular orders received 314 pesos for the same purpose.

What can we surmise from these documents? Intriguingly, the Protestant Reformation in England ushered in a similar shift in pious giving away from the exterior cult and toward the deserving poor. Requests for intercession with the Divine and gifts to hermits, to votive lights, and to the cathedral church had actually risen before the Reformation. A 1547 law instructed the clergy to exhort their neighbors to fill the parish poor chest rather than foment "blind devotions," a sentiment echoed in the Book of Common Prayer. Testators in London, Sussex, Berkshire, the southwest, the northeast, and Norfolk heeded the call, resulting in a rapid increase in gifts to the poor across the country. Although efforts to channel giving toward the poor met with immediate success, it is important to remember that testators were constrained by laws and government policies. "There was no point in investing money in forbidden practices and pious gifts which might shortly be confiscated," historian Ralph Houlbrooke explains.[58]

As the political ground roiled beneath their feet, then, these reformed Catholics groped their way to a novel vision of sovereignty. Between the demotion of illegitimate aristocracies and the promotion of the sober bourgeois liberal, the reformers crossed an ideological bridge fashioned from their notions of Christian virtue. The old, false proofs of authority lay in shambles; only God could offer reliable replacements, and His true followers knew where to look for them.

An Aristocracy of the Heart

An emboldened laity who trained the dictates of conscience on Church and royal authority, of course, was most certainly not what Bourbon adherents of the new piety had anticipated. To attack hierarchy was not to promote democracy, and to stress individuality was not to advocate equality. Well placed in apparatuses of both Church and state, reformers like the Crown-appointed bishops had preached obedience to secular and ecclesiastical authorities. And they did not evince doubt in the process: "One of the sure signs of the pride that goes before a fall," Archbishop Lorenzana declared, "is questioning authority, bad-mouthing superiors' pronouncements, and ... wanting to decide for oneself about topics that should not be debated by inferiors."[59] Not the respect for superiors, but the qualifications of superiority, were up for review.

Nevertheless, by emphasizing the early councils and the internally illuminated individual, reformers launched far-reaching attacks on hierarchies both within the Church and beyond it. Not every professed Christian could be considered a credible guide to matters theological, but all who truly wished to qualify themselves had the tools for disciplined study available to them in this era of the vernacular. Thus, although the high-level reformers we have heard from envisioned a closed-room debate, their theology inadvertently left the doors swinging wide open to all versed in holy texts. Upstarts like Lizardi and Mora walked brazenly through those doors, and it was precisely their knowledge of the Scriptures and the early Church councils that they brandished as their entry tickets to challenge even the most revered authorities.

If the new piety provided an imperative to dismantle power based on corporate or hereditary privileges, it also suggested to its devotees a new rationale for social leadership. Mora, like Veracruz's gente sensata, concluded that exemplars of Christian moderation should rule those who manifested an inability to get a hold of themselves. In the tumultuous post-Independence political climate, numerous candidates for tutelage presented themselves. Peter Guardino notes that the relative political tranquility that prevailed between 1823 and 1828 was shattered by Mexico's default on critical British loans. The ensuing economic crisis roiled the young republic, as did the artisans' and coastal sharecroppers' resentment at a liberal tariff policy. In Mexico City these issues led the aggrieved to sack a clutch of luxurious shops in Mexico City's central square, long a symbol of Spanish merchant domination. Mexico's largest urban uprising in over a century involved perhaps five thousand participants and effectively drove terrified elites from city streets for perhaps a week.[60] With the support of this angry urban underclass as well as mulatto sharecroppers, Independence hero Vicente Guerrero came to power in 1829. His brief rule, Guardino explains, centered on anti-Spanish measures and tariff protection and represented "the most frightening experience of Mexico's ruling class" since parish priest José María Morelos's troops nearly felled the royal government.[61] Within a year, the hombres de bien had deposed Guerrero.

In an 1827 tract, Mora warned that populist demagogues would have free rein in a country where men now walked the "difficult and always dangerous" path of liberty for the first time. Their technique: flatter the popular classes' "passions" and thereby imbue the mob with a serious distrust of those who profess "the maxims of moderation."[62] After the populist Guerrero interlude, Mora became more adamant that the immoderate threatened the republic; radical democracy simply proved too much for him. Limit citizenship to property holders, he proposed in 1830, as had the exemplary "peaceful" countries of America, France, and Germany. In its zeal for "equality," its universal manhood suffrage, Mexico had confused the "wise with the ignorant, the judicious and moderate with the tumultuous and bellicose."[63]

Luckily, a litmus test was readily available to allay the confusion: the wise who should rightly govern held private property (or a salary of 1,000 pesos per year) and monopolized the virtues of beneficence, personal decorum and manners, and love of the public good. The poor not only demonstrated dissipation, they were positively mired in the daily pursuit of basic necessities and therefore could not raise their eyes to higher issues.[64] Although several of the capital's papers backed Mora's proposal, only in 1836 was the franchise officially limited by property and wealth.[65] As we saw in Veracruz, for Mora, the godly individual of enlightened Catholicism looked ahead to free himself from corporate shackles and disdainfully peered back at those who displayed signs of immoderation.

Conclusion

Jean Franco argues that Lizardi envisioned a disciplinary society led by a Europeanized secular intelligentsia. With the economic and political upheaval of the post-Independence period, this Enlightenment ideal could not be implemented, she continues. Instead, it appeared as a series of fictional utopias penned by this aspiring bourgeoisie, as a structuring fantasy for besieged secular philosophes. The tiny learned minority clung to these rational fantasies, surrounded by Latin America's swirling carnival of barbarous masses and profligate elites—or so the argument runs.[66] Franco's literary analysis echoes the historical one of Michael Costeloe. In the giddy first days of freedom, liberal reformers were acutely sensitive to Mexico's backwardness but understood its tremendous potential. "Imbued with and overly dependent upon the utilitarian and rationalist ideologies of Europe," Costeloe summarizes, these optimists "constructed a hypothetical model of their society" and quickly realized that the Church, with its external piety and socially prestigious but nonelected clergy, was a "relic of a bygone theocratic age that had no place in their modern, progressive society."[67]

But Lizardi, Mier, and Mora were not the rootless children of the most secular branch of the French Revolution, but religious radicals dreaming of a godly commonwealth where the reprobates would be under their guidance. Enlightened Catholicism spawned these unexpected and unwanted offspring. Although they tell us nothing of the pious proclivities of the poor, Mexico City wills of the period do register that reform zealots like Mora and Lizardi operated in a milieu where the elite property holders they championed shared their notion of the proper path to God. Ralph Houlbrooke found that English wills "slip out of the realm of the spiritual or sacred" by about 1750; Pierre Chaunu and Michel Vovelle similarly found growing indifference to burial arrangements and pious giving in early eighteenth-century Paris and Provence, which they read as a sign of secularization, of a population increasingly nonchalant about its relationship with God.[68] Although a growing number of nineteenth-century Mexico City testators left much to the discretion of their estate executors, they also filled their wills with requests for modest death rites and gifts to the poor, and in this they resembled more the zealous Protestants of sixteenth- and seventeenth-century England than their indifferent eighteenth-century heirs.

Led by godly secular magistrates like Mora, Mier, and Lizardi (many of them also priests), early nineteenth-century elite Mexicans sought to create a society in conformity with their religion, not remove religion from their society. It quickly became apparent that the righteous should be in charge, and that those who lacked the self-restraint He provided should be effectively excluded. Thus, they officially sought to replace a system with no pretense of equality of opportunity, one of juridically fixed social hierarchies sanctioned by God, with an equally sacral political community built on the fiction of fluidity: the virtuous should rule. Their self-restraint and discipline would manifest themselves in their economic success, and thus the poor could be excluded with no qualms of inequity, for if they were virtuous they would acquire the salary or property to become enfranchised. That self-moderation was a uniquely masculine virtue is demonstrated by women's complete disfranchisement; women possessed of estates remained merely propertied women, not virtuous citizens. Costeloe wonders if the debates swirling around the Church after Independence were a cause or an effect of secularization. The pious proclivities of nineteenth-century testators and the more organized, public campaigns led by enlightened Catholics indicate that Church reformation was not an effect of secularization. But it may have been one of its causes.

chapter 7

The Rise of Medical Empiricism

Enlightened clerics, state bureaucrats, merchants, and emboldened lay intellectuals were not the only ones who demonstrated an affinity for the new piety. Doctors became their fellow travelers, as the interior piety supported the truth claims of the new empirical science and made them acceptable to the self-defined enlightened portion of the population. As we have seen, enlightened piety unseated the divinely ordained monarch and his clerical power brokers and enthroned the internally illuminated individual. Similarly, the new medicine we will explore in this chapter proclaimed individual observation the font of knowledge, dethroning the hoary nostrums of classical authority. Ironically, then, medicine's cultural authority became so powerful that it edged out theology as the dominant language of burial debate, permanently strengthening doctors' authority while further weakening the clergy's intellectual leadership of nineteenth-century society. Beginning roughly around the time of Independence, Veracruz's and Mexico City's burial battle lines had begun to shift. Formerly, the cleric-led enlightened had railed against pompous church burials; now, secular leaders invoked medical verities and the new piety to justify their seizure of all Church-controlled burial spaces. As so often happens, the law of unintended consequences spawned a Frankenstein's monster, and the later clerics found themselves terrorized by their forebears' creation.

The full implications of this development for the course of Mexican modernity becomes evident in the following chapter. But first we need to take up the specific context of medicine in the Spanish Empire. This context demonstrates that complex causal ecology undergirded the rise of medical authority in Mexico; the new piety was not monocausal, and indeed, the two grew up together. The Board of Medical Examiners, the Protomedicato, had provided an institutional structure for promoting the documented practitioner since the fifteenth century, a distinct legacy of the Islamic influence that sets Spain apart from its European neighbors. Furthermore, eighteenth-century New Spain boasted new newspapers that lauded doctors' erudition and lambasted their folk competitors—particularly women—as superstitious and irrational. But while the Protomedicato aggrandized medicine's social authority, it itself became a target of medical reformers who found the institution's reliance on scholastic method archaic, and who promoted a new medicine that had much in common with the new piety. The Protomedicato certainly advanced medicine's authority in general, but it was the rise of this more experimental and clinical medicine that ensured the prominent place of doctors' testimony and public health imperatives in the burial debate. Finally, and most important, I examine the rhetorical bridge that linked reform piety to empirical scientific authority, and from there move in Chapter 8 to the implications of this bloodline for Mexico's disputed modernity.

The Practitioners against the Pretenders

Summing up the energetic campaigns to bolster medicine's status, one reformer declared, "Given that people had no greater desire than that of liberating themselves from sickness and death, what reason could there be for not demanding of the art of curing the same responsibility as demanded of other professions?"[1] A state that measured its wealth in terms of a healthy populace and that engaged in almost constant warfare needed competent medical practitioners, and the eighteenth century witnessed a steady campaign to produce them. In so doing, the organs of power employed several tools to enshrine scientists by denigrating their competition.

Chief among these was a two-pronged drive for official licensing. First officially established in New Spain in 1527, the Real Tribunal del Protomedicato's board of three physicians replaced more whimsical city council efforts to examine and license druggists, physicians, surgeons, and bleeders only after 1646.[2] But from that year forward, a Protomedicato license was required to ply one's medical trade publicly. To receive a license, physicians completed all requirements for the bachelor's degree, which included Latin, in addition to four years of medical study beyond the degree at the Real y Pontifica Universidad de México, served a two-year apprenticeship under a licensed physician, and passed a Protomedicato exam. Romance surgeons, so called because of their complete lack of university-level Latin, underwent a five-year hands-on apprenticeship in a hospital or with a licensed practitioner before taking the exam. All candidates for Protomedicato certification had to provide proof of *limpieza de sangre*, pure Christian lineage, and a baptismal certificate testifying to the bearer's legitimacy.[3]

In addition to licensing medical practitioners who met the requirements, the Protomedicato also policed their competition. Although the undocumented curers' contretemps with the licensing board punctuate the entire colonial period, the eighteenth century witnessed redoubled efforts to firmly delineate the officially sanctioned from the quacks. A flurry of legislation increased the institution's prosecutorial powers over the unlicensed and assigned steeper fines to the undocumented.[4]

Although the state initially encouraged the Protomedicato's licensing campaigns, as part of its larger late eighteenth-century campaign to centralize prosecutorial powers scattered among a welter of corporate entities, it also displayed a keen interest in exerting its own control over medical impostors. A 1795 edict declared that the Protomedicato would continue to license drugstores, but the Audiencia (High Court) now prosecuted those who operated without the proper approvals.[5] Edicts issued in 1798 and 1805 broke with the Protomedicato and Inquisition monopoly to allow all subjects to initiate malpractice proceedings against the unlicensed, and an 1800 law declared that "the King's tribunals"—in this case, the Audiencia— could hear complaints against curanderos (folk healers).[6] Thus, enlightened bureaucrats encouraged men of science to rise on the officially rebuked backs of the undocumented.

Women constituted a special case, as reformers vacillated on whether to bolster midwives' status through licensing or to ban women from the profession entirely. In a 1742 treatise, Spain's influential enlightenment thinker Benito Jerónimo Feijóo y Montenegro (1676–1764) termed women "ignorant of the art" of obstetrics but argued against their total exclusion from midwifery, calling instead for mandatory scientific training for *parteras* (midwives).[7] In New Spain, however, the Bourbons failed to implement a formal educational system for midwives, and obstetrics was taught for the first time in 1768 in the School of Surgery and in 1770 in the Royal Indian Hospital, neither of which admitted female students.[8] The 1793 Mexico City cabildo declared that those who held in their hands "the most precious and delicate of nature's works" required superior moral, scientific, and political accomplishment. Parteras lacked these attributes; they were "lower-class people, without education or polish, even without religion." Dr. Diego Moreno y Peña agreed to instruct these crass *comadres* (fictive kin), but not without Protomedicato approval, which was not forthcoming.[9] To avoid "the harm to humanity" caused by women's ignorance, in 1821 Mexico City's cabildo again considered offering instruction to midwives, but was thwarted by a dearth of funds.[10] So, although women were not banned from midwifery, the enlightened determined that women would not participate in medical practitioners' social ascension; indeed, their exclusion itself reinforced the status of licensed male practitioners.

The Protomedicato's long history of licensing medical practitioners and the state's bolstered prosecutorial powers over the undocumented helped widen the status gap between licensed practitioners and folk healers, but newspapers, a novelty in the New Spain of the late eighteenth century, provided an unparalleled tool for popularizing this distinction. A number of short-lived weeklies dedicated to science, among them *Asuntos varios sobre ciencia y artes* (1772–1773), *Observaciones sobre la física, historia y artes útiles* (1787–1788), and *Mercurio Volante* (1772–1773), as well as the longer-running and more eclectic *Gazeta de México* and *Diario de México*, touted the merits of scientific investigation to Mexico City's highly literate populace.[11] In his inaugural issue, *Mercurio Volante* editor and doctor José Ignacio Bartolache unabashedly championed medicine's rising status and praised the state's reform efforts: "We know that the court has begun to provide an example . . . by reforming studies according to modern ideas of utility and the good of the state. So we have undertaken to communicate to the public in our vulgar Spanish new and curious discoveries. Medicine is not a divinatory or conjectural art, nor is it a frivolous and imperfect discipline, but a science."[12]

The newspapers spelled out and carefully guarded the more rigid boundary between legitimate and illegitimate medical practices, ridiculing midwives and curanderos while lauding the erudition of licensed practitioners. *Mercurio Volante* excoriated midwives—who tended to be Indians, mulattas, and mestizas—as "ridiculously superstitious," and warned readers that "until these comadres learn the art of birthing, which in our time has been written about and perfected by very able men, they should only be counted upon to receive and bathe the child."[13] In a similar attack, a bereaved husband writing under the pseudonym "The Widower" lamented that he had summoned a midwife and not a surgeon for his wife and cursed these "barbarous women," wondering why a culture with "apprenticeships, exams, prizes, and inspectors" for barbers, shoemakers, and tailors would not take similar precautions for "as delicate an act as helping women give birth."[14] The new newspapers drilled the literate on the new distinctions between enlightenment and superstition, the licensed and quacks, reason and irrationality.

Against this backdrop of the Empire-wide rise in medicine's authority, our familiar cabal of enlightened veracruzanos enthusiastically adopted the twin techniques of stricter regulation of science's preserve and vilification of the—often female—interlopers. Leading the Veracruz campaign was cemetery advocate and cabildo member Antonio María Fernández, who in 1789 lamented that pregnant women frequented the city's unlicensed cirujanos (surgeons) or a ragged gaggle of women, who, "in addition to being ignorant, counted among their ranks the old and decrepit and a notorious drunk." Furthermore, he alleged, a kaleidoscopic variety of quacks competed for patients, and even the few Protomedicato-approved practitioners had not registered their titles with the city council.[15]

Sharing Fernández's sentiments but perhaps not his zeal, in 1791 the aldermen finally lumbered into action, ordering all doctors and surgeons to present their official titles for cabildo and Protomedicato approval. The measure succeeded, in part because the official healers seized the opportunity to eliminate their competitors. Surgeons Francisco Hernández and Jacinto Gómez bragged that they routinely spent their off-hours engaged in public service activities, such as attending the numerous prisoners languishing in the city's fetid prisons. The undocumented, in contrast, merely fleeced the public, and their threat could be contained only if apothecaries honored only prescriptions signed by licensed healers. The cabildo agreed with the two surgeons, and sent each of the city's medicine sellers a list of approved practitioners and a warning that a Protomedicato official would slap them with a 100-peso fine for filling any unlicensed curer's requests. At least one apothecary found this measure surprising, candidly asserting that he had always sold to anyone willing to foot the bill. Officials so stringently enforced the measure that when ship's surgeon Roberto Claboro ordered medicines from a Veracruz apothecary, the Protomedicato sent for his papers, and the aldermen dutifully added his name to their list of sanctioned healers.[16]

Apothecaries and their competitors in Veracruz also received city council and Protomedicato attention at the turn of the century. To supplement his meager fees, Dr. Mateo Alvarez concocted and puffed his own remedies. This practice provoked an official investigation by Protomedicato representative José de Avila and the city council, who insisted his patients buy only from the officially approved apothecaries. In 1802, Royal Navy surgeon Estevan Pérez Ximenes returned to a wealthy widow's home to visit an Indian patient whose condition had deteriorated after taking his prescribed medication. Pérez Ximenes noted that the medicine reeked of alcohol and immediately reported the apothecary to the Veracruz City Council, who forwarded an elaborate report to the viceroy and the Protomedicato.[17]

The enlightened thus variously attempted to pry apart the intimate bond between parteras and curanderos like Madre Chepa and her often well-off clients and replace these "impostors" with licensed medical practitioners who employed rational scientific methods, not magic or "superstition." The sensatos fostered doctors' power by discrediting alternative knowledge, thereby cultivating cultural authorities who could be invoked in the campaign against church burial privileges as well as against the poor's slovenly habits. A veritable war had been declared against healers like Madre Chepa and Juan Luis.

But, ominously for the incipient "authorities" being birthed in this process, the enlightened could not corner the market on medical expertise. Indeed, the Veracruz cabildo's efforts to starve out curanderos by cutting off their supplies failed, in part because there were too few doctors to care for the city's expanding population, and in part because most residents continued to vest their trust in the alternative healers. The city council identified an urgent need for more doctors and surgeons in 1798, reporting only seven in the city, and confessing that their efforts to entice practitioners had failed because many feared the city's unhealthy conditions. In 1802, merchant Juan Antonio Ruíz de Albarado lamented that most veracruzanos bypassed the city's doctors to seek relief from "a *negra* or *mulatta* who touted herself as a healer."[18] As we shall see, this trend continued to belie the rising empiricism's claims to hegemony into the national period.

"The Body Is Nature's Truest Book":
The Revolution in Medical Epistemology

As official channels for documentation grew increasingly rigid and extended themselves further into the hinterlands of medical practice, an equally significant shift was underway within the ranks of the sanctioned practitioners. Reformers attacked the traditional bases for physicians' claims to status and social authority: knowledge of Latin, limpieza de sangre, legitimate birth, familiarity with ancient wisdom—all of these paled in importance in comparison with the individual guided by his senses and animated by natural reason. The result was the "surgicalization" of medicine, as more educational emphasis fell on dissections and the clinical practice formerly the exclusive provenance of the lowly surgeon.

Until the eighteenth century, surgery dedicated itself almost exclusively to visible, external ailments and conferred scant prestige on its practitioners; the profession's hands-on approach to wens, gangrene, and syphilitic chancres did little for its image in a society that denigrated manual labor generally. Bloodletting, trussing ruptures, and lancing boils: these were mere practical skills mastered through physical experience, skills far removed from the physician's knowledge of time-worn authorities gained from a university education in Latin.

But the eighteenth century saw the gradual replacement of this unsavory manual association and second-class status with a new epistemology, promoted by the reformers and privileging the empiricism of clinical medicine. Throughout the 1700s, surgeons extended their observations to the body's interior, both through the dissection of corpses and improved surgical techniques. Fueled by the pressure of clinical practitioners themselves, and cosseted by enlightened state officials, surgeons' status equaled that of doctors by 1825.[19]

Throughout the Empire, signs of surgery's newfound respectability were legion. Royal Colleges of Surgery sprang up in Cadiz (1748), Barcelona (1760), and Madrid (1787).[20] In 1798 the state approved a charitable Monte de Piedad for Mexico City's licensed surgeons to provide widows' pensions and money for burials and illnesses.[21] In Guatemala, enlightened medical reformers' agitation for more surgical instruction culminated in the 1804 establishment of the Royal College of Surgery at the General Hospital in Guatemala City, although scant funds stymied its more ambitious projects.[22] Stressing anatomy, practical theory, and physiology, and using modern texts such as the 1751 *Anatomía descriptiva*, New Spain's Royal College of Surgery opened its doors in the Royal Indian Hospital in 1769.[23] The College jealously policed the distinctions between its graduates and the undocumented, and banished its students from barber shops, where, "far from receiving useful instruction they would acquire vices incompatible with the institution's decorum."[24]

The head of the new Mexico City Royal College of Surgery, Andres Montaner i Virgili, a graduate of Cadiz's new surgery school, immediately sought to reform the Protomedicato's educational priorities, persuading the viceroy in 1770 to require all medical candidates to first complete four anatomy courses at the Royal Indian Hospital to qualify for Protomedicato certification.[25] The surgeons kept a close watch on the Protomedicato to ensure compliance with the measure. In 1783, Montaner's colleague, Dr. Manuel Moreno—a dissector, the former rector at Cadiz, and a member along with *Mercurio Volante* editor Bartolache in Mexico City's Economic Society of the Friends of the Country—complained to Viceroy Mayorga that the Protomedicato had approved a doctor's credentials without confirming his completion of the required anatomy courses.[26] Reformers' adamancy about the prominent place of surgery in medical education echoed that of their Guatemalan counterparts: without knowledge of anatomy, surgery, and botany, "no one can call himself a physician."[27] Infiltrating the Protomedicato with Charles III's permission, the new Royal Botanical Garden's enlightened directors reported in 1788 that "charlatans and folk healers infest the kingdom, among them many whom the Protomedicato has furtively licensed without Royal College of Surgery certification."[28] In this rendering, curanderos and scholarly physicians were equally eligible for charlatan status by dint of their mutual ignorance of the latest surgical and clinical medicine. The battleground had clearly shifted.

The College of Surgery's unease with the Protomedicato continued into the nineteenth century, permutating into a bid for autonomy from the institution.[29] In 1804, Director Antonio Serrano reminded Viceroy José de Iturrigaray that a 1798 royal edict gave the Royal College of Surgery, not the Protomedicato, the right to license surgeons, bleeders, dentists, and midwives. Furthermore, delegates should be dispatched to the provinces, which were infested with "a plague of those destroyers of humanity, curanderos," while even in the capital "ignorant and unprincipled women acted as midwives, their knowledge gleaned from a mother, sister, or other relative." The venerable institution responded that it already had provincial delegates to police the unlicensed. Indeed, a 1741 royal edict had extended the Protomedicato's jurisdiction into the provinces.[30]

Even though "modern" authors joined Galen and Hippocrates in the university's curriculum sometime before 1824, reformers in the new educational institutions regarded their battles with the Protomedicato and with the university's educational priorities as pitting modern medicine based on experiment and observation against outdated reverence for old authorities preserved in Latin. The Royal College of Surgery was certainly not alone in criticizing the university and in promoting anatomy, pathology, experimental botany, and the new clinical medicine. At the turn of the century, medical education increasingly reflected reformers' priorities: now all candidates for official certification required the four anatomy courses given by the college of surgery, and, after 1788, a certificate of completion of a course at the Royal Botanical Gardens.[31] In addition, the Royal San Andrés Hospital added a University Chair in Practical Medicine in 1806, and King Charles IV declared it an obligatory subject for all doctors in 1808.[32] The first to hold the coveted position in practical medicine, Dr. Luis José Montaña (1755–1820), who had imbibed Boerhaave under Bartaloche's guidance, rejected verbal pedagogy in Latin for "clinical practice in hospitals, where the eyes more than any of the other senses arrive at the essential truth that is obscured to the ears alone."[33] Although often tagged by reformers as a bastion of moldy tradition, the university, too, bore the reformers' imprint, as Boerhaave's works joined commentaries on Hippocrates in the required curriculum by 1824.[34]

Reformers outside the new educational institutes also weighed in on the new medicine's advantages. In 1821, the Mexico City Council's ever more active Junta Municipal de Sanidad (Sanitation Committee) joined the battle against entrenched authority, declaring war against those "who believe themselves in possession of infallible secrets to cure every sickness, who rely upon ancient rather than modern authors to facilitate their search for rigid doctrines, not truths . . . who lack any knowledge of physiology or anatomy." The innocent but ingenuous public should be protected from these misguided traditionalists, and the Junta ordered the Protomedicato to produce an annual list of approved practitioners—those who had completed the required anatomy courses—for the city council to post in all pharmacies.[35]

The enlightened also used the expanded press and political pamphle-teering to aid the new medical practitioners' break with received wisdom and bid for respectability. As an anonymous *Mercurio Volante* contributor asserted, "Anatomy has taught us that the Ancients had conjectured, and conjectured without cause, the existence of the four humors." It was now clear, he continued, that "physical knowledge of the object of study" was indispensable to the art of curing, "and could only be obtained by dissect-ing cadavers, which is and always has been nature's truest book."[36] Here the anonymous contributor echoed a sentiment frequently expressed by cemetery proponents. To cite just one example, Dr. Tomás Romay, the Havana surgeon we last heard promoting suburban burials, broke with time-honored knowledge to advocate direct personal observation, assert-ing that "the man on his sick bed or the cadaver on the anatomist's table, these books written by nature's own hand, should be the objects of our study and meditation . . . for in this way we can separate the useful truths gleaned by observation and experience from arbitrary hypothesis," and thereby "extract only doctrines in conformity with rigid reason."[37]

"Arbitrary hypotheses" continued to hold sway, however, an anonymous pamphleteer reported in 1820, because the scientific press and the sur-geons, botanists, and clinical physicians outside the university wielded insufficient influence over university medical education, leaving its gradu-ates woefully bereft of clinical instruction. True replicas of the "hero of la Mancha tilting against windmills" and guilty of "servile imitation" of their teachers' stale formulas, these benighted medical men merely applied their pompous wisdom to "illnesses that existed only in their imagination." The author praised Luis Montaña's pedagogical priority of keen observation of natural laws, but felt his focus was an exception among educators. Ani-mated by their "amor propio," he feared, most doctors derived their smug satisfaction of their own merits from flipping a few pages of modern authors, never availing themselves of the wisdom of the natural sciences of chemistry, anatomy, or botany. The result: these misguided folks authored "superstitious miracles" and "chimeras" and were easily confused with the "fanatical midwife" and the "despicable curandero." Noting that he was imbued with the compassion inspired by Saint Augustine, not the vile amor propio, the author hoped his criticisms of medical education would enlighten medical practice.[38]

Although the Protomedicato led the battle to clearly distinguish "scientific knowledge" from "superstition," the enlightened nevertheless inveighed against its outdated mode of arriving at Truth, its slavish devotion to time-worn authority over what one "actually sees." While enlightened state officials regularly invoked medicine's authority in the cemetery campaign, they simultaneously used the state to abet the more modern practitioners in their battle against the Protomedicato's and the universities' entrenched authority. To this end they sponsored medical reforms that stressed recourse to universal reason and empirical observation (sight) as their preferred epistemology. The reformers challenged—but did not topple—official adhesion to the memorization of classical platitudes, particularly the ancient works of Hippocrates, Galen, and the Persian doctor Avicena, all of whose authority derived ultimately from medieval and Renaissance scholars' commentaries. As we shall see, reformers found this latter issue particularly troubling in light of their religious convictions.

The reformers' efforts did not go entirely unrewarded, however. Declaring the Protomedicato indifferent to clinical medicine's advantages and an annoying vestige of the corporate society so anathema to reformers, as early as 1771 Crown advisor and procemetery paladin the Count of Campomanes recommended that the Council of Castile curb the institution's powers.[39] Protomedicato-licensed physicians understood disease as emanating from the inner workings of the body. The ancient theory of the four humors stressed that imbalances in body fluids underlay the temperamental variations that caused all diseases.[40] These humoral imbalances were invisible to the eye, and thus medical knowledge was hypothetical-deductive; discolored urine, for example, indicated such an imbalance, but this imbalance was too minute to be seen and thus examination of the body, dead or alive, was unnecessary. Physical examinations or postmortem dissections, the pathological anatomy so beloved of reformers, had no medical justification in deductive medicine. Thus, in attacking the Protomedicato, reformers like Campomanes sought not to reduce medicine's cultural authority, but to promote the truth claims of empirical medicine. When Spain's University of Alcalá dodged medical reforms in education that centered on Boerhaave's clinical medicine (see below) and claimed that the proposed changes would "render obscure the true merit of ancient authorities," Campomanes frankly declared the university's traditional education responsible for perpetuating "prejudice, sophism, and superficiality in place of science and truth."[41]

Latin, of course, was the language of those odious "sophistries" taught in the universities and a pompous, unnecessary barrier to the exercise of reason. Tagged as an obstacle to individual reflection on doctrine, Latin became the target of both medical and spiritual reformers, who often were one and the same. Recall that spiritual reformers led the campaign that culminated in the publication of a vernacular Spanish Bible. Like priests, doctors who read the sacred script were literally mediating between heaven and earth, sacred and profane. Latin suffused its adepts with divine sanctification; it was not an arbitrarily created representation of God's truth, but an emanation of that truth. But if God—or reason—illuminated man from inside, why employ a rarefied sacred script comprehensible to a small reef of specialists floating on a huge vernacular ocean? Why rely on special mediators between man and God, or between man and natural reason?

The new newspapers' dissemination of scientific information in the vernacular was echoed in calls to end the custom of writing medical prescriptions in the sacred script. Urging the Mexico City Council to "exterminate the barbarous residue of the dark centuries," an anonymous 1820 letter to the editor in the *Noticioso General* asked why doctors should use Latin, when "nothing less than men's lives are at stake . . . and public health requires that medical prescriptions be written in the common language." Hemmed in by legislative precedent, the aldermen reluctantly defended the practice, citing a series of laws that demanded Latin prescriptions.[42] José Fernández de Lizardi, whom we last heard spoofing theatrical religion, also found pompous medical practitioners an enjoyable satirical target: "The simple truth is that this [practice of writing Latin prescriptions] is a practice canonized by the Ancients and without any rational foundation; only doctors and pharmacists interested in exaggerating their importance to sell us the most trivial nonsense engage in it."[43] Manuel Eulogio Carpio (1791–1860), who later became medical reformer Luis José Montaña's star student and a celebrated poet, similarly attacked traditional medical authorities and their Latin-sanctified wisdom, translating Hippocrates into Spanish and arguing that, although Latin enhanced Virgil and Cicero, its use in university teaching was "ridiculous and quixotic pedantry, intolerable, fastidious, and repugnant."[44]

Mexico City's medical reformers were not unique, and their seemingly hyperbolic attack on Latin appears moderate, even tactful, when placed next to the vitriol unleashed by Guatemala's *Gazeta.* This mouthpiece of enlightened medical reformers, many of whom held membership in the country's Economic Society, opined that Latin's exclusiveness suffocated true talent and led to a ridiculous pedantry "bristling with opinions, citations, countercitations, banalities and counterbanalities." Furthermore, the vernacular was everywhere to be preferred because Latin's exclusiveness led only to "moldiness and paralysis."[45] All men could reflect on transparent reason, so why should an ancient language sanctify the speaker's authority or shroud these self-evident truths?

Medical and spiritual reformers' attack on the citadel of Latin, whose defense had been a priority in the Counterreformation's battle with Protestantism, sprang from a shared antagonism toward any mediation between the internally illuminated individual and Truth, whether defined as God's immutable laws "written in each man's breast" or as reason and nature. The illuminated individual's unmediated relationship with the holy text suggested an unmediated relationship with the Book of Creation. Thus, the new piety's popularity made the new medicine's truth claims more plausible. Not surprisingly, reformers throughout the Empire saw no contradiction in championing both.

The relative merits of the unification of the study of surgery and medicine, formerly divided into external and internal jurisdictions, became a touchstone between medical reformers and traditionalists, who believed that the body's inner working remained obscured to the eye. "El Amante de la Humanidad," an anonymous 1820 pamphleteer, felt that surgeons, those "purely technical doctors [operadores]," were now usurping doctors' prerogatives in thrusting themselves into internal medicine. How could a group with only a superficial notion of book-learned humoral medicine justify their expanding jurisdiction? Simple, our author declared: these ridiculous upstarts pointed to their knowledge of medical works written in the Spanish vernacular, and the most audacious even cited what they had learned by observing their patients, whom they tagged "the real books." How absurd! How is it possible that such "barbarous ignoramuses" live among us, he wondered, concluding that surgeons were mere interlopers who should stick to curing external ailments.[46]

But our lover of humanity had missed the epistemological boat, and would be left railing on the shore as Independence dawned. Clinical physicians, surgeons, and their nonmedical allies bent on promoting a healthful, orderly, well-ventilated state had walked off with the prize, and their

monopoly of accepted ways of knowing would only become more completely entrenched within the profession—although not outside of it—as
the nineteenth century progressed. True, the intransigence of the lower
orders repeatedly troubled the new medicine's acolytes, but for the moment they could consider that battle only an incomplete victory, not an
outright defeat.

To Die in the Bosom of Empiricism:
The Epistemic Shift and the Burial Dispute

Even while the medical campaign raged noisily on, the new epistemology
was stealthily winning an equally momentous but undeclared war, one that
centered on burial practices. As the definition of a doctor changed radically
in the eighteenth century, the rhetoric of medicine marched together with
that of enlightened piety among the new cemetery proponents. We shall
follow this expedition and its ultimate implications for modern Mexico in
the coming chapter; for now, we should concentrate on the early era of
diplomatic overlap between the two camps. For the irony of the dispute
rests on its prehistory: empiricism represents not an eruption of the secular into a domain formerly ruled by the sacred, but rather the unforeseen
endpoint of a movement profoundly religious from its inception. The
clerical proponents of the new piety gave birth to the new epistemology,
only to suffer mortally at the hands of their ungrateful heir.

   Crucial to an understanding of this genealogy is recognition of the early
rhetoric of burial. The initial disputes were carried out in two idioms, one
religious, the other more prosaically concerned with sanitation. The combatants themselves clearly saw no contradiction between their twin concerns, and the new medicine's connection to reform piety is assumed. To
listen in on the early days of this bilingual rhetoric, we must return to
Spain, for although reform clerics had proceeded with cemetery construction in Mexico City, Barcelona, and Grenada prior to the well-publicized
1781 epidemic that ravaged the Basque town of Paisages, it was this disaster that provoked the first concerted mobilization against church burials in
the Spanish Empire.

   An emergency meeting of San Sebastian's Junta de Sanidad dispatched
its scientists to determine the epidemic's origins in consultation with local
medical authorities. The Junta's final report concluded that most residents

blamed the church's numerous rotting corpses for the "putrid inflamma-
tory fever," which tormented the sick with headaches, delirium, fever, dry
tongue, and inflamed viscera. Pamplona's archbishop disagreed: the epidemic could just as easily have been brought to Paisages by sailors and by
the stench produced by epidemic victims' unburied bodies, he proposed.[47]
Regardless, the rhetorical point is clear: even a man of God and an opponent of cemeteries did not bother to attribute the scourge to Divine will.
The new scientific form of knowledge offered a field of evidence that both
the cemeteries' proponents and their enemies considered legitimate; disputes in this realm focused not on the relevance of medical testimony but
on its interpretation.

Haunted by the new specter of noxious miasma exuding from rotting
bodies, feces, and refuse, mid-eighteenth-century European burial reformers defined the dead as a threat to the living. As French doctor
Guillume-Lambert Godart's 1767 *Septicologie* succinctly put it, "Air is our
element . . . we contract mortal illness when the air in which we live is
corrupted or filled with putrid miasma," a fact not lost on the enterprising
Felice Fontana (1730–1805), the celebrated Italian anatomist who toured
Europe in 1775 with his "eudiometer," his new invention that purported to
measure the corruption of the air.[48]

The fear of the air that gripped late eighteenth-century commentators
challenged the theological theories of illness prevalent in earlier centuries
and sparked numerous scientific inquiries into the sources of the befouled
environment.[49] At the heart of these investigations stood the "mephitis,"
which one Spanish military doctor arrestingly described as a "place or
object which emits a vapor imperceptible to the eyes, but so lethal that
whoever inhales it, dies within several seconds." Composed of "a volatile
alkali," these gases insinuated themselves not only through the mouth, but
also through the victim's entire superficies. Church congregants risked the
greatest danger of fainting spells, nervous contractions, and nausea, some
believed, because human corpses emitted stronger vapors than did other
decaying matter, and because "in temples the holy spirit enters the body . . .
activating all of the internal powers of the soul . . . so that corporal forces
relax and the body becomes more vulnerable to dangerous air."[50] The most
dogmatic believed that the deadly stench escaped even the most tightly
sealed tombs when activated by the heat generated by the conglomeration
of celebrants—an especially dangerous occurrence, as this same heat

"opened congregants' pores, facilitating the absorption of the deadly venom, the origin of so much evil."[51] Thus, reformers defined churches less as centers of spiritual succor than as corpse-infested threats to bodily health.

Bandied about in Europe and in the reports submitted to the Council of Castile were countless warnings of the death and discomfort wrought by temple burials. Religious dignitaries were not immune to the stench in the early 1780s: during one of his routine pastoral visits, the Archbishop of Cartagena noted that prelates had abandoned the cathedral to hold divine services in the fresher environment of a nearby chapel, and the Bishop of Orihuela lamented that dank, malodorous temples frightened the faithful and stripped the sheen off lamps and gilded altarpieces. A member of the cathedral chapter in Antequera complained that persons of distinction donned special clothes for their obligatory annual parish visit and then discarded them to contain the contamination. Equally troubling, many regular attendees refused the holy water, which came from a well in the church floor. Tortosa's reform bishop related that two-thirds of his flock came to rest in a stench-ridden vault belonging to a popular confraternity. The necessarily frequent openings of the tomb forced the faithful to evacuate the church, and one unfortunate had suffocated before he could escape on one such occasion. The most hyperbolic quip, however, belonged to the Bishop of Zeuta, who blamed "the superstitious" for transforming "buildings destined for the worship of God into fetid theaters of corrupt cadavers." This view was shared by Spain's expanding group of enlightened citizens, according to the Archbishop of Seville, who termed procemetery sentiment a "public belief of all refined, intelligent men."[52]

Spurred into action by their belief in rancid air's hideous effects, burial crusaders judged the dead by medicoscientific criteria, and doctors wielded ever greater authority in interment decisions. In a tour de force of pan-European erudition, the Royal Academy of History's well-documented 1781 published treatise demonstrated a familiarity with the pioneers of clinical medicine based on observation, citing the works of Benito Bails, Boerhaave, Van Swieten, Sauvages, Hoffmann, Verheyen, Ramazini Sánchez Riveyro, Pringle, Joseph Haberman, Tissor, Mead, Vicq d'Azyr, and the medical institutes of Vienna and Paris. Indeed, so important had scientific testimony become that despite the Council of Castile's specific instructions to outline canon law on burials, the 1783 Spanish Royal Academy of

History report contained obsessive excurses into the contaminating presence of cadavers, and repeated that "physicists, doctors, and observers" offered conclusive proof of the health threats posed by church burial.[53] In Spain as in France, doctors' testimony joined pious concern in the campaigns to establish general cemeteries.

In this early period, however, scientific rhetoric gladly shared the stage with the pious concerns of enlightened Catholicism, as we have seen, and bilingual dexterity in these early disputes was not confined to the representatives of the secular Church. If the lay gente sensata of the previous chapter could enact moral transformations in Veracruz, they could also turn their zeal for social meliorism to public health. Those most fluent in the new piety also invariably spoke the language of science and hygiene. Not one to engage in elaborate metaphors and allegories, Viceroy Revillagigedo, last heard proclaiming the new piety, brandished health concerns as a weapon against pernicious social display: "[Church] patrons and others—no matter how distinguished—are not worthy of the abusive custom of church burial, which produces bad humors due to the lack of ventilation." One Veracruz City Council and Junta de Policía member adroitly blended the imperatives of piety and health, stating that he preferred "the general good of an entire people and the health of the most miserable beggar to the pompous and distinguished burials of a few . . . because marking social distinctions only leads to bad consequences." Veracruz Lieutenant Colonel Pedro Laguna confidently stated that together, the maxims of "true religion" and the exigencies of public health overrode even the most distinguished person's burial privileges.[54]

Furthermore, threats to health could spawn threats to the soul, for the dangerous conditions in parish churches dissuaded even the faithful from attending divine services. Don Matias de Lacunra stopped attending Mass entirely; one member of the Junta de Policía often left the church before the consecration of the Host due to the odor, as the soil contained "not only earth, not only fragments, but whole limbs and other body parts with the meat still attached to them."[55] This unpleasant smell, it was asserted, prevented many from appearing at funerals as well. Fortunately, the witnesses concurred, the cemetery, along with the city's new paved streets, had lessened disease in Veracruz.

At the core of this comfortable connivance between the two idioms lay the new piety's and the new medicine's joint starting point: the disciplined individual. Reform medicine and reform piety shared hostility to scholastic method and to rote reverence for the Ancients, advocating instead individual observation and reflection motivated by God in the case of the new piety, and by natural reason, in the case of the new medicine. Recall Haro y Peralta's claim that the sights of the world could distract the pious, but the truly godly could resist these worldly temptations. It is in this context that the carefully disciplined sensate experience that stemmed from scientific reasoning seemed so logical to the enlightened.

This is not to suggest that either school of thought rejected all received wisdom in favor of individual apprehension; certainly, some ancient authorities could be salvaged from the subsequent errors of the centuries. One such reclamation involved the Greek "father of medicine," Hippocrates (c. 460–377 B.C.). Herman Boerhaave (1669–1738), Europe's most influential proponent of clinical medicine and the Dutch doctor cited in the Academy of History's cemetery report, advocated return to the pristine purity of a Hippocrates liberated from the metaphysical accretions of the centuries. Echoing the paeans to the early Church emanating from proponents of "true piety," Boerhaave stressed that original pure doctrines had been perverted by subsequent sects; the task was to cut through the marginalia and return to the source of truth. The illuminated individual should have no need of superfluous commentators. But Boerhaave's Hippocrates, like the Augustine of the religious reformers, bore the marks of contemporary preoccupations: the good doctor stressed Hippocrates as the inspiration for his belief that the only person who could avoid uncertainties was "he who merely learns, accepts, and relates what he actually sees."[56] Even in referring to prior authority, then, the individualist modes of thought required fealty to empiricism; I explore this imperative further in the next chapter.

As late as the 1780s, then, enlightened burial discourse was equally laced with theological and public health justifications, but of a specific and related type. Both sets of justifications implicitly enshrined the rational individual and his unmediated relation to truth. Neither spiritual specialists nor their medical counterparts felt compelled to restrict their arguments to only one strain of reasoning, for the enlightened themselves saw no contradiction between spiritual concerns and an increased interest in physical well-being. Far from being the enemy of piety, rationality was for them its very soul.

Conclusion

The background considered here—a changing medical environment that enlisted the state to uphold one class of healers and that favored the empirical over the received wisdom, a "bilingual" rhetoric of sacred and secular concerns from speakers who did not distinguish between the two—leads us to the final but hollow triumph of the epistemology spawned by the new piety. In the next chapter we will take up the question of how a Christian manner of seeing the world that promoted the individual as the primary unit of faith shed its clerical progenitors in birthing a society that embraced the individual but left the Church hierarchy—at least in its official policies toward burials.

chapter 8

The Heir Apparent

In New Spain, the scientific method that accompanied the new piety grew up to rebel in ways the enlightened clergy could never have anticipated. Indeed, as we saw with Lizardi and Mora, zealous cemetery proponents like Laso de la Vega and Biempico y Sotomayor had unwittingly laid the groundwork for their own diminution as the supreme cultural authority on burials by promoting an individualist theology that downplayed the importance of priestly intercessors and authority in favor of individual self-examination and the imperatives of conscience.

Every Man His Own Physician: The Road Not Taken

The fundamental achievement of the medical revolution we saw in the previous chapter was to establish a new realm of authority: sensate experience carefully moderated by scientific reason. But the new medical professionals' claims to superior knowledge would seem to contradict their philosophy of individual judgment. Why rely on a licensed medical—or any other—authority when one could examine the evidence and make up one's own mind? Although the enlightened used the press to advance modern medicine's authority, the medium also provided a forum for rational individual opinions. The *Diario de México*, for example, provided "The Friend of Mankind" (El Amigo de los Hombres) with a forum to harangue a pharmacist for selling him an overpriced oil that induced severe intestinal pain. The Protomedicato eventually exonerated the accused, but the anonymous contributor wrote back to the paper to challenge the institution's exclusive jurisdiction over the case: "The people's interests are distinct and superior to yours [the Protomedicato's] and to those of any particular person or corporation. . . . And, as the great monarch Tetzcucano Nezahualcoyotl said, a vassal's life is the state's most important concern . . . therefore, that I noticed the abuse is enough justification for me—or any other citizen—to bring the matter before the tribunal of the public."[1]

The Friend of Humanity felt that all citizens in the "public tribunal" could and should pronounce judgment on the errant pharmacist. That medical authority was an affront to equality and reason had been the conclusion of the most radical elements of the French Revolution, who abolished all medical distinctions and educational requirements during the fevered 1789–1794 period and licensed virtually anyone willing to pay a small fee.[2] The anonymous Mexican critic's remarks demonstrate his considerable faith in the people's right to decide for themselves, and little reverence for received wisdom or the expertise of those with official medical knowledge.

If medical reason was self-evident and all could wield it to judge medical matters for themselves, then all men were capable of ordering their own lives according to its precepts. New Spain's scientific journals and newspapers encouraged this sense of individual responsibility by promoting the idea of the body as an object of self-management, an entity that required constant and self-conscious attention to maintain health. Authors believed readers informed by reason were capable of regulating and caring for their own bodies, of subverting the capricious passions and seizing control of their own mortality. As Bartolache informed the *Mercurio Volante*'s literate, elite readers: "If every man lived an orderly and parsimonious existence, there would be so few sick . . . and each man would be his own doctor. No man could hope to have a better doctor than himself nor a more efficacious preservative than a good regimen: all should heed my example and seriously apply themselves to analyzing and ordering their life according to the precepts of reason."[3]

The flip side to this philosophy was that those who shunned the enlightened advice, those who failed to clean and care for their bodies, brought sickness upon themselves—a significant departure from the belief that religious sins provoked divine wrath, which could be borne by wind, water, miasma, and vapors.[4] Just as Veracruz sensatos and Mexico City intellectuals blamed the poor for their own poverty, the sick were now bringing illness upon themselves and thereby endangering upright citizens as well. For some reformers, individual hygiene represented the ultimate etiology of illness, a view that promoted a self-reflexive attitude toward one's own individual body. Cleanliness, indeed, was next to Godliness.

Medical advice printed in the newspapers left no detail to chance; the *Gazetas de México* even offered instruction on the proper care of the teeth.[5] The unreasonable—those who ignored the proffered information—

received little sympathy. Faced with a horrible plague, the 1786 Mexico City Council showed no patience for the medically recalcitrant, blaming the epidemic on the poor's culinary vices, nudity, and recourse to popular medicines prescribed by curanderos. Doctors and cures were readily available; what was lacking were sick people who "truly desired to cure themselves." Although miasma played a role, the poor died "more because of their disorder than from the violence and activity of the bad air." The cabildo despaired of changing a situation in which, "unfortunately, people do not take charge of their own health."[6] The intractable poor haunted reformers' imaginations, bringing sickness upon themselves through their immoderate personal habits—their sinful behavior—and thus endangering everyone's lives. In 1813, the *Diario de México* advised against relocating purveyors of funeral paraphernalia, which they believed provoked epidemics, to the city's outlying impoverished neighborhoods because "the scant cleanliness" of the inhabitants predisposed them to disease. And in response to the 1821 fever epidemic, Dr. Joaquín Guerra recommended that the city council enforce "a practical preservative plan that can be followed by every individual," a plan that advocated personal hygiene, clean clothing, and moderation in food and drink.[7] Reform rhetoric loudly promoted individual responsibility for the body and thus a heightened awareness of the ideal self as a distinct, self-controlled, entity.

This new emphasis on self-control, moderation, and methodical attention to personal health can be understood only in the larger context of the new piety's stress on individual moral transformation guided by God's light to the soul. Recall religious reformers' distrust of sacramental reprieves, of easy absolution for sin, which they believed discouraged the more systematic examination of conscience that led to real moral transformation. The planned and methodical attention to personal hygiene advocated by reformers bore a striking resemblance to the scrutiny of personal sin insisted on by religious reformers. Good works, after all, had little effect on salvation if not properly motivated by God's light. In both cases, the restrained individual's salvation, whether physical or spiritual, depended on adherence to reason. Self-discipline and probity were the highest of virtues, and these virtues could be displayed through studied self-cultivation and restraint, including attention to the body. As we have seen in the writings of Mora and Lizardi, as well as the moderate Veracruz gente sensata, this individual self-cultivation became an increasingly important status index as corporate identification lost its salience. In his advice to artisans, the enlightened Count of Campomanes noted that despite their respectable occupation, their filth rendered them indistinguishable from beggars and vagrants; to make their membership in the community of the enlightened clear, he recommended clean clothes, well-groomed hair, and daily baths.[8]

As radicals encouraged social leveling through the dismantling of hereditary privileges, they simultaneously established new markers of social distinction: in the new newspapers the elite read about themselves as a group defined in opposition to the slovenly, and learned the behaviors that gave them mastery over their own, now individual, body. Self-cultivation, like Veracruz merchants' capital or doctors' "scientific" training, was acquired; here we see a society where expertise, self-control, and merit are edging out birth and corporate privilege as critical markers of social distinction—at least among the self-defined enlightened.

The belief in individual responsibility for mortality provided yet another motivation for their cemetery advocacy: it made death a personal failing rather than the critical moment for community action to ensure immortality. In a similar vein, the new piety's stress on individual moral transformation guided by an interior God made the community's role in salvation less imperative. The campaign to exile the dead from the living, to place them in general cemeteries outside of town, can be understood only in the context of this heightened sense of individual responsibility for health and the attendant conception of death as worldly failure.

A philosophy of individual responsibility for health, however, would seem to militate against the rise of licensed doctors' cultural authority over decisions such as burials. But for the enlightened, the individual was responsible for ordering his life according to the precepts of godly reason, not his own whimsical, irrational inclinations. Demonstrably shirking that responsibility meant forfeiting the privilege of self-determination, as we saw with Mora's attempts to disenfranchise the immoderate. In his 1794 inaugural speech to the enlightened Instituto Asturiano, Crown advisor and prolific author Jovellanos confirmed to his audience that "there being nothing superior to our reason, if we dominate in the natural order of things because of it, we should also rule according to its dictates," an echo of his earlier advice to the King that social engineering be limited to measures "whose utility and possible execution is indicated by reason or confirmed by experience."[9]

But for all of the reformers' claims to the contrary, reason was not a

disembodied, inexorable force marching mankind out of the haze of ancient ignorance and into the light of civilization. As we have seen, the
definition of what constituted reason was forged in social struggle, a
struggle from which some actors predictably emerged with more cultural
clout than others. For enlightened reformers, doctors' testimony became
practically a synonym for reason. Viceroy Revillagigedo battled priests'
fears of diminished revenues and "the general sentiment that provoked
even the most miserable to sell their worldly possessions to ensure their
relatives of church interment," by insisting that new cemeteries be located
according to reason, which he defined as the "dictates of doctors and
surgeons."[10] In an 1813 *Gazetas de México* article attacking *luterías* (stores that
rented funeral paraphernalia) a Cuban doctor thundered that "when public
health is compromised, no obstacle should stand in the way of a politic
informed by the principles of legal medicine." New Spain's hombres sensatos, he reported, found the presence of the dead in temples scandalous
and an offense to public health. In an 1820 report Mexico City Councilman
Casasola championed a new general cemetery constructed according to
"the rules of civil architecture and medical knowledge [*policia medica*]" and
insisted that "no rational man [hombre sensato] likes the prospect of his
dead body infecting the air breathed by the living." A year later, an alderman
recommended building provisional cemeteries west of the capital because
doctors, physicists, and political officials believed the western part of the
city to be less buffeted by winds that could bring miasma into the city. And
to disabuse the public of the widely held notion that Church interment
constituted "proof of having died in the bosom and belief of Catholicism,"
in 1809 Viceroy Beaumont hid behind the cloak of "natural reason" to argue
that the protection of public health demanded suburban cemeteries.[11] As
radicals systematically dismantled the social orders' visually displayed divine mandate, they simultaneously created a new rationale: natural reason,
defined as what promoted physical health, accessible to all reasonable
men, and best interpreted by medical professionals rather than priests,
became an irresistible imperative to action—at least for its advocates.

Animated by this imperative, the enlightened campaigns against burial
customs logically extended beyond cemetery construction. Mortality itself
haunted them, death undaunted in the face of rational social interventions.
Mexico City was to be a tribute to their powers of organization; death had
to be banished, and the comfortable conviviality of the living and deceased
severed. Reformers outlawed rowdy gatherings among the tombs, and a

series of edicts banned refreshment vendors from church cemeteries, even during Holy Week, when sellers jostled for limited space in the streets.[12] Similarly alarmed by death in the capital, in 1812 Intendant Ramón Gutiérrez del Mazo gave the city's luterias four days to relocate their brisk rental business in coffins, shrouds, pillows, beds, and coverings to the suburbs from the city center.[13] An alarmed police superintendent felt this resolution failed the test of justice and reason because the suburb's poor had the same right to health as others and ending the "lugubrious and dirty traffic of the luterias" overrode owners' property rights. The police superintendent felt that the luterias should be permanently closed rather than relocated because "when public health is compromised, no obstacle is too great or cause too small that they do not dictate the use of all of authority's power according to the dictates of legal medicine."[14]

Death had no place in a city increasingly organized according to enlightened notions of public health. And its exaggerated celebration, as diagnosed by enlightened bureaucrats, was particularly irksome to an enlightened class whose power was not evidenced by tacky, irreligious display but by observing, analyzing, and correcting behavior; by scientifically managing the populace; and by prolonging and enhancing physical life through careful moderation in all things. So, although the radical implications of the unmediated individual made a bid for realization in the early nineteenth century, too much was at stake to allow them to triumph. Doctors and their similarly disciplined allies cut off that route and placed themselves firmly in charge of designating "reason"; not surprisingly, reason became synonymous with scientific testimony. Now the task became bringing the undisciplined into line with reasonable dictates, as they had proven themselves reluctant to do so unaided.

Beyond Burials: Taking Empiricism to the Streets

Optimism in every man's ability to improve himself both physically and morally conspired with the oft-quoted belief that the wealth of the kingdom lay in the number and industriousness of its subjects to inspire the enlightened to a new mission: to bring physical and moral salvation to the unreasonable. In this project, they enlisted throughout the Empire two new creatures of the activist, enlightened state: supervisory police power and emboldened municipal health authorities.

Critical to this process was the Empire-wide establishment of neighborhood police and night watchmen, the Alcaldes de Barrio and Guarda Faroles, whom the Veracruz enlightened, as we saw, wielded in their moral reform efforts. Reflecting the enlightened emphasis on observation as a technique of rule, the new police strove to create a Mexico City where objectionable behavior, finding no refuge from the disciplined eyes of power, would wither and die in the light. The dusky interior of the city's numerous taverns particularly irritated reformers, who regarded them as "a cover to commit an infinite number of sins." In 1793, to facilitate *pulquería* (tavern) surveillance and to prevent the "many excesses being committed within," Viceroy Revillagigedo ordered the Alcaldes de Barrio to remove the side walls of all pulquerías as well as the heavy window curtains that adorned the wine taverns; he also insisted that all bars be well lit after 9 P.M. Officials, however, did not limit their scopophilia to the taverns: to break down the barriers that hid the popular classes, the new police systematically destroyed abandoned buildings, placed lanterns in dimly lit alleyways, and removed awnings from porches.[15]

The neighborhood police not only strove to create a more transparent city, they also brought doctors to the less-than-welcoming populous. Whereas a 1585 edict had obliged priests to carry the Host to parishioners in even the most miserable abodes, the eighteenth-century Alcaldes de Barrio ensured that the sick poor, with their "unfounded preoccupations" about medical care, were summarily escorted to a hospital. They also guaranteed that a doctor, surgeon, barber, and midwife resided in every neighborhood and were safely accompanied to the homes of the sick.[16]

In Mexico City, this new health network functioned reasonably well, but not without continuous fine-tuning. Beginning in 1782, the Alcaldes de Barrio did indeed herd the poor into hospitals, instituting a comprehensive sweep of the city during the 1786 plague and scouring neighborhoods for the contagious during a devastating 1797 epidemic.[17] But bringing doctors and midwives to the sick proved fraught with problems. An 1815 viceregal edict threatened to fine doctors who refused to make late-night house calls and lamented the confusion that occurred when masters sent several servants to "the guard, as is customary, to request a doctor, midwife, or confessor," a practice that often resulted in three or four doctors being called out simultaneously. The opposite problem also occurred: after fielding repeated complaints that doctors often were not at home and that messages could not be left for them, in 1819 the last viceroy, Juan Ruíz de

Apodaca, declared a 4-peso fine for doctors' servants who did not keep paper to write the sick person's name and house number, a new possibility in Mexico City, as the Alcaldes de Barrio had numbered each individual home.[18] Finally, in 1821, the Mexico City Council's Junta Municipal de Sanidad initiated an ambitious project to foster prompt and efficient medical attention, posting broadsides with doctors' names and addresses throughout the city and requiring medical personnel to prominently display credentials on their house.[19]

The Alcaldes de Barrio also guarded the increasingly high walls that separated real medical practitioners from the pretenders. When licensed pharmacist Joseph Mariano Pino fell ill in 1794, he discovered the lamentable state of the city's pharmacies and called in the city attorney to advocate his cause. The case eventually landed on Viceroy Revillagigedo's desk, and he ordered the Alcaldes de Barrio, scribes in tow, to check all pharmacy proprietors' credentials. All of this, of course, elicited a storm of protest from the Protomedicato, who convened the pharmacists to review their papers and reiterated that the tribunal denied licenses to undesirables and regularly investigated the city's pharmacies—all of which had the proper permissions.[20]

Empirical zeal, it seemed, could not be safely confined within hospitals and new teaching institutes. Those who discovered in it a new and seemingly irrefutable justification for rule likewise wrought from it new mechanisms of control. In the long run, some of its proponents would discover in this brave new world that empirical epistemology could thrive without true piety, that the political individual could get along nicely without his spiritual twin. But at least for now, the new piety and the new science ran cheek by jowl. Once again, the burial conflicts offer a petri dish for the examination of this social experiment.

The Transfer of Power: Science Ascendant

While the police raked the neighborhoods for malingerers in the battle for reason, the energetic cemetery reformers enrolled the help of the aforementioned Junta Municipal de Sanidad. This move reveals a turning point in the ascendancy of medical over religious authorities in the ongoing burial disputes. Back in 1777 Santa Cruz y Soledad parish priest Gregorio Pérez Cancio had exhumed and transferred his relatives' bodies to his new church and his parish's confraternities had carried the less well-connected dead in elaborate, silk-draped coffins through the streets without interference. But by 1810 secular authorities regularly meddled in the traffic in bodies and bones.[21] The head of the Third Order of San Francisco Hospital, for example, requested state permission to rid his institution's chapel of skeletal fragments to make room for fresh corpses. Viceroy and Archbishop Francisco Javier Lizana y Beaumont asked Dr. Luis Montaña, a former student of *Mercurio Volante* editor José Ignacio Bartolache and a leading proponent of medical science based on observation, and Vicente Ferrer, a surgeon working with a regiment of dragoons in Mexico City, to report on whether the transference threatened public health. The two scientists disagreed on the appropriate resting spot for the remains, but concurred that the bones be transferred at midnight or dawn to protect the population from "the fetid air that could linger momentarily in the streets."[22]

The enlightened also weighed in on the 1805 relocation of the Royal Indian Hospital's dead to the more suburban San Andrés cemetery, where they would rest on an equal footing with deceased non-Indians—a haunting adumbration of the liberals' nineteenth-century campaigns against corporate privileges that would put Indian community lands on the market to "free" individual initiative. Protomedicato head Dr. José Ignacio García Jove joined the hospital's chaplain to oppose the move as unnecessary to public health. The proponents of the new medicine felt differently. Dr. Montaña, who held the University Chair in Practical Medicine, waffled, and wanted to wait until a eudiometer—the apparatus to gauge the air's corruption, made famous by inventor Felice Fontana's European tour—could be imported to scientifically test the cemetery's environs.[23] The other proponent was Dr. Antonio Serrano, the Royal College of Surgery doctor who had made a name for himself as part of a medical committee that rejected humoral analysis and employed anatomic-pathological theory to establish a relationship between diarrhea and hepatic abscesses.[24] Serrano lived near the cemetery and had not only experienced the putrid exhalations, but had observed drunken gravediggers throwing bodies into shallow graves. That anyone would even consider burying within the city shocked Royal Botanical Garden Director Vicente Cervantes, who noted that numerous gravediggers had succumbed to gases that "caused immediate asphyxiation, that produced putrid fevers . . . and that entered our lungs and our humors through normal respiration."[25]

As health concerns and the new piety marched together to arbitrate burial policy, Mexico City's clerics increasingly found their burial practices scrutinized by an emboldened Junta Municipal de Sanidad. In 1819, an indeterminate number of religious elected a representative to warn the Junta of "the grave threat to the Church and humanity represented by suburban burials, which deprived the dead of the living's prayers . . . and packed cadavers in shallow graves without the proper distinction between adults, children, and priests." The Junta functionary sent to have a look around (*hacer una vista de ojos*) the San Lázaro cemetery spared no detail: coffins jutted out of the mud, dogs rummaged nonchalantly for bones, and our keen observer tripped across a skull—which, far from inciting him to philosophical reflection on his own inevitable end, in true Enlightenment style sent him reeling to postpone it. He recommended an immediate cleanup of the site.[26]

In an 1821 circular directed to parish priests, the Junta Municipal de Sanidad criticized their blatant disregard for sanitary burials, exemplified by the mountains of corpses that festered for three or four days awaiting burial in San Lázaro, the suburban cemetery constructed in 1779 by enlightened Archbishop Núñez de Hara y Peralta.[27] Their accusations systematically denied by some of the capital's spiritual leaders, the Junta ordered the ecclesiastical governor to convene and persuade his charges of the "grave threat to humanity" represented by shabby burial practices. The embattled clergy retorted in a letter bristling with anti-Junta sentiment: the problem was not clerical negligence—canonical dispositions and Church rites were rigorously adhered to—but the new cemeteries, where "the pious dead were vilified like Roman slaves and Jews, buried outside the city walls to be fodder for the dogs and wild animals." Indeed, in San Lázaro, pigs rutted among the bodies, and one cleric reported seeing an unseemly character expertly strip a cadaver's clothing, perhaps its mortaja, launder it in a nearby fountain, and then sell it to the *baratillo*'s (flea market's) unsuspecting buyers.[28] The confrontation ended in an apparent stalemate when, by request of the ecclesiastical authorities, the city council tabled the measure until the neighborhood police could "hacer una vista de ojos" and write a full report.

But it is precisely the reformers' beloved "vistas de ojos" that signal the increasing decline of the traditional Church as the mediator of public space. Recall that the funerals, chapels, and festivities of baroque Catholicism had formerly transformed the city into an exaggerated theater of power, and indeed still waged a ritual battle with those of more moderate sensibilities. On this stage the Church displayed the divine mysteries of the faith, but also sanctified the social position of corporate groups by hier-archically arranging the living in religious processions and the dead in holy edifices. The new piety discredited the spiritual motivation of theatrics. As the enlightened state increasingly relied on doctors and those who wielded scientific insights as its urban cultural brokers, it took a seat in the theater of power and transferred the population to the stage. The enlightened state became a spectator, not a performer; it ruled by extending its medical surveillance through new institutions like the Alcaldes de Barrio and Guarda Faroles; and it justified its interventions as much in terms of bodily as spiritual salvation.[29] When ecclesiastics called on the secular authorities to perform a vista de ojos, they effectively paid homage to an epistemology that reduced their authority; the matter would not be settled by learned theological debate, nor would the dispute's outcome be justified in terms of its spiritual significance.

The post-Independence Mexico City cabildo and its Junta Municipal de Sanidad expanded their purview over cemeteries and, although the new piety remained compelling, health imperatives increasingly dominated the enlightened contribution to the cemetery debate. Alderman José Casasola optimistically summed up the situation in an 1821 report: "Although we have not dealt the death blow to cemetery preoccupations, they are debili-tated, and no man who is sensato relishes the idea of his dead body infecting the living's air." Far from gentle resting spots, the capital's burial sites continuously spewed dangerous gases, and, in a comment worthy of our contemporary scene, Casasola felt that "either Mexico City's climate is exceptional, or the capital's inhabitants lived miraculously, encircled as they are by so many causes that conspire against their existence."[30] Sent to have a look at potential provisional cemetery sites, another city council official, Juan Francisco Alzcarate, ventured into that field of horrors, San Lázaro Cemetery, and escaped to declare it a scandal that "rational people, united in civilized societies full of conveniences, tolerate such a cemetery." The rational were indeed upset by dangerous burials, and when the Con-vent of la Merced began tomb construction near its holy water font, a coveted location in the burial hierarchy, the Junta Municipal de Sanidad and the neighborhood police moved in to restore reason.[31]

But, although the dead joined their predecessors in vaults and even rested in fresh new church tombs, no one, not even the bishop, lifted so much as a dead finger without the Junta Municipal de Sanidad's approval. The Junta championed burials in the cemetery just north of the suburban parish of Santa María and urged even the archbishop to approach the cabildo for a burial license. In 1822, the San Lázaro burial site continued to provide the Junta with horror stories aplenty: now the most attractive female dead "fell prey to rapists . . . or provided sustenance to dogs and pigs, the latter destined to feed the living." The situation cried out for a new general cemetery strategy—Alderman Alzcarate's prior project lacked real medical evidence—and the Junta proposed that everyone, "the highest boss to the lowliest citizen, the archbishop to the most humble cleric" should be buried instead at suburban Chapultepec, grave site of Indian emperors.[32] The Junta, not the Church, would conduct monthly visits to ensure that the caretakers rigorously adhered to sanitary guidelines.

The ramifications of this transfer of power dawned only gradually on the still vigorous clergy. But in 1825, an alarmed clergy began to complain about the city council's expanding jurisdiction over the dead. Santa Veracruz parish priest José María Aguirre shunned San Lázaro and received permission from a fellow priest to conduct his dead to a more suburban parish cemetery. But the city council insisted on the unpopular site, and a frustrated Aguirre directed a desperate plea to regional authorities, complaining that the Junta treaded on ecclesiastical jurisdiction—but to no avail. In 1827, Aguirre tried a different tack, petitioning the Junta to open a new cemetery. An organized team of Junta, city council, and police commission dignitaries converged on the proposed site and approved it as a stop-gap measure until the general cemetery opened, in part because the dominant winds would carry the vapors away from the city.[33]

But if Aguirre won the Junta's approval, it was only a momentary respite in a seemingly inexorable process. Medicine's champions were everywhere, not just in organized sanitation committees: Santa Catarina parishioners reported their priest to the Junta, who exacted his promise to cease burials, although the priest claimed to bury only important members of his flock in one of his chapels. In Santa Catarina parish death reeked of privilege now unacceptable to sensatos.[34] Thus ascendant, public health provided the enlightened with a powerful solvent against the prerogatives of the privileged.

Empiricism Enthroned:
Independence and the Reign of Reason

Objectivity, universality, neutrality: by ruling in the name of reason, en-lightened elements in the state glorified these attributes. They claimed for their decrees the force of transparent scientific truths. That this reign of reason arbitrarily favored some forms of knowing over others, and that not all people were considered equally expert at exercising their judgment, had serious consequences for a post-Independence society confronted with the dilemma of who should rule and with what justification.

The rejection of imperial authority opened up the field of state power for new claimants, of whom there was no shortage, as we have seen with Lizardi's and Mora's will to power. One other category of men with state influence cannot be ignored, however. After Independence, doctors and their testimony not only provided the critical link between government and society through institutions like the Junta Municipal de Sanidad; perhaps more striking, they even occupied state offices that allowed them to further advance the cultural credibility of the new medicine. Happily for these men of science, the process of status enhancement detailed in Chapter 7 had already borne fruit by 1821; at the time of Independence, Mexican doctors already enjoyed high status in enlightened circles. Thus, when the chan-nels of power opened up new courses, medical men found themselves well placed to help pilot the ship of state.[35] Although this development may seem unsurprising in the present context, its uniqueness for the era be-comes glaring when we look beyond Mexico for comparisons.

The contrast with English and North American doctors could not be more stark. Paul Starr reports that during the Jacksonian period, state legislatures in the United States voted to do away with medical licensing entirely. North Americans saw physicians' pretensions to exclusive knowl-edge as an affront to their common sense and to a domestic medicine tradition that relied on self-help almanacs. Although Starr acknowledges that U.S. society grew more polarized between rich and poor, rugged individualism flourished, perhaps not ironically, and a deep tension devel-oped between democratic respect for common sense and doctors' claims to specialized knowledge. Starr concludes that in the United States "the democratic interregnum of the nineteenth century was a period of transi-tion when traditional forms of mystification had broken down and the fortress of objectivity had not been built." The state did not even begin to indulge licensed doctors' bid for respectability until the early twentieth century.[36]

England's physicians shared their North American colleagues' woes. Dorothy and Roy Porter argue that in Protestant England doctors had trouble convincing the "priesthood of all believers" of their authority. State control of medicine fell with absolutism in the seventeenth century, opening the arena to a wide variety of practitioners. The eighteenth century, they conclude, has been rightly dubbed the "golden age of quackery" and, well into the nineteenth century, a self-help medical culture combined with a laissez-faire economy and doctors' ineffective treatments to blur the boundaries between men of science and pretenders. Until late in the nineteenth century, official medicine received little state support and exercised little public power.[37]

Whereas almost no British doctor even held state employment before Queen Victoria ascended the throne in 1837, in the 1830s and 1840s Mexican doctors assumed the presidency.[38] When Santa Ana abruptly terminated Dr. Anastasio Bustamante's first presidency in 1833, Bustamante fled to Paris, where he reverted to studying anatomy for three years.[39] Before becoming president, Bustamante had studied medicine and chemistry in Mexico City's Colegio de Mineria (Mining College); he later served as director of San Luis Potosi's military hospital and as General Felix Calleja's personal physician.[40] Meeting with Bustamante during his second presidential stint in 1839, Fanny Calderón de la Barca, wife of the Spanish ambassador to Mexico and dogged, if somewhat haughty, chronicler of Mexican mores, described Bustamante as "fat and pursy—a good man with an honest face . . . his conversation was not brilliant; I do not know apropos to what, I suppose the climate, but it turned the whole time upon medicine. Indeed, he was a doctor and a very bad one he must have been."[41]

As president, Bustamante manifested his preoccupation with medicine by abolishing the Protomedicato and replacing it with the Facultad Médica del Distrito Federal (Federal District Medical Faculty). Surgery's new respectability was reflected in the institute's faculty, which consisted of eight doctor-surgeons and four pharmacists. The new school supervised medical licensing and policed the undocumented.[42]

Nowhere is medical science's tight relationship with the state better illustrated, however, than in the reign of licensed doctor Valentín Gómez Farías (1832–1834) and his chief counselor, theologian José María Luis Mora. Together they created a school of medical science that emphasized the latest French developments in experimental and clinical study and that formally united the study of medicine and surgery. The school taught obstetrics, theoretical and practical pharmacy, and physiology and hygiene under the direction of Manuel Carpio, the relentless champion of vernacular medicine.[43] A year later, midwifery classes were added to the curriculum, a move lauded by liberal newspaper El *Fénix de la Libertad*, which reminded women that if they failed to attend, if they "stuck with their ancient routines," if they "deafened themselves to the voice of nature . . . the authorities would promptly deprive them of their livelihood."[44] Gómez Farías's liberal fellow traveler Casmiro Licéaga headed the new Institute of Medical Sciences. The Institute's founders included Mexico's most prominent physicians, among them a distinguished surgeon who later served as ambassador to France and Italy.[45] Licéaga's inaugural address, printed in its entirety in El *Fénix de la Libertad*, celebrated the doctors' triumph but also warned students that the struggle for status continued and that only "the study of obstetrics, surgical operations, and clinical medicine will protect you from the satire that Molière's descendants rightly direct at charlatanism."[46] Authority based on discipline could never rest.

Doctors' hold on Mexico's slippery reins of state combined with the devastating cholera epidemic to inspire a new flurry of procemetery activity. A circular of 1833 banished all Mexico City cadavers to the suburban convent of Santiago Tlaltelolco, which was due to open as a general cemetery in April 1834. Governor José María Tornel's edict charged the capital's city council with establishing a committee to maintain the site and to record the personal data of the deceased. Recidivist religious communities that persisted in burying in churches would be fined 100 pesos. Indeed, the edict contained a thinly veiled warning to the city's clerics, recounting a cautionary episode from 1805. When Malaga's cathedral chapter had resisted the Junta de Sanidad's attempts to export a priest's body from the cathedral to a suburban cemetery, the King resolved that the secular authorities would summarily exhume all cadavers buried by any religious who flouted the new sanitary laws. Although no bodies were exhumed, the governor's office countered Mexico City nuns' request for cemetery exemption by authorizing medical school director Casmiro Licéaga to inspect and close burial sites not meeting public health standards. Even after the 1833 cholera epidemic abated, the cabildo required each religious order to obtain permission to resume burials.[47]

Death in the Independent State

Many of the priests who wrested permission from the secular authorities to continue church burials may well have felt that in prevailing on the cemetery question, they had emerged triumphant from a protracted siege. But in the most profound sense, their victory was a hollow one: the unreformed Church may have won several small skirmishes, but in hindsight it definitely lost the war. As we have seen, the language of death had already shifted from baroque Catholicism to a radically humble and individual Christianity; it simultaneously included the argot of science and rationalism. And finally, as the nineteenth century waxed into full-blown modernity, the child devoured the parent: even priests and confraternities could now be heard only if they adopted the new tongue.

To appreciate the scope of this alteration, we need only examine a few before-and-after scenarios. In 1780 enlightened Crown servant Jovellanos had assiduously produced evidence from theological tracts and Church edicts to justify general cemeteries.[48] Just fifty years after Jovellanos penned his balanced argument, the Mexico City newspaper *Marimba* was printing lurid descriptions of the "insufferable stench" wafting over the city from a centrally located cemetery, insisting the neighborhood's police perform a vista de ojos to verify their observations. The Mexico City Council ultimately voted to terminate the cemetery and transfer the bodies, to the outrage of the parish confraternity.[49]

Proclaiming its allegiance to "the indisputable dogma of public health as the supreme law," this incensed confraternity adduced a litany of horrors to demonstrate that exhuming bodies threatened public health: in Paris children fainted when corpses were extracted from the San Eustaqio parish; in a Montpelier temple three men died in a corpse-ridden tunnel; a Mexico City woman aborted during an excavation of a church floor; and a Puebla priest transporting bodies to the new suburban cemetery impaled himself on one of the embalmed bones. In case these macabre images failed to sway the secular authorities, the brothers assured them that the cemetery itself was benign; after all, it had been carefully constructed according to medical professors' specifications. Convinced that transporting bodies threatened health, the city council compromised with the confraternity, prohibiting further burials but allowing corpses to remain in hermetically sealed tombs.[50] The reformers, however, did not have to win the exchange; they clearly controlled the terms of its expression: the dead were a public health issue, an issue to be discussed in the language of science.

One final illustration of this sea change in Mexico City cannot be over-looked; certainly it was visible enough to observers in 1845. In May of that year, when the convent of San Diego publicly displayed General Barrera's body parts, the Consejo Superior de Salubridad Pública (CSSP) felt compelled to investigate. Recall that throughout the eighteenth century, the relics of saints and secular dignitaries attracted those who sought succor from sickness or merely a powerful intercessor, and the city's churches and convents competed to have the most holy body parts on display. All of this would have disgusted the CSSP, who, along with the city council's sanitary brigade, declared that General Barrera's heart and entrails emitted an extraordinary stench—not a saintly odor—and should be summarily re-moved from the church where they rested and buried immediately.[51] Scientific testimony increasingly trumped spiritual specialists on entrails as the mortal coil became more mortal and less holy.

The formidable Consejo itself deserves some attention in this context. Established by Casmiro Licéaga in 1841, the CSSP provided licensed practitioners with another institutional base from which to persecute the un-documented and to expand their purview over death. Three doctors, one pharmacist, and one chemist formed the core of the organization, advised by additional pharmacists and doctors from the Institute of Medical Science. Funded by such appropriate sources as a fee for pharmacy inspections and a tax on cadavers, the CSSP supervised the licensing of doctors, surgeons, dentists, pharmacists, phlebotomists, and midwives, and the prosecution of the undocumented. Professional conduct also fell under the consejo's jurisdiction. All official healers registered with the institution, which published the list of approved practitioners in the newspapers and posted it in the city's pharmacies, which were regularly inspected by the organization. Significantly, the group also inspected cemeteries and fielded the still numerous exemption requests.[52]

The collection of the cadaver tax reveals that convent and monastery burials, previously the most popular of burial options, had declined. Suspecting that cemetery administrators withheld fees, the group asked the archbishop to provide them with a list of the dead and to encourage superintendents to collect and forward the funds. The Consejo also asked parish priests to report their dead to the secular authorities, and the city's religious received a circular that reminded them of the tax on all bodies buried in cloister. An 1842 law formalized the requests, mandating a civil license for all burials and requiring priests to file death lists with the Consejo.[53] The ten convents polled by the CSSP admitted to only twenty-one burials among them—a minuscule number, even taking into consideration the possibility of underreporting. So, although the organization initially relied on the bishop's influence to collect fees, more and more bodies trundled out of town for burial in suburban cemeteries. Indeed, where none of the 46 percent of the 1710–1720 testators who had indicated a burial preference chose a cemetery, 75 percent of the 34 percent of opinionated 1850–1860 testators now insisted on burial in the city's new suburban burial grounds.[54]

The CSSP's energetic inspection of burial sites confirms that the secular authorities were defeating the religious communities in the battle for the city's dead. Even the archbishop trod but lightly on the CSSP's jurisdiction and tacitly, albeit unwittingly, acknowledged that medical experts should oversee burials; after visiting several exempt convents, he reassured the CSSP that he had not gone "to scientifically test their suitability for burials"—clearly others were better qualified than a theologian—and that he opposed church burials on both hygienic and theological grounds.[55] The CSSP's official cemetery commission conducted routine inspections and recommended minor changes, such as burying deeper or planting more trees, but also acted ruthlessly to close insalubrious sites perma nently.[56] The commission "saw with its own eyes" the open *nichos* (burial boxes) and putrefying bodies in the parish of San José and immediately banned further burials and ordered all of the exposed bones interred within three days. By 1846, in a special report solicited by Congress, the CSSP boasted that most suburban cemeteries had been recently constructed according to "scientific knowledge and the exigencies of good taste."[57] Some burial grounds, however, continued to promiscuously pile the dead in group graves, "a practice which defied sanitation rules and disgusted the imagination"—and also, we might add, smacked of "the corporate spirit," anathema to many reformers' vision of society. The report to Congress, however, ended on a hopeful note with the group's wish that "in Mexico as in Paris, nobody would be buried without the police's knowledge."[58]

One final example from Veracruz illustrates the creeping medicalization of death in post-Independence Mexico. An 1831 state law penned by the liberals placed local city councils, sanitary commissions, and government officials in charge of selecting suburban cemetery sites; clerics were not part of the process. Emboldened, sanitary committees and the municipal council even meddled in Veracruz's All Souls' Day festivities, declaring during the 1833 cholera epidemic that the customary gathering in the plaza and the swarm of refreshment vendors threatened public health. The same year the Veracruz Sanitary Commission convened a parish priest and several doctors to decide on a new burial site, and by 1839 a civic charity group and the cabildo maintained this new cemetery, requiring for entrance a burial ticket signed by a priest. By 1865, new state laws charged the Veracruz City Council with issuing these entrance tickets, inspecting the cemetery, and keeping a permanent record of all burials.[59] In the nation-state, even the dead proceeded to their final resting place in an orderly fashion, individually labeled and numbered, and presented the proper papers to the authorities.

Although it is well-nigh impossible to pinpoint exact watersheds for cultural and intellectual shifts, it seems that beginning around Independence public health was the language required of all burial dispute participants, although the enlightened continued their bilingual dexterity.[60] But it was not religion that the new medicine threatened, but priestly and community mediation with the Almighty in the realm of death. In terms of burials, Mexican empiricism, like so many ungrateful offspring, forgot its debt to its pious parent as it assumed its full estate.

The Skeptical Majority: The Limits of Empiricism's Legitimacy

Undeniably, doctors used the state to promote their status; they and those who spoke in their idiom controlled the traffic in bodies; they set the terms of the cemetery debate. Yet equally demonstrably they, like enlightened Catholics, presided over a population that remained far from enthralled by their justifications for rule. The consequences of this popular intransigence can safely be called immense. As Antonio Gramsci points out, a successful ruling group must do more than enforce its power through the apparatus of the state; it must also persuade its citizens of the legitimacy of its claims to moral and intellectual leadership. The enlightened in Mexico did neither. If the state increasingly justified its decisions in terms of its ability to foment public health, then its chronic instability should come as no surprise, for few outside of enlightened circles found these claims particularly persuasive.

One form of recalcitrance was the refusal of Mexico City residents to embrace official necrophobia; rather, many seem to have resisted entirely the enlightened's attempt to frame the dead as a public health problem, just as they stubbornly insisted on church burials under a saint's protection. This resistance is clear from the beginnings of the burial campaigns. Cases from around this time and slightly before illustrate what the sensatos were up against. In the late eighteenth century, the Inquisition arrested and questioned an "ill-mannered" Spanish subject who regularly adorned himself with a small bag of hand bones that he had stolen from a cemetery, claiming in his defense that, as everyone knows, human bones prevent fatigue. In another case from 1768, a chocolate seller pried a rib from a skeleton drying in a hospital ossuary. A witness summoned by the Inquisition to testify in the case reported seeing her add a bone fragment to a strong alcoholic drink and justify the act to the nervous witness with "Don't be an idiot, with this in the cup we will improve sales." And when sent to report on the transfer of bones from the cathedral to San Lázaro Cemetery in 1802, one Mexico City Council representative espied several Indians nonchalantly collecting human bones from the site to be processed into gunpowder.[61] Not all Mexico City residents, it appears, shared the sensatos' exaggerated fear of the dead.

Nor did everyone find doctors' scientific testimony self-evident. Most people had little use for their professional insights, and throughout the years bracketing the nineteenth century, doctors' smug self-confidence proved an object of ridicule. In 1797, for instance, the city's most prominent physicians engaged in an ambitious inoculation campaign. Expecting to bask in the populace's gratitude, their Enlightenment hubris was stung by a series of satirical verses plastered throughout the city: "The inoculations are the invention of the poorest and most desperate physician, and those that receive them will express their contrition"; "There is reason to suspect that inoculation is a mistake, and the inoculated infect"; "Suffering Mexico has had time for reflection, and has decided that these doctors brought the infection."[62]

Distrust of doctors' authority was not confined to the occasional satirical verse. As part of a larger work on death and dying, in 1792 Friar Joaquín de

Bolaños wrote a stinging critique of the claims of modern science. In Bolaños's satirical tale, death never left the side of the main protagonist, a Protomedicato-licensed doctor, even when he visited his patients. Bolaños claimed that his readers could easily imagine the effects: there was no sick person whom the good doctor visited who did not recover quickly, because they quickly died, or, as the author more delicately put it: "There is no better remedy for the body's pain than that of separating it from the soul."[63] Small pamphlets and broadsides also lampooned doctors' pretensions. Conversing with an anonymous author, a skeleton from the Cemetery of Santiago Tlaltelolco related a baleful tale to the readers of the tract he starred in: "I had a mild illness, but my family called a doctor, indeed one of the most famous doctors, who declared it a grave illness, and who visited me day and night (because I gave him 4 pesos each visit), he prescribed medicine, the pharmacist botched the prescription . . . and for wanting to restore my health, I brought death upon myself."[64]

The literate were not medicine's only detractors. Reporting that doctors and their medicines terrified "the rabble," to combat a terrible 1824 scourge state officials resorted to a form of authority still more legitimate than scientists among the popular classes. Priests were urged to convince their parishioners "of the obligation to cure themselves under a physician's direction." After only two weeks, the priests reported that the measure was futile, that they could not possibly overcome the deep and widespread distrust of doctors, and that rural areas rarely saw a physician.[65]

Indeed, at the very pinnacle of their political triumph doctors were hit with the 1833–1834 cholera epidemic, whose ravages further deflated their pretensions and sent citizens scrambling for effective relief. Federal District Governor Lorenzo de Zavala personally tended the sick during the epidemic.[66] But there was no cure, and most residents sought solace in the saints rather than in science. Chronicler Guillermo Prieto painted a grim portrait of the desolated city: "The governor banned fruits and other edibles; and even declared chiles rellenos anathema . . . the cemeteries of Santiago Tlaltelolco, San Lázaro, and El Caballito were bursting with bodies . . . inside homes it was fumigation, dousing with vinegar and chlorine [*cloro*] . . . and the numerous candles flickering in front of the Saints. Panic invaded every soul, and people tried even the most contradictory of remedies."[67]

At the same time that doctors' Prometheanism made an easy target for skepticism and ridicule, their competitors flourished. One María Antonia López Rayón transformed her home into a veritable hospital and earned a high reputation for her medical skills in the late eighteenth century. Whereas many healers trained with more experienced curanderos and were "predestined" for their occupation by premature birth, physical oddities, or being born the seventh child, the unlicensed López Rayón had learned from her deceased husband, a surgeon, and her surrogate father, a doctor. Particularly irritating to the Protomedicato were her satisfied patients; she had completely eliminated one man's chronic ulcers, and clients regularly regaled her with small tokens of their gratitude. Given her unofficial status and the stiff competition they felt she represented for the city's numerous approved practitioners, the Protomedicato slapped her with a heavy fine.[68] López Rayón's punishment, however, was an anomaly, as the Protomedicato barely had the resources to prosecute healers who directly competed with the licensed practitioners, as she did, and could not—and did not—even begin to prosecute the ubiquitous folk healers that served the majority of the population beyond the reach of doctors.[69]

Licensed practitioners' small numbers and often higher costs deterred many from seeking their guidance. Although incomplete, the 1811–1812 census reveals only 37 doctors, 50 surgeons, 71 pharmacists, and 218 bleeders residing in the 17 of 31 wards canvassed by the census takers. Comparing these numbers with the Protomedicato's licensing records, historian Luz María Hernández Sáenz found only 17 physicians, 10 surgeons, and 25 pharmacists with official licenses, for a ratio of only 1.81 physicians per 10,000 inhabitants, well below Paris's 3.7 per 10,000. By 1830, only 2.11 physicians and 4.97 surgeons per 10,000 citizens served the population of 170,000. If physicians and surgeons were often simply unavailable, they were also more expensive than unofficial practitioners, although Hernández Sáenz reports that the fees frequently were at least comparable.[70]

Most important, however, the licensed practitioners, despite some genuine successes like the smallpox vaccine, had no clear proof of more efficacious services than did their competitors. There is simply no evidence of clamoring potential patients turned away because they could not get an appointment or foot the bill. Quite the contrary, evidence from both Veracruz and Mexico shows considerable enthusiasm for the alternative healers, at least among the "unenlightened" majority. Curanderos may have been the object of "laughter and satire for the sensatos," as one pamphleteer put it, but those outside their constricted circle found the licensed practitioners' claims more risible.[71]

After Independence, unlicensed curers continued to dominate medical matters despite energetic efforts to eradicate them. The Ministry of Justice argued that the nation should purge itself of the unlicensed, who, like vagrants, "disturbed the peace," and issued an 1842 law that punished the undocumented with military service. Eradication campaigns, however, were underfunded and thus tended to concentrate on only the most visible and vulnerable targets who competed with the licensed practitioners for the elite clients who frequented the documented, usually foreigners. One French doctor, for example, appealed to the CSSP after Tenancingo's judicial authorities "paraded him in front of the town as a 'civil assassin' who had stolen his medical titles." Unlicensed curanderas also concerned the CSSP. The newspaper El *Mosquito Mexicano* wept for the "many victims of the ignorance and impertinence of female intruders in the art of birthing" and lobbied for an official list of the licensed. The CSSP produced the list, but only one partera appeared on the official document sent to pharmacies and newspapers. Nor did the CSSP appear to have the wherewithal to pursue medical interlopers aggressively: the one illegal partera who made it into the archive, a foreigner, caught the group's eye only after she hung out a shingle announcing her profession.[72]

Indeed, the Consejo's impotence to contain this "plague" of alternative practitioners is demonstrated by the well-publicized 1843 case of a cholera victim who died after imbibing a remedy her maid procured from a public market. Sent to investigate, the commissioners reported that "in said places [markets] there have existed from time immemorial small shops vulgarly known as *hervolarías* [herbalists], which sell . . . various substances for energy, as well as plants to which are attributed the cure of all manner of ailments . . . the proprietors lack any scientific knowledge." But the CSSP, for all its scientific know-how, could not command the funds to hire the army of employees needed to supervise these ubiquitous and popular vendors, and, although licensing rules were drawn up, a considerable gap existed between the page and actual practice.[73]

Few outside the ranks of the gente sensata believed that doctors had an exclusive monopoly on remedies for their ills, and even fewer became overwhelmed by the stench of death that so overpowered the CSSP's commissioners. That Mexicans held diverse ideas about the dead, however, nowhere becomes more evident than in the almost continual disputes over Day of the Dead festivities. No sixteenth-century Spaniard or Mexican would have felt entirely at home at an eighteenth- or nineteenth-century Day of the Dead celebration in Mexico City. The festival did indeed weave together elements from each of their traditions, but with the passage of time, a unique festival had been created.

The European Feast of All Souls on November 2 had grown into official prominence out of concern for those among the dead who lacked living friends and family willing to pray for their release from Purgatory. A general Requiem Mass was dedicated therefore to the relief of "all souls." Evidence from fifteenth-century Europe illustrates a folk belief in the dead's ability to return from the grave for a few hours during the feast and enjoy the comforts of bonfires and graveside offerings of food.[74]

In New Spain, indigenous beliefs both complemented and competed with European forms of observance. Each month of the eighteen-month Aztec calendar had its festivals, including several dedicated to the cult of the dead. According to Bernardo de Sahagún, Miccailhuitontli and Miccailhuitl, the Feast of the Dead Little Ones and the Feast of the Dead Adults, featured strung flower decorations and a feast of dog and turkey meat. Sahagún's sixteenth-century native informants revealed that prior to the arrival of the Spanish, people placed death images on reeds of grass and offered them food, tamales, and mazamorra (maize gruel) or stew, and later burned incense to them in pottery burners. Late sixteenth-century Dominican chronicler Diego Durán was saddened when an informant told him that the numerous offerings made by Indians on the Day of Allhallows were for dead children and adults. Durán feared that these Indians gave an indigenous rather than Christian significance to the event: "I suspect that it is an evil simulation . . . the feast has been passed to the Feast of Allhallows in order to cover up an ancient ceremony."[75] A deliberate ruse or merely an indigenous interpretation of a Catholic ritual, festivals for the dead elicited considerable Indian enthusiasm. In 1562 a priest reported that around the time of All Souls' his parishioners offered the deceased enormous quantities of bread and three or four thousand candles, as well as wine, chickens, eggs, and fruit.[76]

In Mexico City, both the Church and the population embraced the festival in the late eighteenth century, but tensions between revelers and the authorities were not uncommon. To avoid disturbances and foment public health, the Royal Indian Hospital closed its cemetery to visitors on All Saints' Day, the day before All Souls, in 1777. Charged with collecting alms for the cemetery's souls, Joseph María de Neve y Romero reported to the viceroy that the flood of donations, especially Indian donations, had been reduced to a trickle after the cemetery's closing, forcing his predecessor to renounce his post. The viceroy, however, was more concerned with controlling the swarm of revelers who filled both the cemetery and the adjacent street, eating, drinking and otherwise undermining the day's somber religious purpose, which the hospital contributed to with a Solemn Mass; he ordered the cemetery doors to remain shut.[77]

Controlling the festivals' meaning proved a constant headache for both secular and religious officials. In a 1791 circular the archbishop reminded his flock that on All Saints' Day both Spaniards and Indians should attend Mass, and Indians should not be forced to work for the Spanish. Chronicler Juan de Viera marveled at the vast array of sugar figures displayed on the Day of the Dead: birds, flowers, fish, beds, coffins, miters, ladies and gentlemen were all for sale for 4 to 6 pesos. Every city corner hosted a vendor, some of whom even stocked expensive silver coffins with miniature figurines of the dead.[78] Visiting Mexico in 1763, traveler Francisco de Ajofrín noted that artisans sold sugar sculptures in the shapes of "coffins, tombs, a thousand figures of the dead, clerics, monks and nuns of all denominations, bishops, and horsemen, for which there is a great market and a colorful fair in the portals of the merchants, where it is incredible to see the crowd of men and women from Mexico City on the evening before and on the Day of All Saints."[79] A 1790 edict prohibited vendors from conglomerating in these entryways and banished them to the streets leading to the Plaza Mayor, which were to be well-lighted for the occasion. The measure also ordered the police to disperse the multitude before nightfall.[80] The same year, the secular authorities brought in police reinforcements during the festival to control the crowds jamming the merchants' portals, where peddlers hawked sweets and the faithful left offerings for the dead.

The festival's exuberance continued to irk post-Independence officials. To prevent people from "turning into an amusement what should in reality be a cause of deep sorrow . . . from turning cemeteries into promenades," the secular authorities closed all burial grounds in 1825. The edict's authors hoped to put an end to the "feasting, dancing and other profane diversions" that mocked cemeteries' holiness. But the festivities continued. Skeletons held congresses in the Santiago Tlaltelolco cemetery, and pamphlets brought their proceedings to the public. During an 1835 gathering described in one pamphlet, the skeleton-president opened the session with these words: "In honor of 2 November, when all mortals have sad memories of us, and because Purgatory has allowed us to leave and roam these Elysian Fields, we are going to form a congress."[81] Night watchmen and newspaper distributors passed out these satirical verses and asked their clients for money for their coffin or for a Day of the Dead offering. According to García Cubas, who labeled the custom "stupid and superstitious," in the evening the lower classes placed tamales, cooked squash, fruit, and sweets on small altars they had built in their homes and lit the candles to prepare for the midnight feast with their departed family members.[82] The sensatos' necrophobia found little resonance in Mexico's raucous cult of the dead.

Fanny Calderon de la Barca, the Scottish wife of the Spanish ambassador, noted the contrast between the Church's somber celebration and the more festive popular commemoration of the Day of the Dead in the early nineteenth century: "Yesterday . . . the day emphatically known as Día de los Muertos—the churches throughout the republic of Mexico present a gloomy spectacle, darkened and hung with black cloth, while in the middle aisle is a coffin, covered also with black and painted with skulls and other emblems of mortality. Everyone attends church in mourning." A year later she ventured beyond the church and discovered a quite different Day of the Dead: "In the eve we walked out under the portals . . . to look at the illumination and at the numerous booths filled with sugar skulls—temptingly ranged in grinning rows, to the great edification of the children. . . . The old women at their booths, with their cracked voices, kept up the constant cry of 'Skulls, niñas, skulls!'—but there were also animals done in sugar, of every species, enough to form specimens for a Noah's ark."[83]

The battle raged throughout the nineteenth century. Early nineteenth-century observer Antonio García Cubas decried the frivolity and celebration that characterized what should have been a day of great sorrow: "Every calendar, without exception, says: '2 November. Commemoration of the Faithful Departed.' What an enormous lie! . . . It should say, so as not to transgress the eighth commandment: 'The Festival of the Faithful Departed.' "[84] Everyone, Cubas explained, went to the cemetery to place candles and flowers on their loved ones' graves.

Cemetery visits, however, irritated health authorities, who in 1848 closed the cemeteries to visitors on the Day of the Dead. In 1874, public health officials repeated this maneuver; *El Siglo XIX*, the capital's most widely circulated newspaper, noted that the authorities had made a last-minute decision and that the cemetery closings thus took the hordes of visitors by surprise. Armed with only flowers and offerings for their dead, women with tear-stained faces beat at the cemetery gates, grappling with the police to enter and daring rows of menacing soldiers with unsheathed bayonets to attack. The newspaper predictably reported that the swarm of sweating protesters inhaled the vapors emanating from the cemetery, causing a greater risk to public health than an unimpeded cemetery visit.[85]

Not all Day of the Dead activities provoked the authorities, however; not surprisingly, orderly, restrained participation received official encouragement. Throughout the nineteenth century the Mexico City Council sponsored a "salon" in the central plaza, complete with chairs, curtains, and even an orchestra, so that spectators could witness the "parade" and "festival" in comfort. Puppetmasters and others, all properly licensed by the cabildo, rigged small theaters around the rim of the plaza and in the adjoining streets. Fruit vendors dotted the cathedral's atrium and the Plaza de la Constitución's garden housed the peddlers that "routinely appeared there on Day of the Dead."[86] Religious authorities also encouraged Day of the Dead activities, after their own lights. Many churches possessed numerous relics, most of which had been seized from the religious communities, and the faithful spent the afternoon of November 1 perusing these holy objects.[87] The same afternoon, priests set up tables decorated with black cloth, Christ figures, skulls, and candles at church entrances to remind the crowds to order suffrages for the dead.[88] Indeed, despite efforts to exile the dead and to inculcate the untutored with a proper sense of disgust, enormous crowds flocked to visit their loved ones on the Day of the Dead. The throngs of visitors so alarmed the Santa Paula Cemetery authorities that they issued an official guide to their cemetery listing each epitaph so that the hordes could satisfy their morbid curiosity from the safety of their homes. In 1848, the city council went one step further, closing all cemeteries on November 2 and dispatching police reinforcements to Santa Paula Cemetery to "avoid potential disorders."[89]

Objects of ridicule, their advice and sensibilities ignored by most Mexicans, doctors nevertheless provided the secular authorities with critical testimony in their battle to end Church control over the dead and their resting places. Santa Ana's 1854 decree for a new municipal cemetery not only ordered individual graves for the poor, but placed the CSSP, not the Church, in charge of choosing an appropriate location. A sensational 1861 piece in the liberal *Monitor Republicano* aided the campaign to redefine sacred space as a threat to mortals rather than a means to immortality. The article applauded the efforts of an alderman and medical doctor who had overseen the extraction of bodies from the Merced Convent—over five hundred bodies, the paper reported, "swimming in infested water that had set like a giant gelatin! A horrible and nauseating spectacle!"[90] In April 1863, as part of a systematic campaign to remove bodies from suppressed convents and thus permanently reduce their revenues, President Benito Juárez granted Dr. Gallardo Fernández authority over all burials in Mexico City, his monthly salary to be paid from municipal funds.[91]

Conclusion

Medical testimony undergirded the liberals' efforts to curb corporate privileges and thereby to create a society composed of nominally equal individuals in the new national republic of Mexico. Nowhere is this struggle better illustrated than in the transfer of death from the Church to the state. When President Benito Juárez ended clerics' economic control of cemeteries in 1859, he also insisted that all crypts be designed for families or individuals, not corporate groups; thus, cemeteries did not merely reflect the liberal imagining of community, but acted as a crucial tool in its creation.[92] Inconceivable to all but the most enlightened in the eighteenth century, a suburban cemetery with individual graves and burial boxes was the ultimate apotheosis of sensato power. The gente sensata's fantasy for the new nation could be read as clearly in the nominally egalitarian, atomized cemetery plots and individual boxes (nichos) as its predecessor had been in the corporate hierarchy of the sanctuary floor.

That this medical empiricism itself owed much to religion was evident even in its hour of triumph, as the 1859 edict proclaimed that the Liberal Party acted in accordance with the Church's primitive discipline. Religion was still very much part of the conversation. Indeed, as a prominent intel lectual heir of Lizardi and Mora, Ignacio Manuel Altamirano, stated in an Independence commemoration speech this same year, the Liberal Party "was the true observer of the gospel as preached by Jesus Christ," and the clergy was "an idol doomed to fall from its pedestal."[93] In his rendering, the liberals had removed religion not from politics, but from the Church. Furthermore, the new piety had stood front and center in the rise of medical authority, effectively discrediting the baroque display of God's approval as a technique and implicitly challenging devotion to authority in favor of the illuminated individual as the origin of knowledge. Ironically, it was in this context that the new medicine's attack on ancient authorities and emphasis on individual observation and *carefully disciplined* sensate experience seemed so eminently reasonable to the enlightened.

But despite the secular authorities' victories and the testators' new burial preferences, doctors' cultural authority remains difficult to assess. On the one hand, they set the terms of the cemetery debate, forcing all participants to speak in the language of science to be taken seriously. Professional medical testimony became synonymous with reason and indisputably facilitated the secular authorities' eventual seizure of authority over the dead and burial grounds from the Church. During the late colonial period, the Protomedicato established firm barriers between the licensed and folk healers and thus nurtured doctors' professional respectability, giving them a status among elites they did not enjoy in the more free-market societies of England and the United States until the late nineteenth century. Enlightened elements in the Bourbon state further cosseted the new medicine's practitioners and their status soared as the eighteenth century wore on, in part because they themselves directly challenged the Protomedicato's reliance on traditional medical authorities. After Independence, the state continued its advocacy of doctors' authority, penalizing interlopers and establishing official schools whose graduates' status depended on their uniform scientific training.

Doctors' powers of cultural suasion, however, were limited to the well-educated, who marked their class membership by patronizing a licensed physician. Most Mexico City residents proved less than dazzled by doctors' claims and continued to flock to alternative, undocumented healers. Nor did most Mexicans share doctors' necrophobia, and some penned biting critiques of the overweening pride of men of science, employing images that illustrated the limits of doctors' power over life. The majority, however, voted with their feet, flocking to the cemeteries on November 2, the Day of the Dead. Thus, although doctors and their allies could harness the state to forward their group interests and could usurp to some degree the clergy's intellectual leadership of society, their rule can hardly be termed hegemonic. A state that justified its rule in terms of its access to "rational" and "scientific" knowledge rested on a shaky ideological foundation indeed when few found these claims persuasive.

conclusion

Beginning in the late eighteenth century, an increasing number of Veracruz and Mexico City elites embraced a simpler, more individual piety. By the mid–nineteenth century, few testators demonstrated the baroque sensibilities so prevalent in the seventeenth and early eighteenth centuries. As we have seen, this enlightened piety radically reconfigured the path to God. Baroque Catholicism's miraculous infusions of divine mercy into the mundane world, its magnificent external prods to piety, the Church's elaborate mediating hierarchy—all came in for criticism from those who felt that God illuminated them from within. The reformed displayed His binding effect on the will through their studied restraint, through the modest funerals and cemetery burials that rejected both sensual stimulation and the saints and the congregation as crucial mediators with the Divine. They faced God alone, with only the Church's minimal mediation, for He was not an exterior force, but always already there in their hearts.

But if enlightened Catholicism helped create the modern individual and thereby eroded ancien régime group identities, it also abetted novel claims to social leadership; it was both a socially destructive and a socially creative force. The reformed wrested from the pared-down piety a new justification for rule: baroque display demonstrated a lack of godly moderation, and they instead opted to observe their social inferiors, not dazzle them. Their economic and political success sprang from God's interior mortification of the senses, and thus they should rule those whose flamboyance or fecklessness revealed their hollow interiors. The new piety sacralized their quite worldly quests, and thus they demoted the religious orders' distance from the world from its lofty spiritual position. In Veracruz the enlightened laity systematically usurped the religious' charitable functions, while throughout the Empire, new institutions like the Alcaldes de Barrio brought surveillance to the city's well-lit streets. And in post-Independence Mexico City, Mora and Lizardi concluded that the Church squandered its vast wealth on the spiritually useless liturgical pomp that undermined morality, rendering it a prime target for reform by the truly godly.

As we have seen, the restoration of the Church to its pristine purity proved a potent rallying cry for the gente sensata. The reformed had no spiritual need for the centuries' accretions of saints, relics, and rank. The internally illuminated could reflect on God's truth in the Scriptures without the aid of Church authorities. Not surprisingly, when the French invasion of the Peninsula provoked a crisis of sovereignty in 1808, enlightened Catholics like the witty and prolific Lizardi wielded their scriptural erudition and knowledge of the early Church councils to justify their participation in a new public sphere of letters.

The authority of popes, bishops, and even parish priests had depended on their privileged relation to the Almighty. The internally illuminated rejected this hierarchical ranking and wished to be shorn of this superfluous barrier to knowledge of God: the divinely illuminated conscience should be freed from the Church's suffocating presence. The Church hierarchy, particularly the Pope, tumbled from their positions of highest worldly font of divine wisdom, and Lizardi brazenly parried with high-ranking religious authorities in Mexico City's lively public sphere. Monarchy, too, had depended on divine sanctification, and the reformed found this justification flimsy, arguing instead for the rule of the propertied, of those who displayed their closeness to God through the individual restraint that found its just reward in economic prosperity. Mexico should be a godly republic ruled by the prosperous, not by those, like priests, born with divinely sanctified juridical privileges. This new vision of society could be read in the new suburban cemeteries as clearly as the ancien régime's juridical hierarchies had been in the church floors.

But enlightened Catholicism alone cannot explain the transference of burials from church chapels under the protection of a particular saint to state-monitored suburban cemeteries. With its distrust of received wisdom and emphasis on the individual's unmediated relationship to scriptural truths, the new piety's clerical proponents perhaps unwittingly abetted the rise of science as the crucial authority in burial decisions. The new empirical medicine of the early nineteenth century rejected time-honored wisdom in favor of the rational individual's observation of the natural world; it made scientifically disciplined sensate experience eminently reasonable. As the nineteenth century progressed, doctors increasingly trumped spiritual specialists in the burial debates, and science became the language required of all participants. By the time the liberals formally secularized the cemeteries in 1859, the Church's loss was a foregone conclusion; by the reformers' lights at least, priests, saints, and communicants had lost their crucial mediating function with God, and doctors should be the reigning authorities on burials.

Mexico's radical Church reformers were far from an anomaly in post-Independence Latin America. In Colombia, Central America, Venezuela, Chile, Peru, and Equador, campaigns to abolish the tithe, reduce ecclesiastical fueros, seize the regular orders' wealth, prune the exuberance of the liturgical calendar, and establish suburban cemeteries raged during the era.[1] Because the Church fell under attack, with few exceptions scholars have ignored religion as an impetus for these reforms. The doyen of Latin American Church history, Lloyd Mecham, found not spiritual or economic motivations for Church reform, but liberal cadres jealous of priests' government positions; others attribute widespread anticlerical measures to the influence of the Enlightenment in Spain in particular and Europe in general—without considering the forceful role of the reformed Church in that Enlightenment.[2]

Evidence of the new piety's contribution to early Latin American liberalism certainly exists, but its popularity outside of small circles of intellectual luminaries remains unexplored. We have already seen reform coteries' procemetery efforts in Lima and Havana. During Colombia's mid-nineteenth-century Church reforms, anticlerical liberals cited apostolic Christianity as a justification to prune Church privileges. Like certain Mexican liberals, they claimed that they, not their opponents, had a true ideological affinity with Christ.[3] For the Peruvian case, Jeffrey L. Klaiber analyzed the intellectual production of a clutch of influential liberals set on creating a less hierarchical Church and found they had continual recourse to "the 'primitive' Church to justify their reform measures."[4]

Our exploration of the rise of enlightened Catholicism among Mexico's urban elites points to the deep religious origins for secularizing the cemeteries in 1859. This measure was part of a larger attack on corporate privileges, best exemplified by the Constitution of 1857, which banned titles of nobility and contained a bill of rights enshrining freedom of speech and of the press. The Constitution also incorporated the 1855 Ley Juárez, which reduced the clerical and military fueros to matters of internal discipline only, as well as the 1856 Ley Lerdo, which banned both the Church and Indian villages from owning land not essential to their day-to-day operations. The stated rationale was the creation of a rural middle class of yeoman farmers; in some places this goal was met, creating a liberal economic constituency.[5]

But we might also add that from the vantage point of enlightened Catholics, the Church had no religious justification for its vast holdings. Furthermore, its privileges were an affront to the theological logic of the internally illuminated, for priests were no closer to God than the gente sensata and thus could assert no justification for special consideration. We cannot understand these economic and political measures outside of the religious context of urban testators' preferences for a reduced Church apparatus and simplified worship, or vocal reformers' efforts to free religion from the Church.

That the reform current within the Church was so strong on the eve of Independence, and that the reformed laity was so influential beyond it, also suggests a new avenue of inquiry for testing the hypothesis that a liberal periphery confronted a conservative center in post-Independence Latin America. In places like Veracruz, Venezuela, and the Palatine lowlands, this liberal crescent housed new mercantile groups who had grown sleek under Bourbon auspices and who now vigorously advocated free trade. They squared off against the colonial highlands, places like the central Andes and central Mexico, where entrenched merchants and artisans sought tariff protection. In short, the theory holds, conservative Catholic highlands battled liberal, anticlerical trading ports. Most significant for our purposes, this hypothesis proposes that this pattern reflects the strength of "the Church" in the central areas, and its weakness on the coast and frontier.[6] But Veracruz's Laso de la Vega was no shrinking violet; especially on the issue of liberal anticlericalism and wider Church reform, the more fruitful agenda would be to ask not where the Church was strongest, but which Church current was most influential where, and among whom. Did Buenos Aires's merchants embrace the new piety? Did Lima's? Did this Augustinian piety then translate into liberal Church and political reforms led by a sacralized laity elsewhere in Latin America? Did it abet the rise of doctors who jockeyed with priests for social leadership?

postscript

All historians think that their period offers the greatest clue to the present, or perhaps the present influences their analysis of the past so much that the two become blurred. My work on the historical genealogy of elite Mexican liberals was no doubt influenced by the havoc currently being wreaked by their twenty-first-century neoliberal heirs. Some of this book was written in 1996 in the spectacularly beautiful Tepotzlán, Morelos, a town of about ten thousand, an hour by bus from Mexico City. Tepoztecos are "self-consciously traditional," I was informed by a local anthropologist who drives a town taxi, "because we know that divided we will be defeated." In the neighborhood where I lived, as in all the barrios, confraternities wended their way through the cobblestone streets collecting for the annual celebration of the patron saint and a seemingly endless array of lesser celebrations. When a group of the wealthy weekenders who have built palatial homes near the town complained about these noisy festivals, a group of townsmen threatened to beat them with sticks. My neighbors likewise demonstrated a profound ecumenism in relation to their health, for the public clinic competed for clients with a host of equally appealing options. Curanderos supplemented antibiotics with herbs, electric massagers, whirlpool baths, and the mysterious healing powers of twins. The more mobile made pilgrimages to the miraculous Christ of Chalma; various neighbors could be counted on to insert an i.v., deliver a baby, or stitch a wound.

Tepotzlán's finest hour struck when several townsmen sold their land to a multinational conglomerate intent on building an eighteen-hole golf course ringed by eight hundred luxury homes. The neoliberal government had already launched its assault on Article 27 of the Constitution, which had enshrined communal property rights since the Revolution. Under the new dispensation of private property, the free market, and individual rights, the land vendors of Tepotzlán felt that their former usufruct claims to common village land had transmogrified into private property rights; and from a legal standpoint, they had a point. But most residents felt differently, and if land issues were somewhat cloudy, the economics of water supply were starkly obvious: the aquifer could support a town or a resort, but not both.

Mexico City and nearby Cuernavaca disgorged a phalanx of government-sponsored scientists, ecologists, and surveyors, who produced reams of paper demonstrating the course's negligible effects; official economists spoke glowingly of the locals to be employed serving margaritas or mowing the green. Tepoztecos responded by barricading the town to federal and state authorities, writing counterreports, and producing guerrilla videos that underlined the disputed area's mythological import to the town. To the promise of service sector jobs, they donned T-shirts on which Revolutionary hero Emiliano Zapata appeared as a golf caddy. Now the same confraternity leaders who collected for the saints reminded their neighbors to board buses for demonstrations in Cuernavaca and Mexico City; protesters chanted that they had come to give the cities "a lesson in dignity."

The movement took on near-messianic fervor with the blessing of the ecstatic parish priest, who spent his afternoons on a loudspeaker quoting from Latin America's prominent liberation theologians. His booming warnings left no room for compromise. The rapacious capitalists and government officials could not escape the "structural situation of sin" that is the global economy! Personal repentance could not save them—they profited from others' misery! To the sacred rights of the individual, he juxtaposed the sanctified community of the humble. Only the universally deserving poor, "God's chosen people," could overturn the system and thereby free both themselves and their sinful oppressors. Surely Archbishop Nuñez de Haro y Peralta was turning over in his grave!

And thus Mexico's elite liberalism continues in its battle to eliminate corporate fueros and enshrine its notion of the rational individual as the country's fundamental constituent. Historians know better than to forecast the future, and certainly powerful forces are on the side of the neoliberal vision.

But nobody tees off in Tepotzlán.

appendix

Mexico City
Notary Archive (AN)
Notary Miguel Blancas
Number 96, vol. 590, 1831
Folios 18–20
December 1st, 1831
TESTAMENT OF CRISTÓBAL PEÑA

In the name of God Our Almighty Lord, Amen. Be it noted and manifested to all who in the present see how I, Don Critóbal Peña, legitimate Son of Don Mariano Peña and Doña Ciriaca García, my parents and lords now deceased and in holy glory, who were residents of the City of Toluca, the city where I am a native although now a citizen of this Capital. Being sick in bed due to the accident that God Our Lord has seen fit to send me, but because of his infinite compassion with all my faculties, comprehension, accomplished memory, and the natural understanding for which I give to His Divine majesty my most revered thanks, believing as I firmly and truly believe and confess to the Almighty and ineffable Mystery of the Beatific Trinity of God the Father, God the Son, and God the Holy Spirit, Three really different persons and only one True God, in the Holy Sacrament of the Altar and in all the other mysteries, articles, and sacraments that the Holy Mother Catholic Church has, believes, confesses, preaches, and teaches, and under whose faith and beliefs I have lived, pretend to live, and want to die as a Catholic and faithful Christian and be of what I love; choosing as I do as my auxiliary patrons and advocates, the Empress of the Heavens and Earth Holy Mother Our Lady conceived in grace from the first instant of her most holy animation to be the worthy mother of the Divine Animated Word; her most chaste and faithful husband the patriarch Señor San José, my Holy Guardian Angel, the Saint of my name, and others of my devotion and heavenly court, to

The original wills that the author describes in the text were in Spanish. The following two samples were translated into English by the author with the help of Ana Maria Aronofski.

intercede for me to Our Lord Jesus Christ to forgive my sins and take my soul to his holy glory, and with this strong hope, afraid of death, a natural thing to all living creatures, its uncertain but unstoppable hour, so it does not assault me and catches me by surprise in the issues having to do with the discharge of my conscience and the good of my soul, I grant that I do and order my testament in the following form and manner:

Firstly, I commend my soul to God Our Lord who raised it and redeemed it with the infinite treasure of his most precious blood, life, passion, and death, and the body I send to the earth, and when it is a corpse I wish for it to be buried in the Church, in the place and locality elected by my estate executor I must name here and to whose disposition I leave these arrangements, asking that it is done with humbleness because that is my will.

I want and request that fifty Masses to be said for my soul and the rest of my intention in churches and altars chosen by my executor.

I request that for the compulsory and pious vows of this Archbishopric, that two silver reales be given to each, and with this asignation of alms I desist and apart them from the right that to my belongings any can claim.

I declare that I am married under the order of Our Holy Mother Church to Doña Francisca García and during our marriage we have not had any children and when we verified it, I had a small capital of about five hundred pesos in a [billiard?] and in reales, and the previously mentioned woman did not bring to my domain any dowry or capital.

I declare that a divorce from the previously mentioned woman is pending in the Archbishopric, and that she has separated from my side, running away after having tried to give me poison to kill me, as it has already been exposed in the Courts, and for which reason I consider her without rights to any of my belongings.

I declare that these are reduced to a house I own in the City of Toluca, marked with the number 4 in the street of San Juan de Dios, free of all mortgage and of which the property title is in my power, and a few household items.

I request that my executor, from the best of my belongings, separate two hundred pesos, and this amount be invested in what I have secretly communicated to him, and nobody, eclesiastic or secular, should obligate him to reveal its contents, because it is enough to say he has accomplished it, because this is my will.

I also request that Don José María de la Peña, my brother, be given fifty pesos; Don Francisco de la Peña, also my brother, twenty-five pesos; Margarita Adan, Manuel Rojo, and Benita Maruri, who are taking care of me in my sickness, fifty pesos to share in equal parts, and also other fifty pesos to distribute among the poor, at my executor's discretion, because this is my will.

I request that the small debts I owe be paid, and to recover what is owed to me, both things already privy to my executor.

And the remnant of the liquidation left of my belongings, debts, rights, and stock or future inheritances that directly or indirectly are received and belong to me, I institute, leave, and name as my Only and Universal Heir, Doña Soledad Peña, my niece, wife of the National Scribe Don José Ximénez de Velasco, and whatever there is, she gets it and takes it with her with the blessings of God our Lord, due to the fact that I do not have forced heirs as the law dictates; I ask her to help her poor sisters with what she kindly is able to do from my belongings, because this is my will.

And to fulfill and pay for this, my testament, I name as executor of my will, trustee and holder of my estate the previously mentioned Don José Ximénez de Velasco, and I give him the powers and faculty required and needed by law so after my death enter into my belongings, make inventory, sell and liquidate into money or out of it, and to spend all the time that were needed, even if it is longer than the time specified by law, because the more he needs I allow him to delay and lengthen in due manner, because this is my will.

And with the present I revoke, anul, give for nullified and with no value, force or effect, others or any wills, codicils, powers of testament, memories and other last dispositions done before this one and granted in writing or word or other manner, for these are not valid or give faith, in court or out of it, except for this present will that I now grant, and want it kept, fulfilled and executed as my final, last, and deliberate wish, in the way and form that is best in the law of the place.

It is dated in the City of Mexico, on the first day of December of the year one thousand eight hundred thirty-one. And I the scribe that presently I am, give faith that I know the grantor, who, although being sick in bed, is in full control of his faculties, sound mind accomplished memory and natural understanding in accordance to the reasons with which he answered the questions and corroborations I asked, and having read it to him, he granted it and signed it, being witnesses Don Agustín Peña, Don José Antonio de la Torre, Don Cristóbal de la Torre, Don Agustín Silva, and Don Manuel Cárdenas from this vecinity.
[Signatures]
Cristóbal Peña
Manuel Blancas National Scribe

Mexico City
Notary Archive (AN)
Notary José Díaz Jimenez
Number 197, Volume 1265 A, 1692

Folios 21v–25
April 22, 1692
TESTAMENT OF JUANA DE ABILA TIRADO

In the name of the Almighty God, Amen. Let all who see this letter know that I, Juana de Abila Tirado, a natural widow from this City of Mexico and her citizen, legitimate daughter of Don Diego de Abila and Doña Lusia Ximénez, natives from the kingdom of Castile, now deceased, being on my feet and in good health, for which I give the Lord my infinite thanks for the many benefits that His Worthy Majesty has done for me, and in my full wisdom and accomplished memory, believing as I believe in the undeniable mystery of the Holy Trinity God Father, Son of God and Holy Spirit, three different persons and only one True God, and in all else that Our Holy mother the Roman Catholic Church confesses, under whose faith and beliefs I have lived and pretend to live and die, like a faithful Catholic, invoking as I should invoke the Sovereign Queen of the Angels Maria Santisima conceived without original sin from the first instant and the glorious Patriarch Señor Don José to be my interceding advocates to their precious son, and to ask Him to forgive my sins and place my soul on the path to salvation; with such hope I make and order my will in the following shape and manner:

—First, I commend my soul to God Our Lord, who created and redeemed it with the infinite cost of his blood, passion and death and the body he sent to the earth that made it, after my death, I want to be buried in the Church of the Limpia Concepción, commonly called Jesús Nazareno, in the vaults that I own in the altar of Santo Ecce Homo, of which I am a founder and patron. I want to be shrouded with the habit of our seraphic Father San Francisco. For the burial I want twenty-four attendants to the priest and a sacristan. The rest of the arrangements I leave to the disposition of my executor.

—Item. I ask that the day of my burial is at a suitable time and if not on the next day, to have a Mass and a vigil while I lie in state, and the cost shall be paid from my estate.

—Item. I order fifty Masses to be said for my soul, paid at the normal price, and such cost shall be paid from my estate.

—Item. I order the compulsory and accustomed vows at four reales each; to the cause of Jerusalem one silver peso, and the same amount to help in the beautification of the venerable Gregorio López.

—Item. I declare that I am a sister of different brotherhoods, such as San Vizente, of the Encarnación, Santo Cristo de los Chinos, Nuestra Señora de la Candelaria, Nuestra Señora de Guadalupe, and San Benito de Palermo, to which I have paid what is customary; and I ask my executor to let their stewards know of my death, and for them to fulfill their obligation to help pay my burial.

—Item. I declare that I was married and veiled in first nuptials to Antonio Ximénez native from San Miguel el Grande, from which marriage I was left without children, I declare this so it is forever known.

—Item. I declare that I passed to second nuptials with Juan de Rojas, and also no children were left from the above mentioned, I declare this so it is known.

—Item. I declare that I was the executor, heiress, and holder of the estate of the named Juan de Rojas, my second husband, who died so poor and with so many debts, that it was with my work and sweat that I could later pay his debts and be able to fulfill his will, I declare this so it is known.

—Item. I declare that I was the executor of Diego Ortiz, a mestizo who died extremely poor as it is well-known, and I paid for his burial and to clear the titles from the adobe hut he left behind in San Hipólito I paid up to forty pesos for the house he lived in, and I had him buried in the vault I own in the altar of Santo Ecce Homo in the Church of Jesús Nazareno. And what remains in my ownership that belonged to this deceased, is a cape of old cloth, three pairs of scissors, four old frames, three saints in ordinary wood slats from the square, two benches and a small table, all of it old. And I order my executor that, after recovering the forty pesos, to give his heirs the titles of this house together with all items I referred to.

—Item. I declare as my own some adobe houses that I bought for father Frai Bernabé Nuñez Depaez, Minister of the Colegio de San Pablo from this City, of the religious Agustinos. These are in Real Street that runs from Monserrat Street to Salto de Agua to the edge of the canal of the Acequia, and on which I spent up to five hundred pesos in their rebuilding, as an estimate.

—Item. I declare also to be my property a mulata slave called Antonia de la Encarnación and some silver bracelets weighing three and a half ounces, a necklace of small pearls with gold ends weighing an ounce and a quarter; I order and request from my executor to give such bracelets and necklace to Nuestra Señora del Rosario de la Congregación which is founded in said church of Jesús Nazareno, with the request that if my executor ever knew of or saw any person wearing such bracelets instead of the Holy Virgin, to take them away and bring them back to the trunk of my estate.

—Item. I declare also to belong to my estate everything that is found inside the house I live.

—Item. I declare and it is my wish that if my orphan Juan de Rojas ever becomes a priest, after becoming ordained, my executor will give him the house I have referred to before and the mentioned slave, Antonia de la Encarnación, two bed sheets, two pillows, one mattress, a bed frame of granadillo wood, a cotton bedspread, three leather stools, a statue of San Esteban, two paintings, two engravings, four medium mirrors, a wooden desk, a pine box, two plates and two silver spoons, and three coconuts with silver decorations. But if the mentioned

Juan de Rojas, my orphan, were not to become a priest, in this case it is my will
that my executor shall not give him the house, the silver or the slave but rather he
should only be given the rest of the objects mentioned in this clause and a blue
cloth to be used as a tablecover. And said house, if it is not for this priest, would
be for a chaplaincy of two sung in the mentioned church of Jesús Nazareno, the
first on the eighth day on which we celebrate his festival, with a Deacon and a
Subdeacon; and the other on the eighth day of the dead, in my altar of Santo Ecce
Homo, for my soul and the souls of my husbands, and the imposition of the value
of such houses, is made by my executor, named as first patron and after his days
to his children and grandchildren, in the preferred order of older to younger and
male to female, and lacking all those named, I name as patron of this pious work,
the Licenciado Diego Calderón Benavides, Presbytery and comisar of the Holy
Tribunal of the Inquisition of this kingdom, second chaplain of said Church, and
when he is not here, the others who will succeed him in that chaplancy, for all to
take care of recovering the credits of such house in order to have these Masses
celebrated.

—Item. I ask and it is my will that Phelipa de la Cruz, my orphan, is given two
shirts, a white pettticoat and a carmine red one, three paintings, one of Jesús
Nazareno, another of the Soledad and another of Nuestra Señora de los Re-
medios, a mattress, a bedspread, a pine box, a statue of the Concepción, a string
of pearls of five threads with corals, two rings—one with eight small emeralds, a
pair of pearl earrings with green stones and she may have half of the china dishes
I have in a box.

—Item. I ask and it is my will that my sister Clara de Rivera, is given a skirt of
manparela with lace, a blue shirt, a black coat with filigree buttons, a white
petticoat and an imperial green one, a cloth to serve as a wrap, a small statue of
San Miguel, a pine box; also, for María, her daughter, a shirt, a petticoat of
imperial green and a white coat; and for Rosa, also a daughter of the named, a
gold ring with eleven red quartz stones, because this is my last will.

—Item. I ask that if at the time of my death if Josepha María were at my home,
she is given a length of imperial red petticoat and a pine box.

—Item. I ask that the same Juan Rojas, my orphan, be given two [unclear?].

—Item. I declare I do not owe anybody any amount, I say it so it is known.

—Item. I declare that I am a patron of the altar of Santo Ecce Homo that stands
in the Church of Jesús Nazareno, the one I paid with my money, and I keep it with
the splendor that it is seen, decorated with ornamental covers, cloths, candle-
holders and candles. And for all of my days, I name as patron of said altar, the
previously named Clara de Rivera, my sister; and after her days, her sons, daugh-
ters and grandchildren and their descendants, being my preference in order from
older to younger and from males to females, so the ones and the others take care

of the decoration of such altar and are buried in the vault that I own in it. And in lacking all of the named and if there is none of my lineage, I name as patrons of such altar the oldest brother and council members of the Congregation of Christ Crucified and Our Lady of the Rosary founded in that church.

—Item. I request that the named Clara de Rivera, my sister, is given a gold and emerald ring.

—And to execute and pay this, my will, the vows and legacies in its contents, I name as my executor and Holder of the Estate, Juana de Abila, my maiden niece, older than twenty-five years old, to whom I give the power to receive, recover, sell into money or out of it among my belongings, and be the executor during all the time that is needed, even if it takes more than the one year provided by law because I extend it.

—And after fulfilling and paying this, my will and its contents, I leave, institute and name for the remnants of my belongings, my Only and Universal Heir, the named Juana de Abila, my niece, for her to inherit and enjoy with God's blessings and mine, honored of having raised her and not having other forced ascendants or descendants as heirs, and I ask her to commend me to God.

—And with the present, I revoke and anul and give for none and to no effect others and any wills, codicils, powers of testament and any other last dispositions previously made or given in writing or word, so they are not valid and do not have faith in court or out of it, except for the will that I grant now, the one I wish is fulfilled and executed as my last will. It is dated in Mexico City on the twenty-second day of the month of April in the year one thousand six hundred ninety-two. I, the notary give faith that I know the grantor and that she shows to be in her full mental capacity and natural memory, and she did not sign it because she said she did not know how to write, at her request, the witnesses who knew how, signed it, and they were Domingo de Peñaflor; Antonio Albarez, Main Officer of the Court of the Town Hall of this City; Bachiller Diego Díaz, Presbitery Main Chaplain of the Convent of Religiosas de San José de Gracia; Antonio de Moctezuma, Master Blacksmith; and Pedro de Chávez, citizens of this City.
[Signatures]
As witness Bachiller Diego Díaz Ximénez
As witness Antonio Albarez
As witness Domingo de Peñaflor
Before José Díaz Ximénez, Royal Scribe
Fee: One Real

archives

MEXICO CITY:

Archivo Histórico de la Secretaría de Salubridad y Assistencia (AHSSA), Archivo General de la Nación (AGN), Archivo Histórico de la Ciudad de México (AHCM), Biblioteca Naciónal, Mexico City (BN), Archivo Histórico de la Mitra (AHM), Archivo de Notarías del Distrito Federal (AN), Instituto Naciónal de Antropologia y Historia (INAH), Archivo Histórico de la Secretaría de Relaciónes Exteriores de México (AHSREM), Centro de Estudios Históricos, Condumex (Condumex), and, Archivo del Catedral de México (ACM)

VERACRUZ:

Archivo Histórico de la Ciudad de Veracruz (AHCV)

MADRID:

Archivo Histórico Naciónal (AHN)

SEVILLE:

Archivo General de Indías (AGI)

AUSTIN:

Benson Latin American Collection (BLAC)

NEWSPAPERS:

La Marimba, El Fénix de la Libertad, El Mercurio Volante, Noticioso General, Gacetas de México, Gazetas de México, El Siglo XIX, El Mosquito Mexicano, El Monitor Republicano, Suplamento al Pensador, El Observador Judicial y de Legislación, Diario de México, El Censor (Madrid), and, El Censor (Veracruz)

notes

Introduction

Unless otherwise specified, all translations are the author's.

1 For other works on death and cemeteries in eighteenth- and nineteenth-century Mexico, see, for example, Anne Staples, "La lucha por los muertos," *Dialogos* 13:5 (September–October 1977), 15–20; Juan Pedro Viqueira, "El sentimiento de la muerte en el México ilustrado del siglo XVIII a través de dos textos de la época," *Relaciones* 2:5 (winter 1981): 27–63; María Dolores Morales, "Cambios en las prácticas funerarias: Los lugares de sepultura en la Ciudad de México, 1784–1857," *Historias* 27 (October 1991–March 1992): 97–105; Francisco de la Maza, *Las piras funerarias en la historia y en el arte de México: Grabados, litografías y documentos del siglo XVI al XIX* (Mexico City: Anales del Instituto de Investigaciones Estéticas, 1946); Verónica Zárate Toscano, "Los nobles ante la muerte en México: Actitudes, ceremonias, y memoria" (Ph.D diss., Colegio de México, 1996).

2 Pamela Voekel, "Peeing on the Palace: Bodily Resistance to Bourbon Reforms," *Journal of Historical Sociology* 5:2 (August 1992): 183–210. The article finds theoretical inspiration in Norbert Elias, who argues that the formation of the "homo-clausus and the modern state go hand in hand," and that this new individual is characterized by his "increased internal compulsions that, more implacably than before, prevent all spontaneous impulses from manifesting themselves directly and motorically in action." See his *The Civilizing Process: The History of Manners*, trans. E. Jephcott (Oxford: Oxford University Press, 1983), especially 258.

3 Albert O. Hirschman, *The Passions and the Interests: Political Arguments for Capitalism before Its Triumph* (Princeton, NJ: Princeton University Press, 1977).

4 Patricia Seed, *To Love, Honor, and Obey in Colonial Mexico: Conflicts over Marriage Choice, 1574–1821* (Stanford: Stanford University Press, 1988), 126–128.

5 Charles A. Hale, *Mexican Liberalism in the Age of Mora, 1821–1853* (New Haven: Yale University Press, 1968), 56, 61, 70.

6 Roger Chartier, *The Cultural Origins of the French Revolution*, trans. Lydia G. Cochrane (Durham, NC: Duke University Press, 1991), 2.

7 The phrase is Gerhard Oestreich's; see his *Neostoicism and the Early Modern State*, ed. Brigitta Oestreich and H. G. Loenigsberger, trans. David McLintock (Cambridge, England: Cambridge University Press, 1981), 33. For a truly illuminating look at the role of interior piety, particularly that of Augustine, in the fashioning of the modern self, see Charles Taylor, *Sources of the Self: The Making of the Modern Identity* (Cambridge, MA: Harvard University Press, 1989), especially 127–142. Also see Paul Kléber Monod. *The Power of Kings: Monarchy and Religion in Europe, 1598–1715* (New Haven: Yale University Press, 1999).

8 In arguing this, of course, I am not suggesting that any particular theology leads inexorably to particular political notions, such as the sovereignty of the people or the right to resist authority, merely that reform piety was part of a complex causal ecology that led to this outcome in Mexico. For a word of caution against monocausal explanations involving theologies, see Wolfgang Reinhard, "Reformation, Counter-Reformation and the Early Modern State: A Reassessment," in *The Counter-Reformation: The Essential Readings*, ed. David M. Luebke (London: Basil Blackwell, 1999), 110. For a comparative study of the differing effects of pietistic religion on the rise of absolutist states, see Mary Fulbrook, *Piety and Politics: Religion and the Rise of Absolutism in England, Würtenberg, and Prussia* (Cambridge, England: Cambridge University Press, 1983).

9 Florencia E. Mallon, *Peasant and Nation: The Making of Postcolonial Mexico and Peru* (Berkeley: University of California Press, 1995), 13.

10 Lyle N. McAlister, "Social Structure and Social Change in New Spain," *Hispanic American Historical Review* 43:3 (August 1963): 349–370; Peter Guardino, *Peasants, Politics, and the Formation of Mexico's National State, Guerrero 1800–1857* (Stanford: Stanford University Press, 1996), 25.

11 McAlister, "Social Structure."

12 Octavio Paz, *Sor Juana Ines de la Cruz o las trampas de la fe*, 3d ed. (Mexico City: Fondo de Cultura Económica, 1983), 45.

13 Nineteenth-century Mexican liberalism is amply detailed in Jesús Reyes Heroles, *El liberalismo mexicano*, 3 vols. (Mexico City: Fondo de Cultura Económica, 1974). Also see Henry C. Schmidt, "Towards the Innerscape of Mexican Historiology: Liberalism and the History of Ideas," *Mexican Studies/Estudios Mexicanos* 8:1 (1992): 117–138. Historians Peter Guardino and Florencia Mallon both argue that "popular liberalism" in Mexico often diverged radically from the "authoritarian" liberalism that forms the subject of Chapter 6 of this book, and that the two were not mutually exclusive domains in the nineteenth century; see Guardino, *Peasants, Politics*. Where I found that these "authoritarian" liberals grounded citizenship in property rights and worked to free homo economicus and the godly conscience from all restraints, Mallon found that in the Sierra de Puebla in the 1860s, peasants located rights in bravery, and "property rights

were tempered by a commitment to solidarity and social justice, while the status of citizen was tied to honorable actions rather than birth, social class, or education" (Mallon, *Peasant and Nation*, 313). For an interesting explanation of the historical genesis of these alternative notions of the self, rights, and citizenship on Mexico's northern frontier in the early nineteenth century, see Ana María Alonso, *Thread of Blood: Colonialism, Revolution, and Gender on Mexico's Northern Frontier* (Tucson: University of Arizona Press, 1995).

14 David A. Brading, "El Jansenismo Español y la caída de la monarquía Católica en México," in *Interpretaciones del siglo XVIII mexicano: El impacto de las reformas borbónicas*, ed. Josefina Zoraida Vázquez (Mexico City: Nueva Imagen, 1992), 187–215.

15 On the diminution of clerical privileges, see Francisco Morales, *Clero y política en México (1767–1834): Algunas ideas sobre la autoridad, la independencia y la reforma eclesiástica* (Mexico City: Secretaría de Educación Pública, 1975); William B. Taylor, *Magistrates of the Sacred: Priests and Parishioners in Eighteenth-Century Mexico* (Stanford: Stanford University Press, 1996); Nancy M. Farriss, *Crown and Clergy in Colonial Mexico, 1759–1821* (London: Cambridge University Press, 1968).

16 Serge Gruzinski, *The Conquest of Mexico: The Incorporation of the Indian Societies into the Western World, 16th–18th Centuries*, trans. Eileen Corrigan (Cambridge, England: Polity Press, 1993), 271.

17 R. H. Tawney, *Religion and the Rise of Capitalism: A Historical Study* (New York: Harcourt, Brace, and Company, 1926); Max Weber, *The Protestant Ethic and the Spirit of Capitalism*, 2d ed., ed. Anthony Giddings, trans. Talcott Parsons (London: George Allen and Unwin, 1976).

18 On the rise of clinical medicine and medical observation, see Michel Foucault, *The Birth of the Clinic: An Archeology of Medical Perception*, trans. A. M. Sheridan (New York: Vintage Books, 1975); Andrew Cunningham and Roger French, eds., *The Medical Enlightenment of the Eighteenth Century* (Cambridge, England: Cambridge University Press, 1990); John Tate Lanning, *The Eighteenth-Century Enlightenment in the University of San Carlos de Guatemala* (Ithaca, NY: Cornell University Press, 1956); José Joaquín Izquierdo, *Montaña y los orígenes del movimiento social y científico de México* (Mexico City: Ediciones Ciencia, 1955).

19 The classics include R. K. Merton, *Science, Technology, and Society in Seventeenth-Century England* (1938; New York: Howard Fertig, 1970); Tawney, *Religion and the Rise*; Weber, *Protestant Ethic*; S. N. Eisenstadt, ed., *The Protestant Ethic and Modernization* (New York: Basic Books, 1968).

20 Dale Van Kley, *The Religious Origins of the French Revolution: From Calvin to the Civil Constitution, 1560–1791* (New Haven: Yale University Press, 1996).

21 I examined wills drawn from all notaries working during each of these three periods, choosing a percentage from each notary that seemed to roughly corre-

spond with the total number of wills written by that notary: as few as one to as many as forty in the case of a notary from the later period. Other than that precaution, the sampling was random. The wills are located in Mexico City's AN archive.

22 Timothy E. Anna, *The Fall of Royal Government in Mexico City* (Lincoln: University of Nebraska Press, 1978), 4–8.

23 The 1791 Veracruz census reported 3,990 residents inside the city's walls; see Veracruz, Veracruz Census, 1791, AHCV, caja 40, vol. 42; Jackie R. Booker, *Veracruz Merchants, 1770–1829: A Mercantile Elite in Late Bourbon and Early Independent Mexico* (Boulder, CO: Westview Press, 1993), 7; Rolph Widemer, "La ciudad de Veracruz en el último siglo colonial (1680–1820): Algunos aspecto de la historia demográfica de una ciudad portuaria," *La palabra y el hombre* 73 (1992): 121–134. Robert Sydney Smith argues that the population merely doubled between 1791 and the 1818 census, which registered 8,934 residents; see his "Shipping in the Port of Veracruz, 1790–1821," *Hispanic American Historical Review* 23 (February 1943): 5.

24 Widemer, "La ciudad," 133.

25 Veracruz, Veracruz Census, 1791, AHCV, caja 40, vol. 42. The census data are confirmed by the parish marriage records for 1798 and 1804, which reveal that 49 percent of Spanish and mestizo males originated in Europe (the two were grouped together), with only 43.7 percent from New Spain and 10.4 percent from Veracruz, in contrast to their brides, none of whom came from Europe and 80 percent of whom had been born in New Spain, particularly in Veracruz (46.7 percent). See Widemer, "La ciudad," 133.

26 W. Taylor, *Magistrates*, especially 299. Also see Gruzinski, *Conquest*, 242–250.

27 The oath's supporters and opponents are thoroughly explored in Timothy Tackett, *Religion, Revolution, and Regional Culture: The Ecclesiastical Oath of 1791* (Princeton, NJ: Princeton University Press, 1986).

28 Juan Viquiera-Alban, *Propriety and Permissiveness in Bourbon Mexico*, trans. Sonya Lipsett-Rivera and Sergio Rivera Ayala (Wilmington, DE: Scholarly Resources, 1999).

29 See, for example, Lorna Jane Abray, *The People's Reformation: Magistrates, Clergy, and Commons in Strasburg, 1500–1598* (Ithaca, NY: Cornell University Press, 1985). Philip Hoffman notes that the Catholic Counterreformation in the Diocese of Lyons, France, succeeded only in urban areas, and even there, folk religion proved intractable to its enticements. Although our concern here is with a reform piety similar to French Jansenism in the eighteenth century, not the earlier Counterreformation, Hoffman's would be an interesting conclusion to test for the case of Mexico; see his *Church and Community in the Diocese of Lyons, 1500–1789* (New Haven: Yale University Press, 1984).

30 This is not to say, of course, that no studies of piety based on wills exist for the Spanish Empire, merely that they do not link their data with the reform movement, and employ categories that make this link problematic. See, for example, José Antonio Rivas Alvarez, *Miedo y piedad: Testamentos Sevillanos del siglo XVIII* (Seville: Diputación Provincial de Sevilla, 1986); David Gonzalez Cruz, *Religiosidad y ritual de la muerte en la Huelva del siglo de la Ilustración*, introduction by León Carlos Alvarez Santaló (Huelva, Spain: Diputación Provincial de Huelva, 1993).

31 A useful introduction to Jansenist theology can be found in Jean Delumeau, *Catholicism between Luther and Voltaire: A New View of the Catholic Reformation*, trans. Jeremy Moser (London: Burns and Oates, 1977), 99–128. Also see Owen Chadwick, *The Popes and European Revolution* (Oxford: Clarendon Press, 1981), 392–446. On Jansenism in Spain, see Émile Appolis, *Les Jansénistes Espagnols* (Bordeaux, France: Sobodi, 1966); Paula de Demerson, *María Francisca de Sales Portocarrero (Condesa de Montijo): Una figura de la Ilustración* (Madrid: Editora Nacional, 1975); Antonio Mestre, *El mundo intelectual de Mayans* (Valencia, Spain: Publicaciones del Ayuntamicnto de Oliva, 1978); María Giovanna Tomsich, *El jansenismo en España: Estudio sobre ideas religiosas en la segunda mitad del siglo XVIII*, introduction by Carmen Martín Gaite (Madrid· Siglo Veintiuno, 1972); Jean Sarrailh, *La España ilustrada de la segunda mitad del siglo XVIII* (Mexico City: Fondo de Cultura Económica, 1957). On Jansenism in Mexico, see the work of one of its most eccentric devotees, Fray Servando Teresa de Mier, *Memorias*, ed. Antonio Castro Leal, 2 vols. (Mexico City: Editorial Porrua, 1946).

32 Van Kley, *Religious Origin*, 7. On the Puritans' critical role in the English Revolution, see Lawrence Stone, *The Causes of the English Revolution, 1529–1642* (London: Routledge and Kegan Paul, 1972), 103.

33 João José Reis, *A morte é uma festa: Ritos fúnebres e revolta popular no Brasil do século xix* (São Paulo, Brazil: Editora Schwarcz, 1991). For more on cemetery revolts during the early nineteenth century in Latin America, see Douglass Creed Sullivan-Gonzalez's lively account of indigenous Guatemalans' adamant desire to continue to rest near their relatives in churches in the early nineteenth century, *Power, Piety, and Politics: Religion and Nation Formation in Guatemala, 1821–1871* (Pittsburgh: University of Pittsburgh Press, 1996), chap. 3.

34 Christopher Haigh, *English Reformations: Religion, Politics, and Society under the Tudors* (Oxford: Clarendon Press, 1993), 15.

1 The Baroque Backdrop

1 These thoughts on the theological rationality of church burials are extracted from the Siete Partidas, the mid-thirteenth-century legal code composed by order of Alfonso X. See Juan M. Rodríquez de la Miguel, compiler, *Pandectas*

hispano-megicanas, o sea código general comprensivo de las leyes generales, útiles y vivas de las Siete partidas, Recopilación novísima, la de Indias, autos y providencias conocidas de Monte Mayor y Beleña, y cédulas posteriores hasta el año de 1820 (Mexico City: Mariano Galván Rivera, 1839), 1:107; Carlos David Malamud Russek, Derecho funerario, introduction by Andrés Sena Rojas (Mexico City: Editorial Porrúa, 1979), 35; Olga López I Miguel, Actitudes collectives davant la mort i discurs testamentari al Mataró del segle XVIII, introduction by Carlos Martínez Shaw (Barcelona: Editorial Rafael Dalmau, 1987), 66.

2   For a particularly lively account of the importance of relics during the Middle Ages, see Patrick J. Geary, Furta Sacra: Thefts of Relics in the Middle Ages (Princeton, NJ: Princeton University Press, 1978). Also see John Dillenberger, Images and Relics: Theological Perceptions and Visual Images in Sixteenth Century Europe (New York: Oxford University Press, 1999); David W. Rollason, Saints and Relics in Anglo-Saxon England (New York: Oxford University Press, 1989).

3   Marina Warner, Alone of All Her Sex: The Myth and the Cult of the Virgin Mary (New York: Vintage Books, 1983), 290.

4   My use of the term Counterreformation to describe early modern Catholicism is perhaps a poor choice, as it can be construed to indicate that Catholic reform was merely a reaction to the Protestant challenge and did not have deeper roots. I have used the term, however, because this is not a book about the Counterreformation, and thus I felt the most widely used term would be the clearest to readers without extensive prior background in Church history.

5   Eugene A. Dooley, "Church Law on Sacred Relics" (Ph.D. diss., Catholic University of America, 1931), 42, 103; H. J. Schroeder, The Canons and Decrees of the Council of Trent (Rockford, IL: TAN Books, 1978), 217.

6   William A. Christian Jr., Local Religion in Sixteenth-Century Spain (Princeton, NJ: Princeton University Press, 1981), 126–141.

7   Ibid., 137–138, 152.

8   Warner, Alone, 296.

9   "Relación breve de la venida de los de la Compañía de Jesús a la Nueva España: Año de 1602," in Relaciones y Crónicas de la Compañía de Jesús en la Nueva España, ed. Francisco González de Cossío (Mexico City: Universidad Nacional Autónoma de México, 1979), 36.

10 See, for example, Mexico City, Will of Antonio de Villasis, 10 July 1749, Notary 144 Ambrosio Ceballos, vol. 873, fols. 61–65; Mexico City, Will of Philipa de la Rosa Pardo de Trejo, 31 August 1748, Notary 206, vol. 1356, fols. 9–11. The mandas forzadas originated with King Philip IV's 1623 law allowing the secular clergy to collect the tax to provide dowries for orphaned girls; it was later expanded to include other religious and secular campaigns. In Mexico City, the cathedral housed a general collector, who carefully registered each contribution

for Masses, mandas, and other pious gifts in a ledger and provided the payer, generally an *albacea* (estate executor), with an official receipt. Throughout the 1620–1860 period, testators contributed from several reales to upward of thousands of pesos per manda for the two to five causes officially sanctioned by the Church or, beginning in the 1840s, by the secular authorities. See Matías Martínez Pereda, "Reflecciones jurídicas sobre la llamada sucesión a favor del alma," *Anales de la Academía Matritense del Notariado* 7 (1953): 171; Mexico City, Receipt of Payment, 20 December 1801, AN, Notary 360, Manuel López de Oquendo, vol. 2336, fol. 86; Mexico City, Will of Josef de la Peña, AN, Notary 206, Andrés Delgado Calmargo, vol. 4813, fols. 27v–28v.

11 Balthasar de Medina, *Vida, martyrio, y beatificación del invicto proto-martyr de el Japón San Felipe de Jesús, patrón de México, su patria, Imperial corte de Nueva España, en el nuevo mundo* (Madrid: Herederos de la Viuda de Juan García Infanzón, 1751), 1–142.

12 Juan Antonio Rivera, *Diario curioso de México* (Mexico City: La Voz de la Religion, 1854), 338.

13 Francisco de Ajofrín, *Diario del viaje que por orden de la sagrada Congregación de Propaganda Fide hice a la América Septentrional en compañía de fray Fermín de Olite, religioso lego y de mi provincia de Castilla* (1763; Mexico City: Instituto Cultural Hispano Mexicano, 1964), 1: 96.

14 Fray Agustín de Vetancourt, "Tratado de la Ciudad de México y las grandezas que la ilustran después que la fundaron Españoles," in *La Ciudad de México en el siglo XVIII (1690–1780): Tres crónicas*, ed. Antonio Rubial García (Mexico City: Consejo Nacional para la Cultura y las Artes, 1990), 129; Juan de Viera, "Breve compendiosa narración de la ciudad de México, corte y cabeza de toda la América septentrional," in Rubial García, *La Ciudad de México*, 208.

15 Mexico City, Viceroy Gálvez, 20 July 1786, AGN, Bandos, vol. 14, no. 34, fol. 101; José Gómez, *Diario curioso y cuaderno de las cosas memorables en México durante el gobierno de Revillagigedo, 1789–1794*, ed. Ignacio Polo y Acosta (Mexico City: Universidad Nacional Autónoma de México, 1986), 245; Mexico City, *Gazetas de México*, 22 August 1786, tomo 2, no. 16, p. 175.

16 Quoted in Warner, *Alone*, 98–100.

17 As Christ made his way up to Calvary, Christian tradition records, a woman named Veronica stepped out of the crowd to mop his face with a hankerchief; the cloth kept the outline of the saviour's face. El Greco's 1580 painting of Saint Veronica memorializes the event; see Alain Saint-Saéns, *Art and Faith in Tridentine Spain (1545–1690)* (New York: Peter Lang, 1995), 17.

18 Alejandro Torres, *Vida del beato Sebastián de Aparicio* (Puebla, Mexico: Fr. Samuel Ortega, Ministro Provincial, 1968), 67, 72. Serge Gruzinski reports on a similar phenomenon in the Mexican countryside in the early seventeenth century,

where friars known as *venerables* became sacred relics on their death, when the faithful often quickly dismembered their body; see his *The Conquest of Mexico: The Incorporation of Indian Societies into the Western World, 16th–18th Centuries*, trans. Eileen Corrigan (Cambridge, England: Polity Press, 1993), 189.

19 Clara García Ayluardo, "Confraternity, Cult and Crown in Colonial Mexico City: 1700–1810" (Ph.D. diss., Cambridge University, 1989), 27.

20 *Gacetas de México*, 1 January 1722, no. 1, in *Testimonios mexicanos: Historiadores 5. Gacetas de México*, ed. Francisco González de Cossio (Mexico City: Secretaría de Educación Pública, 1949), 1:6.

21 *Gacetas de México*, November 1729, no. 24, in González de Cossio, *Testimonios mexicanos*, 1: 212.

22 *Gacetas de México*, November 1733, no. 72, in González de Cossio, *Testimonios mexicanos*, 2: 140.

23 Antonio Rubial García, "Los santos milagreros y malogrados de la Nueva España," in *Manifestaciones religiosas en el mundo colonial americano. Volumen 1: Espiritualidad barroca colonial: Santos y demonios en América*, ed. Clara García Ayluardo and Manuel Ramos Medina (Mexico City: Universidad Iberoamericana, 1993), 71–107; Linda Curcio-Nagy, "Native Icon to City Protectress to Royal Patroness: Ritual, Political Symbolism, and the Virgin of Remedies," *The Americas* 52:3 (January 1996): 367–391. Serge Gruzinski found a "tidal wave of images" in rural areas beginning in the first decade of the seventeenth century, which he attributes to the eradication of the Erasmian tendencies of some of the earlier mendicant friars and the rise of the Jesuits and the secular clergy in New Spain. With its relics and images, baroque Catholicism offered numerous points of access to divine power, and thus numerous opportunities for lay appropriation of these objects and images. Gruzinski notes that by the mid–seventeenth century, Indian nobles claimed direct communication with the saints and thus challenged Spanish control of the supernatural. See his *Conquest*, 193, 221. For a lively account of Christian signs and objects being used for anti-Christian purposes in the rural areas of New Spain, see his *Man-Gods in the Mexican Highlands: Indian Power and Colonial Society, 1520–1800* (Stanford: Stanford University Press, 1989).

24 Juan Manuel de San Vicente, "Exacta descripción de la magnifica corte mexicana, cabeza del nuevo americano mundo, significada por sus esenciales partes, para el bastante conocimiento de su grandeza," in Rubial García, *La Ciudad de México*, 160.

25 Juan de Viera, "Breve compendiosa," 242.

26 Ibid., 226.

27 Peter Brown, "A Dark Age in Crisis: An Aspect of the Iconoclastic Controversy," *English Historical Review*, 88: 346 (January, 1973): 7.

28 Schroeder, *Canons*, 147–148.

29 Victor-L. Tapié, *The Age of Grandeur: Baroque Art and Architecture*, trans. A. Ross Williamson (New York: Frederick A. Praeger, 1961), 41, 57.

30 It has to be seen to be understood, so consult Ichiro Ono's magnificent photographs of the spectacular remains of Mexico's baroque age: *Divine Excess: Mexican Ultra-Baroque* (San Francisco: Chronicle Books, 1996).

31 Cited in Ramón A. Gutiérrez, *When Jesus Came, the Corn Mothers Went Away: Marriage, Sexuality, and Power in New Mexico, 1500–1846* (Stanford: Stanford University Press, 1991), 81.

32 Cited in David A. Brading, *The First America: The Spanish Monarchy, Creole Patriots, and the Liberal State, 1492–1867* (Cambridge, England: Cambridge University Press, 1991), 494–495.

33 Mexico City, "Lutos formados con motivo de lo acaecido en la enfermedad y entierro del sr. Inquisidor D. José Fierro y Torres," 26 Marzo 1768, AGN, Inquisición, vol. 1030, exp. 7, fol. 3.

34 Mexico City, 1818, AGN, Inquisición, vol. 921, exp. 23, fols. 267–271.

35 Mexico City, Asociación de Sacerdotes Difuntos, ACM, "Funerales de señores capitulares," exp. 42, ID 0002, UB E.4.2. (Id. Anterior: no. 420), fols. I–IV.

36 Mexico City, "Sumario de las gracias e indulgencias perpetuas que gozan los hermanos de la ilustre confradia del señor San Homobono . . . ," September 1776, AGN, Bienes Nacionales, leg. 871, exp. 2.

37 In 1785, the Confraternity de las Ánimas del Purgatorio offered, among other things, a blue cloth to wrap the body and the presence of the confraternity's processional standard and lights. See Juan Javier Pescador, *De bautizados a fieles difuntos: Familia y mentalidades en una parroquia urbana: Santa Catarina de México, 1568–1820* (Mexico City: El Colegio de México, 1992), 311, 318.

38 Francisco de la Maza, *Las piras funerarias en la historia y en el arte de Mexico: Grabados, litografías y documentos del siglo XVI al XIX* (Mexico City: Anales del Instituto de Investigaciones Esteticas, Imprenta Universataria, 1946), 14.

39 José Antonio Maravall, *Culture of the Baroque: Analysis of a Historical Structure*, trans. Terry Cochran (Minneapolis: University of Minnesota Press, 1986), 75.

40 Irving J. Leonard, *Baroque Times in Old Mexico: Seventeenth-Century Persons, Places, and Practices* (Ann Arbor: University of Michigan Press, 1959), 9.

41 Solange Alberro and Serge Gruzinski, *Introducción a la historia de las mentalidades* (Mexico City: Cuaderno de Trabajo del Departamento de Investigaciones Históricas 24, Instituto Nacional de Antropología y Historia, 1979), 97; Fernando Martínez Gil, *Actitudes ante la muerte en el Toledo de los Asturias* (Toledo, Spain: Ayuntamiento de Toledo, 1984), 52.

42 Juan Crasset, *La dulce y santa muerte obra que escribió en francés el padre Juan Crasset de*

la Compañía de Jesús, y traduxó en castellano el doctor don Basilio Sotomayor, trans. Basilio Sotomayor (Madrid: Imprenta de Gonzalez, 1728), 19, 243, 246, 341.

43 Mexico City, Will of Bernaude de Medina, 6 July 1640, AN, Notary 336, Gabriel López Ahedo, vol. 2226, fols. 37–46.

44 Rivera, Diario curioso, 20.

45 Antonio de Robles, Diario de sucesos notables (1665–1703), ed. Antonio Leal del Castro (Mexico City: Editorial Patría, 1946), 3:21.

46 Rivera, Diario curioso, 9.

47 Vetancourt, "Tratado," 127; Viera, "Breve compendiosa," 238.

48 Monigotes are discussed in City Attorney José Bernardo Baz's report to the Mexico City Council, 5 May 1817, Actas de Cabildo Originales, 136a, fol. 51. On renting mendicants from the Hospicio de Pobres, see Mexico City, "Carta de José Vara a Gabriel Valverde en que solicita le envíe 24 pobres para asistir al entierro de Félix Villagrán," 5 January 1832, AHSSA, Hospitales y Hospicios, sección Hospicio de Pobres, legajo 1, exp. 12, fols. 1–2.

49 García Ayluardo, "Confraternity," 185. Also see Alicia Bazarte Martínez, Las cofradías de españoles en la ciudad de México (1526–1869) (Mexico City: Universidad Autónoma Metropolitana, Unidad Atzcapotzalco, 1989).

50 García Ayluardo, "Confraternity," 185.

51 Mexico City, Constitution of the Archconfraternity del Cordón de Nuestro Seráfio Padre San Francisco, 22 September 1759, AGN, Cofradías y Archi-Cofradías, vol. 19, exp. 10, fol. 222.

52 García Ayluardo, "Confraternity," 199.

53 Mexico City, Will of Gerónima Antonia de Alciuar, 7 April 1717, AN, Notary 129, Juan de la Colina, vol. 827. fols. 24–26v; Mexico City, Will of Juana Rodríguez, 3 July 1709, AN, Notary 565, Benito Ignacio Rojas, vol. 3895, fols. 50v–55.

54 Mexico City, Congregation of San Pedro, 26 January 1678, AHSSA, Fondo Congregación de San Pedro, libro 7, fol. 256; Mexico City, Friar Mario Antonio de [?] to Congregation of San Pedro, 21 July 1701, AHSSA, Fondo Cofradías, Sección Congregación de San Pedro, Serie Legajos, Legajo 42, exp. 13; Mexico City, Funeral Notification, 8 April 1816, AHSSA, Fondo Congregación de San Pedro, Legajo 87, exp. 22; Mexico City, Francisco de Saavedra to Congregation of San Pedro, 21 February 1643, AHSSA, Fondo Congregación de San Pedro, Legajo 24, exp. 38; Mexico City, Will of Gaspar de Meua, 29 March 1690, AN, Notary 11, Andrés de Almogueras, vol. 43, fols. 52v–55.

55 Zárate Toscano, "Los nobles," 308.

56 Mexico City, 22 April 1788, AGN, Clero Regular y Secular, vol. 21, exp. 3, fol. 63v. For more examples of funeral cards, see Mexico City, Viceroy, 14 and 21 November 1815, AGN, Bandos, vol. 28, exps. 77, 179, fols. 156, 352; Mexico

City, Manuel de Cuevas Moriroi Guerrero, 30 October 1797, AHCM, Funerales y Ceremonias Funerales, vol. 1108, exp. 2.

57 Mexico City, Will of Fr. Manuel de Pedraza, 19 January 1692, AN, Notary 197, José Díaz Jiménez, vol. 1265, fols. 5–10v.

58 Cited in Warner, *Alone*, 285.

59 Alister E. McGrath, *Reformation Thought: An Introduction* (Oxford: Basil Blackwell, 1988), 80.

60 John Bossy, *Christianity in the West 1400–1700* (Oxford: Oxford University Press, 1985), 30. Readers interested in the origins of Purgatory should consult Jacques Le Goff, *The Birth of Purgatory*, trans. Arthur Goldhammer (Chicago: University of Chicago Press, 1981).

61 Bossy, *Christianity*, 55.

62 Carlos M. N. Eire, *From Madrid to Purgatory: The Art and Craft of Dying in Sixteenth-Century Spain* (Cambridge, England: Cambridge University Press, 1995), 109–111.

63 Pedro de Alcántara Fernández, *Manual areglado al ritual romano* (Mexico City: Doña María Rivera, 1748), 144; Mexico City, Guardian of the Franciscan Convent to the Inquisition, 18 March 1768, AGN, Inquisición, vol. 1055, exp. 5, fol. 210.

64 Mexico City, Will of José Muñoz de Castro, 27 July 1694, AN, Notary 390, José Muñoz de Castro, vol. 2564, fols. 142v–150; Mexico City, Will of Bernadino de Herrera, 10 June 1768, AN, Notary 148, Antonio de las Casas Orellana, vol. 879, fols. 60v–63.

65 Mexico City, Will of Ignacio Fuentes, 10 December 1826, AN, Notary 530, Eugenio Pozo, vol. 3551, fols. 90–92; Mexico City, Will of Juana de Ledo y Monno, 19 October 1644, AN, Notary 336, Gabriel López Ahedo, vol. 2227, fols. 74v–76; Mexico City, Will of Francisco Antonio Yñiguez, 9 July 1786, AN, Notary 280, Ignacio José Gonzalez, vol. 1762, fols. 26v–33; Mexico City, Will of Francisco del Castillo, 7 June 1717, AN, Notary 129, Juan de la Colina, vol. 827, fols. 38v–42.

66 Mexico City, Will of Juana Rodríguez, 3 July 1709, AN, Notary 565, Benito Ignacio Rojas, vol. 3895, fols. 50v–55; Mexico City, Will of Isavel Rodríguez, 7 October 1710, AN, Notary 565, Benito Ignacio Rojas, vol. 3895, fols. 108–110v; Mexico City, Will of María Rosa Guerra, 27 January 1718, Notary 397, Miguel Moreno Vezarez, vol. 2630, fols. 13v–19.

67 Gómez, *Diario curioso*, 180.

68 Mexico City, Constitutions of the Archconfraternity del Cordón de Nuestro Seráfico Padre San Francisco, 22 September 1759, AGN, Cofradías y Archicofradías, vol. 19, exp. 10, fols. 216–231. Also see Mexico City, Indulgences given to the Confraternity of el Divino Redentor de Cautivos, 1795, AGN, Bienes

Nacionales, leg. 871, exp. 2. Mexico City, Guardian of the Franciscan Priory to the Inquisition, 18 March 1768, AGN, Inquisición, vol. 1055, exp. 5, fol. 210.

69 Mexico City, Joaquin de León to Sr. Intendente y Juez Politico Ramón Gutiérrez, 7 September 1813, AHCM, Policía de Salubridad, Cementerios y Entierros, vol. 3673, exp. 3, fol. IV. On stripping bodies and vending their mortajas, also see Mexico City, Agustín Iglesias to Junta de Policía, 20 September 1819, AGN, Ayuntamientos, vol. 1, fol. 14.

70 Gómez, Diario curioso, 180. Although canon law did not specify that all of the faithful were entitled to a mortaja, it did oblige priests to bury the poor free of cost. In a 1787 decision, the secular authorities reiterated the prohibition against begging in the streets to raise funds for funerals, insisting that the poor be buried at the parish's expense and that beggars first obtain a license from the secular—not ecclesiastical—authorities to request alms in public. See Mexico City, Real Audiencia, 2 May 1787, AGN, Bandos, vol. 14, no. 59, fol. 225.

71 Gacetas de México, no. 3, 1722, in González de Cossío, Testimonios mexicanos, 1:12.

72 Mexico City, Will of María Florentina d'Arana y Viana, 20 May 1810, AN, Notary 610, Mariano González de la Rosa, vol. 4,087, nf.

73 San Vicente, "Exacta descripción de la magnífica corte mexicana . . . ," 161–162.

74 See, for example, Veracruz, Veracruz City Council to Ecclesiastical Council, 19 February 1796, AHCV, caja 51, vol. 59, fols. 120–122.

75 Schroeder, Canons, 216; Stephen Wilson, Saints and Their Cults: Studies in Religious Folklore and History (Cambridge, England: Cambridge University Press, 1983), 6; Dooley, "Church Law," 51; Keith P. Luria, Territories of Grace: Cultural Change in the Seventeenth-Century Diocese of Grenoble (Berkeley: University of California Press, 1991), 116–117. On the process of becoming a Counter-Reformation saint, see Peter Burke, "How to Become a Counter-Reformation Saint," in The Counter-Reformation: The Essential Readings, ed. David M. Luebke (London: Blackwell, 1999), 129–142. Also see R. Po-Chia Hsia, The World of Catholic Renewal, 1540–1770 (Cambridge, England: Cambridge University Press, 1998), 122–137.

76 This is not to say, however, that elements of the Counter-Reformation Church did not attempt to inculcate the faithful with an appreciation of the saints as moral exemplars rather than purveyors of miracles. See, for example, the efforts in Grenoble, France, described in Luria, Territories of Grace.

77 Recopilación de leyes de los reynos de las Indias, mandadas imprimir, y publicar por la magestad católica del rey don Carlos II, nuestro señor (Madrid: Ilvian de Paredes, 1681), 89v; Madrid, Royal Order, 18 August 1660, AGI, Indiferente, 430, legajo 40, fols. 235–239v. In sixteenth-century Madrid, 435 of the 436 wills examined by historian Carlos M. N. Eire requested burial within a particular church; see his From Madrid, 91.

78 See, for example, Edith Turner and Victor Turner, Image and Pilgrimage in Chris-

tian Culture: Anthropological Perspectives (New York: Columbia University Press, 1978); Diana Webb, *Pilgims and Pilgrimages in the Medieval West* (London: I. B. Tauris, 1999).

79 José Francisco Valdés, *Sermón en que en la translación de los huesos de los religiosos a la capilla de Nuestra Señora de Dolores . . . predicó el Fr. José Francisco Valdes, lector jubilado y calificador del Santo Oficio* (Mexico City: José Antonio de Hogal, 1787), 1–4.

80 Mexico City, Will of Josef de la Peña, A N, Notary 206, Andrés Delgado Calmargo, vol. 1356, fols. 70v–73v; Mexico City, Will of Juana de Abila Tirado, A N, Notary 197, José Díaz Jiménez, vol. 1265, fols. 21v–25.

81 On Our Lady of Guadalupe, see William B. Taylor, "The Virgin of Guadalupe in New Spain: An Inquiry into the Social History of Marian Devotion," *American Ethnologist* 14 (1987): 9–33; Jacques Lafaye, *Quetzalcoatl and Guadalupe: The Formation of Mexican National Conciousness, 1531–1813* (Chicago: University of Chicago Press, 1976); Mexico City, Will of Manuel Antonio Mateos, 22 February 1802, Notary 90, Ignacio Barrera, vol. 577, fols. 7–8.

82 Mexico City, Will of Gervasio del Corral y Sanz, 1 April 1824, A N, Notary 153, Francisco Calapiz y Aguilar, vol. 935, nf.

83 Mexico City, Will of Josefa Rita Rondón, 25 May 1780, A N, Notary 143, José Carballo, vol. 868, nf.; Mexico City, Will of Ana María Guerrero Hinojosa, 13 August 1720, A N, Notary 309, Jerónimo de Herrera, vol. 2113, fols. 92–93; Mexico City, "Constitutions of the Confraternity of San Francisco Xavier en la Santa Veracruz," 16 May 1695, A G N, Cofradías y Archicofradías, vol. 15, exp. 12, fol. 387v.

84 Pescador, *De bautizados*, 303–304.

85 Archbishop of Toledo to Council of Castile, "Informes de los M M . R R Arzobispos, R R. Obispos, y vicarios capitulares, sede-vacante. Colocados por el orden de sus metrópolis y diócesis," in Council of Castile, *Memorial ajustado del expediente seguido en el Consejo, en virtud del orden de S.M. de 24 de Marzo de 1781 sobre establecimiento general de cementerios* (Madrid: Ibarra, 1786), 1.

86 See, for example, Mexico City, Will of Juan Francisco de Guzmán, August 1675, A N, Notary 199, vol. 1308, fols. 92–93v. Some, of course, rejected the Church's burial apparatus entirely; Indians in the area of Xochimilco often buried their dead without any clerical intervention. See Mexico City, Archbishop Alonso Núñez de Haro y Peralta, 1777–1782, A H M, Libro 2 del gobierno del ilustrísimo sr. Dr. Dn. Alonso Nuñez de Haro y Peralta del Consejo de S.M., L9A/8, 1777–1782.

87 Fortino Hipólito Vera, ed., *Colección de documentos eclesiásticos de México, o sea antigua y moderna legislación de la iglesia mexicana* (Amecameca, Mexico: Colegio Católico, 1887), 1:76; *Colección de los Aranceles de obvenciones y derechos parroquiales que han estado vigentes en los obispados de la República Mexicana y que se citan en el*

supremo decreto de 11 de Abril de 1857 (Mexico City: Imprenta de Ignacio Cumplido, 1857), 8.

88 Michael C. Scardaville, "Crime and the Urban Poor: Mexico City in the Late Colonial Period" (Ph.D. diss., University of Florida, 1977), 88.

89 Juan Tejada y Ramiro, ed., *Colección de cánones y de todos los concilios de la Iglesia Española* (Madrid, 1855), 1: 139; Eire, *From Madrid*, 98–99.

90 Francisco Antonio Lorenzana y Butrón, ed., *Concilios provinciales primero, y segundo, celebrados en la muy noble, y muy leal Ciudad de México. Presidiendo el Illmo. y Rmo. Señor D. Fr. Alonso de Montúfar, en los años de 1555, 1565. Dados a luz por El Illmo. Sr. D. Francisco Antonio Lorenzana* (Mexico City: Antonio de Hogal, 1769), 78–79.

91 For examples of the marketing of chapel burial rights, see Mexico City, Will of Juan Cartagena Valdivia, 18 February 1665, AN, Notary 113, Juan de Cartagena Valdivia, vol. 734, fols. 4v–8; Mexico City, Will of Gabriel Guerrero de Luna, 15 May 1661, AN, Notary 112, Gabriel de la Cruz, vol. 773, fols. 24v–26v; Mexico City, Will of Gabriel Guerero de Abila, 13 April 1709, AN, Notary 565, Benito Ignacio Rojas, vol. 3895, fols. 37v–41.

92 Mexico City, Will of Juan Jiménez de Siles, 26 February 1686, AN, Notary 326, vol. 2207, fols. 5v–16; Mexico City, Will of Francisco Chavarri, 24 April 1826, AN, Notary 530, Eugenio Pozo, vol. 3551, nf; Mexico City, Will of Doña Francisca Velasco, 9 October 1661, AN, Notary 5, Nicolas de Arauz, vol. 12, fols. 109v–110v; Mexico City, "Representación que hizo el cura de la parroquia de San José de esta capital Diego Alvarez de Velasco, sobre licencia para construír a su costa . . . un panteón para sepulcro de los cadáveres rexidores de la ciudad," 2 December 1802, AGN, Bienes Nacionales, vol. 550, exp. 23; Veracruz, Veracruz City Council to Viceroy Revillagigiedo, 9 June 1790, AHCV, caja 30, vol. 31, fols. 229–331v; Mexico City, "Plan de las fiestas y distribuciones de gastos, que solicita hacen el illustrísimo y Real Colegio de Abogados en el convento de Nuestra Señora de San Francisco," 9 October 1801, AN, Notary 360, Manuel Lopez de Oquendo, vol. 2336, fols. 102–103; Mexico City, Will of Eugenio Batán, 13 April 1743, AN, Notary 698, vol. 4734, fols. 20v–24; Mexico City, Will of Juana Alvarez de Valdés, 7 December 1681, AN, Notary 636, vol. 4388, fols. 258v–261v.

93 Mexico City, Cathedral Chapter Burial Record of Don Ignacio José Díaz, 24 April 1792, Cathedral Archive, libro 57 of Actas de Cabildo, id 0058, UB E.2.1, 1792–1796, fol. 253v; Mexico City, 19 January 1790, AHSSA, fondo Cofradías, sección Santísima Trinidad, serie Legajos, leg, 1, exp. 11, fols. 1–3. Despite the legal prohibition, however, laypersons were apparently buried near the main altar. Archbishop Núñez de Haro y Peralta, for example, chastised the parish priest of Tenango del Valle for burying Doña Ignacia Alvarez near the main altar. See Mexico City, Archbishop Alonso Núñez de Haro y Peralta Edict, 24 July 1798, in Vera, *Colección de documentos*, 2: 527–528.

2 The Reformation in Mexico City

1 McGrath, *Reformation Thought*, 67–69.

2 Ibid., 55–57.

3 Appolis, *Les Jansénistes*, 10, 18, 249; Demerson, *María Francisca*, 278; John A. Mourant, ed., *Introduction to the Philosophy of Saint Augustine: Selected Readings and Commentaries* (University Park: Pennsylvania State University Press, 1964), 312–319.

4 Alister E. McGrath, *The Intellectual Origins of the European Reformation* (Oxford: Basil Blackwell, 1987), 175–178.

5 Benjamin B. Warfield, *Calvin and Augustine* (Philadelphia: Temple University Press, 1956), 322.

6 John Calvin, *Institutes of the Christian Religion (1559)*, ed. John T. McNeill (Philadelphia: Westminster Press, 1960), 2:1013.

7 Archbishop Alonso Nuñez de Haro y Peralta, *Carta pastoral que el Ilmô. Señor Doctor D. Alonso Nuñez de Haro y Peralta del Consejo de S.M. y Arzobispo de México, dirige a todos sus amados diocesanos sobre la doctrina santa en general, contraída en particular a las más esenciales obligaciones que tenemos para con Dios y para con el Rey* (Mexico City: Don Felipe de Zúñiga y Ontiveros, 1777), 68.

8 José María Laso de la Vega, *Oración panegyrica del gran padre y doctor de la iglesia sr. S. Augustín que en el convento de San Francisco Xavier el Real de Veracruz, del mismo orden dixó (el dia 28 de aug del año de 1780) don Joséph María Lazo de la Vega* . . . (Mexico City: Felipe de Zúñiga y Ontiveros, 1781), viii; Teófanes Egido, "La religiosidad de los ilustrados," in *La época de la Ilustración. Vol. 1: El estado y la cultura*, ed. Miguel Batllori (Madrid: Espasa-Calpe, 1992), 416. Erasmus' influence on Spanish Catholicism of the early sixteenth century is amply detailed in Marcel Bataillon, *Erasmo y España: Estudios sobre la historia espiritual del siglo XVI* (Mexico City: Fondo de Cultura Económica, 1966). On his eighteenth-century revival in Spain, see Antonio Mestre Sanchis, "El redescubrimiento de Fray Luis de León en el siglo XVIII," *Bulletin Hispanique*, 83: 1–2 (1981): 5–64. In New Spain, the early Franciscans acted as the channel for Erasmian thought, although eighteenth-century reformers did not acknowledge this intellectual patrimony; see, for example, Bataillon, *Erasmo y España*, 807–833; John Leddy Phelan, *The Millennial Kingdom of the Franciscans in the New World: A Study of the Writings of Gerónimo de Mendieta* (Berkeley: University of California Press, 1956), 43, 45, 47.

9 Fr. Luis de León, *The Names of Christ (1597)*, trans. and introduction by Manuel Durán and William Kluback (London: SPCK, 1984), 225.

10 Haro y Peralta, *Carta pastoral*, 72.

11 Pedro Rodríguez, Conde de Campomanes, *Discurso sobre la educación popular de los artesanos y su fomento (1775)*, ed. John Reeder (Madrid: Fábrica Nacionál de

Moneda y Timbre, 1975), 129. Campomanes served on the Council of Castile from 1762 to 1791, first as an attorney, then as its president.

12 Haro y Peralta, *Carta pastoral*, 2–3. The clearest statement of the concept of "dead to the law" is the Apostle Paul's: "For I to the law am dead to the law, that I might live unto God" (Galatians 2:19). In these declarations, Núñez de Haro y Peralta echoes other champions of grace against free will, particularly Martin Luther's belief that true faith in Christ's redeeming sacrifice made the Christian "dead to the law," by which Luther meant that the true Christian follows God's laws and Church ceremonies not out of fear of damnation but joyfully, propelled by God's prior love. God for Luther is not a wrathful external force, but a precondition of true Christian charity. See Martin Luther's 1531 "A Commentary on St. Paul's Epistle to the Galatians," in John Dillenberger ed., *Martin Luther: Selections from His Writings* (New York: Anchor Books, 1961), 99–165. Archbishop Haro y Peralta also echoed Erasmus' careful citation of Paul's exhortations to the Galatians: "Wherefore the law was our schoolmaster to bring us unto Christ, that we might be justified by faith. But after that faith has come, we are no longer under a schoolmaster. For ye are all the children of God by faith in Christ Jesus" (Galatians 3: 24–26, cited in Erasmus, *The Enchiridion of Erasmus* [1503], ed. and trans. Raymond Himelick [Bloomington: University of Indiana Press, 1963], 120). For a thorough compendium of Augustine's thoughts on the inferiority of exterior law as compared to interior grace, see Saint Augustine, *An Augustinian Synthesis*, ed. Erich Przywara (New York: Harper and Brothers, 1958), 312–321.

13 Haro y Peralta, "Carta pastoral del 15 de febrero de 1776 a las autoridades del real colegio seminario de Tepotzlán [sic] acerca de la importancia del estado sacerdotal," BN, Lafragua Collection, vol. 1004, pp. 44–45.

14 Miguel Hidalgo de Costilla, "Disertación sobre el verdadero método de estudiar teología escolástica" (1784), *ábside* 17:2 (April–June 1953): 182–183. For more on Hidalgo's theological sensibilities, see Juan Hernández Luna, "El mundo intelectual de Hidalgo," *Historia Mexicana*, 3:4 (October–December 1953):57–177; Gabriel Méndez Plancarte, "Hidalgo reformador intelectual," *ábside* 17:2 (April–June 1953): 135–170; Hugh M. Hamill Jr., *The Hidalgo Revolt: Prelude to Mexican Independence* (Gainesville: University of Florida Press, 1966), especially 61–74; Ernesto de la Torre Villar, "Hidalgo y Fleury," *Historia Mexicana*, 3:4 (October–December 1953): 207–216.

15 Tomsich, *El jansenismo*, 21; William J. Callahan, *Church, Politics, and Society in Spain, 1750–1874* (Cambridge, MA: Harvard University Press, 1984), 70; Lucienne Domergue, "De Erasmo a George Borrow: Biblia y secularización de la cultura española en el Siglo de las Luces," in *La secularización de la cultura española en el Siglo de las Luces: Actas del Congreso de Wolfenbüttel*, ed. Manfried Tietz (Weisbaden: Herzog August Bibliothek Wolfenbüttel, 1992), 57–90.

16 Madrid, El Censor, 20 December 1781, Discurso 46, paragraph 737, and 19 July 1781, Discurso 24, paragraphs 366, 376–379.

17 Seed, To Love.

18 Concilio Provincial Mexicano IV: Celebrado en la ciudad de México el año de 1771 (Queretero, Mexico: Escuela de Artes, 1898), 182. Lorenzana served as archbishop from 1766 to 1772.

19 Don Francisco Fabián y Fuero, Colección de Providencias diocesanas del obispado de la Puebla de los Angeles, hechas y ordenadas por su señor ilustrísima el sr. dr. d. Francisco Fabián y Fuero. Obispo de dicha ciudad y obispado del consejo de su majestad (Puebla, Mexico: Real Seminario Palafoxiano, 1770), 47, edict 14. He served as bishop of Puebla from 1765 to 1773.

20 D. Alonso Nuñez de Haro y Peralta, "Edicto de 20 de octubre de 1774 comunicando al clero de su diócesis que con motivo de su próxima visita a la misma ha dispuesto no se le hagan festejos de ninguna especie," BN Lafragua Collection, vol. 1004, 7.

21 Tomsich, El jansenismo, 61.

22 Fr. Luis de León, The Names, xiii–xiv.

23 Haro y Peralta, Carta pastoral, 86–87.

24 Demerson, María Francisca, 292. On Lorenzana's desire to expose the Eucharist less often, see Appolis, Les Jansénistes, 82; Concilio Provincial Mexicano IV, 111.

25 Don Francisco Antonio Lorenzana, "Aviso pastoral," October 1767, BN, Colección Lafragua, Misc. vol. 994, 4–11.

26 Rev. J. Waterworth, trans., The Canons and Decrees of the Sacred and Ecumenical Council of Trent, Celebrated Under the Pontiffs, Paul III, Julius III, and Pius IV (London: C. Dolman, 1948), 96.

27 Haro y Peralta, Carta pastoral, 227–228.

28 The clerical hierarchy's efforts to inculcate the faithful with an appreciation of the saint's moral rather than miraculous virtues were certainly not unprecedented in the Church. See, for example, Luria, Territories, 115.

29 Mercurio Histórico y Político, 1787, cited in Tomisch, El jansenismo, 136. Michael P. Carroll, Veiled Threats: The Logic of Popular Catholicism in Italy (Baltimore: Johns Hopkins University Press, 1996), 19. The Pope condemned the synod of Pistoia in his Auctorem Fidei of 1794. For more on the synod's influence on Spanish Reform Catholics, see Juan Marichal, "From Pistoia to Cádiz: A Generation's Itinerary," in The Ibero-American Enlightenment, ed. A. Owen Aldridge (Urbana-Champagne: University of Illinois Press, 1974), 97–110.

30 Cited in Tomisch, El jansenismo, 136.

31 Haro y Peralta, "Carta pastora del 15," 54.

32 Mexico City, Archbishop Alonso Núñez de Haro y Peralta to Viceroy Revillagigedo, 24 May 1794, AGN, Cofradías y Archicofradías, vol. 18, exp. 7, fols. 160,

309v; David A. Brading, "Tridentine Catholicism and Enlightened Despotism in Bourbon Mexico," *Journal of Latin American Studies* 15 (May 1983): 12.

33   Fabián y Fuero, *Colección de providencias*, 104, edict 27.

34   Mexico City, Viceroy Revillagigedo, 17 November 1789, AGN, Bandos, vol. 15, exp. 30, fol. 88. On the seventeenth-century celebrations, see Linda Curcio-Nagy, "Giants and Gypsies: Corpus Christi in Mexico City," in *Rituals of Rule, Rituals of Resistance: Public Celebrations and Popular Culture in Mexico*, ed. William H. Beezley, Cheryl English Martin, and William E. French (Wilmington, DE: Scholarly Resources, 1994), 1–26.

35   Mexico City, Royal Order, 19 July 1790, ACM, Actas de Cabildo, Libro 57, fol. 62.

36   Madrid, *El Censor*, 19 July 1781, Discurso 24, paragraphs 366, 376–379.

37   *Concilio Provincial Mexicano IV*, 167; Madrid, *El Censor*, 19 July 1781, Discurso 21, paragraphs 366–380.

38   Mexico City, "Libro de copias de las providencias diocesanas del tiempo del ilustrísimo y excelentísimo señor Dr. Alonso Núñez de Haro y Peralta," 13 November 1795, AHSSA, pamphlet no. 5, fol. 4; Aranjuez, Royal Order, 23 January 1803 and 30 March 1805, AGN, Reales Cédulas Originales, vol. 195, exp. 109, fol. 231.

39   José Joaquín Fernández de Lizardi, "Decimacuarta Conversación del Payo y El Sacristan (1825)," in *Obras V: Periódicos*, ed. María Rosa Palazón Mayoral and Felipe Reyes Palacio (Mexico City: Universidad Nacional Autónoma de México, 1975), 396–397.

40   José Joaquín Fernández de Lizardi, *Correo Seminario de México*, 25 April 1827, in *Obras VI: Periódicos*, 355.

41   Mexico City, Viceroy and Archbishop Francisco Xavier de Lizana y Beaumont, 27 October 1809, AGN, Bienes Nacionales, vol. 910, exp. 23, fol. 1. "Noli foras ire, in teipsum redi; in interiore homine habitat veritas" (Augustine cited in Charles Taylor, *Sources*, 129).

42   *Concilio Provincial Mexicano IV*, 166.

43   Keith Thomas, *Religion and the Decline of Magic* (New York: Scribner, 1971), 74.

44   José Joaquín Fernández de Lizardi, *Testamento del Pensador Mexicano: Ciudadano Fernández de Lizardi. Primera y segunda parte*, ed. Vicente Riva Palacio (Mexico City: Editorial Orientaciones, 1940), 8–9. For Erasmus' critique of devotion to curing saints, see "The Handbook of the Militant Christian (1503)" in *The Essential Erasmus*, ed., John P. Dolan (New York: Penguin Books, 1983), 60.

45   In this, as in so much else, reformers followed Erasmian precedence; see his "The Handbook," 66.

46   Don Gaspar Melchor de Jovellanos, "Informe sobre la disciplina eclesiástica antigua y moderna relativa al lugar de las sepulturas (1783)," in *Biblioteca de autores españoles desde la formación del lenguaje hasta nuestros dias: Obras públicadas e*

inéditas de don Gaspar Melchor de Jovellanos, ed. Miguel Artola (Madrid: Ediciones Atlas, 1956), 5:83. Jovellanos served in a number of Madrid academies and served as Minister of Justice from 1797 to 1798.

47 José Joaquín Fernández de Lizardi, *Obras. VII: Novelas. Vols. 1–2. El periquillo sarniento*, ed. Felipe Reyes Palacio (Mexico City: Universidad Nacional Autónoma de México, 1982), 235.

48 Mexico City, "Sobre asistencia de los religiosos a sacramentos y depósitos de cadáveres entrada la noche," 21 April 1794, AGN, Clero Regular y Secular, vol. 83, exp. 6, fols. 304–332.

49 Mario Góngora, "Estudios sobre el Galicanismo y la 'Ilustración Católica' en América española," *Revista Chilena de Historia y Geografía* 125 (1957): 126.

50 John H. R. Polt, *Gaspar Melchor de Jovellanos* (New York: Twayne Publishers, 1971), 110–111. Also see Brading, *First America*, 510.

51 D. Gaspar Melchor de Jovellanos, "Instrucción que dió a un jóven teólogo al salir de la Universidad, sobre el método que debía observar para perfeccionarse en el estudio de esta ciencia," in *Colección de varias obras en prosa y verso del exmo: Señor D. Gaspar Melchor de Jovellanos* (Madrid: Imprenta de D. León Amarita, 1831), vol. 4.

52 A good introduction to Church governance and debates about the importance of the councils is J. H. Burns and Thomas M. Izbicki, *Conciliarism and Papalism* (Cambridge, England: Cambridge University Press, 1997). In this, as in so much else, reformers followed the precedent of early sixteenth-century Christian humanists. These humanists found in the writings of the early Church Fathers a "holy rhetoric in service of the text," an emphasis on the meaning of Scripture unmediated by the subsequent commentaries of the centuries. See Eugene F. Rice Jr., "The Humanist Idea of Christian Antiquity: Lefévre d'Étaples and His Circle," *Studies in the Renaissance* 9:135 (1962): 132. Erasmus also pointed to the early Church as a paragon of Scripture-center worship and worship uncluttered by numerous mediators and elaborate hierarchies. See Carlos M. N. Eire's discussion of Erasmus and humanistic primitivism in his *War against the Idols: The Reformation of Worship from Erasmus to Calvin* (London: Cambridge University Press, 1986), 28–36.

53 Eire, *From Madrid*, 29.

54 Francisco Antonio Lorenzana y Buitrón, "Aviso pastoral," in *Cartas pastorales y edictos del Ill.mo Señor D. Francisco Antonio Lorenzana y Bútron Arzobispo de México* (Mexico City: Joseph Antonio de Hogal, 1770), 4–11.

55 Ibid., 2–3.

56 Lanning, *Eighteenth Century*, 140. On probalism and other Jesuit thought being banned from the Empire's universities, see Ricardo Krebs Wilckens, "The

Victims of a Conflict of Ideas," in *The Expulsion of the Jesuits from Latin America*, ed. Magnus Mörner (New York: Knopf, 1965), 47–52.

57 Tomisch, *El jansenismo*, 136.

58 Protestant iconoclasm is vividly described in P. Mack Crew, *Calvinist Preaching and Iconoclasm in the Netherlands, 1544–69* (Cambridge, England: Cambridge University Press, 1978); Lee Palmer Wandel, *Voracious Idols and Violent Hands: Iconoclasm in Reformation Zurich, Strasbourg, and Basel* (Cambridge, England: Cambridge University Press, 1995); Eire, *War*; Robert W. Scribner, "Ritual and Reformation," in *The German People and the Reformation*, ed. R. Po-Chia Hsia (Ithaca, NY: Cornell University Press, 1988), 122–144.

59 Josefa Amar y Borbón, *Discurso sobre la educación física y moral de las mujeres*, ed. María Victoria López-Cordón (Madrid: Ediciones Cátedra), 150.

60 Martin Luther and John Calvin cited in Christopher Hill, *Change and Continuity in Seventeenth-Century England* (New Haven: Yale University Press, 1991), 84. Also see Martin Luther, "A Comment on St. Paul's Epistle to the Galatians (1531)," in *Martin Luther: Selections from His Writing*, 112; John Calvin, "Institutes of Christian Religion (1559)," in *John Calvin: Selections from His Writings*, ed. John Dillenberger (New York: Anchor Books, 1971), 414–415. All of these reformers imply that this "integrity of the heart" is a synonym for God's grace to the soul.

61 Haro y Peralta, *Carta pastoral*, 135.

62 Augustin Glazier, *Historie génénerale du movement janséniste despuis se origines jusqu'á nos jours*, 5th ed. (Paris: Librairie Ancienne Honoré Champion, 1924) 1: chap. 1.

63 Demerson, *María Francisca*, 278.

64 Francis Bocanegra cited in Callahan, *Church, Politics*, 5.

65 Tomisch, *El jansenismo*, 43.

66 For a clear statement of this for the Spanish context, see C. C. Noel, "Opposition to Enlightened Reform in Spain: Campomanes and the Clergy, 1765–1775," *Societas* 3:1 (1973): 26–27.

67 Van Kley, *Religious Origins*, 7. That the state-led Spanish enlightenment was a "Catholic enlightenment," is also discussed in Egido, "La religiosidad," 401.

68 Weber, *Protestant Ethic*, especially 155–184.

69 Haro y Peralta, "Carta pastoral del 15," 76–78.

70 Mexico City, Viceroy Bucareli Edict, 29 January 1778, AGN, Ayuntamientos, vol. 194, exp. 12, fol. 17. The 1695 regulations are printed in Robles, *Diario de sucesos*, 3:26. A 1763 reprint of the decree is found in Juan M. Rodríguez de la Miguel, ed., *Pandectas . . .* (Mexico City: Mariano Galvan Rivera, 1839), 1:116.

71 Mexico City, Viceroy Garibay to Mexico City Council, 9 June 1809, AHCM, Actas de Cabildos Regulares, vol. 128a, fols. 171v–172; Madrid, Antonio Porcel to Viceroy, 18 July 1801, AGN, Reales Cédulas Originales, vol. 182, exp. 69, fols. 160–161; Mexico City, Pedro Catalini to Viceroy Iturrigaray, 17 August 1808,

AGN, Criminal, vol. 134, exp. 746, fol. 549; Mexico City, Viceroy Bucareli Edict, 29 January 1778, AGN, Ayuntamientos, vol. 194, exp. 12, fol. 17.

72 Mexico City, Viceroy Bucareli Edict, 29 January 1778, AGN, Ayuntamientos, vol. 194, exp. 12, fol. 17. An 1801 royal order reiterated 1792 and 1794 edicts calling for moderation in the ringing of funeral bells and in coffin decoration; see Madrid, Antonio Porcel to Viceroy, 18 July 1801, AGN, Reales Cédulas Originales, vol. 182, exp. 69, fols. 160–161; Havana, Edict of Doctor Felipe Joseph de Tres-Palacios y Verdeja, 9 January 1792, AGN, Reales Cédulas Originales, vol. 157, exp. 137, fols. 1–9. A 1723 edict that was reissued in 1760 and 1763 is printed in *Novísima recopilación de las leyes de España, mandada formar por el Señor don Carlos IV* (Paris: Don Vicente Salva, 1854), 1:20.

73 Mexico City, Viceroy Bucareli Edict, 29 January 1778, AGN, Ayuntamientos, vol. 194, exp. 12, fol. 17.

74 Madrid, Antonio Porcel to Viceroy Iturrigaray, 14 August 1807, AGN, Reales Cédulas Originales, vol. 199, exp. 43, fol. 3. On efforts to moderate the military's mourning expenditures, see Mexico City, Viceroy Iturrigaray Edict, 6 October 1807, AGN, Bandos, vol. 24, no. 89, fol. 231.

75 Fabian y Fuero, *Colección de providencias*, 417–418.

76 Havana, Edict of Doctor don Felipe Joseph de Tres-Palacios y Verdeja, 9 January 1792, AGN, Reales Cédulas Originales, vol. 157, exp. 137, fols. 1–9; Fabián y Fuero, *Colección de providencias*, 417–418; Mexico City, Viceroy Bucareli Edict, 29 January 1778, AGN, Ayuntamientos, vol. 194, exp. 12, fol. 17.

77 Mexico City, 1793, AGN, Historia, vol. 156, exp. 7, fols. 1–27.

78 Mexico City, *Diario de México*, tomo 2, no. 131, p. 155, cited in Zárate Toscano, "Los nobles," 334. On bell ringing, see Madrid, 18 July 1801, Antonio Porcel to Viceroy, AGN, Reales Cédulas Originales, vol. 182, exp. 69, fols. 160–161. This edict reiterated a royal edict from 1793.

79 *Gazetas de México*, 24 May 1791, vol. 4, no. 34, p. 321; *Diario de México*, 21 November 1805, vol. 52, pp. 218–219.

80 Mestre, *Mundo intelectual*, 283.

81 Brading, "Tridentine Catholicism," 20.

82 Madrid, 14 August 1807, Antonio Porcel to Viceroy Iturrigaray, AGN, Reales Cédulas Originales, vol. 199, exp. 43, fols. 3v–4. Other subjects whose elaborate funerals drew reprimands from the City Council are discussed in Mexico City, City Council, 9 September 1777, AGN, Ayuntamientos, vol. 194, exp. 12, fols. 8–9.

83 Madrid, 14 August 1807, Antonio Porcel to Viceroy Iturrigaray, AGN, Reales Cédulas Originales, vol. 199, exp. 43, fols. 1–2. The Marquesa was wrong about the price for poorhouse residents, which was 1 peso. I thank Silvia Arrom for pointing this out.

84 Mexico City, City Council, 9 September 1777, AGN, Ayuntamientos, vol. 194, exp. 12, fols. 8–9.

85 Mexico City, Viceroy Bucareli Edict, 29 January 1778, AGN, Ayuntamientos, vol. 194, exp. 12, fol. 17.

86 Mexico City, Will of Rafael Sagas, 26 June 1816, AN, Notary 158, José Ignacio Caño y Moctezuma, vol. 961, nf.; Mexico City, Will of Agustína de Olvera y Alzibar, 20 January, 1812, AN, Notary 210, Juan Mariano Díaz, vol. 1402, nf.; Mexico City, Will of José Galindo, 23 February 1823, AN, Notary 530, Eugenio Pozo, vol. 3551, fols. 90–92.

87 Mexico City, Will of Manuel de Marroquín, 14 January, 1815, AN, Notary 158, José Ignacio Caño y Moctezuma, vol. 961, nf.; Mexico City, Will of José Vicente Rodríguez, 19 May 1796, AN, Notary 90, Ignacio de Barrera, vol. 575, fols. 14–19.

88 Mexico City, José Bernardo Baz to City Council, 5 May 1817, AHCM, Actas de Cabildo Originales 136a, fol. 51. The city council went on to say that "due to an interest in humility and economy, some years ago it became customary to conduct private funerals." See Mexico City, City Council to Viceroy, 12 September 1817, AHCM, Actas de Cabildo Originales 136a, fol. 126. In 1820, the city council rejected a plan to eliminate one accompanying priest from the more elaborate funerals and redirect the money saved for cemetery construction, noting that little money would be collected because "most funerals were now conducted privately with little accompaniment." See Mexico City, José María Casasola to City Council, 21 December 1820, AGN, Ayuntamientos, vol. 1, exp. 10, fol. 13v.

89 This description of luxurious funerals is the city attorney's and the cathedral chapter's; see José Bernardo Baz to City Council, 5 May 1817, AHCM, Actas de Cabildo Originales 136a, fol. 60; Mexico City, El Sagrario Parish to City Council, 14 April 1817, AHCM, Actas de Cabildo Originales 136a, fol. 53.

90 Mexico City, El Sagrario Parish to City Council, 14 April 1817, AHCM, Actas de Cabildo Originales 136a, fol. 53, 52v.

91 Mexico City, Will of Ana de Los Angeles, 12 May 1642, AN, Notary 60, Juan de Barrientos, vol. 452, fols. 133v–134v.

92 Mexico City, Will of María Nicolasa Larrión, 1 August 1812, AN, Notary 749, vol. 5, nf.; Mexico City, Poder de Testar de Pedro Ramón Romero de Terreros Rebuesto y Davalos, 9 May 1808, AN, Notary 602, Antonio Ramírez Arellano, vol. 4066, nf. Also see the Count's eulogy, which lauds him as a man who rejected the "opulence of his position" and declared him an enemy of "fuss [fausto] and ambition." Instead, the Count demonstrated the virtues of "modesty, prudence, meekness, and studiousness" and was a major benefactor of the Hospicio de Pobres. His humble funeral, the paper explained, put a fitting

stamp on his virtuous life (Mexico City, 22 October 1809, *Diario de México*, tomo 6, no. 1483, pp. 467–470).

93 Campomanes, *Discurso*.

94 Mexico City, Will of Francisco Jiménez, 28 September 1818, AN, Notary 716, José María Vallejo, vol. 4829, nf. Also see Mexico City, Will of Guillermo de Aguirre, 19 December 1810, AN, Notary 85, Joaquín Barrientos, vol. 561, nf.; Mexico City, Will of Bárbara Rodríguez de Velasco, 12 June 1813, AN, Notary 85, Joaquin Barrientos, vol. 561, nf.

95 See, for example, Mexico City, Will of María Josefa del Rosario Peynado, 1 March 1814, AN, Notary 711, Nicolas de la Vega, vol. 4791, nf.

96 Mexico City, José Ignacio Caño to City Council, 1802, AHCM, Policía de Salubridad, Cementerios y Entierros, vol. 3673, exp. 1, fol. 6v; Mexico City, Joaquin de León to Sn. Intendente y Juez Politico Ramón Gutiérrez, 7 September 1813, AHCM, Policía de Salubridad, Cementerios y Entierros, vol. 3673, exp. 3, fol. 1v.

97 Haro y Peralta, "Carta pastoral del 15," 54.

98 Mexico City, Will of María Guadalupe Ambriz, 5 May 1795, AN, Notary 90, Ignacio de la Barrera, vol. 575, fols. 15–16v.

99 On the rationale for cemetery construction, see, for example, Mexico City, Augustin de Rivero, 12 February 1807, AGN, Gobernación, vol. 2154, caja 2630, exp. 3, fol. 64.

100 Mexico City, Archbishop Alonso Nuñez de Haro y Peralta, 8 November 1779, AGN, Gobernación, vol. 2154, caja 2630, exp. 3, fol. 46. For more on Nuñez de Haro y Peralta's cemetery proposals, see Mexico City, Archbishop Alonso Nuñez de Haro y Peralta, 8 November 1779, BN, Collección Lafragua, 575, fols. 1–3v; Mexico City, Archbishop Alonso Nuñez de Haro y Peralta, 8 November 1779, AGN, Ayuntamientos, vol. 1, fols. 159–159v; Vera, *Colección de documentos*, 2:182–185; San Idelfonso, Royal Order, 15 September 1780, AGN, Reales Cédulas Originales, vol. 119, exp. 152, fols. 323–325.

101 Mexico City, Augustin de Rivero, 12 February 1807, AGN, Gobernación, vol. 2154, caja 2630, exp. 3, fol. 64.

102 Mexico City, Juan Francisco Alzcarate to City Council, 12 August 1821, AGN, Ayuntamientos, vol. 2, exp. 13, fol. 192v.

103 Mexico City, City Council, 9 September 1777, AGN, Ayuntamientos, vol. 194, exp. 12, fols. 8–9.

104 Fernando Benítez, *Historia de la Ciudad de México* (Barcelona: Salvat Editores, 1984), 4:33; Maza, *Las piras*, 17.

105 Mexico City, City Council, 28 and 30 January 1816, AHCM, Actas de Cabildos Regulares, vol. 135, fols. 42, 145.

106 Mexico City, El Sagrario to City Council, 14 April 1817, AHCM, Actas de

Cabildo Originales, vol. 136a, fols. 53, 55v; Mexico City, José Bernardo Baz to City Council, 28 April 1817, AHCM, Actas de Cabildo Originales, vol. 136a, fols. 57–62v.

107   Mexico City, Will of Guillermo Gregoni, 22 February 1810, AN, Notary 418, Manuel Martinez del Campo, vol. 2794; Mexico City, Will of Francisco Xavier Alvarez de Mendez, 25 May 1810, AN, Notary 712, Juan Vicente de Vega, vol. 4811, fols. 39–41.

3   Freeing the Virtuous Individual

1   Bishop Clement constructed a suburban cemetery in Barcelona in 1775. See Peter B. Goldman, "Mitos liberales, mentalidades burguesas, e historia social en la lucha en pro de los cementerios municipales," in *Homenaje a Noel Salomón: Ilustración española e independencia de América*, ed. Alberto Gil Novales (Barcelona: Universidad Autónoma de Barcelona, 1979), 88. On early attempts to build suburban cemeteries in Mexico, see Mexico City, Archbishop Núñez de Haro y Peralta Edict, 8 November 1779, AGN, Gobernación, vols. 2154–2155, caja 2630, exp. 3, fol. 6.

2   Real Academia de la Historia, *Informe dado al consejo por la Real Academia de la Historia en 10 de junio de 1783 sobre la disciplina eclesiástica antigua y moderna relativa al lugar de las sepulturas* (Madrid: Antonio de Sancha, Impresor de la Academia, 1786), vii.

3   Noel, "Opposition," 23.

4   Council of Castile, *Memorial*; Real Academia de la Historia, *Informe*; Real Academia de Medicina, "Informe de la Academia Médica Matritense," AHN, Consejos, 3.151.

5   See, for example, the comments of the bishops of Canarias, Palencia, Cartagena, and Vich in "Informes de los MM.RR Arzobispos, RR. Obispos, y vicarios capitulares, sede-vacante. Colocados por el orden de sus metrópolis y diocesis," in Council of Castile, *Memorial*, 32–33, 58–61, 139, 166–167.

6   Jovellanos, "Informe sobre la disciplina," 5:87. Federico Ponte Chamorro reports that Spanish Christians were buried in churches beginning in the eighth century; see his "Mentalidad religiosa, ritos funerales, y clases sociales en el Madrid decimononico," in *Anales del Instituto de Estudios Madrileños* (Madrid: Consejo Superior de Investigaciones Científicas, 1986), 484.

7   Real Academia de la Historia, *Informe*, 20–21.

8   Cited in Don Ramón Cabrera, "Disertación Historica; en la qual se expone por la serie de los tiempos la varía disciplina que ha observado la Iglesia de España sobre el lugar de las sepulturas," in *Pruebas de ser contrario a la práctica de todas las naciones y a la disciplina eclesiástica, y perjudicial a la salud de los vivos enterrar los*

difuntos en las iglesias y los poblados, ed. Benito Bails (Madrid: Don Benito Bails, 1785), 147.

9 Conde de Cobarrús, "Sanidad pública," in *Cartas,* ed. José Maravall Casesnoves (Madrid: Castellote Editorial, 1973), 6.

10 Huesca, Archbishop of Huesca to Council of Castile, "Informes de los MM.RR Arzobispos," 184.

11 Cortes de la Frontera, Francisco Xavier de Espinosa y Aguilera to Council of Castile, 15 September 1781, AHN, Consejos 3.151, no. 53, fol. 31v.

12 Anonymous Report to the Council of Castile, AHN, Consejos 3.151, no. 52, maps 1181–83, fol. IV.

13 Ibid., fol. 2; Valladolid, Bishop of Valladolid to Council of Castile, "Informes de los MM.RR Arzobispos," 43; Orihuela, Bishop of Orihuela to Council of Castile, "Informes de los MM.RR Arzobispos," 215.

14 Jovellanos, "Informe sobre la disciplina," 5: 104.

15 Council of Castile to King, Madrid, 12 September 1786, AHN, Consejos, leg. 1.032, fols. 155v, 161v–162v, 172v, 173v–174.

16 Julio Antonio Vaquero Iglesias, *Muerte e ideología en la Asturias del siglo XIX* (Madrid: Siglo Veintiuno, 1991), 279–283, 289, 294. The Council of Castile's cemetery debate is also discussed in José Luis Galán Cabilla, "Madrid y los cementerios en el siglo XVIII: El fracaso de una reforma," in *Carlos III, Madrid, y la Ilustración: Contradiciones de un proyecto reformista,* ed. Josef Fontaña (Madrid: Siglo Veintiuno, 1988), 269–271. Also see Goldman, "Mitos liberales," 82–83.

17 Mexico City, 3 April 1787, Real Cédula, AGN, Bienes Nacionales, vol. 910, exp. 23, fols. 14–15v; Rodríquez de la Miguel, *Pandectas,* 1:112; *Novísima recopilación,* 1:18; AGN, Reales Cédulas Originales, vol. 149, exp. 198, fols. 292–305.

18 Real Academia de la Historia, *Informe,* xlii, 98–100. The Bishop of Vich recommended that the King obtain the Pope's permission for *indulgencias* given in cemetery altars; see "Informes de los MM.RR Arzobispos," 167.

19 Tomás Romay, *Descripción del cementerio general de la Havana por el Dr. dn. Tomás Romay, socio numerario de la Sociedad Economica de la Havana en la clase de profesor sobresaliente y académico. Corresponsal de la Real Academia de Medicina de Madrid* (Havana: D. Estevan Joseph Boloña, 1806), 2–9; R. Gutiérrez, "Notas," 1:320.

20 Havana, Bishop Juan Joseph Díaz de Espada y Landa, 20 January 1806, AGI, Santo Domingo, vol. 2258, nf.; Dr. dn. Julian Joseph del Barrio, *Discurso que en la solemne benedición del cementerio general de la Havana, hecha en la tarde del día dos de febrero de 1806, por el ilustrísimo señor D. Juan Joseph Díaz de Espada y Landa, obispo de esta diocesi, pronunció el Dr. dn. Julian Joseph del Barrio, Canonigo de su santa iglesia catedral* (Havana: Estevan Joseph Boloño, 1806), 9.

21 Havana, General Cemetery Rules, 1806, AGI, Santo Domingo, vol. 2258, no. 4, fols. 1–2. The rules governing Santiago de Chile's general cemetery, which

opened in 1823, also proscribed loud display, permitted only small differences among grave markers, and advocated the "utmost simplicity." See *Panteon general. Reglamento del panteon general de Santiago de Chile. Dictado por el supremo gobierno año de 1824* (Santiago: Imprenta Nacional, 1824), 9–10.

22 Madrid, El Ministro del Fiscal, 29 November 1806, AGI, Santo Domingo, vol. 2258, fols. 1–6.

23 Bishop Juan Joseph Díaz de Espada y Landa, *Exhortación a los fieles de la ciudad de Havana, hecha por su prelado diocesano, sobre el cementerio general de ella; y su reglamento, aprobado por el gobierno, con el correspondiente de policía* (Havana: Estevan Joseph Boloña, 1806), 47.

24 Aranjuez, Royal Order, 11 May 1807, AGI, Santo Domingo, vol. 2258, fols. 2–3; Madrid, El Ministro del Fiscal, 29 November 1806, AGI, Santo Domingo, vol. 2258, fol. 2v.

25 Cadiz, Antonio Odoándo de Balmeseda, 30 December 1808, AGI, Santo Domingo, vol. 2258, fols. 1–4.

26 Lima, Archbishop Bartolomé María Heras, 1808, AGN, Bienes Nacionales, vol. 910, exp. 23, fol. 3v.

27 Cited in Pedro Mallo, *Apuntes historicos sobre el estado oriental del Uruguay. Sus medicos, instituciones de caridad, hospitales y cementerios . . . desde el año 1726 hasta el 1810* (Buenos Aires: Imprenta Industrial, 1899), 243–253.

28 Hill, *Change*, 90–93.

29 On the recruitment and establishment of a ministerial and bureaucratic cadre without aristocratic roots, see Miguel Artola, *Antiguo Régime y revolución liberal* (Barcelona: Ariel, 1978), 131–144; David R. Ringrose, *Spain, Europe, and the "Spanish Miracle," 1700–1900* (Cambridge, England: Cambridge University Press, 1996), 315–328. On the split between *colegiales* and *manteistas*, as well as efforts to reform the educational system, see George Addy, *The Enlightenment in the University of Salamanca* (Durham, NC: Duke University Press, 1966). Also see R. Olaechea, "El anticolegialismo del gobierno de Carlos III," *Cuadernos de Investigación, Geográfica e Historia* 2 (1976): 53–90.

30 Jorge Cejudo López, *Bosquejo de política economica española de Campomanes* (Madrid: Taurus, 1984), 12.

31 Appolis, *Les Jansénistes*, 79.

32 Mestre, *Mundo intelectual*, 251.

33 L. Sala Balust, *Visitas y reforma de los colegios mayores de Salamanca en el reinado de Carlos III* (Salamanca: Universidad de Salamanca, 1958), 394.

34 Seville, Bishop of Seville to Council of Castile, "Informes de los MM.RR Arzobispos," 47. Also see Orihuela, Bishop of Orihuela to Count of Floridablanca, 24 March 1781, AHN, Consejos 1.302, fol. 45v.

35 Dr. Don Francisco Fernández, "Disertación físico-legal acerca de los sitios y

parages que se deben destinar para las sepulturas. Se manifiestan los daños y perjuicios que se originan a la salud pública por los entierros dentro de los poblados," AHN, Consejos 3.151, no. 48, fol. 79.

36 Seville, Bishop of Seville to Council of Castile, "Informes de los MM.RR Arzobispos," 68.

37 Benito Bails, ed., *Pruebas de ser contrario a la practica de todas las naciones y a la disciplina eclesiástica, y perjudicial a la salud de los vivos enterrar los difuntos en las iglesias y los poblados* (Madrid: Don Benito Bails, 1785).

38 Dr. Janin, Señor de Camble-Blanco, *El antimefítico ó licor antipútrido y perfectamente correctivo de los vapores perniciosísimos de los dormitorios, comedores, teatros, hospitales, enfermerías, iglesias, cementerios, cuarteles, cárceles, minas, navíos de guerra, lugares comunes, albañales, sumideros, carnicerías, limpías, y mondas* (Madrid: Imprenta Real, 1782).

39 Real Academia de la Historia, *Informe*. Friedrich Hoffmann the Younger (1660–1742), German physician and advocate of the sytematizing of medical knowledge, and François Boissier de Sauvages de Lacroix (1706–1767), published various books on pathology. Hermann Boerhaave (1668–1738), Dutch professor of practical medicine and a champion of clinical medicine. Vicq d'Azyr (1748–1794), French proponent of clinical medicine taught in hospitals. Gerard Freyherr Van Swicten (1689–1762), a student of Boerhaave who reorganized the Vienna medical faculty to emphasize clinical medicine.

40 Jovellanos, "Informe sobre la disciplina," 5: 88. On the Economic Societies, see Robert J. Shafer, *The Economic Societies in the Spanish World, 1763–1821* (Syracuse, NY: Syracuse University Press, 1958), 24–28.

41 Shafer, *Economic Societies*, 20, 85, 50, 92.

42 Asturias, Sociedad Economica del Príncipe de Asturias to Council of Castile, 30 November 1781, in Council of Castile, *Memorial*, 42–43; Demerson, *María Francisca*, 407; Antonio Elorza, *La ideología liberal en la Ilustracion española* (Madrid: Taurus, 1970), 139; Shafer, *Economic Societies*, 48.

43 Soledad Gomez Navarro, "La construccion de cementerios en la provincia de Cordoba, 1787–1833," in *Una arquitectura para la muerte: Actas del I Encuentro Internacional sobre Cementerios Contemporáneos*, ed. Dirección General de Arquitectura y Vivienda de la Consejería de Obras Públicas y Transportes de la Junta de Andalucía (Seville: Junta de Andalucía, 1993), 404, n. 13.

44 Rivas Alvarez, *Miedo y piedad*, 148.

45 Jerez de la Frontera, Tomás de Morila to Príncipe de la Paz, 29 April 1806, AGI, Secretaría, Guerra 7326, exp. 16, fols. 1–12; Madrid, King to Council of Castile, 6 May 1806, AGI, Secretaría, Guerra 7326, exp. 16, fol. 13.

46 See Ruíz de Velasco y Martínez, *Defensa de los cementerios católicos contra la secularización y revindicación de los derechos parroquiales en el entierro y funerales* (Madrid: Baena

Hermnos Impresores, 1907); "Coleccion de providencias sobre cementerios," AHN, Consejos 1.032. At least some rural French parishioners found reform piety an unsavory imposition on their own more exuberant religiosity, whereas others proved more enthusiastic. For the various examples, see Suzanne Desan, *Reclaiming the Sacred: Lay Religion and Popular Politics in Revolutionary France* (Ithaca, NY: Cornell University Press, 1990).

47 "Colección de providencias sobre cementerios," AHN, Consejos 1.032.

48 The edict is printed in Rodríquez de la Miguel, *Pandectas*, 1:35, 1:36. Mexico City, *Noticioso General*, 16 October 1818, no. 436, p. 3, col. 1.

49 Jovellanos, "Informe sobre la disciplina," 5: 104; "Colección de providencias sobre cementerios," AHN, Consejos, leg. 1.032, fol. 18; Bishop of Segovia to Council of Castile, "Informes de los MM.RR Arzobispos," 29.

50 Callahan, *Church, Politics*, 15, 20.

51 María José Zaparaín Yáñez, "La problemática de los cementerios en la provincia de Burgos bajo el reformismo ilustrado," in Direccion General de Arquitectura y Vivienda de la Consejería de Obras Públicas y Transportes de la Junta de Andalucía, *Una arquitectura*, 567–573.

52 Catholic and Protestant visions of public space are expertly discussed in Natalie Davis, "The Sacred and the Body Social in Sixteenth-Century Lyon," *Past and Present* 90 (February 1981): 40–70.

53 Mexico City, Viceroy and Archbishop Francisco Xavier de Lizana y Beaumont, 27 October 1809, AGN, Bienes Nacionales, vol. 910, exp. 23, fols. 1–3; Isidro Sainz de Alfaro y Beaumont, *Circular que dirige el señor gobernador de la sagrada mitra á los párrocos, eclesiásticos, y fieles cristianos del arzobispado de México, sobre ereccion de cementerios fuera de las poblaciones* (Mexico City: Doña María Fernández de Jauregui, 1809), 8–9, 27–28.

54 Huascazaloya, Josef de Azcarate, 26 January 1810, AGN, Bienes Nacionales, vol. 910, exp. 23, fol. 16; Tepexic del Rio, Idelfonso de Esquivel y Vargas, 26 May 1810, AGN, Bienes Nacionales, vol. 910, exp. 23, fols. 18–19; Iguala, José María Vigra, 10 March 1810, Bienes Nacionales, vol. 910, exp. 23, fol. 21. Also see the responses from parish priests in Tepocoacuilco, Amatepec Tlatlaya, Tasco, Michuiahualan, San Andrés Humiltepec, Mextitlan de la Sierra, and Chilcuautla, all of whom stressed a lack of funds for cemetery construction: AGN, Bienes Nacionales, vol. 910, exp. 23.

55 The number of clergy in Irapuato is discussed in David A. Brading, "El clero mexicano y el movimiento insurgente de 1810," *Relaciones* 2:5 (winter 1981): 17. On the failure of cemetery reform in these towns, see Guanajuato, Intendant to Viceroy Venadito, 9 and 12 March 1820, AGN, Ayuntamientos, vol. 2, exp. 8, fols. 96, 98.

56 Guanajuato, Don José Ignacio Rocha to Viceroy Apadaca, 3 July 1818, AGN,

Ayuntamientos, vol. 2, exp. 8, fols. 90–90v; "Causa formado al Presbítero José Antonio Talavera," February 1812 to April 1812, BLAC, Juan E. Hernández y Dávalos Manuscript Collection, HD 4.71.338, fol. IV.

57 Guanajuato, José Ignacio Roca to Viceroy Apadaca, 3 July 1818. AGN, Ayuntamientos, vol. 2, exp. 8, fol. 91.

58 Brading, Una Iglesia asediada: El obispado de Michoacán, 1749–1810 (Mexico City: Fondo de Cultura Económica, 1994), 127, 164.

59 Durángo, Bishop Juan Francisco to Viceroy the Count of Vendito, 6 December 1819, AGN, Ayuntamientos, vol. 2, exp. 11, fols. 155–156.

60 Cortes de la Frontera, Francisco Xavier de Espinosa y Aguilera to Council of Castile, 15 September 1781, AHN, Consejos 3.151, no. 53.

61 Gomez Navarro, "La construcción," 401.

62 Avila Cathedral Chapter, and the bishops of Zamora, Calahorra, and Pamplona to Council of Castile, "Informes de los MM.RR Arzobispos," 73, 91, 138.

63 Vich, Bishop of Vich, "Informes de los MM.RR Arzobispos," 166. Similarly concerned that general cemeteries would sever their occupants from the supplications of the Church community, in 1787 Toledo's Archbishop Francisco Antonio Lorenzana, whom we have seen in Mexico, successfully petitioned the Pope to "concede a privileged altar in every new cemetery, so that the dead not only benefit from the faithful's prayers, but also from sufficient indulgences to liberate their souls from Purgatory." See Toledo, 24 August 1787, Archbishop Don Francisco Antonio Lorenzana to his congregation, BN, Lafragua Collection, letter 13, call no. r282. 4308 mis. 1., fols. 1–2.

64 Cortes de la Frontera, Francisco Xavier de Espinosa y Aguilera to Council of Castile, 15 September 1781, AHN, Consejos 3.151, no. 53, fols. 4v, 6v, 7, 50.

65 Teruel, Bishop of Teruel to Council of Castile, "Informes de los MM.RR Arzobispos," 204.

66 Madrid, Francisco de Arjona to Council of Castile, Madrid, 1803, AHN, Consejos 2.093, exp. 2, fols. 25–27; Vaquero Iglesias, Muerte e ideología, 298; Don Ramón Cabrera, "Disertacion Historica; en la qual se expone por la serie de los tiempos la varía disciplina que ha observado la Iglesia de España sobre el lugar de las sepulturas," in Bails, Pruebas, 73–74.

67 On the royal order of 1804, see Rodríguez de San Miguel, Pandectas, I:114. Novísima recopilación, tomo 1, tit. 3, ley 1, pp. 209–210.

68 Zujar, "Expediente sobre el cementerio en Zujar," 1814, AHN, Consejos 3.151, no. 48, fols. 1–11.

69 Cited in the Gazetas de México, 5 July 1806, tomo 14, no. 54, p. 427. Jose Rámon Rueda López, "Evolucion de los cementerios en la ciudad de Valencia," in Dirección General de Arquitectura y Vivienda de la Consejería de Obras Públicas

y Transportes de la Junta de Andalucía, Una arquitectura, 547–550. On Madrid,
see Leopoldo Tolivar Alas, Dogma y realidad del derecho mortuorio español (Madrid:
Instituto de Estudios de Administración Local, 1983), 170; Manuel Serrano
Laso, "Origin y desarrollo del cementerio público de la ciudad de León hasta
1936," in Dirección General de Arquitectura y Vivienda de la Consejería de
Obras Públicas y Transportes de la Junta de Andalucía, Una arquitectura, 557–
561. Seville's cemetery opened in 1819; see Victor Fernández Salinas, "Cementerios y ciudad en el siglo XIX: La consolidación de los enterramientos extramuros en Sevilla," in Direccion General de Arquitectura y Vivienda de la Consejería de Obras Públicas y Transportes de la Junta de Andalucía, Una arquitectura,
377–382. Zamora, Toledo, and Jaen did not open general cemeteries until the
1830s; see Francisco Javier Lorenzo Pinar, Muerte y Ritual en la edad moderna: El
caso de Zamora 1500–1800 (Salamanca: Universidad de Salamanca, 1991), 216;
Martínez Gil, Actitudes, 86; Juan del Arco Moya, "Religiosidad popular en Jaén
duránte el siglo XVIII: Actitudes ante la muerte," in La religiosidad popular. II. Vida
y muerte: la imaginación religiosa, ed. C. Álvarez Santaló, María Jesús Buxó, and
S. Rodríquez Becerra (Barcelona: Editorial Anthropos, 1989), 309–327. Santiago de Compostela finally built a general cemetery in 1847; see D. González
Lopo, "La evolución del lugar de sepultura en Galicia entre 1550 y 1850: Los
casos de Tuy y Santigo," Obradoiro de Historia Moderna (1990): 2: 175.

70 Of 308 Cadiz Cortes deputies, 30 percent were clerics, 21 percent public administrators, 9 percent military, 7 percent from municipal oligarchies, and 1 percent engaged in commerce. See, for example, François-Xavier Guerra, Modernidad e independencias: Ensayos sobre las revoluciones hispánicos (Mexico City: Fondo de
Cultura Económica, 1993), 101, 115–169. The regular orders were excluded
from participation at the Cadiz Cortes, but 97 out of 308 deputies were secular
clergy, among them three bishops (Callahan, Church, Politics, 92–93). A number
of future Mexican liberals attended the Cortes, among them Lorenzo de Zavala,
Miguel Ramos Arizpe, Juan de Dios Cañedo, and José Mariano Michelena. See
Michael P. Costeloe, La primera república federal de México (1824–1835) (Un estudio de
los partidos políticos independientes), trans. Manuel Fernández Gasalla (Mexico
City: Fondo de Cultura Económica, 1975), 19.

71 Rodríquez de la Miguel, Pandectas, 1:35; AGN, Ayuntamientos, vol. 2, exp. 8,
fol. 72. Also see the archbishop-elect of Mexico City's circular to Mexico City's
religious, which reiterated the Cortes's order: Mexico City, Archbishop-elect to
the Convent of Jesús María, 9 August 1814, AHSSA, Fondo Convento de Jesús
María, legajo 14, exp. 8, fols. 1–iv. For examples of the tumult created by this
order, see Mexico City, Viceroy Calleja, AGN, Ayuntamientos, vol. 2, exp. 8,
fols. 72–84. These pages contain the 4 August 1814 letter from Viceroy Calleja
to authorities in Guadalajara, Yucatan, Leon, Sonora, and Durango and to the

archbishop-elect of Mexico City, and their acknowledgments of receipt of the order.

72 Mexico City, Viceroy Calleja, AGN, Ayuntamientos, vol. 2, exp. 8, fols. 72–84.

73 Guanajuato, Intendant Marañon to Viceroy, 28 November 1816, AGN, Ayuntamientos, vol. 2, exp. 8, fols. 85–85v; Guanajuato, Intendant Marañon to Viceroy Calleja, 23 September 1814, AGN, Ayuntamientos, vol. 2, exp. 8, fols. 77v, 84. On Antonio Pérez Marañon's activities with the Inquisition, see Mexico City, 1798, AGN, Inquisicion, vol. 1325, exp. 6, fols. 1–2.

74 Guanajuato, Intendant Marañon to Viceroy, 28 November 1814, AGN, Ayuntamientos, vol. 2, exp. 8, fol. 85; Guanajuato, Intendant Marañon to Viceroy Calleja, 10 December 1817, AGN, Ayuntamientos, vol. 2, exp. 8, fol. 87; Guanajuato, Intendant to Prior and Prior to Intendant, 7 and 8 March 1820, AGN, Ayuntamientos, vol. 2, exp. 8, fols. 92, 94.

75 The edict is printed in Rodríquez de la Miguel, Pandectas, 1:35, 1:36. Mexico City Noticioso General, 16 October 1818, no. 436, p. 3, col. 1.

76 Sullivan-Gonzalez, Power, chap. 3.

77 Michel Vovelle, Pièté baroque et dèchristianisation en Provence au XVIII e siècle: Les atitudes devant la mort d'apres les clauses des testaments (Paris: Plon, 1973); Pierre Chaunu, La Mort à Paris, 16e, 17e, 18e siècles (Paris: Fayard, 1978), 435–442. Chaunu concludes that "de-Christianization" in Paris began at the end of the seventeenth century, fifty years earlier than in Provence. Philippe Ariès noted that the destruction of St. Innocents cemetery in Paris to build a suburban cemetery provoked no resistance; see his The Hour of Our Death, trans. Helen Weaver (New York: Knopf, 1981), 500. For Bahia, Brazil, see Reis, A morte, 81–86, 185. Jacqueline Thibaut-Payen discusses various incidents of violent reactions to the new cemeteries in rural France; see her Les morts, l'Église et l'État: Recherches d'histoire administrative sur la sépulture et les cimetières dans le ressort du Parlement de Paris aux XVII e et XVIII e siècles (Paris: Éditions Fernand Lanore, 1977), 417.

78 Madrid, El Censor, 26 July 1787, discurso 163, paragraph 633. El Censor regularly produced around 500 copies. Nobles made up only roughly 5 percent of Spain's 10.5 million people in 1797. Far fewer nobles lived in the south, while all Basques were hidalgos; see Elorza, La ideología liberal, 211, 19.

79 Cited in Polt, Gaspar Melchor de Jovellanos, 44–45.

80 Juan Vicente Guemes y Pacheco de Padilla (Conde de Revillagigedo), Informe sobre misiones e instruccion reservada al Marqués de Branciforte 1794, introduction by José Bravo Ugarte (Mexico City: Editorial Jus, 1966), 147.

81 John Lynch, Bourbon Spain, 1700–1808 (Oxford: Basil Blackwell, 1989), 226–227. The Mexican case is discussed in Doris Ladd, The Mexican Nobility at Independence, 1780–1826 (Austin: University of Texas Press, 1976).

82 Nancy M. Farriss offers an elaborate discussion of the absolutist state's rationale for attacking the Church, as well as a meticulous outline of the campaign's repercussions in New Spain; see her *Crown and Clergy*.

83 Elorza, *La ideología liberal*, 38.

84 Carlos Alfonso Forment, "The Formation of Political Society in Spanish America: The Mexican Case, 1700–1830" (Ph.D. diss., Harvard University, 1990), 174.

85 Horst Pietschmann, "Protoliberalismo, reformas borbónicas y revolución: La Nueva España en el último tercio del siglo XVIII," in *Interpretaciones del siglo XVIII Mexicano: El impacto de las reformas borbónicas*, ed. Josefina Zoraida Vásquez (Mexico City: Nueva Imagen, 1992), 28–31; Forment, "The Formation," 171. Lyle McAlister notes that the eighteenth century witnessed a "gradual erosion of a social structure based on estates, corporations and judicial inequality and an outline at least of a new system based on social class." See his "Social Structure," 370. On the Bourbon campaign to grant illegitimate and orphaned children equal status with other subjects, see Aranjuez, Royal Order, 5 January 1794, BN, fondo Franciscanos, caja 133, exp. 1681, fols. 1–2. On "gracias llamada al sacar," see Mexico City, Viceroy Branciforte Edict, 24 July 1795, AGN, Bandos, vol. 18, no. 25, fols. 100–103; Mexico City, Viceroy Branciforte Edict, 25 July 1795, Condumex, 351 VA, A. 27607-C, Misceláneas Reales Cédulas 1795, Pieza no. 2.

86 Serge Gruzinski, "La segunda aculturización: El estado ilustrado y la religiosidad indígena en Nueva España (1775–1800)," *Estudios de Historia Novohispana* 8 (1985): 175–201; Silvio Zavala, ¿El castellano, lengua obligatoria? (Mexico City: Centro de Estudios de Historia de México, Condumex, 1977). William B. Taylor argues that Bourbon social campaigns often had the effect of weakening vertical social bonds in favor of more horizontal ones; see his *Magistrates*, 26.

87 Mexico City, City Council, 14 August 1782, AHCM, Actas de Cabildo: Borradores, vol. 457-A; San Lorenzo, 5 November 1782, AEAM, Instruccion Pública, vol. 2475, exp. 34, fols. 19–20. In 1786, seven months after the formation of the new schools, the *Gazetas de México* reported twenty-seven in operation; see Mexico City, *Gazetas de México*, 8 August 1786, vol. 2, no. 15, pp. 168–169. For more on the escuelas pías in Mexico City, see Dorothy Tank de Estrada, "The 'Escuelas Pías' of Mexico City: 1786–1820," *The Americas* 31:1 (July 1974): 51–72.

88 Farriss, *Crown and Clergy*.

89 Madrid, Royal Order, 14 January 1773, *Novísima recopilación de las leyes de España*, tomo 1, libro 1, titulo 4, ley 5 (Madrid, 1805), 26; Guillermo Floris Margadant, *Carlos III y la iglesia novohispana* (Mexico City: Biblioteca del Claustro de Sor Juana, 1983), 39.

90 Mexico City, "Causa formada a peticion de Petra Escolasa Durán para haver

extraido los comisarios de la Acordada a su hermano Juan Durán del cementerio de Santa Catarina Mártir, donde se hallaba refugiado," 22 July 1782, AGN, Bienes Nacionales, vol. 731, exp. 5, fols. 1–11. The routine nature of ecclesiastical asylum can be seen in Mexico City parish priest Gregorio Pérez Cancio's casual accounting of offering asylum in 1782 to a Pardo soldier he believed to have been falsely accused of stealing his captain's horse. See Gregrio Pérez Cancio, *La Santa Cruz y Soledad de Nuestra Señora: Libro de fábrica del templo parroquial. Años 1773–1784* (Mexico: Instituto Nacional de Antropología e Historia, 1970), 206. The European history of the cemetery as a place of asylum from the secular authorities is discussed in Ariés, *Hour*, 63–71.

91 Mexico City, *Gazetas de México*, 18 December 1787, vol. 2, no. 47, pp. 463–466. In August 1788 Viceroy Manuel Antonio Flores reported that he had complied with the order to extract refugees from churches; see San Lorenzo, 11 November 1789, King to Viceroy Flores, AGN, Reales Cédulas Duplicados, vol. 177, exp. 1, fol. 490. The order was reissued in 1797; see Aranjuez, 7 April 1797, AGN, Reales Cédulas Originales, vol. 166, exp. 172, fol. 262.

92 William B. Taylor argues that parish priests' role as teacher became increasingly important in late eighteenth-century New Spain; see his *Magistrates*, 161.

93 Conde de Campomanes, *Discurso sobre la educación popular y fomento de la industria popular* (Madrid: Don Antonio de Sancha, 1774), xxxii; Ramón Cabrera, "Disertación Historica," 146.

94 Hamill, *Hidalgo Revolt*, 80–85.

95 *El Censor*, 19 October 1786, discurso 127, paragraphs 1136–1138.

96 This change is discussed in Colin M. Maclachlan, *Spain's Empire in the New World: The Role of Ideas in Institutional and Social Change* (Berkeley: University of California Press, 1988).

97 Campomanes, *Discurso*, cxxxvi. Jovellanos echoed Campomanes's thoughts, declaring that "the greatest wealth of the state consists in an abundant population"; see his "Población in España," in *Biblioteca de autores Españoles desde la formación del lenguaje hasta nuestros días. obras publicadas e inéditas de Don Gaspar Melchor de Jovellanos*, ed. Don Miguel Artola (Madrid: Ediciones Atlas, 1956), 56:595.

98 See Brading, *First America*, 81.

99 Maríano Baena del Alcazar, *Los estudios sobre administración en la España del siglo XVIII, con el discurso sobre el gobierno municipal de José Agustín Ibáñez de la Rentería* (Madrid: Instituto de Estudios Políticos, 1968), 24.

100 Juan de Cabrera, *Crisis política. Determina el más florido imperio y la mejor institucion de príncipes y ministros* (Madrid, 1719).

101 Bernardo Ward, *Proyecto Económico* (Madrid: D. Joachin Ibarra, Impresor de Camara de S.M., 1762), 206.

102 Hipólito Villarroel, *México por dentro y por fuera bajo el gobierno de los vireyes, o sea enfermedades políticas que padece la capital de esta Nueva España* (Mexico City: Impresor de Alejandro Valdes, 1831), 108.

103 Both David A. Brading and William B. Taylor suggest that the Bourbon state unwittingly cut itself loose from divine purpose by emphasizing a more secular justification for its projects; see Taylor, *Magistrates*, 151–152; Brading, "El jansenismo," 198, 214.

4 The Battle for Church Burials

1 Gregorio M. de Guijo, *Diario, 1648–1664*, ed. Manuel Romero de Terreros, 2d ed. (Mexico City: Editorial Porrúa, 1986), 183, 212.

2 Veracruz, Intendant Miguel de Corral and Parish Priest Laso de la Vega to Viceroy Revillagigedo, 23 June 1790, AGN, Gobernación 3a, legajo 2154, caja 2630, ex. 2, cuaderno 10, fol. 135. On the prices of parish tombs, see the burial records contained in AGN, Veracruz Defunciones. On the wages of urban artisans in Mexico City, see Scardaville, "Crime and the Urban Poor," 88.

3 Veracruz, 14 October 1777, burial record of D. Manuel Joséf de Aizparisa, AGN, Veracruz Defunciones, rollo 2366, no. 42719. On Gil's intermediary role in the cochineal trade, see Brian R. Hamnet, *Política y comercio en el sur de México, 1750–1821* (Mexico City: Instituto Mexicano de Comercio Exterior, 1976), 61–62. Veracruz, 20 July 1779, burial record of D. Juan Francisco Ximénez, AGN, Veracruz Defunciónes, rollo 2366, no. 42719; Veracruz, 19 August 1756, burial record of D. Antonio de la Ganda, AGN, Veracruz Defunciones, rollo 2366, no. 42719; Veracruz, 16 August 1771, burial record of D. Pedro de Caldes, AGN, Veracruz Defunciones, rollo 2366, no. 42719.

4 Veracruz, Convent of la Merced, Fr. Francisco Orozco, Fr. Pedro Rodríguez, Fr. Bernabe de San Felipe, and Fr. Domingo de Ormas to Governor Intendant Miguel de Corral, 28 and 29 May 1790, AGN, Gobernación 3a, legajo 2154, caja 2630, exp. 2, cuaderno 10, fols. 78–83.

5 Mexico City, Viceroy Revillagigedo to the Marqués de Bajamar, 1790, AGN, Correspondencia de Virreyes 2a, vol. 30, letter 69, fol. 82.

6 As a counterweight to papal authority, the Spanish state appointed national vicars for the Franciscans (1776), the Trinitarians (1784), the Carthusians (1784), and the Augustinians (1786). See Callahan, *Church*, 27.

7 Mexico City, Friar Tomás Mercado to Veracruz Augustinians, Mexico, 15 June 1790, AGN, Gobernación 3a, legajo 2154, caja 2630, exp. 2, cuaderno 10, fols. 132–132v.

8 Veracruz, José María Laso de la Vega to Viceroy Revillagigedo, 30 June 1790, AGN, Gobernación 3a, legajo 2154, caja 2630, exp. 2, cuaderno 10, fol. 149;

Mexico City, Viceroy Revillagigedo to Govenor Intendant Miguel de Corral and José María Laso de la Vega, 14 July 1790, AGN, Gobernación 3a, legajo 2154, caja 2630, exp. 2, cuaderno 10, fol. 189; Veracruz, José María Laso de la Vega to Viceroy Revillagigedo, 27 September 1790, AGN, Gobernación 3a, legajo 2154, caja 2630, exp. 2, cuaderno 10, fol. 227. Also see Mexico City, Viceroy Revillagigedo to Govenor Intendant Miguel de Corral and José María Laso de la Vega, 3 November 1790, AGN, Gobernación 3a, legajo 2154, caja 2630, exp. 2, cuaderno 10, fol. 229.

9 Veracruz, Governor Intendant Miguel de Corral to Viceroy Revillagigedo, 29 December 1790, AGN, Gobernación 3a, legajo 2154, caja 2630, exp. 2, cuaderno 10, fol. 252.

10 On Barbara Bauza's death and burial, see Veracruz, burial record of Barbara Bauza, 30 April 1790, AGN, Veracruz Defunciones, rollo 2367, no. 42720. Her husband's geneology is found in Veracruz, 28 September 1769, AGN, Inquisición, vol. 1174, exp. 3, fol. 20. Bauza's husband served as the secretary of the Third Order of San Francisco; see Veracruz, Francisco José de las Piedras, 1 November 1792, AGN, Gobernación 3a, legajo 2154, caja 2630, exp. 1, fol. 1.

11 Mexico City, Viceroy Revillagigedo, 29 February 1792, AGI, Estado, vol. 21, no. 4, fol. 5v; Mexico City, Viceroy Revillagigedo to Veracruz City Council, 17 May 1790, AHCV, caja 30, vol. 31, fol. 229v; Veracruz, José María Laso de la Vega to Viceroy Revillagigedo, 14 July 1790, AGN, Gobernación 3a, leg. 2154, caja 2630, exp. 2, cuaderno 10, fol. 191; Mexico City, Viceroy Revillagigedo to José María Laso de la Vega, 21 July 1790, AGN, Gobernación 3a, leg. 2154, caja 2630, exp. 2, cuaderno 10, fol. 196.

12 Veracruz, Governor Intendant Corral to Viceroy Revillagigedo, 4 June 1790, AGN, Gobernación 3a, leg. 2154, caja 2630, exp. 2, cuaderno 10, fol. 62; Veracruz, Veracruz City Council to Viceroy Revillagigedo, 9 June 1790, AHCV, caja 30, vol. 31, fols. 330–331v.

13 Mexico City, Viceroy Revillagigedo to Marqués de Bajamar, 3 June 1790, AGN, Correspondencía de Virreyes, ser. 2a, vol. 30, letter 69, fol. 182. The Dominicans had argued that one of the prime reasons for burying Cabeza de Vaca in their convent was that the group had no designated space in the cemetery. Veracruz, Governor Intendant Miguel de Corral to Viceroy Revillagigedo, 29 December 1790, AGN, Gobernación 3a, legajo 2154, caja 2630, exp. 2, cuaderno 10, fol. 252.

14 Mexico City, Revillagigedo to Intendant of Puebla, 13 July 1790, AGN, Reales Cedulas Duplicadas, vol. 188, exp. 1, fol. 130; Mexico City, Viceroy Revillagigedo to Intendant Miguel del Corral and Parish Priest José María Laso de la Vega, 17 May 1790, AGN, Gobernación 3a, legajo 2154–2155, caja 2630, exp. 1, fol. 52. On the Regular Orders receiving the order from Revillagigedo, see the priors'

letters to Laso de la Vega, Veracruz, 28 and 29 December 1790, AGN, Gobernación 3a, legajo 2154, caja 2630, exp. 1, fols. 263–269.

15 Mexico City, Viceroy Revillagigedo to Governor Intendant Miguel de Corral, 31 July 1790, AGN, Reales Cedulas Duplicadas, vol. 188, exp. 1, fols. 127–131. On the move to request Masses only from the Regular Orders, see José María Laso de la Vega to Viceroy Revillagigedo, Veracruz, 14 December 1790, AGN, Gobernación 3a, legajo 2154, exp. 2, cuaderno 10, fol. 235.

16 As this law had presented a particular problem in the Indies, where many subjects lived too far from churches to ensure burial, in 1554 Charles V ordered that prelates bless rural burial grounds; this law was reissued by Philip IV. See ley 11 libro 1 tit. 18, in *Recopilación de leyes*; Mexico City, Real Audiencia, 2 May 1787, AGN, Bandos, vol. 14, no. 59, fol. 225.

17 Veracruz, José María Laso de la Vega to Viceroy Revillagigedo, 23 June 1790, AGN, Gobernación 3a, legajo 2154, exp. 2, cuaderno 10, fol. 127v; Veracruz, José María Laso de la Vega and Governor Intendant Miguel de Corral to Viceroy Revillagigedo, 14 and 29 December 1790, AGN, Gobernación 3a, legajo 2154, exp. 2, cuaderno 10, fols. 235, 253.

18 These earlier petitions are discussed in Veracruz, Veracruz City Council to King, 18 August 1804, AGN, Ayuntamientos, vol. 1, exp. 3, fol. 61. The appeals of an infantry lieutenant and a man of commerce are mentioned in Aranjuez, Royal Order, 6 May 1794, AGN, Ayuntamientos, vol. 1, exp. 8, fol. 210. Nancy M. Farriss reports that the Council of the Indies was consistently more conservative than the King's enlightened ministers; see her *Crown*, 104.

19 Veracruz, Veracruz City Council to Viceroy Revillagigedo, 9 June 1790, AHCV, caja 30, vol. 31, fols. 229–331v. The viceroy later insisted that city council members be buried in the hermitage, prompting them to appeal to the intendant and to the bishop of Puebla, as well as the Council of the Indies. See Puebla, Bishop Biempico y Sotomayor to Veracruz City Council, 14 March 1792, AHCV, caja 37, vol. 39, fol. 281; Veracruz, Intendant Miguel del Corral to Veracruz City Council, 26 June 1792, AHCV, caja 37, vol. 39, fols. 287–287v.

20 Veracruz, Veracruz City Council meeting, 29 November 1790, INAH, Veracruz Microfilm Collection, rollo 13, libro 83, fols. 259v–260. Esteves and Echeverría were the two permanent aldermen on the City Council. Veracruz, Veracruz City Council meeting, n.d., AHCV, caja 32, vol. 34, fol. 576v.

21 On disease in Veracruz, see Romeo Cruz Velásquez, "Los hospitales en el Puerto de Veracruz durante 1760–1800," Tesis de Licenciatura, Universidad de Veracruz, 1992.

22 Veracruz, Teniente del Alguacil Sebastián de Vega, 23 February 1792, INAH, Veracruz Microfilm Collection, rollo 14, libro 5, fol. 25.

23 Veracruz, "Cuentos de los diputados de fiestas," Veracruz City Council, 1791–1792, AHCV, caja 37, vol. 39, fols. 87–110.

24 Veracruz, Veracruz City Council to Viceroy Revillagigedo, 9 June 1790, AHCV, caja 30, vol. 31, fols. 229–231v; Mexico City, Viceroy Revillagigedo to José María Laso de la Vega, 23 June 1790, AGN, Gobernación 3a, legajo 2154, caja 2630, exp. 2, cuaderno 10, fol. 23. On the Veracruz City Council's advocate in Madrid, see Veracruz, Veracruz City Council Meeting, 14 August 1794, Veracruz, INAH, Veracruz Microfilm Collection, rollo 16, libro 87, fol. 60.

25 Veracruz, burial record of Miguel Laso de la Vega, November 1791, AGN, Veracruz Defunciones, rollo 2367, no. 42720; Veracruz, burial record of Doña Josépha Britto, 17 July 1770, AGN, Veracruz Defunciones, rollo 2366, no. 342719.

26 Veracruz, Governor Intendant Miguel de Corral and José María Laso de la Vega to Viceroy Revillagigedo, 25 May 1791, AGN, Gobernación 3a, legajo 2154, caja 2630, exp. 2, cuaderno 10, fol. 294v.

27 Madrid, King to Viceroy Revillagigedo, 26 November 1791, AGN, Reales Cedulas Originales, vol. 150, exp. 190, fol. 285; San Lorenzo, King to Viceroy Revillagigedo, 9 October 1791, AGN, Reales Cedulas Originales, vol. 150, exp. 84, fols. 133–137.

28 Mexico City, Viceroy Revillagigedo to Marqués de Balamar, 29 February 1792, AGN, Correspondencía de Virreyes, ser. 1a, vol. 168, exp. 371, fol. 17v. Also see Mexico City, Viceroy Revillagigedo to Marqués de Balamar, 30 March 1792, AGN, Correspondencía de Virreyes, ser. 1a, vol. 164, exp. 422, fols. 59–59v; Mexico City, Viceroy Revillagigedo to Marqués de Balamar, 29 February 1792, AGI, Estado, vol. 21, no. 4, fols. 1–2.

29 Mexico City, Viceroy Revillagigedo to Marqués de Balamar, 31 March 1792, Correspondencía de Virreyes, ser. 1a, vol. 168, exp. 384, fol. 27; Veracruz, Intendant Miguel de Corral to Viceroy Revillagigedo, 25 January 1792, AGN, Gobernación, leg. 2154–2155, caja 2630, exp. 12, fols. 15–17.

30 The King's decision to allow exceptions to cemetery burial came too late in the case of Echeverría, who was buried in the cemetery on 13 May 1791 in a crypt in the burial ground's chapel. He died a Franciscan Tertiary and the Order accompanied his body to the cemetery. See Veracruz, burial record of Juan José de Echeverría, 13 May 1791, AGN, Veracruz Defunciones, rollo 2367, no. 42720.

31 Veracruz, José María Laso de la Vega and Miguel de Corral to Viceroy Revillagigedo, 25 May 1791, AGN, Gobernación, leg. 2155, caja 2630, exp. 13, fol. 294v.

32 Veracruz, Veracruz City Council Meeting, 8 February 1792, INAH, Veracruz Microfilm Collection, rollo 14, libro 85, fols. 38v–40v.

32   Mexico City, Viceroy Revillagigedo to Veracruz City Council, 1 February 1792, AHCV, caja 37, vol. 39, fol. 272.

34   Mexico City, Viceroy Revillagigedo, 16 March 1792, AGN, Gobernación 3a, legajo 2154, vol. 2630, exp. 4, fol. 11v; Puebla, Bishop Biempico y Sotomayor, 16 March 1792, AGN, Gobernación 3a, legajo 2154, vol. 2630, exp. 4, fol. 123; Puebla, Bishop Biempico y Sotomayor, 1 April 1792, AGN, Gobernación 3a, legajo 2154, vol. 2630, exp. 4, fol. 14v.

35   Veracruz, Intendant Antonio Cardenas to Viceroy Revillagigedo, 1791, AGN, Historia, vol. 314, exp. 9, fol. 14.

36   Veracruz, burial record of Doña Gregoria Evaiedo, 4 June 1796, AGN, Veracruz Defunciones, rollo 2367, no. 42720. Isabela Gil, for example, gave a large but unspecified sum to the head of the Confraternity of Nuestra Señora de la Consolación, housed in the Convent of La Merced; see Veracruz, burial record of Isabela Gil, 21 July 1796, AGN, Veracruz Defunciones, rollo 2367, no. 42720. Josefina Muriel reports that the Confraternity of the Rosary often rented a house to the Hospital of San Carlos in the eighteenth century; see her *Hospitales de la Nueva España: Fundaciones de los siglos XVII and XVIII* (Mexico City: Editorial Jus, 1960), 2:229.

37   Veracruz, Constitutions of the Confraternity of San Benito de Palermo, 18 March 1759, AGN, Cofradías y Archicofradías, vol. 5, exp. 1, fol. 30v.

38   Pope Alexander VII, "Indulgencias y gracias concedidas por la santidad del papa Alejandro VII (de felice memoria) a la cofradía de la Coronación de nuestro señor Jesús Cristo llamada vulgaramente de San Benito de Palermo . . . año del señor de 1674. La cuál esta fundada por authoridad ordinaria en el convento de frayles menores de la observacia de nuestro padre San Francisco de esta ciudad de la Nueva Veracruz," Condumex, Miscelaneas Indulgencias Siglo 18, no. 3, pieza no. 2, 1767. For a brief description and illustrations of Mexico City patentes, see Clara García Ayluardo and Alicia Bazarte Martínez, "Patentes o sumarios de indulgencias, documentos importantes en la vida y en la muerte," in *Visiones y Creencias IV: Anuario Conmemorativo del V centenario de la llegada de España a America* (Mexico City: Universidad Autónoma Meteropolitana, 1992), 117–140.

39   Mexico City, Viceroy Revillagigedo to Marques de Balamar, 31 March 1792, Correspondencia de Virreyes, ser. 1a, vol. 168, exp. 384, fol. 27; Veracruz, Don Sebastián de Bobadilla, José Ramírez de Aguilera, Pedro Antonio de Garay y Llano, Pedro de Moreno, et al., 4 June 1793, AGN, Gobernación 3a, legajo 2154, caja 2630, exp. 2, fol. 5. On Pedro Antonio de Garay y Llano's efforts to found the Confraternity of La Escuela de Christo, see Miguel Lerdo de Tejada, *Apuntes históricos de la heroica ciudad de Veracruz. Precedidos de una noticia de los descubrimientos hechos en la islas y en el continente Americano . . .* (Mexico City: Imprenta de Ignacio Cumplido, 1850), 422.

40 Veracruz, patent of the confraternity of Nuestro Padre Jesús Nazareno, n.d., AGN, Gobernación 3a, legajo 2154, caja 2630, exp. 2, fols. 130–130v; Veracruz, 30 November 1793, AGN, Correspondencia de Virreyes 2a, vol. 27 fol. 144; Veracruz, burial record of Doña Beatriz de Real, 15 September 1802, AGN, Veracruz Defunciónes, rollo 2367, no. 42720; Veracruz, burial record of Don Francisco José de Ortega, 20 July 1794, AGN, Veracruz Defunciones, rollo 2367, no. 42720.

41 Count of Floridablanca, *Instrucción reservada para la dirección de la junta de estado*, ed. Cayetano Alcazar (Madrid: M. Aguilar, 1897), 124.

42 Campomanes, *Discurso*, 91.

43 Sarah T. Nalle, *God in la Mancha: Religious Reform and the People of Cuenca, 1500–1650* (Baltimore: Johns Hopkins University Press, 1992), 168.

44 Veracruz, Parish Priest Laso de la Vega to Veracruz City Council, 21 February 1782, AHCV, caja 25, vol. 26, fol. 253; Veracruz, Head of the Confraternity of Nuestra Señora de la Soledad to Veracruz City Council, 21 February 1782, AHCV, caja 25, vol. 26, fol. 29. For more on the invitations to dress the wooden angels, see Veracruz, Veracruz City Council to Ecclesiastical Council, 19 February 1796, AHCV, caja 51, vol. 59, fols. 120–122; Veracruz, Ecclesiastical Council to Veracruz City Council, 18 February 1796, INAH, Veracruz Microfilm Collection, rollo 18, libro 89. Veracruz, Veracruz City Council Meeting, 6 June 1796, INAH, Veracruz microfilm collection, rollo 16, libro 87.

45 Veracruz, 30 November 1793, AGN, Correspondencia de Virreyes 2a, vol. 27, fol. 144; Veracruz, 1793, AGN, Bienes Nacionales, vol. 1536, exp. 8.

46 Lerdo de Tejada, *Apuntes*, 338–339.

47 Madrid, Royal Order, 8 March 1791, AGN, Cofradías y Archicofradías, vol. 18, exp. 1, fols. 1–2; San Idelfonso, Royal Order, 10 September 1794, AGN, Reales Cedulas Originales, vol. 228, exp. 133, fol. 301; Brading, *Una Iglesia*, 150–151. On receipt of the order in Veracruz, see Veracruz, Governor of Veracruz, 31 August, 1791, AGN, Correspondencia de Diversas Autoridades, vol. 45, exp. 60, fol. 145.

48 Mexico City, Archbishop Alonso Nuñez Haro y Peralta to Viceroy Revillagigedo, 24 May 1794, AGN, Cofradías y Archicofradías, vol. 18, exp. 7, fols. 160, 309v; Brading, "Tridentine," 12.

49 San Idelfonso, Royal Order, 10 September 1794, AGN, Reales Cedulas Originales, vol. 228, exp. 133, fol. 301; Veracruz, Intendant Miguel de Corral to Viceroy Revillagigedo, 17 May 1792, Mexico City, Viceroy Revillagigedo to Council of the Indies, 28 June 1794, AGN, Correspondencia de Virreyes, ser. 2a, vol. 27, letter 368, fols. 213–214; Veracruz, Governor of Veracruz, 1792, AGN, Correspondencia de Diversas Autoridades, vol. 46, exp. 66, fol. 1; Aranjuez, Antonio Porcel to Viceroy, 23 January 1803, AGN, Reales Cedulas Originales,

vol. 190, letter 8, fols. 13–14; Veracruz, Intendant Miguel de Corral to Viceroy Revillagigedo, 17 May 1792, Mexico City, Viceroy Revillagigedo to Council of the Indies, 28 June 1794, AGN, Correspondencia de Virreyes, ser. 2a, vol. 27, letter 368, fols. 213–214; Veracruz, Governor of Veracruz, 1792, AGN, Correspondencia de Diversas Autoridades, vol. 46, exp. 66, fol. 1; Aranjuez, Antonio Porcel to Viceroy, 23 January 1803, AGN, Reales Cedulas Originales, vol. 190, letter 8, fols. 13–14.

50   Many of Veracruz's secular officials belonged to the Franciscan Tertiaries; see, for example, Veracruz, Veracruz City Council Meeting, 24 April 1807, AHCV, caja 88, vol. 99, fol. 26; Veracruz, Third Order Meeting, 17 April 1759, AHCV, caja 82, vol. 93, fols. 618–619.

51   Juan B. Iguiñiz, *Breve Historia de la Tercera Orden hasta nuestros días* (Mexico City: Editorial Patria, 1951), 11; *Sumario de las Indulgencias, gracias, y privelegios autenticos que ganan y gozan los hermanos de la Tercera Orden de Penitencia de N.P. San Francisco . . .* (Mexico City: D. Maríano de Zuñiga y Ontiveros, 1802), 17, 25.

52   Gabriel Berdu, *Tratado del Tercer Orden del Querubico Patriarca Santo Domingo de Guzman, de su origen, reglas, gracias, e excelencias . . .* (Mexico City: D. Felipe de Zúñiga y Ontiveros, 1777), 39; Friar Manuel de Santa Teresa, *Instructorio espiritual de los terceros, terceras, y beataṣ de nuestra Señora del carmen . . .* (Mexico City: D. Felipe de Zúñiga y Ontiveros, 1782), 66.

53   *Libro de las constituciones del V. Orden Tercero de Penitencia de N.S.P.S Francisco: . . . Mandadas guardar á todas las Terceras Ordenes por el M.R.P. Comisario visitador, Presidente de Capítulo, y R.y V. Definitorio de esta Providencia del Santo Evangelio año de 1783* (Mexico City: D. Josef de Zúñiga y Ontiveros, 1796), 26–29; Pope Benedict XIII, *Constitución de nuestro santissimo señor, el Señor Benedicto Papa XIII en favor de la Tercera Orden de N.P.S. Francisco* (Mexico City: Joseph Bernardo de Hogal, 1726), 1.

54   *Libro de las constituciones*, 26–29; Pope Benedict XIII, *Constitución*, 1.

55   Antonio López Matoso, "Viaje de perico ligero al país de los moros (1815–1816)," in *Cien Viajeros en Veracruz: Crónicas y relatos. Tomo II, 1755–1816*, ed. Martha Poblett Miranda (Veracruz: Gobierno del Estado de Veracruz, 1992), 204.

56   Veracruz, burial record of don Sancho Ruíz de Villogar, 28 My 1785, AGN, Veracruz Defunciónes, rollo 2366, no. 42719; Veracruz, burial record of don José García de la Larra, 11 May 1778, AGN, Veracruz Defunciones, rollo 2366, no. 42719; Veracruz, burial record of Don Miguel Francisco de Herrera, 3 September 1777, AGN, Veracruz Defunciónes, rollo 2366, no. 42719. For a brief description of the parish's presbetery, see Lerdo de Tejada, *Apuntes históricos*, 322.

57   Veracruz, Head Brother of the Third Order Sebastián Pérez, 1792, AGN, Gobernación 3a, legajo 2154, caja 2630, exp. 1, fol. 11; Veracruz, Governor Intendant

to Viceroy Revillagigedo, 24 March 1792, AGN, Gobernación 3a, legajo 2154, caja 2630, exp. 1, fol. 13; Puebla, Bishop to Viceroy Revillagigedo, 1 April 1792, AGN, Gobernación 3a, legajo 2154, caja 2630, exp. 1, fol. 15; Mexico City, Viceroy Revillagigedo to Governor Intendant of Veracruz, 19 June 1792, AGN, Gobernación 3a, legajo 2154, caja 2630, exp. 1, fol. 17.

58 Veracruz, Frey Francisco de Orosco to Veracruz Governor Intendant Don Diego García Panes, 27 October 1795, AGN, Hospitales, vol. 143, exp. 10, fols. 338v–339; Veracruz, R. Diego de Ossa, Head Brother of San Juan de Montes Claros to Vicario de Veracruz, 1622, AGN, Hospitales, vol. 18, exp. 10, fols. 69–73; Puebla, Bishop of Tlaxcala Don Alonso de la Mota y Escobar, 9 February 1622, AGN, Hospitales, vol. 18, exp. 11, fols. 74–76; Christon I. Archer, *El ejército en el México borbónico, 1760–1810,* trans. Carlos Valdés (Mexico City: Fondo de Cultura Económica, 1983), 63.

59 Veracruz, Antonio María Fernandez, 14 May 1789, INAH, Veracruz Microfilm collection, rollo 12, 1789, fol. 174v. On the four hospitals operating in Veracruz in 1789, see Velásquez, "Los hospitales," especially 110–125.

60 Veracruz, Viceroy Revillagigedo to Governor Intendant of Veracruz, 9 June 1790, Veracruz, AGN, Gobernación 3a, legajo 2154, caja 2630, exp. 2, fol. 65; Veracruz, Antonio de Sola, Head Captain of the Hospital de San Juan de Montesclaros, 29 April 1700, AGI, Contratación, vol. 466, no. 6, fols. 1–4v; Veracruz, Parish Priest Laso de la Vega to Viceroy Revillagigedo, 21 June 1790, AGN, Gobernación 3a, legajo 2154, caja 2630, exp. 1, fol. 110; Veracruz, Parish Priest Laso de la Vega to Veracruz City Council, 25 June 1794, INAH, Veracruz Microfilm Collection, rollo 16, vol. 87, fol. 181; Veracruz, Governor Intendant Antonio Cardenas to Prior of San Juan de Montes Claros Santiago Luga, 26 June 1794, INAH, Veracruz Microfilm Collection, rollo 16, vol. 87, fol. 182; Veracruz, Friar Manuel José Mandeo to Parish Priest José M. Laso de la Vega, 10 January 1791, AGN, Gobernación 3a, legajo 2154, caja 2630, exp. 2, fol. 281; Veracruz, Governor Intendant of Veracruz, 6 April 1790, Gobernación 3a, legajo 2154, caja 2630, exp. 2, fol. 32.

61 Veracruz, Parish Priest Bartolome Borrero to Governor Diego García Panes, 7 October 1795, AGN, Hospitales, vol. 143, exp. 10, fol. 319; Veracruz, Governor Diego García Panes to Prior of Montes Claros Francisco Orosco, 7 October 1795, AGN, Hospitales, vol. 143, exp. 10, fol. 319v; Veracruz, Governor Intendant Cardenas, 7 November 1795, AGN, Hospitales, vol. 143, exp. 10, fol. 342; Veracruz, Fray Francisco Orosco, 9 November 1795, AGN, Hospitales, vol. 143, exp. 10, fol. 343v; Veracruz, Bartolome Borrero, 9 November 1795, AGN, Hospitales, vol. 143, exp. 10, fol. 344; Veracruz, Cardenas, 11 November 1795, AGN, Hospitales, vol. 143, exp. 10, fols. 344–345v; Veracruz, Fray Francisco Orosco to Governor Intendant don Diego García Panes, 28 November 1795, AGN,

Hospitales, vol. 143, exp. 10, fol. 346v; Veracruz, Parish Priest José María Laso de la Vega to Governor Intendendent Diego García Panes and Fray Francisco Orosco, 23 April 1796, AGN, Hospitales, vol. 143, exp. 10, fol. 352.

5 Piety, Power, and Politics

1 Puebla, Bishop Biempico y Sotomayor to King, 1792, AGI, Estado, vol. 21, no. 4, fols. 3, 9; Puebla, Bishop Biempico y Sotomayor, 16 March 1792, AGN, Gobernación 3a, legajo 2154, caja 2630, exp. 4, fol. 124.

2 Bishop Biempico y Sotomayor, "Carta pastoral del Illmo. Sr. obispo de la Puebla de Los Angeles dirigida al clero de su diócesis en el año de 1792," Condumex, Miscelánea, Cartas Pastorales, Puebla, no. 1, folleto no. 8, fol. 57; Puebla, Bishop Biempico y Sotomayor, 28 March 1792, AGN, Gobernación 3a, legajo. 2154, caja 2630, exp. 4, fol. 1.

3 Laso de la Vega, *Oración panegírica, que en la festividad de N.S de Guadalupe . . .* (Puebla, Mexico: Seminario Palafoxiana, 1794), 1–2. Laso de la Vega also appears in the documentation as Lazo de la Vega.

4 Laso de la Vega, *Oración panegyrica del gran padre . . .* (Mexico City: Felipe de Zúñiga y Ontiveros, 1781), xii, xii–4.

5 There are no extant wills for this period of Veracruz history, so these statistics are based on the information on burials contained in wills that were filed with the parish and noted in the parish burial book. The burial records I examined were those of the white population, as the casta records have disappeared. I examined the information from four hundred wills contained in the parish burial records for the years 1742 to 1809. These records can be found in Mexico City, AGN, Archivo Parroquial de la Iglesia Catedral de Veracruz, Diocesis de Veracruz, Estado de Veracruz, Defunciones 1742–1789 and 1790–1809, Mexico, SMM, rollos 2366, no. 42719 and 2367, no. 42720.

6 Veracruz, Burial record of Beatriz de Real, 15 September 1802, AGN, Veracruz Defunciones, rollo 2367, no. 42720; Veracruz, Burial record of Juan Bautista de Alvizuri, 30 October 1806, AGN, Veracruz Defunciones, rollo 2367, no. 42720.

7 Veracruz, Veracruz City Council Meeting, 18 February 1792, AHCV, caja 37, vol. 39, fol. 276; Veracruz, Don Eligio Uztáriz, 28 February 1792, Gobernación 3a, legajo 2154, vol. 2630, exp. 4, fols. 60v–61v.

8 Veracruz, Don José María Laso Vacarino, 28 February 1792, Gobernación 3a, legajo 2154, vol. 2630, exp. 4, fols. 68v–70.

9 Ibid., fols. 97–99.

10 Veracruz, Eligio Uztáriz, 28 February 1792, Gobernación 3a, legajo 2154, vol. 2630, exp. 4, fols. 68v–69v; Veracruz, Juan Manuel Muñoz, Remigio Fernández, José María Laso Vicariño, Francisco de la Torre, 28 February 1792, Gobernación 3a, legajo 2154, vol. 2630, exp. 4, fols. 92v, 64v, 68v–71v, 84v.

11   Veracruz, Veracruz City Council, 5 November 1806, AGN, Ayuntamientos, vol. 1, exp. 8, fol. 262; Puebla, Bishop Biempico y Sotomayor, 1792, AGI, Estado 21, no. 4., fol. 13.

12   The 1791 Veracruz census reported 3,990 residents inside the city's walls; see Veracruz, Veracruz census, 1791, AHCV, caja 40, vol. 42. Velásquez, "Los hospitales," 116–121; Booker, Veracruz Merchants, 7; Rolf Widemer, "La ciudad," 121–134. Robert Sydney Smith argues that the population merely doubled between 1791 and the 1818 census, which registered 8,934 residents; see his "Shipping," 5. Pierre Chaunu reports similar figures to those of Smith; see his "Veracruz en la segunda mitad del siglo XVI y primera del XVII," Historia Mexicana 36:9 (April–June 1960), 543. Richard E. Boyer and Keith A. Davies, Urbanization in 19th Century Latin America: Statistics and Sources (Los Angeles: UCLA Press, 1973), 48.

13   Christiana Renate Borchant de Moreno, Los mercaderes y el capitalismo en la ciudad de México: 1759–1778 (Mexico City: Fondo de Cultura Económica, 1984), 61.

14   Matilde Souto Mantecon, "El consulado de comerciantes de Veracruz" (Master's thesis, Universidad Nacional Autónoma de México, Departamento de Filosofía y Letras, 1989), 4.

15   Booker, Veracruz Merchants, 20–21.

16   Hamnet, Política y comercio, 61–66. John E. Kicska disputes Hamnet's contention that Veracruz traders were interlopers in the Oaxaca trade, arguing instead that the Mexico City Merchants Guild was overwhelmed by the volume of trade and thus reluctantly tolerated the Veracruz contingent; see his Empresarios coloniales, familias, y negocios en la ciudad de México durante los Borbones (Mexico City: Fondo de Cultura Económica, 1986), 111–112.

17   Humberto Tandron, El comercio de Nueva España y la controversia sobre la libertad de comercio, 1796–1821 (Mexico City: Instituto Mexicano de Comercio Exterior, 1976), 9–10.

18   Eduardo Arcila Farías, Reformas económicas del siglo XVIII en la Nueva España (Mexico City: SepSetentas, 1984), 1:106, 132; Lerdo de Tejada, Apuntes históricos 1:333.

19   Smith, "Shipping," 11.

20   Guadalupe Jiménez Codinach, "An Atlantic Silver Entrepot: Veracruz and the House of Gordan and Murphy," in Atlantic Port Cities: Economy, Culture, and Society in the Atlantic World, ed. Franklin W. Knight and Peggy K. Liss (Knoxville: University of Tennessee Press, 1991), 158.

21   Antonio de Ulloa, "Descripción geográfica-física de una parte de la Nueva España," in Antonio Ulloa y la Nueva España: Con dos apéndices documentales, ed. Francisco Solano (Mexico City: Universidad Autónoma de México, 1979), 27–28; cited in Souto Mantecon, "El consulado," 49.

22   Booker, Veracruz Merchants, 25.

23   Souto Mantecon, "El consulado," 61.

24 José María Laso de la Vega to Viceroy Revillagigedo, Veracruz, 27 September
    1790, AGN, Gobernación 3a, legajo 2154, caja 2630, exp. 2, cuaderno 10, fol.
    227. Also see Viceroy Revillagigedo to Governor Intendant Miguel de Corral
    and José María Laso de la Vega, Mexico City, 3 November 1790, AGN, Goberna-
    ción 3a, legajo 2154, caja 2630, exp. 2, cuaderno 10, fol. 229. Mexico City,
    Viceroy Revillagigedo to Marqués de Balamar, 31 March 1792, Correspondencia
    de Virreyes, ser. 1a, vol. 168, exp. 384, fol. 27; Veracruz, Intendant Miguel de
    Corral to Viceroy Revillagigedo, 25 January 1792, AGN, Gobernación, leg.
    2154–2155, caja 2630, exp. 12, fols. 15–17.

25 Veracruz, Eligio Uztáriz, 28 February 1792, Gobernación 3a, legajo 2154, vol.
    2630, exp. 4, fol. 68v–69v; Veracruz, Antonio María Fernández, 14 May 1789,
    INAH, Veracruz Microfilm Collection, rollo 12, libro 83, tomo 2, fols. 174–176.

26 See, for example, Veracruz, Miguel Ignacio de Miranda, 10 March 1792, AHCV,
    caja 37, fol. 278.

27 Mexico City, Viceroy Revillagigedo to Marqués de Balamar, 31 March 1792,
    AGN, Correspondencia de Virreyes, ser. 1a, vol. 168, exp. 384, fol. 27; Veracruz,
    Don Sebastián de Bobadilla, José Ramírez de Aguilera, Pedro Antonio de Garay
    y Llano, Pedro de Moreno, et al., 4 June 1793, AGN, Gobernación 3a, legajo
    2154, caja 2630, exp. 2, fol. 5. On Pedro Antonio de Garay y Llano's efforts to
    found the Confraternity of La Escuela de Cristo, see Lerdo de Tejada, *Apuntes
    históricos*, 422. Other merchants also played prominent roles in the city's con-
    fraternities. Juan de Vieyra y Sousa and Antonio Frediani, for example, both
    served as majordomos of the Confraternity of Nuestro Padre Jesús Nazareno,
    located in the convent of Padres Predicadores. See Veracruz, Patent of the
    Confraternity of Nuestro Padre Jesús Nazareno, n.d., AGN, Gobernación 3a,
    legajo 2154, caja 2630, exp. 2, fols. 130–130v.

28 Veracruz, Remigio Fernández, 28 February 1792, AGN, Gobernación 3a, legajo
    2154, caja 2630, exp. 4, fols. 66–66v. Also see Juan Manuel Muñoz, 20 February
    1792, fol. 95v. Veracruz, Veracruz City Council, 23 September 1791, INAH,
    Veracruz Microfilm Collection, rollo 14, libro 84, fols. 693–695v.

29 Veracruz, José Ignacio de Uriarte, 20 February 1792, AGN, Gobernación 3a,
    legajo 2154, caja 2630, exp. 4, fols. 115, 112, 75v; Veracruz, Veracruz City
    Council, 24 February 1792, INAH, Veracruz Microfilm Collection, rollo 14,
    libro 85, fol. 30v.

30 Veracruz, Veracruz City Council Meeting, 8 and 24 February 1792, INAH, Vera-
    cruz Microfilm Collection, rollo 12, libro 83, fols. 30v, 38v–40v; Veracruz,
    Francisco Antonio de la Torre, 28 February 1792, AGN, Gobernación 3a, legajo
    2154, caja 2630, fol. 84v.

31 Veracruz, Veracruz City Council Meeting, 15 February 1803, INAH, Veracruz
    Microfilm Collection, rollo 29, libro 95, fols. 445–446; Veracruz, Veracruz City
    Council to King, 18 August 1804, AGN, Ayuntamientos, vol. 1, exp. 3, fol. 6ov.

32   On the royal order of 1804, see Rodriquez de la Miguel, *Pandectas*, 1:114. On the Ayuntamiento's pledge, see Veracruz, Veracruz City Council to King, 18 August 1804, AGN, Ayuntamientos, vol. 1, exp. 3, fol. 58.

33   Veracruz, Veracruz City Council to King, 18 August 1804, AGN, Ayuntamientos, vol. 1, exp. 3, fol. 61v. A bill to the city council for cemetery maintenance can be found in Veracruz, Veracruz City Council, 18 July 1806, AHCV, caja 77, vol. 87, fol. 432, and caja 81, vol. 92, fol. 65.

34   Humbolt, *Ensayo político*, 4:158.

35   Christopher Hill, *Change and Continuity in Seventeenth-Century England* (New Haven: Yale University Press, 1991), 90–93.

36   Rolf Widemer explains that beginning in 1780 and peaking in 1800 an agricultural crisis hit the area around Veracruz. Unable to obtain the money to pay taxes, peasants fled to the city in search of work; see his "La ciudad," 133.

37   Ibid., 133.

38   Veracruz, Veracruz Census, 1791, AHCV, caja 40, vol. 42.

39   On the fluidity of ethnic categories among the seventeenth-century Mexico City poor, even on the level of individual self-identification, see R. Douglass Cope, *The Limits of Racial Domination: Plebian Society in Colonial Mexico City* (Madison: University of Wisconsin Press, 1994), 49–67. The case of mulatto parish priest Laso de la Vega illustrates the problem: the 1791 census taker, after meticulously noting the ethnic categories of the priest's maids and servants, as well as every one of his neighbors, omitted his status entirely, perhaps boggled by a darkskinned individual exercising so important a position as parish priest. See Veracruz, Veracruz Census, 1791, caja 40, vol. 42, fol. 87.

40   Giovanni Francesco Gemelli Carreri, *Le Mexique a la fin du XVIie siècle un par un voyaguer italien Gemelli Careri*, ed. Jean Pierre Berthe (Paris: Calmann-Lévy, 1968), 209.

41   Veracruz, "Noticías de la antigua Veracruz de Padre Andrés de Rivas, provincial de la Companía de Jesús," AGN, Historia, vol. 31, exp. 1, fol. 17v; López Matoso, "Viaje," 203.

42   Thomas Gage, *A New Survey of the West Indies: or, The English American his Travail by Sea and Land* (London: E. Corte, 1655), 23.

43   Ajofrín, *Diario del viaje*, 1:35.

44   Henry George Ward, *México en 1827* (Mexico City: Fondo de Cultura Económica, 1985), 67; Ulloa, "Descripción," 76.

45   Cope, *The Limits*, 86–105.

46   Veracruz, Veracruz Census, 1791, AHCV, caja 42, vol. 40, fols. 15, 33; Veracruz, Veracruz Census, 1797, INAH, Veracruz Microfilm Collection, rollo 20, libro 19, fols. 302–307.

47   Veracruz, Veracruz Merchant Guild to Governor Intendant Diego García Panes, 21 November 1796, INAH, Veracruz Microfilm Collection, rollo 20, libro 19,

fol. 43; Veracruz, Thomas de Aguirre and José Ignacio de Uriarte to Veracruz Merchant Guild, 14 November 1796, INAH, Veracruz Microfilm Collection, rollo 20, libro 19, fols. 45–45v. On Veracruz's black militia units, see Pedro Alonso O'Crouley O'Donnel, "Idea compendiosa del reino de la Nueva España, 1764," in Martha Poblett ed., *Cien viajeros en Veracruz: Crónicas y relatos. Tomo II, 1755–1816*, ed. Martha Poblett (Veracruz: Gobierno del Estado de Veracruz, 1992), 65. Also see Joséph Antonio de Villa-Señor y Sanchez, *Theatro Américano: Descripción general de los reynos y provincias de la Nueva España y sus jurisdicciónes* (Mexico City: Don Joséph Bernardo de Hogal, 1746), 274.

48 Veracruz, Thomas de Aguirre and José Ignacio de Uriarte to Veracruz Merchant Guild, 14 November 1796, INAH, Veracruz Microfilm Collection, rollo 20, libro 19, fol. 45v.

49 Veracruz, 1804, Francisco de Paula Garay, INAH, Veracruz Microfilm Collection, rollo 20, libro 19, fol. 45v.

50 Veracruz, 28 January 1723, AGN, Inquisición, vol. 798, exp. 8, fols. 125–157.

51 Veracruz, 16 January 1778, AGN, Inquisición, vol. IIII, exp. 57, fols. 448–458.

52 R. Douglass Cope persuasively argues that the Mexico City poor were not enthralled with elites' notions of racial hierarchy, and thus race and ethnicity were not the primary fissures dividing the poor. Instead, the poor were linked to elite patrons rather than each other by a need to work, and to work in the city's small-scale industries with only a handful of employees each; see his *The Limits*, 86–105.

53 Michael C. Scardaville, "(Hapsburg) Law and (Bourbon) Order: State Authority, Popular Unrest, and the Criminal Justice System in Bourbon Mexico City," *The Americas* 50:4 (April 1994): 508–511.

54 Veracruz, Antonio María Fernández, 14 May 1789, INAH, Veracruz Microfilm Collection, rollo 12, libro 83, fol. 169; Ulloa, "Descripción," 76.

55 Antonio Gramsci, *Selections from the Prison Notebooks*, ed. and trans. Quinten Hoare and Geoffrey Nowell Smith (London: Lawrence and Wishart, 1971), 123–209. For a suggestive use of Gramsci's ideas on how dominant groups employ universalist claims for their particular agendas, see Elliott Gordon Young, "Deconstructing La Raza: Identifying the Gente Decente of Laredo, 1904–1911," *Southwest Historical Quarterly* (October 1994): 226–259. On the exclusions inherent in projects of group constitution, see Jessica Chapin, "From Irca to Orca: Apprehending the Other in 'Your San Antonio Experience,'" *Journal of Historical Sociology* 7:1 (March 1994): 102–112.

56 Veracruz, Antonio María Fernández, 14 May 1789, INAH, rollo 12, libro 83, fols. 169–175. Natalie Davis has offered an interesting critique of the theory that Protestant critiques of "hypocritical good works" underlay sixteenth-century European efforts to stop indiscriminate almsgiving and enact disciplinary mea-

sures to uproot the poor from idleness. She urges us to consider whether new poor laws "do not flow as naturally from Erasmian views of education and order, as they do from Protestant ones about works and Church policies." See her "Poor Relief, Humanism, and Heresy," in *Society and Culture in Early Modern France: Eight Essays by Natalie Davis* (Stanford: Stanford University Press, 1965), 20. For more on "Erasmian" charity, see Linda Martz, *Poverty and Welfare in Habsburg Spain: The Example of Toledo* (London: Cambridge University Press, 1983), especially 7–14. For a more general introduction to these debates, see Carter Lindberg, *Beyond Charity: Reformation Initiatives for the Poor* (Minneapolis: Fortress Press, 1993).

57 Lerdo de Tejada, *Apuntes históricos*, 1:378; Manuel B. Trens, *Historia de la H. Ciudad de Veracruz y de su Ayuntamiento* (Veracruz: Ayuntamiento de Veracruz, 1955), 54; Booker, *Veracruz Merchants*, 111; Veracruz, Veracruz City Council, 1797, INAH, rollo 21, libro 90, fol. 21v.

58 Campomanes, *Discurso*; Trens, *Historia*, 54.

59 Mexico City, Viceroy Revillagigedo to Veracruz City Council, 6 February 1795, INAH, rollo 17, libro 88, fol. 73; Veracruz, Viceroy Revillagigedo to City Council, 29 March 1794, INAH, rollo 16, libro 87, fol. 110; Veracruz, Antonio María Fernández, 14 May 1789, INAH, rollo 12, libro 83, fol. 176v; Veracruz, Remigio Fernández, 28 February 1792, AGN, Gobernación 3a, legajo 2154, caja 2630, exp. 4, fols. 66–66v; Veracruz, Veracruz City Council, 23 September 1791, INAH, Veracruz Microfilm Collection, rollo 14, libro 84, fols. 693–695v; Veracruz, Juan Manuel de Muñoz, 20 February 1792, AGN, Gobernación 3a, legajo 2154, caja 2630, exp. 4, fol. 95v.

60 Trens, *Historia*, 55; Veracruz, Veracruz City Council to Veracruz Merchants Guild, 12 May 1801, INAH, rollo 27, libro 94, fol. 362; Cruz Velásquez, "Los hospitales," 143.

61 Cruz Velásquez, "Los hospitales," especially 110–125.

62 Muriel, *Los Hospitales*, 2:26–28.

63 Cruz Velásquez, "Los hospitales," 126; Lerdo de Tejada, *Apuntes históricos*, 404–405.

64 Veracruz, Veracruz City Council, 16 July 1802, INAH, Veracruz Microfilm Collection, rollo 27, libro 94, fol. 261–261v; Veracruz, City Council, 1807, AHCV, caja 82, vol. 93, fols. 574–616; Trens, *Historia*, 47; Veracruz, Veracruz City Council, 14 June 1798, INAH, rollo 22, libro 91, fol. 203; *Veracruz y Oaxaca en 1798* (Mexico City: Editorial Vargas Reas, 1946), 12.

65 Veracruz, José María Quiros, 21 October 1797, AHCV, caja 58, vol. 67, fols. 115–121v; Veracruz, Veracruz City Council, 2 June 1801, INAH, Veracruz Microfilm Collection, rollo 27, libro 94, fol. 332. It is unclear when the Alcaldes de Barrio were established in Veracruz or when the Veracruz City Council divided the city

into wards; by 1810, however, both measures were in practice; see Veracruz, Veracruz City Council, 18 May 1810, AHCV, caja 93, vol. 108, fols. 253–253v; Veracruz, Veracruz City Council, 17 April 1810, AHCV, caja 87, vol. 98, fol. 438.

66 Veracruz, Francisco García Puertas, 18 June 1804, INAH, Veracruz Microfilm Collection, rollo 20, libro 19, fol. 48v; Veracruz, Francisco García Puertas, 18 June 1804, INAH, Veracruz Microfilm Collection, rollo 20, libro 19, fol. 52v.

67 Veracruz, Martín Sánchez y Serrano, 3 August 1804, INAH, Veracruz Microfilm Collection, rollo 20, libro 19, fol. 57; Veracruz, Francisco García Puertas, 18 June 1804, INAH, Veracruz Microfilm Collection, rollo 20, libro 19, fol. 50.

68 Madrid, El Censor, 19 October, 1786, tomo 6, discurso 127, paragraph 1136.

69 See Weber, Protestant Ethic.

70 For a suggestive discussion on grace and free will in reform thought, see Van Kley, Religious Origins, 51–53, 60–62.

71 Puebla, Bishop Biempico y Sotomayor, 29 February 1792, AGN, Gobernación 3a, legajo 2154, exp. 4, fol. 41; Mexico City, Augustín de Rivero, 12 February 1807, AGN, Gobernación 3a, legajo 2154, exp. 3, fols. 70v–71.

72 Amar y Borbón, Discurso, 150.

73 See the June 1790 exchange of letters among Viceroy Revillagigedo, the Veracruz City Council, and Intendant Miguel de Corral found in Veracruz, AHCV, caja 30, vol. 31, fol. 230v; and in Mexico City, AGN, Gobernación 3a, legajo 2154, caja 2630, exp. 2, fols. 62v, 66, 76.

6   The Ideology Articulated

1 David A. Brading, The Origins of Mexican Nationalism (Cambridge, England: Centre for Latin American Studies, Cambridge University, 1985), 24.

2 Michael Costeloe, Church and State in Independent Mexico: A Study of the Patronage Debate, 1821–1857 (London: Royal Historical Society, 1978), 30–32.

3 F. Guerra, Modernidad e independencias, 13, 85, 89, 101, 290, 338. The classic work on the public sphere that Guerra follows is Jürgen Habermas, The Structural Transformation of the Public Sphere: An Inquiry into a Category of Bourgeois Society, trans. Thomas Burger (Cambridge, MA: MIT Press, 1989). Stanley C. Green, The Mexican Republic: The First Decade, 1823–1832 (Pittsburgh: University of Pittsburgh Press, 1987), 94–99. On the new public sphere of letters in Latin America, see Angel Rama, The Lettered City, ed. and trans. John Charles Chasteen (Durham, NC: Duke University Press, 1996). Although not concerned with Lizardi specifically, Michael Costeloe attributes the explosion of criticism against the Church to the effects of European liberal and secular influences on the upper classes, who nevertheless retained their allegiance to religion; see his Church and State, 32.

4 Numerous authors locate Lizardi's roots in the European—especially French—Enlightenment. See, for example, Nancy Vogely, "El Periquillo Sarniento: The Problem of Mexican Independence" (Ph.D. diss., Stanford University, 1980), 4, and her "The Concept of 'the People' in El Periquillo Sarniento," Hispania 70:3 (September 1987): 461; Fernando Alegría, Historia de la novela hispanoamericana, 3d. ed. (Mexico City: Ediciones de Andrea, 1966), 21; Nöel Solomón, "La crítica del sistema colonial de la Nueva España en El Periquillo Sarniento," Cuadernos Americanos 138:1 (January–February 1965): 171; Jefferson Rea Spell, "The Intellectual Background of Fernández de Lizardi as Reflected in El Periquiillo Sarniento," Proceedings of the Modern Language Association 71 (1956): 414–432; Jean Franco, "Waiting for a Bourgeoisie: The Formation of the Mexican Intelligentsia in the Age of Independence," in Critical Passions: Selected Essays, ed. Mary Louise Pratt and Kathleen Newman (Durham, NC: Duke University Press, 1999), 476–493. Dieter Janik also finds European Enlightenment influences in Lizardi's works; see his "La noción de sociedad en el pensamiento de Lizardi y de sus contemporaneos," Cahiers des Amériques latines 10 (1990): 41. Although not concerned with Lizardi's works, historian Juan Viquiera-Alban also points to the French influence on enlightened Mexico City elites at the turn of the century; see his Propriety and Permissiveness in Bourbon Mexico, trans. Sonya-Lipsett Rivera and Sergio Rivera Ayala (Wilmington, DE: Scholarly Resources, 1999), xvi.

5 Hale, Mexican Liberalism, 160.

6 Ibid., 164, 163; José María Luis Mora, "Estado de la moral publica," in El clero, la educación, y la libertad (Mexico City: Empresas Editoriales, 1950), 118–121.

7 José María Luis Mora, "Disertación sobre bienes eclesiásticos (1834)," in Obras Completas: José María Luis Mora. Vol. 3: Obra Política, ed. Lillian Briseño Senosiain, Laura Solares Robles, and Laura Suárez de la Torre (Mexico City: SEP, 1986), 167.

8 Jean Franco, "Waiting," 482. Also see Jean Franco, "La heterogenidad peligroso: Escritura y conrol social en vísperas de la independencia mexicana," Hispamérica 12 (1983): 9–10.

9 Franco, "La heterogenidad," 22, 12.

10 Franco, "Waiting," 477, 478.

11 Fernández de Lizardi, El pensador mexicano, no. 9, 3 December 1812, in Obras III: Periódicos, 87.

12 This is not to say, of course, that Lizardi ignored all Enlightenment thinkers. We have heard Campomanes and Jovellanos rehearsing the new piety's fundamental tenets, and it was these thinkers, as well as the theologians they frequently cited, whom Lizardi found inspirational. That the "Church's first centuries were the best and most efflorescent" was the lesson he gleaned from Campomanes's 1769 Juicio imparcial, which, like his own Correo Semanario de México,

wended its way through the labyrinth of Church history to demonstrate the papacy's usurpation of power. This text had an authoritative ring to it, El Pensador noted, because King Charles III sponsored the work and "the wise Count of Campomanes" and others of the Council of Castile edited and approved it. See José Joaquín Fernández de Lizardi, *Correo semanario de México*, 25 April 1827, in *Obras VI*, 361. Two French theologians in particular are frequently cited by Lizardi and other Reform Catholics: Claude Fleury (1640–1723) and Jaques-Bénigne Bossuet (1627–1704), both of whom challenged the Pope's influence on the monarchy. On Fleury and Bossuet, see, for example, Fernández de Lizardi, "Vigesimasegunda conversación del Payo y el Sacristán," and "Vigesimatercia conversación del Payo y el Sacristán," in *Obras V*, 494, 504; Brading, *First America*, 500.

13   José Joaquín Fernández de Lizardi, "Repique brusco al Campanero por el Pensador Mexicano (1820)," in *Obras X: Foletos (1811–1820)*, ed. María Rosa Palazón Mayoral and Irma Isabel Fernández Arias (Mexico City: Universidad Autónoma de México, 1981), 303.

14   Fernández de Lizardi, *El pensador mexicano*, no. 13, 25 November 1813, in *Obras III*, 233.

15   Fernández de Lizardi, "El sedicioso manifiesto del Obispo de Sonora. Impugnado por El Pensador en la sexta conversación del Payo y el Sacristán (1825)," in *Obras V*, 328–329. The Bishop of Sonora, Bernardo Martínez y Ocejo, was no stranger to Mexico's public sphere of letters, having contributed to the *Diario de México* and published numerous pastoral letters, including the 1824 *La soberanía del Altísimo* that so provoked Lizardi. Ironically, the bishop had earlier served as the first teacher of ecclesiastical history in the Real y Pontifica Universidad de México. On the bishop's career, see Fernández de Lizardi, *Obras V*, 310 n. 15.

16   Mexico City, José María Luis Mora to British and Foreign Bible Society of London, 17 July 1829, cited in Pedro Gringoire, "El 'Protestantismo' del doctor Mora," in *Lecturas de Historia Mexicana 5: Iglesia y Religiosidad*, ed. Pilar Gonzalbo Aizpuru (Mexico City: El Colegio de México, 1992), 121.

17   W. P. Stevens, *Zwingli: An Introduction to His Thought* (Oxford: Clarendon Press, 1992), 134, 136.

18   Fernández de Lizardi, *Correo semanario de México*, no. 9, 17 January 1827, in *Obras VI*, 147–148. Readers who doubt Lizardi's knowledge of ecclesiastical history, or his insistence about returning the Church to its parsimonious early structure, should consult the twenty-four editions of the *Correo semanario de México* he penned in 1826 and 1827. The paper meticulously detailed the history of the papacy from the first century to the nineteenth. See *Obras VI*, 7–378.

19   Fernández de Lizardi, "Vigesimarprima conversación del Payo y el Sacristán," 21 June 1825, in *Obras V*, 482. A copy of this papal encyclical of 24 September 1824 can be found on pages 524–528.

20   Fernández de Lizardi, *Correo semanario de México*, 22 November 1826, in *Obras VI*, 13. For another Reform Catholic's reaction to the encyclical, see Fr. Servando Teresa de Mier, *Discurso del D. Dr. Servando Teresa de Mier sobre la enciclica del Papa León XII* (Mexico City, 1825).

21   Mora, "Disertación sobre bienes," in *Obras Completas*, 3:170–173; Brading, *First America*, 650.

22   Fernando Perez Memen, *El episcopado y la Independencia de México (1810–1836)* (Mexico City: Editorial Jus, 1977), 281–336, especially 286, 289, 295, 322.

23   W. Eugene Shields, "Church and State in the First Decade of Mexican Independence," *Catholic Historical Review* 28 (July 1942): 206–211; Anne Staples, *La iglesia en la primera república federal mexicana* (Mexico City: SepSetenas, 1976), 18–31.

24   Costeloe, *Church and State*, 5; Anne Staples, "Clerics as Politicians: Church, State, and Political Power in Independent Mexico," in *Mexico in the Age of Democratic Revolutions, 1750–1850*, ed. Jaime Rodríguez O. (Boulder, CO: Lynn Rienner, 1994), 225.

25   Mexico City, 17 April 1823, Fray Servando Teresa de Mier, *Diario de las sesiones del Congreso Constituyente de México*, tomo IV, cited in Reyes Heroles, *El liberalismo*, 1: 288. Mier was one of the Independence era's most eccentric personalities and prolific writers; see, for example, Edmundo O'Gorman, ed., *Antología del pensamiento político americano: Fray Servando Teresa de Mier* (Mexico City: Imprenta Universitaria, 1945). A useful English translation of his memoirs is Susana Rotker, ed., *The Memoirs of Fray Servando Teresa de Mier*, trans. Helen Lane (New York: Oxford University Press, 1998). For more on his life, see Brian R. Hamnett, *Revolución y contrarevolución en México y el Peru: Liberalismo, realeza y seperatismo, 1800–1824* (Mexico City: Fondo de Cultura Económica, 1978), 260–268; Brading, *First America*, 588–600; Brading, *The Origins*, 32–37.

26   Timothy Tackett, *Becoming a Revolutionary: The Deputies of the French National Assembly and the Emergence of a Revolutionary Culture (1789–1790)* (Princeton, NJ: Princeton University Press, 1996), 288–289.

27   José Joaquín Fernández de Lizardi, *The Itching Parrot*, trans., Katherine Anne Porter (Garden City, NY: Doubleday, Doran, 1942), 236.

28   Fernández de Lizardi, *El periquillo sarniento* (1816), in *Obras VII: Novelas*, 242.

29   Fernández de Lizardi, "Segunda conversación del Payo y El Sacristán (1825)," in *Obras V*, 281.

30   Mexico City, *El Fenix de la Libertad*, 12 February 1834, tomo 4, no. 25, fol. 2, col. 3; fol. 3, cols. 1–3; fol. 4, col. 1. Mexico City, *El Fenix de la Libertad*, 24 February 1834, tomo 4, no. 43, fols. 2–3, cols. 3, 1–3.

31   Fernández de Lizardi, *Testamento*, 8–9.

32   Mexico City, AN, Wills.

33   Campomanes, *Discurso*, 113.

34   Calvin, *Institutes*, 2: 1013; Haro y Peralta, *Carta pastoral*, 20, 68.

35   Saint Augustine, The City of God (426), ed. Vernon J. Bourke (Garden City, NJ: Image Books, 1958), 310.

36   Fernández de Lizardi, "El egoísta y su maestro," 4 October 1813, and "Sobre una materia interestante," 16 December 1813, in Obras III, 295, 271–272. See Vogeley, "El Periquillo Sarniento," 90–92.

37   Fernández de Lizardi, "Sobre una materia," 271–272.

38   Francois Javier Guerra notes that on 7 November 1811, seven thousand copies of the Diario de México were distributed in Mexico City alone, enough for one out of twenty of the capital's 140,000 persons to have their own copy, from which he concludes that Mexico had a high rate of literacy compared to other areas of Latin America; see his Modernidad, 281. The Diario de México was founded in 1805.

39   Mexico City, Diario de México, 31 March 1808, tomo 7, no. 914, p. 261; Mexico City, Diario de México, 14 July 1809, tomo 11, no. 1382, pp. 54–55. Juan Viquiera Alban also notes that moderation became increasingly central to some elites' definition of virtue in the late eighteenth century, but he ascribes this to French influence; see his Propriety and Permissiveness.

40   Mexico City, Diario de México, 13 August 1811, tomo 15, no. 20146, pp. 193–194.

41   Campomanes, Discurso, 129.

42   Mora, "Abolicion de los privilegios del clero y la milicia," in El clero, 53; Mora, "Disertación sobre bienes," 219, 231.

43   Fernández de Lizardi, "El sedicioso manifiesto del Obispo de Sonora. Impugnado por El Pensador en la sexta conversación del Payo y el Sacristán (1825)," in Obras V, 327–328.

44   Fernández de Lizardi, Correo semanario de México, 17 January 1827, in Obras VI, 145.

45   Fernández de Lizardi, "Razones contra insolencias. O respuesta de El Pensador al padre Soto (1820)," in Obras X, 381–382.

46   Fernández de Lizardi, "Avisos de El Pensador (1812)," in Obras X, 86.

47   Fernández de Lizardi, "Suplamento extraordinario al pensador mexicano," 12 October 1813, in Obras III, 310.

48   Fernández de Lizardi, "Contesta El Tío a Juanillo," 27 December 1813, in Obras III, 369.

49   Fernández de Lizardi, El periquillo, 235.

50   On the violence that could be provoked when Christians redefined the exterior cult as "frozen wealth," see Wandel, Voracious.

51   Mora, "Disertación sobre bienes," 203.

52   Fernández de Lizardi, El periquillo, 208.

53   This information is based on a statistical analysis of wills found in Mexico City, AN.

54   B. Ward, Proyecto económico, 200.

55 Mexico City, Will of Cristobal Peña, 1 December 1831, AN, Notary 96, Miguel Blancas, vol. 590, fols. 6–8; Mexico City, Will of Don José Mariano Fernandez de Cordova, 11 April 1830, AN, Notary 164, Manuel Carrillo, vol. 973, fols. 5–8.

56 Mexico City, Will of Guadalupe Ceballos, 31 August 1859, AN, Notary 43, Tomas Avilar, vol. 305, nf.

57 Mexico City, Will of María Josefa de Avendaño y Orduña, 18 September 1717, AN, Notary 254, Juan Clemente Guerrero, vol. 1,664, nf.; Will of Manuel de Marraguín, 14 January 1815, Notary 158, José Ignacio Caño y Moctezuma, vol. 961, nf.

58 Ralph Houlbrooke, Death, Religion, and the Family in England, 1480–1750 (Oxford: Clarendon Press, 1998), 116–118, 122, 128.

59 Archbishop Francisco Antonio de Lorenzana, Cartas pastorales y edictos del Ill.mo Señor D. Francisco Antonio Lorenzana y Búitron, Arzobispo de México (Mexico City: Joseph Antonio de Hogal, 1770), carta 3.

60 Silvia M. Arrom, "Popular Politics in Mexico City: The Parián Riot, 1828," Hispanic American Historical Review 68:2 (May 1988): 245–268; Guardino, Peasants, Politics, 123–127; Harold Sims, La expulsión de los españoles de México (1821–1828) (Mexico City: Fondo de Cultura Económica, 1974), 51–52.

61 Guardino, Peasants, Politics, 127, 123–127. Michael Costeloe also tags the Parián riot as a definitive moment in the gente decente's separation from the poor; see his La primera república, 214–216.

62 Mora, "Discurso sobre los medios de que se vale la ambición para destruir la libertad (1827)," in Obras Completas, 1:177.

63 Mora, "Discurso sobre la necesidad de fijar el derecho de ciudadanía en la República y hacerlo esencialmente afecto a la propiedad," in Obras Completas, 1:370.

64 Ibid., 374.

65 Richard Andrew Warren, "Vagrants and Citizens: Politics and the Poor in Mexico City, 1808–1836" (Ph.D. diss., University of Chicago, 1994), 195.

66 Franco, "Waiting."

67 Costeloe, Church and State, 175.

68 Houlbrooke, Death; Chaunu, La Mort; Vovelle, Piètè baroque.

7 The Rise of Medical Empiricism

1 Mexico City, Don José Bernardo Baz Report, 1820, AHCM, Policía de Salubridad. Juntas de Sanidad, vol. 3685, exp. 12, fol. 1. John Tate Lanning reports that in Guatemala doctors were seen as a servile profession until the late eighteenth century, when public opinion began to accord them more respect; see his Eighteenth-Century, 207–208.

2   Gordon Schendel, *Medicine in Mexico: From Aztec Herbs to Betatrons* (Austin: University of Texas Press, 1968), 99.

3   John Tate Lanning, *The Royal Protomedicato: The Regulation of the Medical Professions in the Spanish Empire*, ed. John Jay Tepaske (Durham, NC: Duke University Press, 1985), 72, 264, 266.

4   A 1741 Royal Edict granted New Spain's Protomedicato the privilege of examining and certifying doctors in the provinces where they resided, ending the need for a costly journey to the capital and significantly reducing the number of unendorsed physicians; see Aranjuez, Royal Order, 19 April 1741, AHSSA, Salubridad Pública, sec. Presidencia, serie Secretaría, caja 1, exp. 13, fol. 1. A 1799 viceregal edict required that all phlebotomists and those barbers who bled patients or extracted teeth obtain Protomedicato permission; only those dedicated to shaving could remain undocumented; see *Gazetas de México*, 15 April 1799, vol. 9, no. 34, p. 267; Mexico City, Viceroy Miguel José de Azanza Edict, 29 March 1799, AGN, Bandos, vol. 20, exp. 18, fol. 19. In 1803, Viceroy José de Iturrigaray informed all intendants that henceforth Protomedicato officials would certify even phlebotomists in their districts; see Mexico City, Viceroy Iturrigaray to all Intendants, 29 August 1803, AGN, Protomedicato, vol. 3, fols. 177–178v.

5   Lanning, *Eighteenth-Century*, 234.

6   San Lorenzo, Royal Order, 27 October 1798, AGN, Historia, vol. 102, exp. 13, fols. 9–14v; Manuel de Jesús Febles, *Noticia de las leyes y órdenes de policía que rigen a los profesores del arte de curar. Dispuestas por Manuel de Jesús Febles* (Mexico City: Imprenta del Ciudadano Alejandro Valdés, 1830), 2.

7   Benito Jerónimo Feijóo, "Uso mas honesto de la arte obstétrica (1742)," in *Obras*, ed. Ivy L. McClelland (Madrid: Taurus, 1985), 161.

8   Dr. Nicolas León, ed., *La obstetricia en México: Notas bibliográficas, étnicas, históricas, documentarias y críticas, de los orígenes históricos hasta el año de 1910* (Mexico City: La Viuda de F. Díaz de León, 1910), 26.

9   Mexico City, City Council, 25 May 1793, AHCM, Médicos y Boticas, 1776–1850, exp. 3, fols. 14–16.

10 Mexico City, City Council, 19 February 1821, AHCM, Policía de Salubridad, Juntas de Sanidad, vol. 3685, exp. 17, fol. 22v.

11 Martha Eugenia Rodríguez, "La medicina científica y su difusión en Nueva España," *Estudios de historia novohispana* 12 (1992): 190.

12 José Ignacio Bartoloche, *Mercurio Volante* (1772–1773), ed. Roberto Moreno (Mexico City: Universidad Nacional Autónoma de México, 1979), 8–9.

13 *Mercurio Volante*, 17 October 1772, no. 1, p. 1. Naomi Quezada asserts that parteras tended to be Indians and mestizas; see her spectacular *Enfermedad y*

maleficio: El curandero en el México colonial (Mexico City: Universidad Nacional Autónoma de México, 1989), 22–23.

14 *Diario de México,* reproduced in N. León, *La obstetricia en México,* 223–224.

15 Veracruz, Antonio María Fernández, 12 May 1789, INAH, rollo 12, libro 83, fols. 173–174.

16 Veracruz, Veracruz City Council, 9 November 1791, INAH, rollo 14, libro 84, fols. 697–698; Veracruz, Francisco Hernández and Jacinto Gómez to Veracruz City Council, 30 June 1796, INAH, rollo 18, libro 89, fols. 167–174, 303v. Doctors' petitions to be included on the Veracruz City Council's list can be found in Veracruz, Veracruz City Council, 1802, INAH, Veracruz Microfilm Collection, rollo 27, libro 95, fol. 19; Veracruz, Veracruz City Council, 1803, INAH, Veracruz Microfilm Collection, rollo 28, libro 95, fols. 75v, 84. Also see Veracruz, Dr. Joaquín Ablanedo, 15 September 1809, AGN, Protomedicato, vol. 1, exp. 6, fols. 14–15.

17 Veracruz, Veracruz City Council, 29 August 1800, INAH, Veracruz Microfilm Collection, rollo 24, libro 93, fols. 291–305; Mexico City, Protomedicato, 1802, AGN, Protomedicato, vol. 1, exp. 2, fols. 1–38v.

18 Veracruz, Veracruz City Council, 31 October 1798, INAH, Veracruz Microfilm Collection, rollo 22, libro 91, fol. 215; Veracruz, Juan Antonio Ruiz de Albarado, 1802, INAH, Veracruz Microfilm Collection, rollo 28, libro 95, fol. 229.

19 N. León, *La obstetricia,* 225.

20 On Cadiz and Barcelona, see Dorothy Tank de Estrada, "Médicos," in *Historia de las profesiones en México,* ed. Josefina Z. Vásquez (Mexico City: Colegio de México, 1982), 41. On Madrid, see Agustín Albarracín, "La medicina española en Columbia," *Cuadernos Hispanoamericanos* 427 (October 1989): 37.

21 San Lorenzo, Royal Edict, 15 November 1798, AGN, Bandos, vol. 22, exp. 38, fols. 94–97.

22 Lanning, *Eighteenth-Century,* 296.

23 Rómulo Velasco Ceballos, *La cirugía Mexicana en el siglo XVIII* (Mexico City: Archivo Histórico de la Secretaría de Salubridad y Asistencia, 1946), 80–81; Aranjuez, Royal Edict, 20 May 1768, AGN, Protomedicato, vol. 3, exp. 15, fols. 5–5v. In 1780 the Viceroy ordered the Real Hospital de Amor to provide dead bodies to the Royal College of Surgery for dissections; see Velasco Ceballos, *La cirugía Mexicana,* 447.

24 *Gazetas de México,* 7 November 1807, vol. 14, no. 93, p. 736.

25 Mexico City, Protomedicato, 1772, AHSSA, fondo Salubridad Pública, sección Presidencia, serie Secretaría, caja 1, exp. 9, fols. 1–3; Mexico City, Viceroy Marqués de Croix Edict, 10 April 1770, AGN, Bandos, vol. 5, exp. 67, fol. 247; Rodríquez, "La medicina científica," 183; Tank de Estrada, "Médicos," 42. Interestingly, in 1621, anatomy had been an obligatory course for doctors at the

National University of Mexico, and in 1645 Viceroy Palafox ordered all doctors to attend dissections. See Schendel, *Medicine in Mexico*, 85–86, 98.

26   Cited in Velasco Ceballos, *La cirugía Mexicana*, 205–206. *Gazetas de México*, 2 October 1787, tomo 2, no. 42, p. 416.

27   Manuel de Molina, 1782, cited in Lanning, *Eighteenth-Century*, 281.

28   Mexico City, Martin de Sessé, Vicente Cervantes, and Juan del Castillo to King, 26 September 1788, AGN, Historia, vol. 527, exp. 8, fols. 1–2; *Gazetas de México*, 5 August 1788, tomo 3, no. 13, p. 125.

29   For the new Royal Botanical Garden's directors similar attempts to wrest the licensing of apothecaries from the Protomedicato, see Aranjuez, Royal Order, 19 April 1741, AHSSA, Salubridad Pública, sec. Presidencia, serie Secretaría, caja 1, exp. 13, fol. 1; Mexico City, Martin de Sessé, Vicente Cervantes, and Juan del Castillo to King, 26 September 1788, AGN, Historia, vol. 527, exp. 8, fols. 2–3v; Mexico City, Vicente Cervantes to Viceroy Iturrigaray, 21 September 1804, AGN, Protomedicato, vol. 3, exp. 16, fol. 338v.

30   Mexico City, Dr. Antonio Serrano to Viceroy Iturrigaray, 15 December 1804, AGN, Protomedicato, vol. 3, exp. 15, fols. 1, 7–8v; Mexico City, Protomedicato Director José Ignacio García Jove y Capelón to Viceroy Iturrigaray, 31 December 1804, AGN, Protomedicato, vol. 3, exp. 16, fols. 27–34; Aranjuez, Royal Order, 19 April 1741, AHSSA, Salubridad Pública, sec. Presidencia, serie Secretaría, caja 1, exp. 13, fol. 1.

31   On the 1788 decision, see Velasco Ceballos, *La cirugía mexicana*, 207–208.

32   Mexico City, Viceroy Marqués de Croix Edict, 10 April 1770, AGN, Bandos, vol. 5, exp. 67, fol. 247; M. Rodríquez, "La medicina científica," 183; Tank de Estrada, "Médicos," 42; Schendel, *Medicine in Mexico*, 116.

33   Cited in Izquierdo, *Montaña*, 209; cited in Ignacio Chávez, *México en la cultura médica* (Mexico City: Fondo de Cultura Económica, 1987), 69.

34   Luz María Hernández Sáenz reports that it is unclear when, exactly, Boerhaave and other modern authors were added to the curriculum, although in 1774 several public lectures mentioned the works of Boerhaave and his illustrious students; see her *Learning to Heal: The Medical Profession in Colonial Mexico* (New York: Peter Lang, 1997), 27, 29.

35   Mexico City, Joaquín Guerra to City Council, 26 February 1821, AHCM, Médicos y Boticarios, 1776–1850, exp. 12, fols. 1–3.

36   "Memoria de un anónimo sobre la importancia de la anatomía para la medicina," *Mercurio Volante* 3 February 1773, no. 15, p. 1, col. 1. José Joaquín Fernández de Lizardi also regarded bodies as doctors' rightful books, even libraries; see his *Chanzas y Veras de El Pensador Méxicano. Diálogo entre el autor y un licenciado* (Mexico City: Doña María Fernández de Jáuregui, 1813). On the battle to replace scholasticism with empiricist medicine in Spain, see Luis S. Granjel,

"Panorama de la medicina española durante el siglo XVIII," *Revista de la Universidad de Madrid* 9 (1960): 675–702.

37   Cited in José Lopez Sánchez, *Tomás Romay y el origin de la ciencia en Cuba* (Havana: Academia de Ciencias, 1964), 136.

38   *Es culpable el que se calle en perjuicio de los hombres* (Mexico City: D. Alejandro Valdés, 1820), 4, 6, 8, 11.

39   Michael E. Burke, *The Royal College of San Carlos: Surgery and Spanish Medical Reform in the Late Eighteenth Century* (Durham, NC: Duke University Press, 1977), 41.

40   Roy Porter, *The Greatest Benefit to Mankind: A Medical History of Humanity* (New York: Norton, 1997), 57.

41   The Count of Campomanes's 1771 remark is cited in Burke, *The Royal College*, 52.

42   *Noticioso General*, 18 December 1820, no. 776, p. 3, col. 2; Mexico City, City Council, 20 December 1820, AHCM, Policía de Salubridad, Juntas de Sanidad, vol. 3685, exp. 14, fol. 1.

43   José Joaquin Fernández de Lizardi, *Suplemento al Pensador*, 27 September 1813, p. 13, col. 1.

44   Manuel Carpio, *Aforismos y Pronósticos de Hipócrates. Seguidos del artículo pectoriloquo del diccionario de ciencias médicas. Traducidos al Castellano, los primeros del Latín, y el último del Francés* (Mexico City: Mariano Ontiveros, 1823), 1.

45   *Gazeta de Guatemala*, 3 February 1800, 159–162, cited in Lanning, *Eighteenth-Century*, 33, also see 37–38.

46   *El Amante de la Humanidad, Destierro de charlatanes y abuso de cirujanos* (Mexico City: Imprenta de Juan Bautista de Arizpe, 1820), 3, 4.

47   Marquis de Basecourt to Council of Castile, Report of Junta de Sanidad, Council of Castile to King, in Council of Castile, *Memorial ajustado*, 18–20, 155–158v.

48   Cited in Richard A. Etlin, *The Architecture of Death: The Transformation of the Cemetery in Eighteenth-Century Paris* (Boston: MIT Press, 1987), 16, 31, 30. For a more detailed discussion of the science of eudiometry and the European debates about the air's pernicious effects, see Simon Schaffer, "Measuring Virtue: Eudiometry, Enlightenment and Pneumatic Medicine," in Cunningham and French, *Medical Enlightenment*, 281–319.

49   Alain Corbin, *El Perfume o el Miasma: El olfato y lo imaginario social. Siglos XVIII y XIX*, trans. Carlota Vallée Lazo (Mexico City: Fondo de Cultura Económica, 1987).

50   San Roque, Dr. Mauricio de Echandi, "Expediente sobre que se forme un campo santo en la ciudad de Algeciras a instancia de la representación del Conde de Revillagigedo, en el año pasado de 1780," AHN, Consejos 3.151, no. 49, fols. 10–11v; San Roque, 13 August 1780, "Memoria remitida por d. Mauricio de Echandi, protomédico del ejército," AHN, Consejos 1.032, fols. xxxii–xxxiii. Echandi's career is outlined in Miguel Parrilla Hermid, "El Doctor

Mauricio Echandi Montalvo," *Revista del Instituto José Cornide de Estudios Coruñeses* 8–9 (1972–1973): 247–255.

51   Anonymous report to Council of Castile, 1781, AHN, Consejos, 3.151, no. 52, maps 1181–83.

52   Archbishop of Orihuela to Conde de Floridablanca, 24 March 1781, AHN, Consejos, vol. 1.302, fol. 45v. See the 1781 reports from the church hierarchy of Orihuela, Antequea, and Tortosa in AHN, Consejos, vol. 1.302, fols. 45v, 71, and 34, respectively. Zeuta, Archbishop of Zeuta to Council of Castile, "Informes," 63; Seville, Archbishop of Seville to Council of Castile, "Informes," 68.

53   Real Academia de la Historia, *Informe*, x, xxxiii, xlvii, xliv–lv, 1, 45.

54   Mexico City, Viceroy Revillagigedo to Veracruz City Council, 17 May 1790, AHCV, caja 30, vol. 31, fols. 224–226; Veracruz, Don Eligio Uztáriz, 28 February 1792, AGN, Gobernación 3a, legajo 2154, vol. 2630, exp. 4, fols. 60v–62; Veracruz, Don Pedro Laguna, 28 February 1792, AGN, Gobernación 3a, legajo 2154, vol. 2630, exp. 4, fols. 100v–103v. For similar statements contained in the report, see fols. 79v and 119.

55   Veracruz, Don Matías de Lacunra, 28 February 1792, AGN, Gobernación 3a, legajo 2154, vol. 2630, exp. 4, fol. 110v; Veracruz, Don Remigio Fernández, 28 February 1792, AGN, Gobernación 3a, legajo 2154, vol. 2630, exp. 4, fols. 66–66v.

56   Herman Boerhaave, "On Commending the Study of Hippocrates (1701)," cited in Andrew Cunningham, "Medicine to Calm the Mind: Boerhaave's Medical System and Why It Was Adopted in Edinburgh," in Cunningham and French, *Medical Enlightenment*, 50. Medical theses in Mexico show evidence of familiarity with Boerhaave beginning in 1770; see Lanning, *Royal Protomedicato*, 334. Bartaloche's students, including Chair of Practical Medicine José Luis Montaña, read Boerhaave in their course in physiology; see Izquierdo, *Montaña*, 80.

8   The Heir Apparent

1   Mexico City, *Diario de México*, 25 September 1813, tomo 2, no. 87, fols. 3–4; Mexico City, *Diario de México*, 5 October 1813, tomo 2, no. 97, fols. 1–4.

2   See, for example, Toby Gelfand, "From Guild to Profession: The Surgeons of France in the 18th Century," *Texas Reports on Biology and Medicine* 32 (1974): 121–134.

3   Bartoloche, *Mercurio*, 133. For a suggestive analysis of the importance of medical advice to the rise of the notion of the body as an individual responsibility in the context of the French Revolution, see Dorinda Outram, *The Body and the French Revolution: Sex, Class, and Political Culture* (New Haven: Yale University Press, 1989), 41–68.

4 For an example of blaming illness on sin, see Cayetano de Cabrera y Quintero, *Escudo de Armas de México: escrito por el presbítero cayetano de Cabrera y Quintero para comemorar el final de la funesta epidemia de Matlazahuatl que asoló a la Nueva España entre 1736 y 1738 (1743)* (Mexico City: Instituto Mexicano de Seguridad Social, 1981), 59. Juan Javier Pescador discusses manifestations of God's wrath in his *De bautizados*, 275–276.

5 *Gazetas de México*, 21 August 1787, vol. 2, no. 40, p. 398. For other examples of medical advice plied by the new periodicals, see *Gazetas de México*, 7 April 1784, vol. 1, no. 7, p. 61; *Gazetas de México*, 13 March 1787, vol. 2, no. 30, pp. 314–315.

6 Mexico City, City Council to Viceroy Galvez, 1786, AHCM, Policía de Salubridad, Epidemias, vol. 3674, exp. 4, fols. 21–22, cited in Donald B. Cooper, *Epidemic Disease in Mexico City, 1761–1813: An Administrative, Social, and Medical Study* (Austin: University of Texas Press, 1965), 80.

7 *Diario de México*, 28 January 1813, vol. 1, pp. 159–160, cited in Cooper, *Epidemic Disease*, 159; Mexico City, Dr. Joaquín Guerra to City Council, 12 March 1821, AHCM, Policía de Salubridad, Juntas de Sanidad, vol. 3685, exp. 27, fol. 27.

8 Campomanes, *Discertación*, 187.

9 Don Gaspar Melchor de Jovellanos, "Oración Inaugural del Instituto Asturiano (1794)" in *Biblioteca de autores Españoles*, 46: 320; Don Gaspar Melchor de Jovellanos, "Discurso sobre los medios de promover la felicidad del principado (1781)," in *Biblioteca de autores Españoles desde la formacion del lenguaje hasta nuestros dias: Obras publicadas e inéditas de Don Gaspar Melchor de Jovellanos*. Multiple vols., ed. Don Miguel Artola. Madrid: Ediciones Atlas, 1956. 50: 438.

10 Mexico City, Viceroy Revillagigedo to Archbishop, 16 September 1790, AGN, Correspondencia de Virreyes, serie 2a, vol. 21, carta 71, fols. 130–132v. The importance of doctors' testimonies in the campaign for general cemeteries was also evident in Guadalajara, where during the 1786 plague City Attorney Antonio López armed himself with medical testimony to combat ecclesiastical opposition to a suburban cemetery. See María Angeles Galvez Ruíz, "La consolidación de la conciencia regional en Guadalajara: El gobierno del intendente Jacobo Ugarte y Loyola (1791–1798)," (Ph.D. diss., Universidad de Grenada, 1993), 331–342. In Montevideo in 1789 the City Council invited the area's doctors to a meeting to discuss a new general cemetery; see the discussion printed in Mallo, *Apuntes históricos*, 235–267. The Protomedicato was formally in charge of Lima's new suburban cemetery, which was in operation by 1814; see Archbishop of Lima Bartolomé María de Heras's remarks at the benediction of the general cemetery, in Lima, 1814, AGN, Bienes Nacionales, vol. 910, exp. 23.

11 Mexico City, "Informe de los perjuicios de las luterías, targeas, y cementerios, dada al sr. superintendente de policía, por el doctor don Florencio Pérez y Comoto, de la Real Sociedad Patriótica de la Havana, y consultor de la de Guatemala," *Diario de México*, 28 January 1813, tomo. 1, no. 40, pp. 157, 159, 160;

Mexico City, José M. Casasola to City Council, 21 December 1820, AGN, Ayunta-mientos, vol. 2, exp. 10, fols. 1, 10v; Mexico City, 1821, Juan Francisco Azcarate report to City Council, AGN, Ayuntamientos, vol. 2, exp. 13, fol. 189; Mexico City, Report of Viceroy Beaumont, 27 October 1809, AGN, Bienes Nacionales, vol. 910, exp. 12, fol. 1.

12   Mexico City, "Bando de la Real Sala de Crimen," 1 October 1766, printed in Eusebio Ventura Beleña, *Recopilación sumaria de todos los autos acordados de la real audiencia y sala de crimen de esta Nueva España, y providencias de su superior gobierno* (Mexico City: D. Felipe de Zúñiga y Ontivero, 1787), 1: 4. Repeated efforts to ban vendors from cemeteries had been ineffective because market judges charged vendors for licenses and therefore respected only the edict of the viceroy who issued it, reissuing licenses with the advent of a new viceroy to collect the fees. See Mexico City, Francisco Sosa to King and Supreme Council of the Indies, 26 February 1804, AGN, Reales Cédulas Originales, vol. 195, exp. 40, fols. 1–2.

13   Mexico City, Ramón Gutierrez de Mazo to Mexico City Council, 12 February 1812, AHCM, Actas de Cabildo Originales, vol. 137; Mexico City, Ramón Gu-tierrez de Mazo to City Council, 21 February 1812, AHCM, Policía de Salubridad, vol. 3668, exp. 6. It appears that the luterías did a thriving business. During a 1798–1799 Crown fundraising campaign the *alquiladores de lutos* were among the more generous donors; see Mexico City, "Contributions of the alquiladores de lutos," 17 June 1799, AGN, Donativos y Préstamos, vol. 18, exp. 2, fols. 221–221v.

14   Mexico City, Superintendent of Police, *Diario de México*, 28 January 1813, vol. 1, no. 40, pp. 157–159.

15   Mexico City, Alcalde de Barrio 13 to Juez Mayor Jacobo, 12 October 1807, AGN, Policía, vol. 34, exp. 6, fol. 85v; Mexico City, Viceroy Revillagigedo "Ordenanzas de Pulquerías," 25 January 1793, AGN, Bandos, vol. 17, fol. 32. On the curtains, see *Gazetas de México*, 17 February 1789, vol. 3, no. 25, p. 4; Scardaville, "Crime," 219. Mexico City, Maestro Mayor to [Caño?], 3 November 1802, AHCM, Policía en General, vol. 3629, exp. 122, fol. 3; Mexico City, Real Junta de Policía to Viceroy Revillagigedo, 2 March 1791, AHCM, Alumbrado, vol. 345, exp. 7, fol. 12; Mexico City, "Sobre los defectos notados por el alcalde de cuartel menor 23," 1791, AHCM, Política en General, vol. 3629, exp. 140, fol. 3.

16   Fortino Hipólito Vera, ed., *Notas del compendio histórico del Concilio III Mexicano* (Amecameca, Mexico: Colegio Católico, 1879), 59; Viceroy Mayorga, *Ordenanza de la división de la nobilísima ciudad de México en cuarteles, creación de los alcaldes de ellos, y reglas de su gobierno* . . . (Mexico City: Mariano Joseph de Zúñiga y Ontiveros, 1782), 9. On the Guarda Faroles escorting medical personnel to private homes, see Mexico City, "Report of Alcalde de Barrio 11," AHCM, Alumbrado, vol. 345, exp. 8; Mexico City, Viceroy Revillagigedo Edict, 7 April 1790, AGN, Bandos,

vol. 15, fol. 159; Mexico City, "Guarda Faroles Reports," 28 July 1794, 6 May 1795, 17 December 1795, AGN, Policía, vol. 20, fols. 170–171, 183v, 202. Before the Alcaldes de Barrio had begun to collect the sick poor, their function had been performed by the Brotherhood of St. John of the Cross; see Mariano Cuevas, *Historia de la iglesia en México* (El Paso, TX: Editorial Revolución Católica, 1928), 3: 335.

17 Mexico City, Viceroy Galvez to Jueces Mayores, 21 April 1786, AHCM, Policía de Salubridad, Epidemias, vol. 1, exp. 4, fols. 3; Mexico City, Francisco Antonio Crespo, Modesto de Salcedo, and Miguel Antonio Batallez y Basco to Viceroy Galvez, April 1786, AHCM, Policía de Salubridad. Epidemias, vol. 1, exp. 4, fols. 8, 10, 17. On the 1797 epidemic, see Cooper, *Epidemic*, 118. For more on the Alcaldes' role in bringing the sick to the hospitals, see Mexico City, City Council, 29 March 1821, AHCM, Actas de Cabildo, Impresas, vol. 671a, fols. 227–228.

18 Mexico City, Viceroy Calleja Edict, 4 April 1815, AGN, Policía, vol. 34, exp. 18, fols. 313–313v; Mexico City, 1 October 1819, Order of Viceroy Conde de Venadito, recopied in Febles, *Noticia de las leyes*, 77–78. On house numbers, see "Residencia de Revillagigedo," Mexico City, AGN, Historia, vol. 60, exp. 2, fol. 17. The 1790 census reported 51 doctors and 227 surgeons, barbers, and bleeders residing in the city; see *Gazetas de México*, 10 January 1792, vol. 1, p. 9.

19 Mexico City, City Council, January 1821, AHCM, Policía de Salubridad. Juntas de Sanidad, vol. 3685, exp. 17, fols. 5–12.

20 Mexico City, Joseph Mariano Pino to Fiscal de lo Civil, June 1794, and Protomedicato to Viceroy Branciforte, 11 August 1796, AGN, Protomedicato, vol. 3, exp. 3, fols. 1–38.

21 Pérez Cancio, *La Santa Cruz*, 125.

22 Mexico City, "Sobre transladar la huesamenta de los cadáveres al hospital de Terceros de San Francisco a la capilla de la fábrica," 29 March 1810, AGN, Hospitales, vol. 39, exp. 7, fol. 7.

23 Cited in Etlin, *The Architecture of Death*, 16, 31, 30.

24 Schendel, *Medicine in Mexico*, 116.

25 Mexico City, Dr. Luis Montaña, Dr. Jove, Dr. Vicente Fernández to Juez Privativo del Hospital Real, August and September 1805, AGN, Ayuntamientos, vol. 1, exp. 5, fols. 4v–5v, 12–13, 29.

26 Mexico City, Agustín Iglesias to Señores de la Junta de Policía, 29 September 1819, AGN, Ayuntamientos, vol. 1, exp. 8, fol. 101; Mexico City, Ignacio Pico to City Council, 29 September 1819, AGN, Ayuntamientos, vol. 1, exp. 8, fol. 103.

27 On the 1779 establishment of San Lázaro cemetery, see Mexico City, Juan Francisco Alzcarate to City Council, 1821, AGN, Ayuntamientos, vol. 2, exp. 13, fol. 186v.

28 Mexico City, "Circular a las parroquias de esta capital sobre el modo de enterrar los cadáveres," 18 November 1821, AGN, Ayuntamientos, vol. 2, exp. 12, fol. 9; Mexico City, José Ignacio Ormaechea to Parish Priests, 26 February 1821, AGN, Ayuntamientos, vol. 2, exp. 12, fol. 14.

29 For examples of secular authorities performing vistas de ojos, see Mexico City, City Council, 22 September 1815, AHCM, Actas de Cabildo Regulares, vol. 134, fol. 248; Mexico City, City Council, 20 April 1790, AHCM, Juntas de Policía, Actas Originales, vol. 449a, fol. 6v.

30 Mexico City, Alderman José Casasola, 1821, AGN, Ayuntamientos, vol. 2, exp. 15, fols. 215v, 214v.

31 Mexico City, Juan Francisco Alzcarate to City Council, 12 August 1821, AGN, Ayuntamientos, vol. 2, exp. 13, fols. 6–6v; Mexico City, Junta de Sanidad, 23 January 1821, AHCM, Policía de Salubridad, Cementerios y Entierros, vol. 3673, exp. 6, fols. 1–7.

32 Mexico City, Archbishop Don Pedro Fontes to City Council and Agustín Espinosa to City Council, 17 and 21 April, AGN, Bienes Nacionales, legajo 715, exp. 28, fols. 1–2v; Mexico City, Junta de Policía proposal for a general cemetery, 15 April 1822, AGN, Ayuntamientos, vol. 3, exp. 3, fols. 2, 4–5.

33 Mexico City, María Aguirre to Gobierno del Distrito Federal, 12 September 1825, AHCM, Policía de Salubridad, Cementerios y Entierros, vol. 3673, exp. 10, fol. 10; Mexico City, City Council Report, 21 August 1827, AGN, Ayuntamientos, vol. 3, exp. 4, fols. 1–7v.

34 Mexico City, Eusebio Sánchez Pareja to City Council, 11 October 1827, AHCM, Policía de Salubridad, Cementerios y Entierros, vol. 3673, exp. 12, fols. 1–3.

35 On lawyers' powers in the new nation, see Richard N. Sinkin, The Mexican Reform, 1855–1876: A Study of Liberal Nation-Building (Austin, TX: Institute of Latin American Studies, 1979), especially 45–47. For a suggestive analysis of the importance of doctors and medical testimony to the exercise of power in the eighteenth century, see Michel Foucault, Power/Knowledge: Selected Interviews and Other Writings, 1972–1977, ed., Colin Gordon, trans. Colin Gordon, Leo Marshall, John Mepham, and Kate Soper (New York: Pantheon Books, 1980), especially 165–182.

36 Paul Starr, The Social Transformation of American Medicine: The Rise of a Sovereign Profession and the Making of a Vast Industry (New York: Basic Books, 1982), 17, 30–37, 59. Also see Richard Shryock, Medicine and Society in America, 1660–1860 (Ithaca, NY: Cornell University Press, 1962), 2–9, 15; Robert Derbyshire, Medical Licensure and Discipline in the United States (Baltimore, MD: Johns Hopkins University Press, 1969), especially 2–3. Starr, Social Transformation, 81. Also see William J. Rothstein on doctors' failure to obtain licensing laws in the early nineteenth century: American Physicians in the 19th Century: From Sects to Science (Baltimore, MD: Johns Hopkins University Press, 1985), 73.

37 Dorothy Porter and Roy Porter, *Patient's Progress: Doctors and Doctoring in Eighteenth-Century England* (Stanford: Stanford Univeristy Press, 1989), 18, 139; Roy Porter, *Disease, Medicine and Society in England, 1550–1860,* 2d ed. (Cambridge, England: Cambridge University Press, 1995), 40, 44.

38 R. Porter, *Disease, Medicine,* 44.

39 Sonia Flores G. and José Sanfilippo B., *Anastasio Bustamante y las institucines de salubridad en el siglo XIX (documentos médicos)* (Mexico City: Facultad de Médicina, Universidad Autónoma de México, n.d), xxvi.

40 Green, *Mexican Republic,* 67. On Bustamante's official status as doctor, see Alicia Hernández Torres and Francisco Fernández del Castillo, *El Tribunal del Protomedicato en la Nueva España, segun el archivo Histórico de la Facultad de Medicina* (Mexico City: Universidad Nacional Autónoma de México, 1965), 43.

41 Fanny Calderon de la Barca, *Life in Mexico: The Letters of Fanny Calderon de la Barca. With New Material from the Author's Private Journals,* ed. Howard T. Fisher and Marion Hall Fisher (Garden City, NY: Anchor Books, 1970), 107.

42 Mexico City, Anastasio Bustamante Edict, 26 November 1831, AHCM, Médicos y Boticas, 1776–1850, exp. 16, fol. 1; *La salubridad y higiene pública en los Estados Unidos Mexicanos* (Mexico City: Casa Metodista de Publicaciones, 1910), ixxv.

43 *El Fenix de la Libertad,* 26 December 1833, tomo 3, no. 148, fol. 2, cols. 1–2; Manuel Dublán and José María Lozano, eds., *Legislación mexicana o colección completa de las disposiciones legislativas expedidas desde la Independencia de la República* (Mexico City: Imprenta del Comercio, 1867–1904), 2: 654.

44 *El Fenix de la Libertad,* 13 February 1834, tomo 4, no. 45, fol. 4, cols. 2–3.

45 Guillermo Prieto, *Memorias de mis tiempos (1828–1840)* (Mexico City: Editorial Patria, 1958), 209–210; *Diccionario Porrúa: Historia, biografía y geografía de México,* 5th ed. (Mexico City: Editorial Porrúa, 1986), n.p.

46 *El Fénix de la Libertad,* 10 December 1833, tomo 3, no. 132, fol. 2, cols. 2–3 and fol. 3, cols. 1–2.

47 Federal District, Edict of Governor José María Tornel, 15 December 1833, AGN, Gobernación, sección S/S, caja 161, exp. 9, fol. 2; *El Fenix de la Libertad,* 19 December 1833, tomo 3, no. 141, fol. 1, col. 1; Federal District, Edict of Governor José María Tornel, 15 December 1833, AHSSA, fondo Salubridad Pública, sección Higiene Pública, serie Inspección de Panteones, caja 1, exp. 1, fol. 1; Mexico City, "Bando para la regulación de los panteones en el Distrito Federal," 15 December 1833, AHSSA, fondo Salubridad Pública, sección Higiene Pública, serie Inspección de Panteones, caja 1, exp. 1, fol. 1. The edict is also cited in Dublán and Lozano, *Legislación mexicana,* 2: 647. Mexico City, San Juan de la Penitencia Vicar to José María Tornel, 24 September 1834, AHCM, Policía de Salubridad. Cementerios y Entierros, vol. 3673, exp. 23, fol. 8. Licéaga was the director of the Institute of Medical Sciences, which had been established by Gómez Farías.

48   The edict is printed in Rodríquez de la Miguel, *Pandectas*, 1:35, 1:36. *Noticioso General*, 16 October 1818, no. 436, p. 3, col. 1. Ruíz de Velasco y Martínez, *Defensa de los cementerios católicos*, 378; Madrid, Royal Order, 18 August 1818, AGN, Reales Cédulas Originales, vol. 219, exp. 134, fols. 134–135.

49   *La Marimba*, 3 May 1832, vol. 1, no. 15., p. 1. For an example of an earlier vista de ojos performed by the Junta de Sanidad on tombs in the Merced convent, see Mexico City, "Representación del Regidor don Eusebio García sobre estarse fabricando sepulcros en el convento de la Merced," 23 May 1821, AHCM, Policía de Salubridad. Cementerios y Entierros, vol. 3673, exp. 6, fol. 1. Mexico City, "Cementerios: sobre que se haga una vista de ojos en el de la Santa Veracruz," City Council, AHCM, Policía de Salubridad, Cementerios y Entierros, vol. 3673, exp. 14, fols. 7–10. The confraternity was established in 1824 and boasted among its members President Guadalupe Victoria; it opened its cemetery in 1827. See Lauro E. Rosell, *Iglesias y conventos coloniales de México: Historia de cada uno de los que existen en la ciudad de México*, 2d ed. (Mexico City: Editorial Patria, 1961), 31; *Constituciones de la muy ilustre Archicofradía de Cuidadanos de la Santa Veracruz, mandandos observar por acuerdo de su junta general celebrada en 29 de Febrero de 1824* (Mexico City: Imprenta del Cuidadano Alejandro Valdés, 1824).

50   Mexico City, Sala de Juntas de la muy ilustre Archicofradía de Ciudadanos de la Santa Veracruz, "Exposición en que la ilustre Archicofradía de Ciudadanos de la Santa Veracruz, solicita del Supremo Gobierno la persistencia de su panteón," 10 May 1833, Condumex, Miscelania Papeles, Varios Autores, no. 3, pieza no. 41, no. 47733-c; Mexico City, "Cementerios: sobre que se haga una vista de ojos en el de la Santa Veracruz," 7 August 1833, City Council, AHCM, Policía de Salubridad. Cementerios y Entierros, vol. 3673, exp. 14, fols. 15–15v.

51   Mexico City, Consejo Superior de Salubridad to City Council, 15 May 1845, AHCM, Policía de Salubridad, Cementerios y Entierros, vol. 3673, exp. 36, fols. 1–iv; Mexico City, Consejo Superior de Salubridad, 15 May 1845, AHSSA, fondo Salubridad Pública, sección Higiene Pública, serie Inspección de Panteones, caja 1, exp. 19, fol. 1; Mexico City, City Council to José Ignacio Duran, 1845, AHSSA, fondo Salubridad Pública, sección Presidencia, serie Secretaría, caja 3, exp. 28, fol. 1.

52   Mexico City, Consejo de Salubridad, 4 January 1841, AGN, Gobernación sec. S/S, caja 247, exp. 3, fols. 21–31; Mexico City, "Ordenamiento de arreglo de estudios Médicos y exámenes de profesores y policía en ejercicio de las facultades de medicina en el departamento de México," AHSSA, carpeta 24, fols. 23–31; Fernando Martínez Cortés, *De los miasmas y efluvios al descubrimiento de las bacterias patógenas: Los primeros cincuenta años del Consejo Superior de Salubridad* (Mexico City: Bristol-Myers Squibb, 1993), 35, 42–45; Mexico City, María Lavin de Vieyra to Consejo, 2 June 1841, AHSSA, fondo Salubridad Pública, sección

Presidencia, serie Secretaría, caja 2, exp. 20, fol. 1; Mexico City, Guarda de Alumbrado to Consejo Superior de Salubridad, Mexico City, Consejo Superior de Salubridad to *Siglo XIX*, 22 February 1844, AHSSA, fondo Salubridad Pública, serie Ejercicio de Medicina, caja 2, exp. 46, fol. 1.

53 Mexico City, Leopoldo Río de la Loza to Governor, 23 February 1842, AHSSA, fondo Salubridad Pública, sección Presidencia, serie Secretaría, caja 2, exp. 50, fol. 1; Mexico City, Archbishop to Consejo Superior de Salubridad, 4 May 1842, AHSSA, fondo Salubridad Pública, sección Higiene Pública, serie Inspección de Panteones, caja 1, exp. 9, fol. 4; Mexico City, Consejo de Salubridad to convents of San Francisco, Santa Catalina, La Concepción, and Santa Isabela, 9 June 1845, AHSSA, fondo Salubridad Pública, sección Higiene Pública, caja 1, exp. 20, fols. 1–2; "Police Orders Concerning Cadavers," 28 March 1842, in Dublán and Lozano, *Legislación mexicana*, 4:134; Mexico City, Convent of La Concepción to Consejo Superior de Salubridad, 1845, AHSSA, fondo Salubridad Pública, sección Higiene Pública, serie Inspección de Panteones, caja 1, exp. 21, fol. 1.

54 Mexico City, AN, Wills. During the 1810–1820 period, 55 percent of testators indicated a burial preference, with 13 percent electing a cemetery burial.

55 Mexico City, Archbishop to José María Bocanegra, 18 August 1843, AGN, Gobernación, sección S/S, 1843, D.F. Policía de Salubridad: Cementerios, fol. 7.

56 On these routine visits to cemeteries and *panteones* (pantheons), see, for example, Mexico City, Visit to Colegio de San Fernando, 8 November 1843, AHSSA, fondo Salubridad Pública, sección Higiene Pública, serie Inspección de Panteones, caja 1, exp. 13, fols. 1–4; Mexico City, Visit to Campo Florida, 7 May 1850, AHSSA, fondo Salubridad Pública, sección Higiene Pública, serie Inspección de Panteones, caja 1, exp. 27.

57 Mexico City, Consejo de Salubridad to City Council, 13 November 1848, AHCM, Policía de Salubridad, Cementerios y Entierros, vol. 3673, exp. 41, fols. 1–5; Mexico City, Consejo Superior de Salubridad to Congress, 9 December 1846, AHSSA, fondo Salubridad Pública, sección Higiene Pública, serie Inspección de Panteones, caja 1, exp. 23, fol. 7v. Founded in 1841, the Consejo Superior de Salubridad had five titled members, including three doctors, one pharmacist and one chemist; it also counted on seven auxiliary members, all of whom were faculty members at the Institute of Medical Sciences; see Martínez Cortés, *De los miasmas*, 13.

58 Mexico City, Consejo Superior de Salubridad to Congress, 9 December 1846, AHSSA, fondo Salubridad Pública, sección Higiene Pública, serie Inspección de Panteones, caja 1; exp. 23, fols. 7v, 10.

59 Veracruz, State Congress of Veracruz, 14 March 1831, AHCV, caja 193, vol. 261,

fols. 89–96; Veracruz, El Censor, 29 October 1833, fol. 3, cols. 1–2; Veracruz, Veracruz City Council, 17 December 1833, AHCV, caja 170, vol. 231, fols. 1043–1055; Veracruz, Veracruz City Council, 18 October 1839, AHCV, caja 165, vol. 223, fol. 198; Veracruz, Veracruz City Council, 1 April 1865, AHCV, caja 227, vol. 317, fols. 130–156.

60   Veracruz, Veracruz City Council to Intendant Carlos Irrutia, 27 April 1810, AHCV, caja 93, vol. 108, fols. 239–244.

61   Mexico City, Inquisition, AGN, Inquisición, vol. 1268, fol. 250; Mexico City, Inquisition vs. María Antonia Básquez de Acuña, 7 July 1768, AGN, Inquisición, vol. 1055, exp. 5, fols. 185–210; Mexico City, José Ignacio Cano to City Council, 1802, AHCM, Policía de Salubridad, Cementerios y Entierros, vol. 3673, exp. 1, fol. 6v.

62   Mexico City, Fernando Fernández de San Salvador, 20 September 1797, AGN, Historia, vol. 44, exp. 14, fols. 1–1v; Mexico City, Luis Montaña to Viceroy Branciforte, 29 September 1797, AGN, Historia, vol. 44, exp. 14, fols. 24–31v. The verses are also discussed in Cooper, Epidemic Disease, 130.

63   Fray Joaquín de Bolaños, La Portentosa vida de la muerte. Emperatriz de los sepulcros, vengadora de los agravios del Altísimo y muy señora de la humana naturaleza (1792), ed. Agustín Yáñez (Mexico City: Universidad Autónoma Nacional de México 1994), 140–146. This text is discussed in Viqueira, "El sentimiento," 27–63.

64   Las calaveras borrachas claman por el chinguirito (Mexico City: Hipólito Lagarza, 1836), 1.

65   Mexico City, City Council, 13 July 1824, AHCM, Policía de Salubridad, vol. 3668, exp. 15, fol. 1; Mexico City, Bishop to City Council, 27 July 1824, AHCM, Policía de Salubridad, vol. 3668, exp. 15, fols. 3–3v.

66   Martínez Cortés, De los miasmas, iv; Miguel Angel Cuenya and Elsa Malvido, El cólera de 1833: Una nueva patología en México. Causas y efectos (Mexico City: Instituto Nacional de Antropología e Historia, 1992), 82–83. On Gómez Farías's medical training, see Dr. Ernesto Lemoine, "La praxis política de Gómez Farías," in Memoria de las mesas redondas sobre las ideas de Valentín Gómez Farías y José María Luis Mora (Mexico City: Instituto Dr. José María Luis Mora, 1982), 53–65.

67   Prieto, Memorias, 69–70.

68   Mexico City, "Causa formada contra D. María Antonia López Rayón, por curandera," 3 January 1791, AGN, Protomedicato, vol. 7, exp. 4, fols. 1–17. On curandero training and curing techniques, see Quezada, Enfermedad y maleficio, especially 35–37, 82–91.

69   Hernández Sáenz, Learning to Heal, 252.

70   Ibid., 228–230, 251, 255.

71   El Amante de la Humanidad, Destierro de charlatanes, 1.

72   Dublán and Lozano, Legislación mexicana, 4: 108; El Observador Judicial y de Legislación, 26 May 1842, tomo 1, no. 15, pp. 347–348; Mexico City, City Council to

Consejo Superior de Salubridad, 22 April 1845, AHSSA, fondo Salubridad Pública, sección Ejercicio de Medicina, caja 2, exp. 73; Tenancingo, Dr. Pablo Lefubure to Consejo Superior de Salubridad, 30 July 1846, AHSSA, fondo Salubridad Pública, sección Ejercicio de Medicina, caja 2, exp. 77; *El Mosquito Mexicano*, 7 May 1841, tomo 9, no. 37, p. 1, col. 1; Mexico City, Consejo Superior de Salubridad, 1842, AHSSA, fondo Salubridad Pública, sección Ejercicio de Medicina, caja 1, exp. 8; Mexico City, María de Jesús Blea to Consejo Superior de Salubridad, 1842, AHSSA, fondo Salubridad Pública, sección Ejercicio de Medicina, caja 2, exp. 2, fol. 1; Mexico City, M. Bires to Secretary of the Consejo Superior de Salubridad, 26 January 1842, AHSSA, fondo Salubridad Pública, sección Presidencia, serie Secretaría, caja 2, exp. 38, fol. 20.

73 Mexico City, Consejo Superior de Salubridad, 22 January 1843, AHSSA, fondo Salubridad Pública, sección Ejercicio de Medicina, caja 2, exp. 44; Mexico City, Consejo Superior de Salubridad, 22 January 1843, AHSSA, fondo Salubridad Pública, sección Ejercicio de Medicina, caja 2, exp. 44, fol. 4.

74 Bossy, *Christianity*, 32–33.

75 Cited in Elizabeth Carmichael and Chloe Sayer, *The Skeleton at the Feast: The Day of the Dead in Mexico* (Austin: University of Texas Press, 1991), 31, 28.

76 Vera, *Notas del compendio*, 92–93.

77 Mexico City, Joseph María de Neve y Romero, 1777, INAH, Hospital Real de Naturales, rollo 44, vol. 81, exp. 8, fols. 124–124v, 229v; Juan Pedro Viqueira, "La Ilustración y las fiestas populares en la ciudad de México (1730–1821)," *Cuicuilco* 14–15 (July–December 1984): 17; Carmichael and Sayer, *Skeleton*, 43–44.

78 Mexico City, Edict of the Archbishop, 26 October 1791, cited in Vera, *Colección de documentos*, 3: 663; Viera, "Breve compendiosa," 280.

79 Cited in Carmichael and Sayer, *Skeleton*, 46.

80 Gómez, *Diario curioso*, 308; Mexico City, Alcalde Report, 21 October 1790, AGN, Criminal, vol. 33, fols. 184–190.

81 Mexico City, [?] to City Council and Federal District Governor, 23 September 1825, AGN, Ayuntamientos, vol. 3, exp. 3, fol. 1; *El congreso de los muertos en días de Todos Santos en Santiago Tlaltelolco* (Mexico City: A. Rangel, 1835), 1.

82 Antonio García Cubas, *El libro de mis recuerdos. Narraciones históricas, anécdotas y de costumbres mexicanas anteriores al actual estado social. Ilustradas con más de trescientos fotograbados* (Mexico City: Editorial Patria, 1950), 511, 513.

83 Calderón de la Barca, *Life in Mexico*, 349, 541–542.

84 García Cubas, *El libro*, 498.

85 Mexico City, Superior Order, 31 October 1848, AHCM, Policía de Salubridad. Cementerios y Entierros, vol. 3673, exp. 39, fols. 1–2; Mexico City, *Siglo XIX*, 25 October 1875, p. 3, col. 2.

86 See the descriptions of the festival from the years 1824, 1860, 1861, 1864, 1866,

1867, and 1869 in Mexico City, City Council, AHCM, Festividades, Noviembre y Todos Santos, vol. 1065, exps. 2, 3, 4, 5, 7, 8, 11, 13.

87 Ignacio M. Altmarino, El Renacimiento, 6 November 1869, p. 252; García Cubas, El libro, 509–510.

88 García Cubas, El libro, 513.

89 Mexico City, 1843, Biblioteca Nacional, Collección Lafragua, no. 707, necrologías no. 5, documento no. 26; Panteón de San Pablo (Mexico City: Antonio Díaz, 1843); Mexico City, Juan María Flores to City Council, 31 October 1848, AHCM, Policía de Salubridad, Cementerios y Entierros, vol. 3673, exp. 39, fol. 1.

90 Mexico City, Santa Anna, Municipal Cemetery Decree, 18 July 1854, AHCM, Panteones, vol. 3454, exp. 1, fol. 1; Mexico City, Santa Anna, Municipal Cemetery Decree, 14 July 1854, AGN, Gobernación, legajo 221, caja 315, exp. 2, fol. 367; Mexico City, El Monitor Republicano, 3 August 1861, p. 4, col. 1. Charles Hale characterizes the Monitor Republicano as a liberal mouthpiece; see his Mexican Liberalism, 12.

91 Mexico City, President of the Republic Benito Juárez to City Council, 10 April 1863, AHCM, Policía de Salubridad, vol. 3668, exp. 68, fols. 1–2. On Dr. Gallardo Fernández's removal of bodies from closed convents, see fol. 3.

92 Martín Luis Guzmán, ed., Leyes de Reforma: Gobiernos de Ignacio Comonfort y Benito Juárez (1856–1863) (Mexico City: Empresas Editoriales, 1947), 153–154; Veracruz, Benito Juárez Edict, 31 July 1859, AHSSA, fondo Salubridad Pública, serie Higiene Pública, sección Inspección de Panteones, caja 1, exp. 49, fols. 1–6; Benito Juárez Edict, 31 July 1859, AGN, Gobernación, leg. 1030, exp. 4, no. 14.

93 Ignacio Manuel Altamirano, Discursos (Paris: Biblioteca de la Europa y America, 1892), 18, 20. David A. Brading also notes that Altamirano found the Church, not religion, to be the main problem in Mexico; see his First America, 658.

Conclusion

1 J. Lloyd Mecham, Church and State in Latin America: A History of Politico-Ecclesiastical Relations (Chapel Hill: University of North Carolina Press, 1934), 504; David Bushnell, The Making of Modern Colombia: A Nation in Spite of Itself (Berkeley: University of California Press, 1993), 51, 56; Mary P. Holleran, Church and State in Guatemala (New York: Columbia University Press, 1949), 76–88.

2 Mecham, Church and State, 503. Ralph Lee Woodward Jr., "The Liberal-Conservative Debate in the Central American Federation, 1823–1840," in Liberals, Politics and Power: State Formation in Nineteenth-Century Latin America, ed. Vicent C. Peloso and Barbara Tenenbaum (Athens: University of Georgia Press, 1996), 66, 76.

3 Bushnell, Making, 110.

4 Jeffrey L. Klaiber, *Religion and Revolution in Peru, 1824–1976* (Notre Dame, IN: University of Notre Dame Press, 1977), 19, 5–22.

5 For a good summary of this process, see Alan Knight, "The Peculiarities of Mexican History: Mexico Compared to Latin America, 1821–1992," *Journal of Latin American Studies* 24 (Quincentenary Supplement, 1992): 120–122.

6 Ibid., 120; Donald F. Stevens, *The Origins of Instability in Early Republican Mexico* (Durham, NC: Duke University Press, 1991), 76–77, 113. Stevens and a battery of modern computer technology tested Brading's hypothesis by examining the geogaphical backgrounds of elite political leaders; he found that the far north and far south produced proportionally more liberals (77–87). The liberal crescent that had been described by Brading included the area from Guerrero through Michoacán, Jalisco, part of Guanajuato, Zacatecas, and San Luis Potosí to Veracruz; see his "Creole Nationalism and Mexican Liberalism," *Journal of Interamerican Studies and World Affairs* 15 (May 1973): 185–186. Also see Sinkin, *Mexican Reform*, 37–38.

bibliography

PRIMARY SOURCES

Abad y Queipo, Manuel. "La población Novohispana en 1799." In *México en el siglo XIX: Antología de fuentes e interpretaciones históricos.* Ed. Alvaro Matute. Mexico City: Universidad Nacional Autónoma de México, 1973.

Ajofrín, Friar Francisco de. *Diario del viaje que por orden de la sagrada Congregación de Propaganda Fide hice a la América Septentrional en compañía de fray Fermín de Olite, religioso lego y de mi provincia de Castilla (1763).* 2 vols. Mexico City: Instituto Cultural Hispano Mexicano, 1964.

Alcántara Fernández, Pedro de. *Manual areglado al ritual romano.* Mexico City: Doña María Rivera, 1748.

Alfaro y Beaumont, Isidro Sainz de. *Circular que dirige el señor gobernador de la sagrada mitra á los párrocos, eclesiásticos, y fieles cristianos del arzobispado de México, sobre erección de cementerios fuera de las poblaciones.* Mexico City: Doña María Fernández de Jauregui, 1809.

Altamirano, Ignacio Manuel. *Discursos.* Paris: Biblioteca de la Europa y America, 1892.

———. *El Renacimiento,* 6 November 1869, p. 252.

Amar y Borbón, Josefa. *Discurso sobre la educación físcia y moral de las mujeres.* Ed. María Victoria López-Cordón. Madrid: Ediciones Cátedra, nd.

Arrillaga, Basilo José, ed. *Recopilación de leyes, decretos, bandos, reglamentos, circulares, y providencias de los supremos poderes y otras autoridades de la república Mexicana. Formada de orden del Supremo Gobierno por el lic. Basilo José Arrillaga.* 27 vols. Mexico City: Imprenta de J. M. Fernández de Lara, 1835.

Augustine, Saint. *An Augustinian Synthesis.* Ed. Erich Przywara. New York: Harper and Brothers, 1958.

———. *The City of God (426).* Ed. Vernon J. Bourke. Garden City, NJ: Image Books, 1958.

Báez Macías, Eduardo. "Ordenanzas para el establecimiento de Alcaldes de Barrio en la Nueva Espana: Ciudades de Mexico y San Luis Potosí." *Boletín del Archivo General de la Nación,* 10: 1–2 (1969): 12–38.

Bails, Benito, ed. *Pruebas de ser contrario a la practica de todas las naciones y a la disciplina eclesiástica, y perjudicial a la salud de los vivos enterrar los difuntos en las iglesias y los poblados*. Madrid: Don Benito Bails, 1785.

Barrio, Dr. dn. Julian Joseph del. *Discurso que en la solemne benedición del cementerio general de la Havana, hecha en la tarde del día dos de febrero de 1806, por el ilustrísimo señor D. Juan Joseph Díaz de Espada y Landa, obispo de esta diocesi, pronunció el Dr. dn. Julian Joseph del Barrio, Canonigo de su santa iglesia catedral*. Havana: Estevan Joseph Bolõno, 1806.

Bartoloche, José Ignacio. *Mercurio Volante (1772–1773)*. Ed. Roberto Moreno. Mexico: Universidad Nacional Autónoma de México, 1979.

Berdu, Gabriel. *Tratado del Tercer Orden del Querubico Patriarca Santo Domingo de Guzman, de su origen, reglas, gracías, e excelencias. Compuesto por el Dr. Gabriel Berdu, capellan penitenciario de la Santa Iglesia Metropolitana de Valencia, y Profesor del mismo Tercer Orden, y Comisario de el Santo Oficio*. Mexico City: D. Felipe de Zúñiga y Ontiveros, 1777.

Bolaños, Fray Joaquín de. *La Portentosa vida de la muerte. Emperatriz de los sepulcros, vengadora de los agravios del Altísimo y muy señora de la humana naturaleza (1792)*. Ed. Agustín Yañez. Mexico: Universidad Nacional Autónoma de México, 1994.

Cabrera, Juan de. *Crisis política. Determina el más florido imperio y la mejor institución de príncipes y ministros*. Madrid, 1719.

Cabrera, Ramón. "Disertacion Histórica; en la qual se expone por la serie de los tiempos la varía disciplina que ha observado la Iglesia de España sobre el lugar de las sepulturas." In *Pruebas de ser contrario a la práctica de todas las naciones y a la disciplina eclesiástica, y perjudicial a la salud de los vivos enterrar los difuntos en las iglesias y los poblados*, ed. Benito Bails. Madrid: Don Benito Bails, 1785.

Cabrera y Quintero, Cayetano de. *Escudo de Armas de México: escrito por el presbítero cayetano de Cabrera y Quintero para comemorar el final de la funesta epidemia de Matlazahuatl que asoló a la Nueva España entre 1736 y 1738 (1743)*. Mexico City: Instituto Mexicano de Seguridad Social, 1981.

Calderon de la Barca, Fanny. *Life in Mexico: The Letters of Fanny Calderon de la Barca. With New Material from the Author's Private Journals*. Ed. Howard T. Fisher and Marion Hall Fisher. Garden City, NY: Anchor books, 1970.

Calvin, John, *Institutes of the Christian Religion (1559)*. Ed. John T. McNeill. Philadelphia: Westminster Press, 1960.

———. *John Calvin: Selections from His Writings*. Ed. John Dillenberger. New York: Anchor Books, 1971.

Camble-Blanco, Dr. Janin, Señor de. *El antimefítico ó licor antipútrido y perfectamente correctivo de los vapores perniciosísmos de los dormitorios, comedores, teatros, hospitales, enfermerías, iglesias, cementerios, cuarteles, cárceles, minas, navíos de guerra, lugares comunes, albañiles, sumideros, carnicerías, limpías, y mondas*. Madrid: Imprenta Real, 1782.

Campomanes, Conde de (Pedro Rodríguez). *Discertación sobre la educación popular de los artesanos y su fomento (1775)*. Ed. John Reeder. Madrid: Fábrica Nacionál de Moneda y Timbres, 1975.

——. *Discurso sobre la educación popular y fomento de la industria popular*. Madrid: Don Antonio de Sancha, 1774.

Carpio, Manuel. *Aforismos y Pronósticos de Hipócrates. Seguidos del artículo pectoriloquo del diccionario de ciencias médicas. Traducidos al Castellano, los primeros del Latín, y el último del Francés*. Mexico City: Mariano Ontiveros, 1823.

Cobarrús, Conde de. "Sanidad pública." In *Cartas*, ed. José Maravall Casesnoves. Madrid: Castellote Editorial, 1973.

Colección de los Aranceles de obvenciones y derechos parroquiales que han estado vigentes en los obispados de la República Mexicana y que se citan en el supremo decreto de 11 de Abril de 1857. Mexico City: Imprenta de Ignacio Cumplido, 1857.

Concilio Provincial Mexicano IV: Celebrado en la ciudad de México el año de 1771. Queretero, Mexico: Escuela de Artes, 1898.

Constituciones de la muy ilustre Archicofradía de Cuidanos de la Santa Veracruz, mandandos observar por acuerdo de su junta general celebrada en 29 de Febrero de 1824. Mexico City: Imprenta del Cuidadano Alejandro Valdes, 1824.

Council of Castile. *Memorial ajustado del expediente seguido en el Consejo, en virtud del orden de S.M. de 24 de marzo de 1781 sobre establecimiento general de cementerios*. Madrid: Ibarra, 1786.

Crasset, Juan. *La dulce y santa muerte obra que escribío en francés el padre Juan Crasset de la Compañía de Jesús, y traduxó en castellano el doctor don Basilio Sotomayor*. Trans. Basilio Sotomayor. Madrid: Imprenta de Gonzalez, 1728.

Devoti, Felix. *Discurso sobre el cementerio general que se ha erigido extramuros de la ciudad de Lima por el orden, zelo, y beneficencia de su excmo. señor virey don José Fernando de Abascal y Sousa, por Felix Devoti, profesor de medicina*. Guadalajara, Mexico: José Fruto Romero, 1814.

Dublán, Manuel, and José María Lozano. *La Legislación mexicana o colección completa de las disposiciones legislativas expedidas desde la Independencia de la República*. 30 vols. Mexico City: Imprenta del Comercio, 1876–1912.

El Amante de la Humanidad. Destierro de charlatanes y abuso de cirujanos. Mexico City: Imprenta de Juan Bautista de Arizpe, 1820.

El congreso de los muertos en días de Todos Santos en Santiago Tlaltelolco. Mexico City: A. Rangel, 1835.

Erasmus. *The Enchiridion of Erasmus (1503)*. Ed. and trans. Raymond Himelick. Bloomington: University of Indiana Press, 1963.

——. *The Essential Erasmus*. Ed. John P. Dolan. New York: Penguin Books, 1983.

Es culpable el que se calle en perjuicio de los hombres. Mexico City: D. Alejandro Valdés, 1820.

Espada y Landa, Juan Joseph Díaz de. *Exhortación a los fieles de la ciudad de Havana, hecha por su prelado diocesano, sobre el cementerio general de ella; y su reglamento, aprobado por el gobierno, con el correspondiente de policía.* Havana: Estevan Joseph Boloña, 1806.

Fabián y Fuero, Franciscisco. *Colección de providencias diocesanos del obispo de la Puebla de Los Angeles Dr. Don Francisco Fabián y Fuero.* Puebla, Mexico: Imprenta Palafoxiana, 1770.

Febles, Manuel de Jesús. *Noticia de las leyes y órdenes de policía que rigen a los profesores del arte de curar. Dispuestas por Manuel de Jesús Febles.* Mexico City: Imprenta del Ciudadano Alejandro Valdés, 1830.

Feijoo, Benito Jerónimo. "Uso mas honesto de la arte obstetrica (1742)." In *Obras.* Ed. Ivy L. McClelland. Madrid: Taurus, 1985.

Fernández de Lizardi, José Joaquín. *Chanzas y Veras de El Pensador Méxicano. Díalogo entre el autor y un licenciado.* Mexico City: Doña María Fernández de Jáuregui, 1813.

——. *Obras VII: Novelas. Vols. 1–2. El periquillo sarniento.* Ed. Felipe Reyes Palacios. Mexico City: Universidad Nacional Autónoma de México, 1982.

——. *Obras. Vols. 1–7.* Ed. María Rosa Palazón Mayoral and Felipe Reyes Palacios. Mexico City: Universidad Autónoma de México, 1975.

——. *Testamento del Pensador Mexicano: Ciudadano Fernández de Lizardi. Primera y segunda parte.* Ed. Vicente Riva Palacio. Mexico City: Editorial Orientaciones, 1940.

——. *The Itching Parrot.* Trans. Katherine Anne Porter. Garden City, NY: Doubleday, Doran, 1942.

Floridablanca, Conde de. *Instrucción reservada para la dirección de la junta del estado.* Ed. Cayetano Alcazar. Madrid: M. Aguilar, 1897.

Gage, Thomas. *A New Survey of the West Indies: or, The English American his Travail by Sea and Land.* London: E. Corte, 1655.

García Cubas, Antonio. *El libro de mis recuerdos. Narraciones históricas, anécdotas y de costumbres mexicanas anteriores al actual estado social. Ilustradas con más de trescientos fotograbados.* Mexico City: Editorial Patria, 1950.

Gemelli Carreri, Giovanni Francesco. *Le Mexique a la fin du XVIie siècle un par un voyaguer italien Gemelli Careri.* Ed. Jean Pierre Berthe. Paris: Calmann-Lévy, 1968.

Gómez, José. *Diario curioso y cuaderno de las cosas memorables en México durante el gobierno de Revillagigedo, 1789–1794.* Ed. Ignacio Polo y Acosta. Mexico City: Universidad Nacional Autónoma de México, 1986.

González de Cossio, Francisco, ed. *Relaciones y Crónicas de la Compañía de Jesús en la Nueva España.* Mexico City: Universidad Nacional Autónoma de México, 1979.

——, ed. *Testimonios mexicanos. Historiadores. Gacetas de México.* 3 vols. Mexico City: Secretaría de Educación Pública, 1949.

Gonzalez Polo y Acosto, Ignacio. "Compendio de providencias de policía de la ciudad de México del segundo conde de Revillagigedo." *Boletín del Instituto de Investigaciónes Bibliograficas* 17–18 (1977–1978), vols. 14–15.

Guerra, José. *Fecunda nube del cielo Guadalupano, y mystica paloma del estrecho polomar de el Colegio Apostolico de Nuestra Señora de Guadalupe. Relación breve de la vida exemplar del V.P.F. Antonio Margil de Jesús, predicador apostolico, fundador de los tres colegios de estas Indias Occidentales. Comisario del S. Oficio, Examinador Synodal del Obispado de Guadalajara, y ex-prefecto de las misiones Propaganda Fide.* Mexico City: Joseph Bernardo de Hogal, 1726.

Guijo, Gregorio M. de. *Diario, 1648–1664.* 2 vols. 2d. ed. Ed. Manuel Romero de Terreros. Mexico City: Editorial Porrúa, 1986.

Guzmán, Martín Luis, ed. *Leyes de Reforma: Gobiernos de Ignacio Comonfort y Benito Juárez (1856–1863).* Mexico City: Empresas Editoriales, 1947.

Haro y Peralta, D. Alonso Núñez de. *Carta pastoral que el Ilmô. Señor Doctor D. Alonso Nuñez de Haro y Peralta del Consejo de S.M. y Arzobispo de México, dirige a todos sus amados diocesanos sobre la doctrina sana en general, contraída en particular a las más esenciales obligaciones que tenemos para con Dios y para con el Rey.* Mexico City: Don Felipe de Zúñiga y Ontiveros, 1777.

Humbolt, Alejandro de. *Ensayo politico sobre el reino de la Nueva España.* 5 vols. Ed. Vito Allessio Robles. Mexico City: Editorial Pedro Robredo, 1941.

Jovellanos, Don Gaspar Melchor de. *Colección de varias obras en prosa y verso del exmo: Señor D. Gaspar Melchor de Jovellanos.* Madrid: Imprenta de D. León Amarita, 1831.

——. "Discurso sobre los medios de promover la felicidad del principado (1781)." In *Biblioteca de autores Españoles desde la formación del lenguaje hasta nuestros dias: Obras publicadas e inéditas de Don Gaspar Melchor de Jovellanos.* Mutiple vols., edited by Don Miguel Artola. Madrid: Ediciones Atlas, 1956.

——. "Informe sobre la disciplina ecclesiástica antigua y moderna relativa al lugar de las sepulturas (1783)." In *Biblioteca de autores españoles desde la formación del lenguaje hasta nuestros dias: Obras públicas e inéditas de don Gaspar Melchor de Jovellanos.* Multiple vols. Ed. Miguel Artola. Madrid: Ediciones Atlas, 1956.

——. "Oración Inaugural del Instituto Asturiano (1794)." In *Biblioteca de autores Españoles desde la formacion del lenguaje hasta nuestros dias: Obras publicadas e inéditas de Don Gaspar Melchor de Jovellanos.* Multiple vols. Ed. Don Miguel Artola. Madrid: Ediciones Atlas, 1956.

——. "Población en España." In *Biblioteca de autores Españoles desde la formación del lenguaje hasta nuestros días. Obras publicadas e inéditas de Don Gaspar Melchor de Jovellanos.* Multiple vols. Ed. Don Miguel Artola. Madrid: Ediciones Atlas, 1956.

Las calaveras borrachas claman por el chinguirito. Mexico City: Hipólito Lagarza, 1836.

Laso de la Vega, José María. *Oración panegirica, que en la festividad de N.S de Guadalupe, celebrada el día doce de deciembre del año de 1793, en la paroquia de la Nueva Veracruz, dixo su parroco Dr. D. Joseph María Laso de la Vega, quien la dedica al muy ilustre ayuntmiento de aquella ciudad.* Puebla, Mexico: Seminario Palafoxiana, 1794.

——. *Oración panegyrica del gran padre y doctor de la iglesia sr. S. Augustin que en el convento de San Francisco Xavier el Real de Veracruz, del mismo orden dixo (el dia 28 de Agosto del año de 1780) don Joséph María Lazo de la Vega, clerigo presbytero del obispado de la Puebla de los Angeles, colegial que fue por beca real por opposicion del Colegio de San Ildefonso, de la misma ciudad, doctor por la Real y Pontífica Universidad de México, opositor a la canongia lectoral de la santa iglesia de puebla, y a la magistral de la de Oaxaca, calificador del Santo Oficio, y su comisario en la Ciudad de Veracruz, cura interino, y juez ecclesiástico de la real fortaleza de San Juan de Ullua.* Mexico City: Felipe de Zúñiga y Ontiveros, 1781.

León, Fr. Luis de. *The Names of Christ* (1597). Trans. and introduction by Manuel Durán and William Kluback. London: s p c k, 1984.

Lerdo de Tejada, Miguel. *Apuntes históricos de la heroica ciudad de Veracruz. Precedidos de una noticia de los descubrimientos hechos en las islas y en el continente Americano, y de las providencias dictadas por los reyes de España para el gobierno de sus nuevas posesiones, desde el primer viaje de don Cristobal Colon, hasta que se emprendio la conquista de México.* Mexico City: Imprenta de Ignacio Cumplido, 1850.

Libro de las constituciones del V. Orden Tercero de Penitencía de N.S.P.S Francisco: Sacadas de las que hizo el illmõ. Señor don Fr. Antonio Trejo Obispo de Cartajena, y Vicario general de la Regular Observancia: confirmadas por N.SS. P. Urbano VIII, y nuevamente modificadas y añadidas otras peculiares por los Hermanos de la Mesa de dicho V.orden en México. Mandadas guardar á todas las Terceras Ordenes por el M.R.P. Comisario visitador, Presidente de Capítulo, y R.y V. Definitorio de esta Providencia del Santo Evangelio año de 1783. Mexico City: D. Maríano Josef de Zúñiga y Ontiveros, 1796.

López Matoso, Antonio. "Viaje de perico ligero al país de los moros (1815–1816)." In *Cien viajeros en Veracruz: Crónicas y relatos. Tomo II, 1755–1816,* ed. Martha Poblett. Veracruz: Gobierno del Estado de Veracruz, 1992.

Lorenzana y Bútrón, Francisco Antonio. *Cartas pastorales y edictos del Ill.mo Señor D. Francisco Antonio Lorenzana y Bútron, Arzobispo de México.* Mexico City: Joseph Antonio de Hogal, 1770.

——, ed. *Concilios provinciales primero, y segundo, celebrados en la muy noble, y muy leal Ciudad de México. Presidiendo el Illmo. y Rmo. Señor D. Fr. Alonso de Montúfar, en los años de 1555, 1565. Dados a luz por El Illmo. Sr. D. Francisco Antonio Lorenzana.* Mexico City: Antonio de Hogal, 1769.

Luther, Martin. *Martin Luther: Selections from His Writings.* Ed. John Dillenberger. New York: Anchor Books, 1961.

Mayorga, Viceroy Martin de. *Ordenanza de la división de nobilísima ciudad de México en cuarteles, creación de los alcaldes de ellos, y reglas de su gobierno: dada y mandada observar por el Exmo. señor don Martin de Mayorga, Virrey, Gobernador, y Capitán General de esta Nueva España.* Mexico City: Mariano Joseph de Zúñiga y Ontiveros, 1782.

Medina, Balthasar de. *Vida, martyrio, y beatificación del invicto proto-martyr de el Japón San Felipe de Jesús, patron de México, su patria, Imperial corte de Nueva España, en el nuevo mundo.* Madrid: Herederos de la Viuda de Juan García Infanzón, 1751.

Mier, Fr. Servando Teresa de. *The Memoirs of Fray Servando Teresa de Mier.* Ed. Susana Rotker. Trans. Helen Lane. New York: Oxford University Press, 1998.

——. *Memorias.* 2 vols. Ed. Antonio Castro Leal. Mexico City: Editorial Porrua, 1946.

——. *Discurso del D. Dr. Servando Teresa de Mier sobre la enciclica del Papa León XII.* Mexico City, 1825.

Mora, José María Luis. *El clero, el estado, y la economia nacional.* Mexico City: Empresas Editoriales, 1950.

Mora, José María Luis. *Obras sueltas de José Luis Mora, ciudadano Mexicano (1837).* Mexico City: Editorial Porrúa, 1963.

Mora, José María Luis. *Obras Completas. Vol. 3: Obra Política.* Ed. Lillian Briseño Senosiain, Laura Solares Robles, and Laura Suárez de la Torre. Mexico City: SEP, 1986.

Novísima recopilación de las leyes de España, mandada formar por el Señor don Carlos IV. Paris: Don Vicente Salva, 1854.

O'Crouley O'Donnel, Pedro Alonso. "Idea compendiosa del reino de la Nueva España, 1764." In *Cien viajeros en Veracruz: Crónicas y relatos. Tomo II, 1755–1816,* ed. Martha Poblett. Veracruz: Gobierno del Estado de Veracruz, 1992.

Ordenanzas para el nuevo establecimiento de alcaldes de quartel de la ciudad de la Puebla de los Angeles de N.E. Puebla, Mexico: Don Pedro de la Rosa, 1796.

Ordenanzas, que para el establecimiento de alcaldes de barrio en esta ciudad de Vallodolid de Michoacan ha extendido su Corregidor Intendente en virtud de superiores órdenes del exmo Señor Virrey. Mexico City: Mariano Joseph de Zúñigay y Ontiveros, 1796.

Ossorio, Fr. Diego. *Manual para administrar los Santos Sacramentos. Arreglado al Ritual Romano, con el orden de bendiciones, exequias, procesiones, y otras cosas necessarias.* Mexico City: Imprenta del Nuevo Rezado, de Doña María de Ribera, 1748.

Panteón de San Pablo. Mexico City: Antonio Díaz, 1843.

Panteón general. Reglamento del Panteón general de Santiago de Chile. Dictado por el supremo gobierno año de 1824. Santiago, Chile: Imprenta Nacional, 1824.

Pérez Cancio, Gregorio. *La Santa Cruz y Soledad de Nuestra Señora: Libro de fábrica del templo parroquial. Años 1773–1784.* Mexico City: Instituto Nacional de Antropología e Historia, 1970.

Pope Benedict XIII. *Constitucion de nuestro santissimo señor, el Señor Benedicto Papa XIII en favor de la Tercera Orden de N.P.S. Francisco.* Mexico City: Joseph Bernardo de Hogal, 1726.

Prieto, Guillermo. *Memorias de mis tiempos (1828–1840).* Mexico City: Editorial Patria, 1958.

Pública Vindicacion del Ilustre Ayuntameinto de Santa Fé de Guanajuato justificando su conducta moral y politica en la entrada y crimenes que cometieron en aquella ciudad las huestes insurgentes agabilladas por sus coriféos Miguel Hidalgo, Ignacio Allende. Mexico City: Mariano Joseph de Zúñiga y Ontiveros, 1811.

Real Academia de la Historia. *Informe dado al consejo por la Real Academia de la Historia en 10 de junio de 1783 sobre la disciplina eclesiástica antigua y moderna relativa al lugar de las sepulturas.* Madrid: Antonio de Sancha, Impresor de la Academia, 1786.

Recopilación de leyes de los reynos de las Indias, mandadas imprimir, y publicar por la magestad católica del rey don Carlos II, nuestro señor Madrid: Ilvian de Paredes, 1681.

Revillagigedo, Conde de. *Informe sobre las misiones e instrución reservada al Marqués de Branciforte.* Introduction by José Bravo Ugarte. Mexico City: Editorial Jus, 1966.

Rivera, Juan Antonio. *Diario curioso de México.* Mexico City: La Voz de la Religion, 1854.

Robles, Antonio de. *Diario de sucesos notables (1665–1703).* 3 vols. Ed. Antonio Leal del Castro. Mexico City: Editorial Patría, 1946.

Rodríquez de la Miguel, Juan M., ed. *Pandectas hispano-megicanas, ó sea código general comprensivo de las leyes generales, útiles y vivas de las Siete partidas, Recopilación novívisa, la de Indias, autos y providencias conocidas de Montemayor y Beleña, y cédulas posteriores hasta el año de 1820.* Mexico City: Mariano Galvan Rivera, 1839.

Romay, Tomás. *Descripción del cementerio general de la Havana por el Dr. dn. Tomás Romay, socio numerario de la Sociedad Economica de la Havana en la clase de profesor sobresaliente y académico. Corresponsal de la Real Academia de Medicina de Madrid.* Havana: D. Estevan Joseph Boloña, 1806.

San Vicente, Juan Manuel de. "Exacta decripción de la magnifica corte mexicana, cabeza del nuevo americano mundo, significada por sus esenciales partes, para el bastante conocimiento de su grandeza." In *La ciudad de México en el siglo XVIII (1690–1780): Tres crónicas,* ed. Antonio Rubial García. Mexico City: Consejo Naciónal para Las Culturas y Las Artes, 1990.

Santa Teresa, Friar Manuel de. *Instructorio espiritual de los terceros, terceras, y beatas de nuestra Señora del carmen: dispuesto por f. Manuel de Santa Teresa, Carmelita Descalzo, Lector de Sagrada Escritura, ex-Definidor, y prior que fue de los conventos de Zelaya y Toluca, y vicario del Santo Desierto: Quien lo dedica a la misma Santisima virgin. A expensas de la venerable Tercera Orden de Nuestra Señora del Carmen de Sr. s.Joseph de la Ciudad de Toluca.* Mexico: D. Felipe de Zúñiga y Ontiveros, 1782.

Sequeira y Arango, Manuel de. "El cementerio." In *Poesias del Coronel D. Manuel de Sequeira y Arango,* ed. Manuel de Sequeira y Caro. Havana: Imprenta del Gobierno, 1852.

Sumario de las Indulgencias, gracías, y privelegios autenticos que ganan y gozan los hermanos de la Tercera Orden de Penitencia de N.P. San Francisco, como consta de las bulas y decretos apostolicos que se citan, y especialmente segun el tenor de la bula Benedicto XVIII, que llamamos el mare-magnum, cuya reviviscencia hizo nro. SSmo. P. Clemente XIV en todo y por todo su contenido. Dispuesto y Ordenado por el R.P. Fr. Miguel Tadeo de Guevara, lector jubilado, y Comisario Visitador del Venerable Orden Tercero de esta corte. Mexico City: D. Maríano de Zuñiga y Ontiveros, 1802.

Tejada y Ramiro, Juan. Colección de cánones y de todo los concilios de la Iglesia Española. 5 vols. Madrid, 1855.

Thompson, Waddy. Recollections of Mexico. New York: Wiley and Putnam, 1846.

Ulloa, Antonio de. "Descripción geográfica-física de una parte de la Nueva España, 1777." In Cien viajeros en Veracruz: Crónicas y relatos. Tomo II, 1755–1816, ed. Martha Poblett. Veracruz: Gobierno del Estado de Veracruz, 1992.

Valdes, José Francisco. Sermón en que en la translación de los huesos de los religiosos a la capilla de Nuestra Señora de Dolores, fabricada a solicitud del r.p. guardián fr. Pascual Eguia, notario del Santo Oficio, y difinidor de la providencia de S. Diego de México predicó el Fr. José Francisco Valdes, lector jubilado y calificador del Santo Oficio. Mexico City: José Antonio de Hogal, 1787.

Ventura Beleña, Eusebio. Recopilación sumaria de todos los autos acordados de la real audiencia y sala de crimen de esta Nueva España, y providencias de su superior gobierno. 2 vols. Mexico City: D. Felipe de Zúñiga y Ontivero, 1787.

Vera, Fortino Hipólito. Colección de documentos ecclesiásticos de México, o sea antigua y moderna legislación de la iglesia mexicana. 3 vols. Amecameca, Mexico: Colegio Catolico, 1887.

———. Notas del compendio histórico del Concilio III Mexicano. Amecameca, Mexico: Colegio Católico, 1879.

Veracruz y Oaxaca en 1798. Mexico City: Editorial Vargas Reas, 1946.

Vetancourt, Friar Agustín de. "Tratado de la Ciudad de México y las grandezas que la ilustran después que la fundaron Españoles." In La Ciudad de México en el siglo XVIII (1690–1780). Tres crónicas, ed. Antonio Rubial García. Mexico City: Consejo Nacional para la Cultura y las Artes, 1990.

Viera, Juan de. "Breve compendiosa narración de la ciudad de México, corte y cabeza de toda la America septentrional." In La Ciudad de México en el siglo XVIII (1690–1780). Tres crónicas, ed. Antonio Rubial García. Mexico City: Consejo Nacional para la Cultura y las Artes, 1990.

Villarroel, Hipólito. México por dentro y por fuera bajo el gobierno de los vireyes, o sea enfermedades políticas que padece la capital de esta Nueva España. Mexico City: Impresor de Alejandro Valdes, 1831.

Villa-Señor y Sánchez, José Antonio de. Theatro Americano. Descripción general de los reynos y provincias de la Nueva España y sus jurisdicciónes. Mexico City: Don Joseph Bernardo de Hogal, 1746.

Ward, Bernardo. Proyecto Económico. Madrid: D. Joachin Ibarra, Impresor de Camara de S.M., 1762.

Ward, Henry George. México en 1827. Mexico City: Fondo de Cultura Económica, 1985.

SECONDARY SOURCES

Abray, Lorna Jane. *The People's Reformation: Magistrates, Clergy, and Commons in Strasburg, 1500–1598.* Ithaca, NY: Cornell University Press, 1985.

Addy, George. *The Enlightenment in the University of Salamanca.* Durham, NC: Duke University Press, 1966.

Albarracín, Agustín. "La medicina española en Colombia." *Cuadernos Hispanoamericanos* 427 (October 1989): 12–32.

Alberro, Solange, and Serge Gruzinski. *Introducción a la historia de las mentalidades.* Mexico City: Cuaderno de Trabajo del Departamento de Investigaciones Historicas 24, Instituto Nacional de Antropología y Historia, 1979.

Alegría, Fernando. *Historia de la novela hispanoamericana.* 3d. ed. Mexico City: Ediciones de Andrea, 1966.

Alonso, Ana María. *Thread of Blood: Colonialism, Revolution, and Gender on Mexico's Northern Frontier.* Tucson: University of Arizona Press, 1995.

Anna, Timothy. *The Fall of Royal Government in Mexico City.* Lincoln: University of Nebraska Press, 1978.

Appolis, Émile. *Les Jansénistes Espagnols.* Bordeaux, France: Sobodi, 1966.

Archer, Christon I. *El ejército en el México borbónico, 1760–1810.* Trans. Carlos Valdés. Mexico City: Fondo de Cultura Económica, 1983.

——. *The Army in Bourbon Mexico, 1760–1810.* Albuquerque: University of New Mexico Press, 1977.

Arcila Farías, Eduardo. *Reformas económicas del siglo XVIII en la Nueva España.* 2d ed. 2 vols. Mexico City: SepSetentas, 1974.

Arco Moya, Juan del. "Religiosidad popular en Jaén durante el siglo xviii: Actitudes ante la muerte." In *La religiosidad popular. II. Vida y muerte: La imaginación religiosa,* ed. C. Álvarez Santaló, Maria Jesús Buxó, and S. Rodriquez Becerra. Barcelona: Editorial Anthropos, 1989.

Ariés, Philippe. *El hombre ante la muerte.* Trans. Mauro Armiño. Madrid: Taurus Ediciones, 1983.

——. *The Hour of Our Death.* Trans. Helen Weaver. New York: Knopf, 1981.

Arrom, Silvia M. "Popular Politics in Mexico City: The Parián Riot, 1828." *Hispanic American Historical Review* 68:2 (May 1988): 245–268.

Artola, Miguel. *Antigua Régime y revolución liberal.* Barcelona: Ariel, 1978.

Baena del Alcazar, Mariano. *Los estudios sobre administración en la España del siglo XVIII, con el discurso sobre el gobierno municipal de José Agustín Ibáñez de la Rentería.* Madrid: Instituto de Estudios Politicos, 1968.

Balust, L. Sala. *Visitas y reforma de los colegios mayores de Salamanca en el reinado de Carlos III.* Salamanca: Universidad de Salamanca, 1958.

Bataillon, Marcel. *Erasmo y España: Estudios sobre la historia espiritual del siglo XVI.* Mexico City: Fondo de Cultura Económica, 1966.

Bazarte Martínez, Alicia. *Las cofradías de españoles en le ciudad de México (1526–1869).* Mexico City: Universidad Autónoma Metropolitana, Unidad Atzapotzalco, 1989.

Benítez, Fernando. *Historia de la Ciudad de México.* 7 vols. Barcelona: Salvat Editores, 1984.

Booker, Jackie R. *Veracruz Merchants, 1770–1829: A Mercantile Elite in Late Bourbon and Early Independent Mexico.* Boulder, CO: Westview Press, 1993.

Borchant de Moreno, Christiana Renate. *Los mercaderes y el capitalismo en la ciudad de México: 1759–1778.* Mexico City: Fondo de Cultura Económica, 1984.

Bossy, John. *Christianity in the West 1400–1700.* Oxford: Oxford University Press, 1985.

Boyer, Richard E., and Keith A. Davies. *Urbanization in 19th Century Latin America: Statistics and Sources.* Los Angeles: UCLA Press, 1973.

Brading, David A. "Creole Nationalism and Mexican Liberalism." *Journal of Interamerican Studies and World Affairs* 15 (May 1973): 139–190.

——. "El clero mexicano y el movimiento insurgente de 1810." *Relaciones* 2:5 (winter 1981): 5–26.

——. "El jansenismo Español y la caída de la monarquía Católica en México." In *Interpretaciones del siglo XVIII mexicano: El impacto de las reformas borbónicas,* ed. Josefina Zoraida Vázquez. Mexico City: Nueva Imagen, 1992.

——. *The First America: The Spanish Monarchy, Creole Patriots and the Liberal State.* Cambridge, England: Cambridge University Press, 1991.

——. *The Origins of Mexican Nationalism.* Cambridge, England: Centre for Latin American Studies, Cambridge University, 1985.

——. "Tridentine Catholicism and Enlightened Despotism in Bourbon Mexico." *Journal of Latin American Studies* 15 (May 1983): 1–23.

——. *Una Iglesia asediada: El obispado de Michoacán, 1749–1810.* Mexico City: Fondo de Cultura Económica, 1994.

Brown, Peter. "A Dark Age in Crisis: An Aspect of the Iconoclastic Controversy." *English Historical Review,* 88: 346 (January, 1973): 1–27.

Burke, Michael E. *The Royal College of San Carlos: Surgery and Spanish Medical Reform in the Late Eighteenth Century.* Durham, NC: Duke University Press, 1977.

Burke, Peter. "How to Become a Counter-Reformation Saint." In *The Counter-Reformation: The Essential Readings,* ed. David M. Luebka. London: Blackwell, 1999.

Burns, J. H., and Thomas M. Izbicki. *Conciliarism and Papalism.* Cambridge, England: Cambridge University Press, 1997.

Bushnell, David. *The Making of Modern Colombia: A Nation in Spite of Itself.* Berkeley: University of California Press, 1993.

Callahan, William J. *Church, Politics, and Society in Spain, 1750–1874.* Cambridge, MA: Harvard University Press, 1984.

Calleja Folguera, María del Carmen. "La reforma sanitaria en la España ilustrada." Ph.D. diss., Universidad Complutense de Madrid, 1988.

Carmichael, Elizabeth, and Chloe Sayer. *The Skeleton at the Feast: The Day of the Dead in Mexico.* Austin: University of Texas Press, 1991.

Carroll, Michael P. *Veiled Threats: The Logic of Popular Catholicism in Italy.* Baltimore: Johns Hopkins University Press, 1996.

Cejudo López, Jorge. *Bosquejo de política economica española de Campomanes.* Madrid: Taurus, 1984.

Chadwick, Owen. *The Popes and European Revolution.* Oxford: Clarendon Press, 1981.

Chapin, Jessica. "From Irca to Orca: Apprehending the Other in 'Your San Antonio Experience.' " *Journal of Historical Sociology* 7:1 (March 1994): 102–112.

Chartier, Roger. *The Cultural Origins of the French Revolution.* Trans. Lydia G. Cochrane. Durham, NC: Duke Univerity Press, 1991.

Chaunu, Pierre. *La Mort à Paris, 16e, 17e, 18e siècles.* Paris: Fayard, 1978.

——. "Veracruz en la segunda mitad del siglo XVI y primera del XVII." *Historia Mexicana* 36:9 (April–June 1960): 540–563.

Chávez, Ignacio. *México en la cultura medica.* Mexico City: Fondo de Cultura Económica, 1987.

Christian, William A., Jr. *Local Religion in Sixteenth-Century Spain.* Princeton, NJ: Princeton University Press, 1981.

Cooper, Donald B. *Epidemic Disease in Mexico City, 1761–1813: An Administrative, Social, and Medical Study.* Austin: University of Texas Press, 1965.

Cope, Douglass R. *The Limits of Racial Domination: Plebian Society in Colonial Mexico City.* Madison: University of Wisconsin Press, 1994.

Corbin, Alain. *El Perfume o el Miasma: El olfato y lo imaginario social. Siglos XVIII y XIX.* Trans. Carlota Vallée Lazo. Mexico City: Fondo de Cultura Económica, 1987.

Costeloe, Michael P. *Church and State in Independent Mexico: A Study of the Patronage Debate, 1821–1857.* London: Royal Historical Society, 1978.

——. *La primera república federal de México (1824–1835) (Un estudio de los partidos políticos independientes).* Trans. Manuel Fernández Gasalla. Mexico City: Fondo de Cultura Económica, 1975.

Crew, P. Mack. *Calvinist Preaching and Iconoclasm in the Netherlands, 1544–69.* Cambridge, England: Cambridge University Press, 1978.

Cuenya, Miguel Angel, and Elsa Malvido. *El colera de 1833: Una nueva patologia en México. Causas y efectos.* Mexico City: Instituto Nacional de Antropología e Historia, 1992.

Cuevas, Mariano. *Historia de la iglesia en México.* 5 vols. El Paso, TX: Editorial Revolucíon Catolica, 1928.

Cunningham, Andrew. "Medicine to Calm the Mind: Boerhaave's Medical System and Why It Was Adopted in Edinburgh." In *The Medical Enlightenment of the Eighteenth Century*, ed. Andrew Cunningham and Roger French. Cambridge, England: Cambridge University Press, 1990.

Cunningham, Andrew, and Roger French, eds. *The Medical Enlightenment of the Eighteenth Century*. Cambridge, England: Cambridge University Press, 1990.

Curcio-Nagy, Linda. "Giants and Gypsies: Corpus Christi in Mexico City." In *Rituals of Rule, Rituals of Resistance: Public Celebrations and Popular Culture in Mexico*, ed. William H. Beezley, Cheryl English Martin, and Wilham E. French. Wilmington, DE: Scholarly Resources, 1994.

———. "Native Icon to City Protectress to Royal Patroness: Ritual, Political Symbolism, and the Virgin of Remedies." *The Americas* 52:3 (January 1996): 367–391.

Davis, Natalie. "Poor Relief, Humanism, and Heresy." In *Society and Culture in Early Modern France: Eight Essays by Natalie Davis*. Stanford: Stanford University Press, 1965.

———. "The Sacred and the Body Social in Sixteenth-Century Lyon." *Past and Present* 90 (February 1981): 40–70.

Delumeau, Jean. *Catholicism between Luther and Voltaire: A New View of the Catholic Reformation*. Trans. Jeremy Moser. London: Burns and Oates, 1977.

Demerson, Paula de. *María Francisca de Sales Portocarrero (Condesa de Montijo): Una figura de la Ilustración*. Madrid: Editora Nacional, 1975.

Derbyshire, Robert. *Medical Licensure and Discipline in the United States*. Baltimore, MD: Johns Hopkins University Press, 1969.

Desan, Suzanne. *Reclaiming the Sacred: Lay Religion and Popular Politics in Revolutionary France*. Ithaca, NY: Cornell University Press, 1990.

Diccionario Porrúa: Historia, biografía y geografía de México. 5th ed. Mexico City: Editorial Porrúa, 1986.

Dillenberger, John. *Images and Relics: Theological Perceptions and Visual Images in Sixteenth Century Europe*. New York: Oxford University Press, 1999.

Domergue, Lucienne. "De Erasmo a George Borrow: Biblia y secularización de la cultura española en el Siglo de las Luces." In *La secularización de la cultura española en el Siglo de las Luces: Actas del Congreso de Wolfenbüttel*, ed. Manfried Tietz. Weisbaden: Herzog August Bibliothek Wolfenbüttel, 1992.

Dooley, Eugene A. "Church Law on Sacred Relics." Ph.D. diss., Catholic University of America, 1931.

Egido, Teófanes. "La religiosidad de los ilustrados." In *La época de la Ilustración*. Vol. 1: El estado y la cultura, ed. Miguel Batllori. Madrid: Espasa-Calpe, 1992.

Eire, Carlos M. N. *From Madrid to Purgatory: The Art and Craft of Dying in Sixteenth-Century Spain*. Cambridge, England: Cambridge University Press, 1995.

———. *War against the Idols: The Reformation of Worship from Erasmus to Calvin*. London: Cambridge University Press, 1986.

Eisenstadt, S. N., ed. *The Protestant Ethic and Modernization*. New York: Basic Books, 1968.

Elias, Norbert. *The Civilizing Process: The History of Manners*. Trans. E. Jephcott. Oxford: Oxford University Press, 1983.

Elorza, Antonio. *La ideología liberal en la Ilustracion española*. Madrid: Taurus, 1970.

Etlin, Richard A. *The Architecture of Death: The Transformation of the Cemetery in Eighteenth-Century Paris*. Boston: MIT Press, 1987.

Farriss, Nancy M. *Crown and Clergy in Colonial Mexico, 1759–1821*. London: Cambridge University Press, 1968.

Fernández Salinas, Victor. "Cementerios y ciudad en el siglo XIX: La consolidación de los enterramientos extramuros en Sevilla." In *Una arquitectura para la muerte: Actas del I Encuentro Internacional sobre los Cementerios Contemporáneos*, ed. Dirección General de Arquitectura y Vivienda de la Consejería de Obras Públicas y Transportes de la Junta de Andalucía. Seville: Junta de Andalucía, 1993.

Flores G., Sonia, and José Sanfilippo B., eds. *Anastasio Bustamante y las instituciones de salubridad en el siglo XIX (documentos médicos)*. Mexico City: Facultad de Médicina, Archivalia Médica, Nueva Epoca 2, Universidad Nacional Autónoma de México, n.d.

Flynn, Maureen. *Sacred Charity: Confraternities and Social Welfare in Spain, 1400–1700*. Ithaca, NY: Cornell University Press, 1989.

Forment, Carlos Alfonso. "The Formation of Political Society in Spanish America: The Mexican Case, 1700–1830." Ph.D. diss., Harvard University, 1990.

Foucault, Michel. *Power/Knowledge: Selected Interviews and Other Writings, 1972–1977*. Ed. Colin Gordon. Trans. Colin Gordon, Leo Marshall, John Mepham, and Kate Soper. New York: Pantheon Books, 1980.

———. *The Birth of the Clinic: An Archeology of Medical Perception*. Trans. A. M. Sheridan. New York: Vintage Books, 1975.

Franco, Jean. "La heterogenidad peligroso: Escritura y control social en vísperas de la independencia mexicana." *Hispamérica* 12 (1983): 3–24.

———. "Waiting for a Bourgeoisie: The Formation of the Mexican Intelligentsia in the Age of Independence." In *Critical Passions: Selected Essays*, ed. Mary Louise Pratt and Kathleen Newman. Durham, NC: Duke University Press, 1999.

Fulbrook, Mary. *Piety and Politics: Religion and the Rise of Absolutism in England, Würtenberg, and Prussia*. Cambridge, England: Cambridge University Press, 1983.

Galán Cabilla, José Luis. "Madrid y los cementerios en el siglo XVIII: El fracaso de una reforma." In *Carlos III, Madrid, y la Illustracion: Contradiciones de un proyecto reformista*, ed. Josef Fontaña. Madrid: Siglo Veinteuno, 1988.

Galvez Ruíz, María Angeles. "La consolidación de la conciencia regional en

Guadalajara: El gobierno del intendente Jacobo Ugarte y Loyola (1791–1798)."
Ph.D. diss., Universidad de Grenada, 1993.

García Ayluardo, Clara. "Confraternity, Cult and Crown in Colonial Mexico City:
1700–1810." Ph.D. diss., Cambridge University, 1989.

García Ayluardo, Clara, and Alicia Bazarte Martínez. "Patentes o sumarios de in-
dulgencias, documentos importantes en la vida y en la muerte." In *Visiones y
Creencias IV: Anuario Conmemorativo del V centenario de la llegada de España a America.*
Mexico City: Universidad Autónoma Meteropolitana, 1992.

García Ayluardo, Clara, and Manuel Ramos Medina, eds. *Manifestaciones religiosas en
el mundo colonial americano. Volumen 1: Espiritualidad barroca colonial: Santos y demonios en América.* Mexico City: Universidad Iberoamericana, 1993.

Geary, Patrick J. *Furta Sacra: Thefts of Relics in the Middle Ages.* Princeton, NJ: Princeton University Press, 1978.

Gelfand, Toby. "From Guild to Profession: The Surgeons of France in the 18th
Century." *Texas Reports on Biology and Medicine* 32 (1974): 121–134.

Glazier, Augustin. *Historie génénerale du mouvement janséniste depuis se origines jusqu'á
nos jours.* 2 vols. 5th ed. Paris: Librairie Ancienne Honoré Champion, 1924.

Goldman, Peter B. "Mitos liberales, mentalidades burguesas, e historia social en
la lucha en pro de los cementerios municipales." In *Homenaje a Noël Salomón:
Ilustración española e independencia de América,* ed. Alberto Gil Novales. Barcelona:
Universidad Autónoma de Barcelona, 1979.

Gómez Navarro, Soledad. "La construcción de cementerios en la provincia de Cór-
doba, 1787–1833." In *Una arquitectura para la muerte: Actas del I Encuentro Internacional sobre los Cementerios Contemporáneos,* ed. Dirección General de Arquitectura y
Vivienda de la Consejería de Obras Públicas y Transportes de la Junta de Andalucía. Seville: Junta de Andalucía, 1993.

Góngora, Mario. "Estudios sobre el Galicanismo y la 'Ilustración Católica' en
América española," *Revista Chilena de Historia y Geografía* 125 (1957): 96–152.

Gonzalez Cruz, David. *Religiosidad y ritual de la muerte en la Huelva del siglo de la Ilustración.* Huelva, Spain: Diputación Provincial de Huelva, 1993.

González de Cossío, Francisco, ed. *Relaciones y Crónicas de la Compañía de Jesús en la
Nueva España.* Mexico City: Universidad Nacional Autónoma de México, 1979.

———, ed. *Testimonios mexicanos: Historiadores 5. Gacetas de México.* Mexico City: Secretaría de Educación Pública, 1949.

González Lopo, D. "La evolución del lugar de sepultura en Galicia entre 1550 y
1850: Los casos de Tuy y Santiago." *Obradoiro de Historia Moderna* (1990): 170–189.

Gramsci, Antonio. *Selections from the Prison Notebooks.* Ed. and trans. Quinten Hoare
and Geoffrey Nowell Smith. London: Lawrence and Wishart, 1971.

Granjel, Luis S. "Panorama de la medicina española durante el siglo XVIII." *Revista
de la Universidad de Madrid* 9 (1960): 675–702.

Green, Stanley C. *The Mexican Republic: The First Decade, 1823–1832*. Pittsburgh: University of Pittsburgh Press, 1987.

Gringoire, Pedro. "El 'Protestantismo' del doctor Mora." In *Lecturas de Historia Mexicana 5: Iglesia y religiosidad*, ed. Pilar Gonzalbo Aizpuru. Mexico City: Colegio de México, 1992.

Gruzinski, Serge. *The Conquest of Mexico: The Incorporation of the Indian Societies into the Western World, 16th–18th Centuries*. Trans. Eileen Corrigan. Cambridge, England: Polity Press, 1993.

——. "La segunda aculturización: El estado ilustrado y la religiosidad indígena en Nueva España (1775–1800)." *Estudios de Historia Novohispana* 8 (1985): 175–201.

——. *Man-Gods in the Mexican Highlands: Indian Power and Colonial Society, 1520–1800*. Stanford: Stanford University Press, 1989.

Guardino, Peter. *Peasants, Politics, and the Formation of Mexico's National State, Guerrero 1800–1857*. Stanford: Stanford University Press, 1996.

Guerra, François-Xavier. *Modernidad e independencias: Ensayos sobre las revoluciones hispánicas*. Mexico City: Fondo de Cultura Económica, 1993.

Gutiérrez, Ramón A. *When Jesus Came, the Corn Mothers Went Away.: Marriage, Sexuality, and Power in New Mexico, 1500–1846*. Stanford: Stanford University Press, 1991.

Habermas, Jürgen. *The Structural Transformation of the Public Sphere: An Inquiry into a Category of Bourgeois Society*. Trans. Thomas Burger. Cambridge, MA: MIT Press, 1989.

Haigh, Christopher. *English Reformations: Religion, Politics, and Society under the Tudors*. Oxford: Clarendon Press, 1993.

Hale, Charles A. *Mexican Liberalism in the Age of Mora, 1821–1853*. New Haven: Yale University Press, 1968.

Hamill, Hugh M., Jr. *The Hidalgo Revolt: Prelude to Mexican Independence*. Gainesville: University of Florida Press, 1966.

Hamnet, Brian R. *Política y comercio en el sur de México, 1750–1821*. Mexico City: Instituto Mexicano de Comercio Exterior, 1976.

——. *Revolución y contrarevolución en México y el Peru: Liberalismo, realeza y seperatismo, 1800–1824*. Mexico City: Fondo de Cultura Económica, 1978.

Hernández Luna, Juan. "El mundo intelectual de Hidalgo." *Historia Mexicana* 3:4 (October–December 1953): 155–177.

Hernández Sáenz, Luz María. *Learning to Heal: The Medical Profession in Colonial Mexico*. New York: Peter Lang, 1997.

Hernández Torres, Alicia, and Francisco Fernández del Castillo. *El Tribunal del Protomedicato en la Nueva España, segun el archivo Histórico de la Facultad de Medicina*. Mexico City: Universidad Nacional Autónoma de México, 1965.

Hidalgo de Costilla, Miguel. "Disertación sobre el verdadero método de estudear teología escolástica (1784)." *ábside* 17:2 (April–June 1953).

Hill, Christopher. *Change and Continuity in Seventeenth-Century England.* New Haven: Yale University Press, 1991.

Hirschman, Albert O. *The Passions and the Interests: Political Arguments for Capitalism before Its Triumph.* Princeton, NJ: Princeton University Press, 1977.

Hoffman, Philip. *Church and Community in the Diocese of León, 1500–1789.* New Haven: Yale University Press, 1984.

Holleran, Mary P. *Church and State in Guatemala.* New York: Columbia University Press, 1949.

Houlbrooke, Ralph. *Death, Religion, and the Family in England, 1480–1750.* Oxford: Clarendon Press, 1998.

Hsia, R. Po-Chia. *The World of Catholic Renewal, 1540–1770.* Cambridge, England: Cambridge University Press, 1998.

Iguíñiz, Juan B. *Breve Historia de la Tercera Orden hasta nuestros días.* Mexico City: Editorial Patria, 1951.

Izquierdo, José Joaquín. *Montaña y los origenes del movimiento social y científico de México.* Mexico City: Ediciones Ciencia, 1955.

Janik, Dieter. "El *Periquillo Sarniento* de J. J. Fernandez de Lizardi: Una normativa vacilante (sociedad—naturaleza y religion—razon)." *Ibero-Amerikanisches Archiv* 13 (1987): 49–60.

———. "La noción de sociedad en el pensamiento de Lizardi y de sus contemporaneos." *Cahiers des Amériques latines* 10 (1990): 38–50.

Jiménez Codinach, Guadalupe. "An Atlantic Silver Entrepot: Veracruz and the House of Gordan and Murphy." In *Atlantic Port Cities: Economy, Culture, and Society in the Atlantic World, 1650–1850,* ed. Franklin W. Knight and Peggy K. Liss. Knoxville: University of Tennessee Press, 1991.

Kicska, John E. *Empresarios coloniales, familias, y negocios en la ciudad de México durante los Borbones.* Mexico City: Fondo de Cultura Económica, 1986.

Klaiber, Jeffrey L., *Religion and Revolution in Peru, 1824–1976.* Notre Dame, IN: University of Notre Dame Press, 1977.

Kléber Monod, Paul. *The Power of Kings: Monarchy and Religion in Europe, 1598–1715.* New Haven: Yale University Press, 1999.

Knight, Alan. "The Peculiarities of Mexican History: Mexico Compared to Latin America, 1821–1992." *Journal of Latin American Studies* 24 (Quincentenary Supplement, 1992): 99–144.

La salubridad y higiene pública en los Estados Unidos Mexicanos. Mexico City: Casa Metodista de Publicaciónes, 1910.

Ladd, Doris. *The Mexican Nobility at Independence, 1780–1826.* Austin: University of Texas Press, 1976.

Lafaye, Jacques. *Quetzalcoatl and Guadalupe: The Formation of Mexican National Conciousness, 1531–1813*. Chicago: University of Chicago Press, 1976.

Lancaster, Roger. *Thanks to God and the Revolution: Popular Religion and Class Consciousness in the New Nicaragua*. New York: Columbia University Press, 1988.

Lanning, John Tate. *The Eighteenth-Century Enlightenment in the University of San Carlos de Guatamala*. Ithaca, NY: Cornell University Press, 1956.

——. *The Royal Protomedicato: The Regulation of the Medical Professions in the Spanish Empire*. Ed. John Jay Tepaske. Durham, NC: Duke University Press, 1985.

Leduc, Alberto, Luis Lara Pardo, and Carlos Roumagnac. *Diccionario de geografía, historia, y biografía mexicanas*. Mexico City: Librería de la Viuda de Bouret, 1910.

Le Goff, Jacques. *The Birth of Purgatory*. Trans. Arthur Goldhammer. Chicago: University of Chicago Press, 1981.

Lemoine, Dr. Ernesto. "La praxis política de Gómez Farías." In *Memoria de las mesas redondas sobre las ideas de Valentín Gómez Farías y José María Luis Mora*. Mexico City: Instituto Dr. José María Luis Mora, 1982.

Leonard, Irving J. *Baroque Times in Old Mexico: Seventeenth-Century Persons, Places, and Practices*. Ann Arbor: University of Michigan Press, 1959.

Lindberg, Carter. *Beyond Charity: Reformation Initiatives for the Poor*. Minneapolis: Fortress Press, 1993.

López I Miguel, Olga. *Actitudes collectives davant la mort I discurs testamentari al Mataró del segle XVIII*. Introduction by Carlos Martínez Shaw. Barcelona: Editorial Rafael Dalmau, 1978.

López Sánchez, José. *Tomás Romay y el origin de la ciencia en Cuba*. Havana: Academia de Ciencias, 1964.

Lorenzo Pinar, Francisco Javier. *Muerte y ritual en la edad moderna: El caso de Zamora 1500–1800*. Salamanca, Spain: Universidad de Salamanca, 1991.

Luebke, David M., ed. *The Counter-Reformation: The Essential Readings*. London: Basil Blackwell, 1999.

Luria, Keith P. *Territories of Grace: Cultural Change in the Seventeenth-Century Diocese of Grenoble*. Berkeley: University of California Press, 1991.

Lynch, John. *Bourbon Spain, 1700–1808*. Oxford: Basil Blackwell, 1989.

Maclachlan, Colin M. *Spain's Empire in the New World: The Role of Ideas in Institutional and Social Change*. Berkeley: University of California Press, 1988.

Mallo, Pedro. *Apuntes historicos sobre el estado oriental del Uruguay. Sus medicos, instituciones de caridad, hospitales y cementerios . . . desde el año 1726 hasta el 1810*. Buenos Aires: Imprenta Industrial, 1899.

Mallon, Florencia E. *Peasant and Nation: The Making of Postcolonial Mexico and Peru*. Berkeley: University of California Press, 1995.

Maravall, José Antonio. *Culture of the Baroque: Analysis of a Historical Structure*. Trans. Terry Cochran. Minneapolis: University of Minnesota Press, 1986.

Margadant, Guillermo Floris. *Carlos III y la iglesia novohispana.* Mexico City: Biblioteca del Claustro de Sor Juana, 1983.

Marichal, Juan. "From Pistoia to Cádiz: A Generation's Itinerary." In *The Ibero-American Enlightenment,* ed. A. Owen Aldridge. Urbana-Champagne: University of Illinois Press, 1974.

Martínez Cortés, Fernando. *De los miasmas y efluvios al descubrimiento de las bacterias patógenas: Los primeros cincuenta años del Consejo Superior de Salubridad.* Mexico City: Bristol-Myers Squibb, 1993.

Martínez Gil, Fernando. *Actitudes ante la muerte en el Toledo de los Asturias.* Toledo, Spain: Ayuntamiento de Toledo, 1984.

Martinéz Pereda, Matías. "Refleciones jurídicas sobre la llamada sucesión a favor del alma." *Anales de la Academía Matritense del Notariado* 7 (1953): 151–189.

Martz, Linda. *Poverty and Welfare in Habsburg Spain: The Example of Toledo.* London: Cambridge University Press, 1983.

Maza, Francisco de la. *Las piras funerarias en la historia y en el arte de México: Grabados, litografías y documentos del siglo XVI al XIX.* Mexico City: Anales del Instituto de Investigaciones Esteticas, 1946.

McAlister, Lyle N. *The Fuero Militar in New Spain, 1754–1800.* Gainesville: University of Florida, 1957.

McAlister, Lyle N. "Social Structure and Social Change in New Spain." *Hispanic American Historical Review* 43:3 (August 1961): 349–370.

McGrath, Alister E. *Reformation Thought: An Introduction.* Oxford: Basil Blackwell, 1988.

———. *The Intellectual Origins of the European Reformation.* Oxford: Basil Blackwell, 1987.

Mecham, J. Lloyd. *Church and State in Latin America: A History of Politico-Ecclesiastical Relations.* Chapel Hill: University of North Carolina Press, 1934.

Méndez Plancarte, Gabriel. "Hidalgo reformador intelectual." *Ábside* 17:2 (April–June 1953): 135–170.

Merton, R. K. *Science, Technology, and Society in Seventeenth-Century England.* 1938. New York: Howard Fertig, 1970.

Mestre Sanchis, Antonio. *El mundo intelectual de Mayans.* Valencia, Spain: Publicaciones del Ayuntamiento de Oliva, 1978.

Mestre Sanchis, Antonio. "El redescubrimiento de Fray Luis de León en el siglo XVIII." *Bulletin Hispanique* 83:1–2 (1981): 5–64.

Morales, Francisco. *Clero y política en México (1767–1834): Algunas ideas sobre la autoridad, la independencia y la reforma eclesiástica.* Mexico City: Secretaría de Educación Pública. 1975.

Morales, María Dolores. "Cambios en las prácticas funerarias: Los lugares de sepultura en la Ciudad de México, 1784–1857." *Historias* 27 (October 1991–March 1992): 97–105.

Mourant, John A., ed. *Introduction to the Philosophy of Saint Augustine: Selected Readings and Commentaries*. University Park: Pennsylvania State University Press, 1964.

Muriel, Josefina. *Hospitales de la Nueva España: Fundaciones de los siglos XVII and XVIII*. 2 vols. Mexico City: Editorial Jus, 1960.

Nalle, Sarah T. *God in la Mancha: Religious Reform and the People of Cuenca, 1500–1650*. Baltimore: Johns Hopkins University Press, 1992.

Noel, C. C. "Opposition to Enlightened Reform in Spain: Campomanes and the Clergy, 1765–1775." *Societas* 3:1 (1973): 21–43.

Oestreich, Gerhard. *Neostoicism and the Early Modern State*. Ed. Brigitta Oestreich and H. G. Loenigsberger. Trans. David McLintock. Cambridge, England: Cambridge University Press, 1981.

O'Gorman, Edmundo, ed. *Antología del pensamiento político americano: Fray Servando Teresa de Mier*. Mexico City: Imprenta Universitaria, 1945.

Olaechea, R. "El anticolegialismo del gobierno de Carlos III." *Cuadernos de Investigación, Geográfica e Historia* 2 (1976): 53–90.

Ono, Ichiro. *Divine Excess: Mexican Ultra-Baroque*. San Francisco: Chronicle Books, 1996.

Outram, Dorinda. *The Body and the French Revolution: Sex, Class, and Political Culture*. New Haven: Yale University Press, 1989.

Parrilla Hermid, Miguel. "El Doctor Mauricio Echandi Montalvo." *Revista del Instituto José Cornide de Estudios Coruñeses* 8–9 (1972–1973): 247–255.

Paz, Octavio. *Sor Juana Ines de la Cruz o las trampas de la fe*. 3d ed. Mexico City: Fondo de Cultura Económica, 1983.

Pérez Memen, Fernando. *El episcopado y la Independencia de México (1810–1836)*. Mexico City: Editorial Jus, 1977.

Pescador, Juan Javier. *De bautizados a fieles difuntos: Familia y mentalidades en una parroquia urbana: Santa Catarina de México, 1568–1820*. Mexico City: Colegio de México, 1993.

Phelan, John Leddy. *The Millennial Kingdom of the Franciscans in the New World: A Study of the Writings of Gerónimo de Mendieta*. Berkeley: University of California Press, 1956.

Pietschmann, Horst. "Protoliberalismo, reformas borbónicas y revolución: La Nueva España en el último tercio del siglo XVIII." In *Interpretaciones del siglo XVIII Mexicano: El impacto de las reformas borbónicas*, ed. Josefina Zoraida Vásquez. Mexico City: Nueva Imagen, 1992.

Polt, John H. R. *Gaspar Melchor de Jovellanos*. New York: Twayne Publishers, 1971.

Ponte Chamorro, Federico. "Mentalidad religiosa, ritos funerales, y clases sociales en el Madrid decimononico." In *Anales del Instituto de Estudios Madrileños*. Madrid: Consejo Superior de Investigaciones Científicas, 1986.

Porter, Dorothy, and Roy Porter. *Patient's Progress: Doctors and Doctoring in Eighteenth-Century England.* Stanford: Stanford University Press, 1989.

Porter, Roy. *Disease, Medicine and Society in England, 1550–1850.* 2d ed. Cambridge, England: Cambridge University Press, 1995.

———. *The Greatest Benefit to Mankind: A Medical History of Humanity.* New York: Norton, 1997.

Quezada, Naomi. *Enfermedad y maleficio: El curandero en el México colonial.* Mexico City: Universidad Nacional Autónoma de México, 1989.

Rama, Angel. *The Lettered City.* Ed. and trans. John Charles Chasteen. Durham, NC: Duke University Press, 1996.

Reinhard, Wolfgang. "Reformation, Counter-Reformation and the Early Modern State: A Reassessment." In David M. Luebke, ed., *The Counter-Reformation: The Essential Readings.* London: Basil Blackwell, 1999.

Reis, João José. *A morte é uma festa: Ritos fúnebres e revolta popular no Brasil do século XIX.* São Paulo, Brazil: Editora Schwarcz, 1991.

Reyes Heroles, Jesús. *El liberalismo mexicano.* 3 vols. Mexico City: Fondo de Cultura Económica, 1974.

Rice, Eugene F., Jr. "The Humanist Idea of Christian Antiquity: Lefévre d'Étaples and His Circle." *Studies in the Renaissance* 9:135 (1962): 122–140.

Ringrose, David R. *Spain, Europe, and the "Spanish Miracle," 1700–1900.* Cambridge, England: Cambridge University Press, 1996.

Rivas Alvarez, José Antonio. *Miedo y Piedad: Testamentos Sevillanos del siglo XVIII.* Seville: Diputación Provincial de Sevilla, 1986.

Rodríquez, Martha Eugenia. "La medicina científica y su difusión en Nueva España." *Estudios de historia novohispana* 12 (1992): 179–193.

Rollason, David W. *Saints and Relics in Anglo-Saxon England.* New York: Oxford University Press, 1989.

Rosell, Lauro E. *Iglesias y conventos coloniales de México: Historia de cada uno de los que existen en la ciudad de México.* 2d ed. Mexico City: Editorial Patria, 1961.

Rotker, Susana, ed. *The Memoirs of Fray Servando Teresa de Mier.* Trans. Helen Lane. New York: Oxford University Press, 1998.

Rothstein, William J. *American Physicians in the 19th Century: From Sects to Science.* Baltimore, MD: Johns Hopkins University Press, 1985.

Rueda López, José Ramón. "Evolución de los cementerios en la ciudad de Valencia." In *Una arquitectura para la muerte: Actas del I Encuentro Internacional sobre los Cementerios Contemporáneos,* ed. Dirección General de Arquitectura y Vivienda de la Consejería de Obras Públicas y Transportes de la Junta de Andalucía. Seville: Junta de Andalucía, 1993.

Ruíz de Velasco y Martínez, Don Francisco. *Defensa de los cementerios católicos contra la* secularización y revindicación de los derechos parroquiales en el entierro y funerales. Madrid: Baena Hermnos Impresores, 1907.

Russek, Carlos David Malamud. Derecho funerario. Introduction by Andrés Sena Rojas. Mexico City: Editorial Porrúa, 1979.

Saint-Saéns, Alain. Art and Faith in Tridentine Spain (1545–1690). New York: Peter Lang, 1995.

Sarrailh, Jean. La España ilustrada de la segunda mitad del siglo XVIII. Mexico City: Fondo de Cultura Económica, 1957.

Scardaville, Michael C. "Crime and the Urban Poor: Mexico City in the Late Colonial Period." Ph.D. diss., University of Florida, 1977.

——. "(Hapsburg) Law and (Bourbon) Order: State Authority, Popular Unrest, and the Criminal Justice System in Bourbon Mexico City." The Americas 50:4 (April 1994), 500–521.

Schaffer, Simon. "Measuring Virtue: Eudiometry, Enlightenment and Pneumatic Medicine." In The Medical Enlightenment of the Eighteenth Century, ed. Andrew Cunningham and Roger French. Cambridge, England: Cambridge University Press, 1990.

Schendel, Gordon. Medicine in Mexico: From Aztec Herbs to Betatrons. Austin: University of Texas Press, 1968.

Schmidt, Henry C. "Towards the Innerscape of Mexican Historiology: Liberalism and the History of Ideas." Mexican Studies/Estudios Mexicanos 8:1 (1992): 117–138.

Schroeder, H. J. The Canons and Decrees of the Council of Trent. Rockford, IL: TAN Books, 1978.

Scribner, Robert W. "Ritual and Reformation." In The German People and the Reformation, ed. R. Po-Chia Hsia. Ithaca, NY: Cornell University Press, 1988.

Seed, Patricia. To Love, Honor, and Obey in Colonial Mexico: Conflicts over Marriage Choice, 1574–1821. Stanford: Stanford University Press, 1988.

Serrano Laso, Manuel. "Origen y desarrollo del cementerio público de la ciudad de León hasta 1936." In Una arquitectura para la muerte: Actas del I Encuentro Internacional sobre los Cementerios Contemporáneos, ed. Dirección General de Arquitectura y Vivienda de la Consejería de Obras Públicas y Transportes de la Junta de Andalucía. Seville: Junta de Andalucía, 1993.

Shafer, Robert J. The Economic Societies in the Spanish World, 1763–1821. Syracuse, NY: Syracuse University Press, 1958.

Shields, W. Eugene. "Church and State in the First Decade of Mexican Independence." Catholic Historical Review 28 (July 1942): 206–228.

Shyrock, Richard. Medicine and Society in America, 1660–1860. Ithaca, NY: Cornell University Press, 1962.

Sims, Harold. La expulsión de los españoles de México (1821–1828). Mexico City: Fondo de Cultura Económica, 1974.

Sinkin, Richard N. *The Mexican Reform, 1855–1876: A Study of Liberal Nation-Building*. Austin, TX: Institute of Latin American Studies, 1979.

Smith, Robert Sydney. "Shipping in the Port of Veracruz, 1790–1821." *Hispanic American Historical Review* 23 (February 1943): 5–20.

Solomón, Nöel. "La crítica del sistema colonial de la Nueva España en El *Periquillo Sarniento*." *Cuadernos Americanos* 138:1 (January–February 1965): 158–176.

Souto Mantecon, Matilde. "El consulado de comerciantes de Veracruz." Master's thesis, Universidad Nacional Autónoma de México, Departamento de Filosofía y Letras, 1989.

Spell, Jefferson Rea. "The Intellectual Background of Fernández de Lizardi as Reflected in El *Periquillo Sarniento*." *Proceedings of the Modern Language Association* 71 (1956): 414–432.

Staples, Anne. "Clerics as Politicians: Church, State, and Political Power in Independent Mexico." In *Mexico in the Age of Democratic Revolutions, 1750–1850*, ed. Jaime Rodríguez O. Boulder, CO: Lynn Rienner, 1994.

——. *La iglesia en la primera república federal mexicana*. Mexico City: SepSetenas, 1976.

——. "La lucha por los muertos." *Dialogos* 13:5 (September–October 1977): 15–20.

Starr, Paul. *The Social Transformation of American Medicine: The Rise of a Sovereign Profession and the Making of a Vast Industry*. New York: Basic Books, 1982.

Stevens, Donald F. *The Origins of Instability in Early Republican Mexico*. Durham, NC: Duke University Press, 1991.

Stevens, W. P. *Zwingli: An Introduction to His Thought*. Oxford: Clarendon Press, 1992.

Stone, Lawrence. *The Causes of the English Revolution, 1529–1642*. London: Routledge and Kegan Paul, 1972.

Sullivan-Gonzalez, Douglass Creed. *Power, Piety, and Politics: Religion and Nation Formation in Guatemala, 1821–1871*. Pittsburgh: University of Pittsburgh Press, 1996.

Tackett, Timothy. *Becoming a Revolutionary: The Deputies of the French National Assembly and the Emergence of a Revolutionary Culture (1789–1790)*. Princeton, NJ: Princeton University Press, 1996.

——. *Religion, Revolution, and Regional Culture: The Ecclesiastical Oath of 1791*. Princeton, NJ: Princeton University Press, 1986.

Tandron, Humberto. *El comercio de Nueva España y la controversia sobre la libertad de comercio, 1796–1821*. Mexico City: Instituto Mexicano de Comercio Exterior, 1976.

Tank de Estrada, Dorothy. "Médicos." In *Historia de las profesiones en México*, ed. Josefina Z. Vásquez. Mexico City: Colegio de México, 1982.

——. "The 'Escuelas Pias' of Mexico City: 1786–1820." *The Americas* 31:1 (July 1974): 51–72.

Tapié, Victor-L. *The Age of Grandeur: Baroque Art and Architecture*. Trans. A. Ross Williamson. New York: Frederick A. Praeger, 1961.

Tawney, R. H. *Religion and the Rise of Capitalism: A Historical Study*. New York: Harcourt, Brace, and Company, 1926.

Taylor, Charles. *Sources of the Self: The Making of Modern Identity*. Cambridge, MA: Harvard University Press, 1989.

Taylor, William B. *Magistrates of the Sacred: Priests and Parishioners in Eighteenth-Century Mexico*. Stanford: Stanford University Press, 1996.

——. "The Virgin of Guadalupe in New Spain: An Inquiry into the Social History of Marian Devotion." *American Ethnologist* 14 (1987): 9–33.

Tenenbaum, Barbara A. *The Politics of Penury: Debts and Taxes in Mexico, 1821–1856*. Albuquerque: University of New Mexico Press, 1986.

Thibaut-Payen, Jacqueline. *Les morts, l'Église et l'État: Recherches d'histoire administrative sur la sépulture et les cimetières dans le ressort du Parlement de Paris aux XVIIe et XVIIIe siècles*. Paris: Éditions Fernand Lanore, 1977.

Thomas, Keith. *Religion and the Decline of Magic*. London: Scribner, 1971.

Thompson, E. P. *The Poverty of Theory and Other Essays*. New York: Monthly Review Press, 1978.

Tolivar Alas, Leopoldo. *Dogma y realidad del derecho mortuorio español*. Madrid: Instituto de Estudios de Administración Local, 1983.

Tomsich, María Giovanna. *El jansenismo en España: Estudio sobre ideas religiosas en la segunda mitad del siglo XVIII*. Introduction by Carmen Martín Gaite. Madrid: Siglo Veintiuno, 1972.

Torre Villar, Ernesto de la. "Hidalgo y Fleury." *Historia Mexicana* 3:4 (October–December 1953): 207–216.

Torres, Alejandro. *Vida del beato Sebastián de Aparicio*. Puebla, Mexico: Fr. Samuel Ortega, Ministro Provincial, 1968.

Trens, Manuel B. *Historia de la H. Ciudad de Veracruz y de su Ayuntamiento*. Veracruz, Mexico: Ayuntamiento de Veracruz, 1955.

Turner, Edith, and Victor Turner. *Image and Pilgrimage in Christian Culture: Anthropological Perspectives*. New York: Columbia University Press, 1978.

Van Kley, Dale. *The Religious Origins of the French Revolution: From Calvin to the Civil Constitution, 1560–1791*. New Haven: Yale University Press, 1996.

Vaquero Iglesias, Julio Antonio. *Muerte e ideología en la Asturias del siglo XIX*. Madrid: Siglo Veintiuno, 1991.

Velasco Ceballos, Rómulo. *La cirugía Mexicana en el siglo XVIII*. Mexico City: Archivo Histórico de la Secretaría de Salubridad y Assistencia, 1946.

Velásquez, Romeo Cruz. "Los hospitales en el Puerto de Veracruz durante 1760–1800." Tesis de Licenciatura, Universidad de Veracruz, 1992.

Viqueira-Alban, Juan Pedro. "El sentimiento de la muerte en el México ilustrado del siglo XVIII a través de dos textos de la época." *Relaciones* 2:5 (winter 1981): 27–63.

——. "La Ilustración y las fiestas populares en la ciudad de México (1730–1821)." *Cuicuilco* 14–15 (July–December 1984): 17–34.

——. *Propriety and Permissiveness in Bourbon Mexico.* Trans. Sonya Lipsett-Rivera and Sergio Rivera Ayala. Wilmington, DE: Scholarly Resources, 1999.

Voekel, Pamela. "Peeing on the Palace: Bodily Resistance to Bourbon Reforms." *Journal of Historical Sociology* 5:2 (August 1992): 183–210.

Vogely, Nancy. "*El Periquillo Sarniento*: The Problem of Mexican Independence." Ph.D. diss., Stanford University, 1980.

——. "The Concept of 'the People' in *El Periquillo Sarniento.*" *Hispania* 70:3 (September 1987): 456–478.

Vovelle, Michel. *Piètè baroque et dèchristiamsation en Provence au XVIIIe siècle: Les atitudes devant la mort d'apres les clauses des testaments.* Paris: Plon, 1973.

Wandel, Lee Palmer. *Voracious Idols and Violent Hands: Iconoclasm in Reformation Zurich, Strasbourg, and Basel.* Cambridge, England: Cambridge University Press, 1995.

Warfield, Benjamin B. *Calvin and Augustine.* Philadelphia: Temple University Press, 1956.

Warner, Marina. *Alone of All Her Sex: The Myth and the Cult of the Virgin Mary.* New York: Vintage Books, 1983.

Warren, Richard Andrew. "Vagrants and Citizens: Politics and the Poor in Mexico City, 1808–1836." Ph.D. diss., University of Chicago, 1994.

Waterworth, Ra. J., trans. *The Canons and Decrees of the Sacred and Ecumenical Council of Trent, Celebrated Under the Pontiffs, Paul III, Julius III, and Pius IV.* London: C. Dolman, 1948.

Webb, Diane. *Pilgrims and Pilgrimages in the Medieval West.* London: I. B. Tauris, 1999.

Weber, Max. *The Protestant Ethic and the Spirit of Capitalism.* 2d ed. Ed. Anthonoy Giddings. Trans. Talcott Parsons. London: George Allen and Unwin, 1976.

Widemer, Rolph. "La ciudad de Veracruz en el último siglo colonial (1680–1820): Algunos aspecto de la historia demográfica de una ciudad portuaria." *La palabra y el hombre* 73 (1992): 121–134.

Wilckens, Ricardo Krebs. "The Victims of a Conflict of Ideas." In *The Expulsion of the Jesuits from Latin America,* ed. Magnus Mörner. New York: Knopf, 1965.

Wilson, Steven. *Saints and Their Cults: Studies in Religious Folklore and History.* Cambridge, England: Cambridge University Press, 1983.

Woodward, Ralph Lee, Jr. "The Liberal-Conservative Debate in the Central American Federation, 1823–1840." In *Liberals, Politics and Power: State Formation in Nineteenth-Century Latin America,* ed. Vicent C. Peloso and Barbara Tenenbaum. Athens: University of Georgia Press, 1996.

Young, Elliott Gordon. "Deconstructing La Raza: Culture and Ideology of the

Gente Decente of Laredo, 1904–1911." *Southwest Historical Quarterly* (October 1994): 226–59.

Zaparaín Yáñez, María José. "La problematica de los cementerios en la provincia de Burgos bajo el reformismo ilustrado." In *Una arquitectura para la muerte: Actas del I Encuentro Internacional sobre los Cementerios Contemporáneos*, ed. Dirección General de Arquitectura y Vivienda de la Consejería de Obras Públicas y Transportes de la Junta de Andalucía. Seville: Junta de Andalucía, 1993.

Zárate Toscano, Verónica. "Los nobles ante la muerte en México: Actitudes, ceremonias, y memoria." Ph.D. diss., Colegio de México, 1996.

Zavala, Silvio. *¿El castellano, lengua obligatoria?* Mexico City: Centro de Estudios de Historia de México, Condumex, 1977.

index

Pamela Voekel is an Assistant Professor
in the Department of History at the
University of Montana.